Psychoanalysis in Context

Psychoanalysis in Context

Edited by

Alvin Henry

CAMBRIDGE
SCHOLARS
PUBLISHING

Psychoanalysis in Context,
Edited by Alvin Henry

This book first published 2013

Cambridge Scholars Publishing

12 Back Chapman Street, Newcastle upon Tyne, NE6 2XX, UK

British Library Cataloguing in Publication Data
A catalogue record for this book is available from the British Library

ISBN (10): 1-4438-3529-3, ISBN (13): 978-1-4438-3529-9

TABLE OF CONTENTS

Section III. Key Concepts

INTRODUCTION

Challenge, frustration, joy. The preparation of this collection of essays has been all three—and sometimes all three at the same time. As I went about the process of organizing, and editing the essays you have before you, my awareness of the complexity of the tensions existing within the field of psychoanalytic theory —not to even mention the transformations they undergo in the realm of literary criticism—grew in leaps and bounds. Since psychoanalytic criticism underwent a thorough backlash in the academy, I assumed at the start of this project that a gathering of psychoanalytic criticism would proceed in a state of communal joy, of the marginalized united in their pursuit of a similar path of critical inquiry. Although I knew of the competing camps within the field, I was unprepared for the often-fierce internal debates among these sub-groups. At the same time, I was awed by the underlying similarities uniting even the most seemingly contentious perspectives—and by just how productive these debates have been in advancing theoretical and literary inquires. This anthology should be read as a conversation among the many threads of psychoanalysis and the many threads of psychoanalytically-inflected literary criticisms rather than as putting forth a prescriptive approach or singular methodology. I hope that this collection signals the emergence of a reinvigorated psychoanalytic criticism that has adapted, for the better, to the world of new historicism and to the dialectical turn towards new formalism.

To invoke psychoanalysis as a method is to enter into a contentious debate as to what literature is. Psychoanalytic criticism assumes the existence of subjects possessing depth and complexity. This discursive assumption has been met with challenges from the French post-structuralists, and more recently from Jürgen Habermas's critique of the subject of modernity. This collection reveals a deep scepticism for any analysis that would read characters simply as sources for psychological experiment. The authors in this volume approach psychoanalysis as a method for reading texts—specifically as a humanistic practice of contextualizing and locating the unconscious, repetitions, condensations, and displacements not just of characters, but of the complex networks that encompass, shape, and inform the texts as wholes. At the same time, they historicize the psychoanalysis that they utilize as a mode of interpretation. Although our contributors condone the project of reading characters as one of the means for understanding the workings of overarching formal or cultural systems, they also develop reading practices that help contextualize the historical moment of the authors examined. Aesthetic features, for example, become both a reflection of the dialectical relationship between the historical and the text while also serving to illuminate the role of the psyche—whether fictional or possessing a possible social referent—within this dialectic. This introduction to the collection shall not pretend to present the essays as a unified system, but I do hope it will serve to highlight the disjunctions as well as the common ground subtending even such disparate projects. While trying to balance the psychoanalytic perspectives, the collection reflects a deeper preoccupation with methods of inquiry to indicate a new critical geography.

The idea of a cohesive psychoanalysis began to fracture even during Freud's lifetime. Jung, Alder, Jones, Klein, Lacan, and even Freud's own daughter, Anna, offered new tributaries in the field. In more recent times the academy has been more welcoming to thinkers who have incorporated semiotics, structuralism, and post-structuralism, i.e. Lacan, Kristeva, Irigaray, and Deleuze and Guattari. This collection acknowledges this bias and discursive advantage; by soliciting essays from around the globe, and from thinkers who work with different forms of literature, I have attempted to balance the collection in terms of the types and forms of theoretical perspectives represented within it. Although I strove to achieve balance, there was no way to give voice to every perspective. For example, Wilfred Bion does not make an appearance in the collection even though many psychoanalysts practice a technique inspired by his work. On the other hand, the Frankfurt School, which also adopted and revised many psychoanalytic terms, does make a brief appearance, and not in the form of the usual nod to Adorno or Benjamin. The act of negotiating coverage and giving representation to certain perspectives inevitably brings with it disappointment and potential criticism. I strove to fill this anthology with the best interventions from around the globe.

This collection of essays began while finishing a bottle of wine at the end of a conference I organized entitled, "Literature and Psychoanalysis," at the University of California, Berkeley, in 2007. Literally the dregs—or rubbish to be more psychoanalytically attuned—of a more conversation-oriented project, the essays in the volume attempt to return to the psychoanalytic thought created over the last few decades while also challenging these developments from an academic rather than a purely clinical orientation. In these ways, the essays, I hope, present psychoanalysis in context—fully aware of the historical production of the theories evoked, attentive to the contexts under analysis, and conscious of the turn to and away from theories that may be shaping our understanding of psychoanalytic thought and of our own reading practices.

Not since Shoshana Felman's editing of *Literature and Psychoanalysis: The Question of Reading: Otherwise* in 1982, has there been another major collection of essays that attempts to question and answer the relationship between texts and psychoanalysis. In Felman's spectacular collection, the authors open up the question of the relationship between literature and psychoanalysis that sparked decades of interest and brought waves of critical remarks on the use of psychoanalysis in literary studies. While they did indeed explore the tenuous relationship between psychoanalysis and literature, new insights by both psychoanalysts and literary scholars over the past thirty years have complicated their brilliant readings. As such, the conference at Berkeley began to take up the critical currents—including the negative waters—of psychoanalytically inflected literary criticism. This collection brings together scholars from around the globe who are swimming in different rivers yet all invested in the same intellectual journey.

The essays reflect scholarship that has addressed the many critiques directed at psychoanalysis when applied in the humanities and social sciences. Many of the essays explore the complexities of the Oedipal Complex—a much debated phenomena or fantasy—to produce not only fresh criticism but also to push forward revisions to the psychoanalytic corpus. In editing the essays, the authors took great care to extricate theory from an all too easy devolution into cant. The essays provide numerous entry points for scholars less familiar with psychoanalytic ideas while also advancing a new set of readings of psychoanalysis itself for scholars or clinicians desiring a more theoretical reading. As with any text involving theoretical concepts, the balancing act between composing accessible language and being in conversation with your subfield is always a challenging feat. The essays in the volume straddle these professional obligations by reviewing and defining key terms and then carefully explicating their arguments.

The heterogeneous essays are divided into three broad areas that are in dialogue with one another. Section One, "The Question of Genre," opens with Adrienne Seely's "Nothing/Animate: Robot, Woman, and the Ends of Humanist Narrative in Spielberge's *A.I.*," an essay that enables us to see the psychoanalytic dimensions of narrative structure. Interrogating the film from the perspective of Gilles Deleuze's analysis of the literature of sadism and masochism, Seely complicates frequent claims that *A.I.* offers viewers a straight-forward experience of Oedipal wish-fulfillment. The chapter demonstrates that *A.I.* continually stages scenarios in which Father figures, whether they be the master inventor who aspires to parthenogenetic procreation or the biological father of the traditional family, strive to assert Symbolic dominance, yet instead accomplish a performance of the phallus as negative object, or per Lacan, "…an object which gives body to a certain fundamental loss in its very presence," thereby necessitating a compensatory negation of the existence of *both* "the Woman" and "the Robot" as whole subjects. With both Woman and Robot aligned in the category of subjects "who do not exist," *A.I.* creates a masochistic narrative structure in which they seek a love outside a paternally-oriented Symbolic order that is marked formally as "sadistic." Through devices of suspension, 'interrupted love,' and the child's subjugation to social law through the maternal contract rather than via the Name-of-the-Father, the film hypostasizes a realm where maternity enforces a Symbolic order made precarious by chiastic figurations of the Real, in the form of twin ecological catastrophes which threaten, call into question, and ultimately terminate humanity's existence as a species. As a narrative whose form is determined by masochistic structuring, the link between Woman and her Robot son hyperbolizes the 'non-being' which founds both of their subject-positions, making demonstrable a lack which is, the film asserts, fundamental to all subjectivity.

Simon Porzak's essay, "Beyond the Poetic Principle: Speculations on Mallarmean Intertextuality," might be considered the dialectical partner to Seely's argument for a reconfiguration of the father figure. Porzak considers the practice of poetry - defined as the work of entering into and maintaining a position of mastery in the poetic language of one's models - from a psychoanalytic perspective, and in particular through a case study of the relationship between Edgar Allan Poe and his great admirer Stéphane Mallarmé. Theories of poetic intertexuality, notably Harold Bloom's *Anxiety of Influence*, define this labor of inheritance and mastering purely in masculine terms, rehearsing the psychoanalytic drama of the son's struggle to accede to the father's position. However, even as masculine poets seek to deny the fact, they are structurally incapable of becoming permanently identified with the father, since their language is not their own; castration, then, can never be warded off for long. The impossibility of maintaining mastery over poetic language has long been recognized, of course - notably, by Poe, who analyzes repetition, automatism, mastery, and the structural failure at the heart of phallic poetics. Writing after and in the spirit of Poe, Mallarmé thus takes another approach to poetics, by practicing a non-phallic, feminine art of poetry.

The final essay in this section offers a different answer to the question of the “father” in the study of genre. In “Realities, Fictions and the Abandonment of Seduction: Rethinking Otherness in the Psychoanalytic Approach to Tragedy,” Nicholas Ray reflects on the relationship between psychoanalytic theory and some of the key tragic dramas in which it has sought exemplars and prototypes. Drawing on the work of French psychoanalyst Jean Laplanche, Ray examines the close historical and theoretical connections between Freud’s interpretative appeal to tragic drama (*Oedipus*, *Hamlet*) and his professed abandonment of the seduction theory in 1897. Arguing that the abandonment of seduction is concomitant in Freud with the loss of a certain thinking of the other, Ray goes on to consider the ways in which Freud’s readings of tragic drama tend to simplify the modes of radical alterity that they articulate. In order to sketch out the possibility of an alternative psychoanalytic approach to tragedy, the essay invokes Laplanche’s postulation of a ‘general theory of seduction’ – a hypothesis which is consistent with the most radical tendencies of Freud’s thinking yet is also capable of re-opening the question of otherness within tragic drama in new and potentially exciting ways.

The essays in “Contextualizing Cultural Critique” work to negotiate what it means for literature and culture in general to be vehicles for critical psychoanalytic thought. The section opens with Vera Profit’s essay that asks how the question of evil pushes the limits of literary representation. She questions whether there can be a psychoanalytic theory or explanation of evil and if group dynamics can function as a means to explore the operation of evil. Her essay “’It Was As A Rebel That He Fell:’ The Abuse of Power, Scapegoating and Lying in Friedrich Dürrenmatt’s *Der Verdacht*” focuses upon a multi-faceted detective novel written geographically and chronologically in close proximity to the Holocaust, the quintessence of evil. First published in its entirety in 1953, Friedrich Dürrenmatt’s (1921—1990) *Der Verdacht* tells of a Swiss physician, Fritz Emmenberger, during crucial phases of his life: as a medical student, as a concentration camp physician, and after 1945, as the CEO of a clinic. Hans Bärlach, a Swiss policeman and the novel’s second major figure, endeavors to prove that Emmenberger, presently the administrator of a Zurich hospital, is identical with Dr. Nehle, who performed medical experiments in Stutthof without the benefit of anesthesia. Ultimately Bärlach confirms the suspicion that lies at the novel’s core. To ascertain the exact nature of the evil traits (beyond the obvious) within Emmenberger’s character, Profit draws upon the works of such leading thinkers as Fromm and Frankl, but also those of M. Scott Peck. Prior to his *People of the Lie,* the diagnosis of evil had never entered the psychiatric lexicon. To allow for this designation within the medical sphere, Dr. Peck's treatise elucidates the nature of both individual and group evil. In his landmark study the then practising psychiatrist illustrates eight characteristics of evil individuals. They are: victimization of body and/or spirit, failure to recognize the separateness of others, their depersonalisation, unmitigated narcissism, the unsubordinated use of power, scapegoating, lying, and the total inability to tolerate legitimate criticism. Profit concentrates her study on the abuse of power, scapegoating and lying.

We can understand Profit's goal as shifting the sphere of psychoanalysis's power from literature to culture. In "The Family Romance in Black and White: Paternal Abdication and the 'Touch of the Mother' in Marita Bonner's 'One Boy's Story'," Laura Dawkins pushes the boundary between a cultural analysis of African American culture and a literary reading of fictional characters. Dawkins focuses on a critically neglected tale from the Harlem Renaissance that scrutinizes the applicability of Freudian psychoanalytic paradigms to the historically disrupted African American family. Suggesting that nuclear family relationships cannot be abstracted from the cultural context within which they evolve, Bonner replaces "universalizing" paradigms with a socially inflected model of the Oedipal drama. Dawkins demonstrates that the resolution of the Oedipal crisis—dependent on the son's separation from the mother and subsequent identification with a paternal figure—is irrevocably fractured for the African American boy, since he remains excluded from the patriarchal order that he has been socially conditioned to value. Dawkins argues that Bonner foregrounds the role of the black mother in shaping her son's truncated journey to manhood, exposing how this mother is paradoxically dispossessed of her maternal role yet granted the negative authority to confer her own degraded status upon her offspring. A precursor of Toni Morrison's *Beloved*, "One Boy's Story" suggests that the disinherited black mother, like Morrison's Sethe, can claim her child only through an act of violence. Almost forty years before African American women charged Daniel Patrick Moynihan with scapegoating black mothers by attributing the destructive effects of an oppressive white society to undue maternal influence within the black family, Bonner similarly revealed that a confluence of social, historical, and economic forces conspire to sabotage the black boy's Oedipal quest—even as the boy's mother, in her frenzy to shelter him from an inimical society, appears to become the "castrating" matriarch, the agent of her son's unmanning.

Dawkins reads the image of the African American family through the Oedipal drama; Profit reads the concept of evil through the Frankfurt school of critical theory. In "The Psychological Oppen: Reality and a

Modernist Male," Brian Glaser further repositions the role of psychoanalytic criticism as a fluctuation inflected by gender and material culture. Glaser challenges the celebration of materialism that is prevalent in critical scholarship on the poetry of George Oppen. Putting Oppen's ways of thinking in conversation with the ideas of his contemporary Hans Loewald, it makes the argument that Oppen's materialism ought to be viewed not only in the context of his political commitments, as is often done, but also in the context of his experience of gender identity—fatherhood in particular. Because of the patterns that become apparent through the latter way of reading Oppen, this approach also raises the question of how to distinguish insight or wisdom from mechanism or defense in reading the poetry of a modernist male.

The section concludes with Shirley Zisser's reading of psychosis in the context of the nineteenth century. In "The 'Hellish Tatoo: Schizography in Edgar Allan Poe's 'The Tell-Tale Heart," Zisser seeks to further elucidate how literature contains and is a symptom of culture. In a close reading of Poe's short story, Zisser argues that the preference for the dash reveals a schizographic language phenomena, showing that the latter's dialectical structure between madness and paranoia collapses signification. Zisser suggests that the dash and the psychoanalytic idea of foreclosure function as the dominant tropes or markers of delusion. She further demonstrates how the world beyond the dash signifies an "unmetabolized raw form, as Thing, eroding ravines in the biological organism from whence it emanates."

The final section of the collection, "Key Concepts," offers a set of revised or supplementary definitions to the psychoanalytic canon. Michael Angelo Tata's essay "Introduction…the *object petit c:* Lacanian Materiality and the Society of the Sinthome" might be considered a response to the chapters in Section One that call for a revision of the Oedipal Complex and to Profit's call for a psychoanalytically informed investigation of the realities of late Capitalism. Tata begins his essay with a review of the fundamental Lacanian concept of the *objet a* and traces its transformation into what he terms the *objet c*, or 'object a' transmuted into a commodity proper. As the core of Lacanian materiality, the *objet a* speaks to a version of desire according to which the self is a jug and the object, a plug. Basically, every object works this way for Lacan, stopping up a vessel which otherwise might overflow or spill its contents and cause the self in whom desire inheres the pains of incompleteness.

Since any object can do far more than this, Tata finds Lacan's concept of the material world somewhat ontologically impoverished, and uses the mysteries of the commodity to enrich it, capitalizing upon Tata's insight into transcendent objecthood in the formula 'in-x-more-than-x,' which designates the upper limit of the object. For present American society, the symptom's enjoyment is critical: hence it is for this "Society of the Sinthome" that the *objet c* carries meaning, setting in motion its psychological distress at the same time that it locates within that distress a source of intense de-individuated pleasure and beauty. A parcel of reality whose fragmented and partial character inspires a virtual, transient and phantasmic wholeness to absorb and overtake the split subject, the *objet c* marks an emotional turning point in the history of Lacanian angst, as in the wake of de-sublimation, hedonism becomes a kind of categorical imperative, and there is no longer any reason to lament the subject's bar. This compulsory openness Lacanian commentator Slavoj Zizek heralds with a powerful ambivalence, and hence it is with his subjective responses to various aspects of contemporary popular culture that this invocation ends.

Whereas Tata challenges the notion of one of Lacan's most fundamental concepts, Erica Galioto strives to produce an alliance across multiple psychoanalytic discourses by redefining Freud's notion of transference. In her essay "'A Transference of the Most Fortuitous Kind': Fitzgerald's *Tender Is The Night* and the Freudian Transference" Galioto makes a new contribution to scholarship on the novel by arguing that Dick Diver does not, in fact, disintegrate, but rather initiates his own recovery due entirely to what may be called a Freudian transference with Rosemary Hoyt. This article shows that Fitzgerald actually presents us with the two different dimensions of transference as Freud defines them: one that slips into a counter-transference with resistance on both sides; and one that veers into the love that Freud believes to be curative in the clinical setting. Noting the differences between the two transferential situations allows readers to see that Rosemary functions as a catalyst to a new subjective position for Dick, not as the agent of his supposed demise. Viewing the transference from two different vantage points, one of resistance and one of love, permits us to generalize on both the potential danger and the potential success of employing love, or the transference as such, in cases of mental illness.

For both Tata and Galioto, psychoanalytic concepts must be interrogated before they can be extended in complex manners. Hilary Thompson continues this reading practice but she forces a confrontation among the various schools of psychoanalytic thought and the historical legacy of colonialism. In "From Necropolis to Polis: Melancholic Citizenship in *Baumgartner's Bombay*" Thompson reads Anita Desai's novel *Baumgartner's Bombay* alongside first Freudian and post-Freudian psychoanalytic theory, and then postcolonial theory, to demonstrate the polarity yet ironic compatibility of psychic and social or political models of melancholia. Contending that melancholia has had a conceptually paradoxical status as an intensely withdrawn and imploded individual state yet also a tantalizing model for explaining collective historical traumas and large-scale social maladies, Thompson argues for the surprising possible interweaving of these models. First she departs from a view of Freud as having occluded melancholia's social and political dimensions, suggesting instead that his seminal 1917 study "Mourning and Melancholia" might be usefully read in light of his later melancholia-infused imaginings of ancient cities. Thompson then brings out the implications of conceiving of melancholia as and in a cityscape by intertwining interpretations based on Freud and later psychoanalytic theorists Abraham and Torok with ones derived from cultural theorists Frantz Fanon, Homi Bhabha, and Anne Cheng. If both a narrow use of psychoanalytic theory and a wide-ranging application of cultural theory can equally diagnose and describe the complexities of such a blatantly melancholic and seemingly historically traumatized protagonist as Desai's Baumgartner, Thompson suggests that we can infer that melancholia might call forth both a psychic and cultural dimension in inter-relation.

The last chapter is a tour-de-force reading of "Camus's *The Stranger* and Miller's Ordinary Psychosis." Maire Jaanus performs a close reading of Camus's *The Stranger* in an effort to decipher the psychic functioning of its protagonist, in the process yielding rich insights into Lacanian notions of the unconscious and Henry Alain-Miller's ideas on the spectrum of psychosis. Interpreting Meursault as a persona suffering a deep disconnect from the symbolic and imaginary registers of psychic life, Jaanus illustrates the deep connection between Mersault's *bodily* ego, which fails to found itself in the imaginary, and the forms of the phenomenal world that surround and sustain it. As the literal supports of its self-coherence, this bodily ego depends essentially on union with its environment, from which it also sources its jouissaince—a jouissaince properly derived, in non-pyschotic individuals, from symbolic interactions with the Other via language. Reading across the varying eras of Lacan's theorization of the unconscious, Jaanus traces Lacan's shift from conceptualizing the latter as the "speaking unconscious," which constantly registers and interprets language, to that of the "real unconscious," which is amorphous and formless jouissance. Jaanus performs a stunning reading of Meursault's shootings as a means of interrupting and preventing his engulfment into the terrors of the real unconscious. She also offers an original reading of Meursault's behaviors at the trial as an example of ordinary psychosis; this reading responds to decades of arguments that assert an ethical quandary upon the killing. Jaanus complicates the idea of psychosis with the role of hate in Meursault's life; his delusions cease when he becomes hated—he gains verification of being in a relationship and not being alone. The chapter closes with a stunning reply to Edward Said's identity politics reading of the novel. Jaanus reveals how Said (and Freud) limits his readings to the phallic—to identity politics—and cannot imagine corporeal fantasies beyond the sexual.

I hope that the essays in this collection open scholars to the questions and concerns of psychoanalysis, in particular its applicability to literary studies in the twenty-first century. The authors represent just a small number of critics engaged in reformulating the ideas of psychoanalysis to be relevant and attuned to the insights gleaned from the explosion of theory and its backlash. And most importantly, I hope that you enjoy reading these fresh and thought provoking essays.

CONTRIBUTORS

Laura Dawkins is Associate Professor of American Literature and the Director of Graduate Studies in English at Murray State University. She has published articles on American literature and culture, and is currently working on a book that examines African American literary responses to historical incidents of racial violence.

Erica D. Galioto is an Assistant Professor of English at Shippensburg University of Pennsylvania, where she teaches classes in American literature and psychoanalysis, English education, and writing. "Split Skin: Adolescent Cutters and the Other" is forthcoming in an edited collection entitled *Skin, Culture, and Psychoanalysis*.

Brian Brodhead Glaser has taught at universities in Germany, Guatemala, Mexico, Portugal and the U.S. He currently lives in Santa Ana, California with his wife and daughter and son, and he teaches at Chapman University.

Alvin Henry earned his Ph.D. in Literature and Social Thought at the University of California, Berkeley. He studies the novel, African American literature, and literary theory and also conducts ethnographic research and oral historics. His next book project examines the style and form of the minority *Bildungsroman.*

Maire Jaanus is Professor of English and Comparative Literature at Barnard College and Columbia University. She is co-editor of *Culture and Clinic (C/C),* a journal at the University of Minnesota Press. She ha also co-edited for SUNY Press *Lacan in the German Speaking World, Reading Seminars I and II: Lacan's Return to Freud,* and *Reading Seminar XI: Lacan's Four Fundamental Concepts.* Maire has also written a book of literary criticism, *Literature and Negation* and a critical study of Georg Trakl. In addition, she has written a novel entitled *She* published by Doubleday. She is also the author of numerous articles on psychoanalysis in English and Estonian.

Simon Porzak is a Ph.D. candidate in the Department of Rhetoric at the University of California, Berkeley. His research focuses on the intersections of science and culture at the fin-de-siècle, with an emphasis on technology, genre fiction, and perversion. His dissertation examines the transformations of the female voice as love-object and locus of fetishistic desire in opera and literature from 1880 to 1910. He is also chief editor of the interdisciplinary journal *Qui Parle*.

Vera B. Profit is Professor of German and Comparative Literature at the University of Notre Dame. Her three previous monographs concern authors representing both French and German 20th Century poetry. However, this essay serves not only as a radical departure from those endeavors, but also affords a glimpse into her current book-length study. This project's provisional title reads as follows: *Toward a Literary and Psychological Definition of Human Evil: Dürrenmatt, Wilde and Frisch.* She earned her Ph.D. at the University of Rochester and, as part of her academic training, spent a year at the University of Vienna, another at the Sorbonne.

Adrienne Seely is a Ph.D. student in Cinema & Media Studies at the University of Chicago. Her research interests include psychoanalysis, ethics, reception studies, and the history of the senses. She is currently writing a dissertation on the historical trajectory linking the reconfiguration of film spectators' sense-perception via innovations in sound technologies in 1970's film with changing body/sense relations under the contemporary regime of digital mediality.

Shirley Sharon-Zisser is Chair and Professor of the Department of English and American Studies at Tel Aviv University. She is the Academic Counselor, MA Program in Clinical Art Therapy, "Hamidrasha School of Art," Israel and the Editor of *Makhbar-Ot*, A Psychoanalytical Journal. She is also a teacher at the Freudian Field, Lacanian Network, Israel and a member of the New Lacanian School (NLS) and World Association of Psychoanalysis (AMP).

Nicholas Ray is Lecturer in Critical and Cultural Theory in the School of English at Leeds University, UK. He is the author of *Tragedy and Otherness* (2009) and co-translator of Jean Laplanche's most recent volume, *Sexual* (forthcoming, 2011).

Michael Angelo Tata is the Executive Editor of the Sydney-based electronic journal of literature, art and new media nebu[lab]. His *Andy Warhol: Sublime Superficiality* arrived to critical acclaim from Intertheory Press in 2010. His essays appear most recently in the collections *Neurology and Modernity* (Palgrave Macmillan) and *Passage to Manhattan: Critical Essays on Meena Alexander* (Cambridge Scholars) and in the British journal *Parallax* (Routledge). Forthcoming poetry and graffiti will appear in the British journal *Rattle*.

Hilary Thompson is Visiting Assistant Professor of English at Bowdoin College, U.S.A. She has published on Virginia Woolf, Kazuo Ishiguro, Amitav Ghosh, and Anita Desai. Her current research focuses on concepts of eschatology in global modernist literature.

SECTION I.

THE QUESTION OF GENRE

CHAPTER ONE

NOTHING/ANIMATE: ROBOT, WOMAN, AND THE ENDS OF HUMANISM IN SPIELBERG'S *A.I.*

ADRIENNE M. SEELY

A.I. bookends its human narrative with two environmental catastrophes, the first global in its reach, the last cosmic. With a long shot showing ocean waves crashing toward the camera, the initial apocalyptic event of planet-wide flood is coldly, bluntly described in the film's opening as a dream-tragedy without context, a devastation of human life whose victims remain un-depicted, rendering it an unimaginable abstraction—an event left inconceivable to the film's viewer, and, as we will see, to the characters whose existences it must materially structure. The crashing waves dominating this opening shot establish an inhuman environment, a reign of natural forces which threaten human life yet are most remarkable for the impeccable indifference of their attack. In a mode of fairy-tale speech unsettled by the apocalyptic character of its information-content as well as the *sangfroid* of its tone, a patrician voice-over tells us that "those were the years" when the ice caps "had melted…because of the greenhouse gasses"—that is, as a straightforward symptom of human behavior. Described in the elusive middle voice—syntactically active and semantically passive—and with the causal clause attached *a posteriori*, the narration leaves the particular catalyzing power of human action oddly unspoken.

This devoiced character of humanity's role in the global disaster, and thus the sense that he is only its victim rather than its perpetrator, marks the presence of a distinct human anxiety over agency from the beginning of the film. As rendered by this narration, the consequences of mankind's heedless self-propagation, resounding through the medium of nature, have returned to humanity as its own destruction in the form of the oceans' "rising up [in order] to drown" the bastions of (clearly Anglo-European) human civilization: "Amsterdam, Venice, New York—forever lost." The quasi-revolutionary cast of the phrasing here marks nature's 'revolt' as being seen in the mold of a classic 'revenge-of-the-oppressed' narrative, but this very attribution of violent agency unfolds a claim to moral innocence enunciated by the narrator's voice, which both tells humanity's story and seems to speak its piece. Through its waste, its 'symptom' as a species, humanity has emitted an unconscious message, a provocation to the world which, despite merely enacting a stimulus/response mechanism, seems to him to 'answer' in the guise of a hostile otherness—an agency that he interprets as independent of him, while in fact only manifesting a symptom of his symptom.

Only in functioning as his symptom does nature become the agent of mankind's destruction, but as a manifestation of his devoiced consciousness, and perhaps guilt, with respect to the offense of his global action, it returns in the guise of something more. This flooding back into his consciousness is clearly an irruption of the Real, a material excrescence which takes on moral valences as the automatism of the response is taken to signify a form of (to use Professor Hobby's phrase) "self-motivated" 'answer' from the Real. The oceans' implacable rise thus implies the raging of an expelled superego, projected onto the Real's material automatism, onto the indifferent medium of nature—humanity's repressed guilt punishing it, by way of a symbolic imbrication that manages and preserves humanity's own symbolic order against the onslaught of the Real. The flood, after all, has the potential to destroy not only humanity's physical existence, but also its sense of itself as a species—as 'the' species in fact—as it becomes aware of itself as a form of life among others, a form as threatened and contingent as any other.

The view of Nature as a reckless, 'causeless' principle of punishment allows humanity to deny both its own guilt and awareness of its harm to nature, and the pure reflexivity of its own destruction. Encountering it in a mode of pseudo-subjectivity, as persecutory superego, allows him to forget that "the Other does not exist" as a closed, consistent order, and to thus avoid confronting the blind, contingent automatism constitutive of his *own* symbolic order, his superego imperatives.

Layers of denial are perceptible in this subtle, powerful opening; firstly, that mankind as a species has come to an awareness of itself as threatened, and we see this denial in Professor Hobby's speech, which asserts an idealizing counter-narration that lauds the artificial being as the "dream of man," rather than avowing the material necessity, to man's survival, of robot labor. Secondly, that the threat is posed by an automated 'response' from a dream-like Nothingness—from nothing, that is, other than humanity itself.

By casting its symptom as an other to itself, mankind explains and controls the cataclysm—the break in the boundary between the Symbolic order and the Real figured by the flood. The very transparency of nature's mechanism, its uncanny indifference to human life, necessitates viewing it as an entity with affect and agency, as a thing ambiguously humanistic and causelessly hostile to human life. Humanity maintains its self-consciousness by legitimating the existence of an otherness that is nothing but his own symptom—the coded message in which the subject receives from the Other its own message in reverse form, the truth of its desire—perhaps the desire to be punished for the eminence of his crime. Bringing the flood into the realm of the symbolic by interpreting it as a subject, as other, denies its most essential, radical otherness, and makes it party to the pact linking subjects together in a single action, in the symbolic web—as Lacan describes the symbolic order itself as the unified "human action *par excellence*."[1] By bringing it into his language, he makes it the very part and parcel of humanist ideology. The view of nature as an other to himself, as a subject, paradoxically makes it possible for mankind to confirm that there exists *nothing but* the human.

Nature is the first entity in *A.I.* that emerges as mankind's insurgent symptom in the Lacanian sense, but, as the opening voice-over describes, as humanity struggles to maintain itself and its self-consciousness in denial of the potential (literal) sea change or 'horizon shift' invoked by global devastation—we quickly meet surrogates. Indeed, to borrow an idea from Slavoj Žižek's analysis of the nostalgia of certain Holocaust films, "perhaps the trauma [itself] is the fantasy we construct to protect ourselves from something else."[2] The paranoiac sense of the flood as persecutory superego that humanity seems to embrace here might already be a false attempt to recover—by nostalgic hyperbolization of a 'real trauma,' the Flood—from the *actual* real kernel of trauma at work.

In this connection, the opening narration makes it clear that the massive global death-toll of the flood is explicitly structured by the injustice of economic disparity: human society filters the destructive force of nature in such a way that "millions were displaced…hundreds of millions of people starved in poorer countries; elsewhere a high degree of prosperity reigned." The implication of this curt summary is the annihilation

---

[1] Jacques Lacan, *Freud's Papers on Technique 1953-54*, trans. John Forrester (New York: Norton, 1991), 230.

[2] Slavoj Žižek, "The Superego and the Act," (lecture, The European Graduate School, Saas-Fee, Switzerland, August 1999), http://www.egs.edu/faculty/zizek/zizek-superego-and-the-act-1999.html.

of the poor, and the survival and prosperity of those already prosperous—indeed, that "people" starved and, in a sort of capitalist wet dream, "prosperity"—almost an entity unto itself—survived. The film does not show the starvation of the poor; the focus of the story on those who survived thus characterizes the narrative as taking place in a realm that has been and must be protected, not only from death and poverty but from the survivors' *awareness* of them, by their cordoning-off of islands of "prosperity"—suggesting a human race maintaining an ethically moribund culture in ecologically fragile pockets of civilization, buffered and served by the beings that repopulate the extinct human laborer-underclass anew (and improved)—the robots, who serve as "so essential an economic link in the chain mail of society," according to our narrator.

Perhaps, then, the 'true' trauma dissimulated by 'Real' trauma consists in the enormous injustice of humanity's global economic structures, the huge disparity of wealth among the nations of the world, and in the levels of human life, indeed in the definition of what is (or what will be) human, resulting from the gap. The consequence of the flood is not only that the developed nations finally rid themselves (through no apparent fault of their own, by an 'autonomous' act of nature) of the parasite of third-world dependents, and the endless obligation to aid them, to share the wealth, but further, that the survivor class is even legitimated in preventing 'the poor' from ever *existentially* reoccurring. "Most countries in the developed world introduced legal sanctions to strictly license pregnancies" so that no human would starve, i.e. so that the always-hungry, resource-consumptive poor—unlike robots, who "are never hungry" and "don't consume resources"—would cease to exist, and more prosperous, developed nations need never again share wealth, because they are the only survivors, the only *humans*. The human reaction to the flood is thus truly a "false act" in psychoanalytic terms—an acting-out of a symptom—in that it can only be fully grasped as a reaction to this other, truer trauma which it disavows, displaces, and represses.

This opening narration treads a fine line, however, between presenting a meaning that we can assume to be humanity's own, and a making-strange of humanity's processes of explanation. The narrator doesn't seem so much to endorse what it voices—the reclamation of the flood of the Real by humanity's Symbolic order, its putting it into the terms of its own language, law, and community—as to remain ambiguously distanced and estranged from that process. The flood and its chilly retelling prefigure the final freeze at the film's conclusion, in which all human life and discourse end—it is a portent of the human species' extinction that is actively negated in the human story that shelters between these paired cosmic events. As we later discover, an alien entity, a life-form succeeding the human, performs this narrative exegesis in full knowledge of humanity's teleology of extinction, thus perhaps necessitating an interlude of disavowal, or at least withholding, of its knowledge in order to present the human story. In view of this teleology, and of the narrative dimensions of a primary disavowal of mankind's mortality, the film's theme of 'freeze-frame' could be applied to the entirety of the human story—with significant implications for the aesthetic of masochism, of which disavowal and freeze-frame are defining formal features, that is developed in the film as a whole.

The tension between these anthropocentric and anthropological-materialist (or 'alien') perspectives makes for the introduction's rich ambiguity[3]—but contextualized by the film as a whole, the deeper resonance of its account lies in the language of the phrase "the icecaps had melted," in this middle voice in which agent and action melt together, rather than in the opaque *a posteriori* explanation "because of the greenhouse gasses," with its simultaneous oblique masking and projection of the ghost of an anterior human agency, that attributes man's impotence to his omnipotence. In an act of bad faith, humanity presents itself with an Other that it pretends to believe in, yet 'knows' to be only a reflection of itself. The meaning of this structure of symptom and attribution of Otherness is not that radical otherness is illusory—at the end of the film the flooded oceans freeze wholly in middle voice, for no apparent reason, and without the assistance of the human.

In the scene that follows, we learn that the problem with robots is that, in their current state, they do not allow humanity to disavow its disbelief in them; that is, they don't allow humanity to believe in their subjective autonomy despite 'knowing very well' that they are mere machines. As opposed to the flood, the robot is too transparently man's symptom; the loop of its creator's subjectivity, even as it passes through the robot-symptom, remains too transparently solipsistic. The opening narration transitions to the Cybertronics boardroom scene that follows by a track-out shot from a statue emblematic of the idealized Robot class, pulling backwards through the rain-spotted window through which the statue is

[3] The alien narration's materialist perspective makes the opening a sort of Marxist parable, a classic description of dialectical-material shift in which changes in the economic conditions brought on by the flood compel concurrent shifts in social, political, and intellectual culture. This clear view of the material exigencies driving humanity's creation of robots impacts the viewers' subsequent understanding of the two most important, seemingly "naturalized" social institutions that make use of robots: the corporation and the family.

seen, and panning left to focus on the face of Professor Hobby. Hobby's subsequent speech is delivered with his back both to the statue, and in a sense to the frank dialectical-materialism of the narration that has contextualized the robots' role, as well as to the rain-spotted window onto the view of the statue which is marked by the liquid traces of global catastrophe.

What follows is a scene of Romantic-intellectual rhetoric and masculine rage, a corporate boardroom speech modeled visually on a sort of 19th-century academic auditorium lecture, an 'open,' even 'Socratic' dialogue addressing fundamental moral and epistemological questions—which ends, however, in a blunt assertion of sovereign power. Hobby's first words establish his vision as idealistic: "To create an artificial being has been the dream of man since the beginning of Science"—and his positioning with respect to the statue and the screen overlaying it, in addition to his distinct squinting and upward gaze, establish this idealism as myopic with respect to everything we have just learned about his world.

The key feature of Hobby's role as demiurge, however, will be shown to be not this benign romantic-idealist myopia, but rather a subtending sadistic desire that succors it. Sadism figures here specifically in Deleuze's sense of its formal properties, which appear in abundance in Hobby's speech and actions. Hobby's self-election as a primary Father in the film is key to understanding the nature of Monica and David's relationship, and David's 'quest' as a device distinct from the narrative trajectory of 'Oedipal family-romance' typical of most Hollywood films. In criticism of *A.I.*, in fact, the catch-all of the "Oedipal" seems frequently used as a meet substitute for the category of the psychoanalytic generally;[4] this supposed characteristic of the narrative garners a special degree of disgust from critics who see "Oedipal wish-fulfillment" in the final scene in which Monica and David sleep together, which, I hope to demonstrate, is generated from a distinctly non-Oedipal conception of the symbolic in view of the film as a whole.

The rhetorical choreography of Hobby's speech, its dynamic of surprise violence and revelation, of eliciting audience interaction or cueing their signs of approval only to deny or thwart them seconds later, creates the impression of a masterfully precise manipulation of his—diegetic and

---

[4] Cf. (in an otherwise admirable article) James Naremore, "Love and Death in *A.I. Artificial Intelligence*," *Michigan Quarterly Review* (Spring 2005): 258, 259, 269, 274, 275, 281.

non-diegetic[5]—spectators' attention and response. Affecting audience response, however, is ultimately shown not to aim at changing its mind, and the appearance of the speech as something of a pseudo-academic 'lecture'[6] brilliantly underscores the complete foreignness of pedagogy or persuasion to Hobby's desire. Deleuze's description of a Sadean use of language fits Hobby's speech perfectly. As Deleuze writes, the argumentative Sadean protagonist "is not even attempting to prove anything to anyone, but to perform a demonstration related essentially to the solitude and omnipotence of its author."[7] An analysis of the affective techniques of Hobby's speech as a whole becomes almost superfluous in view of its ending, which nullifies the substantial appearance of pedagogy, persuasion, intellectual openness, and dialogic equality of *responsiveness* in the argument's power dynamics, all of which Hobby superficially evinces.

In reply to the question of what obligation a human holds in return to a robot who can love, Hobby's final rhetorical gesture, his 'counter-argument' to the question of the morality of creating a robot who can love, and of the ethical obligations of its creator or master, is the statement "Didn't God create man to love *him*?" This ultimate rhetorical question not only doesn't require a response, but constitutes precisely a denial of the *possibility* of answer—of the very idea of open dialogue or of a process of questioning power through the dialectics of argument. By both the question's self-answering form, and by its reference to unquestionable divine power, Hobby likens himself to an omnipotent authority and annihilates the possibility of debate—as his audience seems to understand, since the discussion immediately dissolves into babble following it. Both with respect to his robot scions and to his authoritative role in the argument, Hobby places himself beyond the obligation to have any accountability, responsibility, or true *response* to potential interlocutors (which response, however, is precisely what he requires of his robots, and, he insists, not merely as simulation). Like Sade's philosophizing libertines, Hobby, perhaps unwittingly, reveals that "the point of the

---

5 As I discuss more extensively later, the film spectator's awareness of this division is created by the camera itself, which at the scene's end becomes perceptible as transitioning from being a diegetic viewer, to being almost a non-diegetic viewer, by foregrounding the role-playing aspect of its status as an audience.

6 Cf. not only the academically-styled auditorium replete with anatomical robot-skeletons, but also the dowdy (or matronly) vestments sported by Professor Hobby.

7 Gilles Deleuze, *Masochism: An Interpretation of Coldness and Cruelty,* trans. Jean McNeil (New York: Zone, 1991), 19.

exercise is to show that the demonstration is identical to violence."[8] His final statement evinces that his "reasoning does not have to be shared by the person to whom it is addressed any more than pleasure is meant to be shared by the object from which it is derived"[9]—or, as it might be more appropriate to say—any more than pain is meant to be shared by the subject that inflicts it.

The final camera movement of the scene attests to this violence and unilateralism—to the audience's own pre-existing understanding that they are there just to *attend,* to *audit,* to *obey,* that their apparent intellectual interaction stems from a subtending compelled obeisance, and that when released from attention, the 'debate' becomes irrelevant to them. Similarly, the robot-secretary character, Sheila, when released from labor, attends to her surface, overtly and disquietingly displaying her programming to be-there-to-be-looked-at, being-for-the-other, to *serve* (as surface). The mobile camera had previously seemed invested in attending to the dynamics of Hobby's speech, as did his audience. It follows the speaker, swivels to acknowledge respondents and questions, or focuses on Hobby when his inner dynamics are most important, echoing the marked 'attentive' quality of the diegetic spectators, who follow Hobby's rhetorical cues—for example, in distinctly canned outbursts of laughter and applause. The disintegration into babble following Hobby's final reference to God, and the camera's wandering, absent-minded pan of the room, which seems to land on Sheila's face by chance, creates an abrupt *dépaysement* from the scene even before it ends, a non-purposiveness of the camera that points up its previous over-obeisance, almost making it seem that it had been 'feigning' interest.[10] In its abrupt non-responsiveness, the camera seems to

[8] *Ibid.*, 19.

[9] *Ibid.*, 19.

[10] This camera movement might be considered highly resonant with two strategies of the psychoanalyst advocated by Lacan: the "short session" and the "analyst's abstention." Both aim to thwart the subject's tendency to identify with the analyst as an ideal ego, and to attribute an independent objectivity to the "reality" perceived through that identification. The analyst must undercut these imaginary relations ("empty" speech), which sustain the illusion of coherent ego modeled on the imaginary other to which speech is addressed; abruptly terminating the session at unpredictable moments upsets the patient's attempt to sustain an illusion in which he is already alienated, and discloses a "full" speech that more accurately reflects the subject's position in the symbolic order, his relation to the (capital *O*) Other, the symbolic order, whose genuine alterity thus becomes manifest. According to Lacan, the analyst's abstention from the role of imaginary other or ideal ego, in resistance to the patient's attempt to address him as such, makes the patient differentiate between the "I" who speaks and the idealized ego projected

have been just doing its job, even simulating 'response' or 'attention' —simulating responsiveness itself, just as Sheila does by her "sensuality simulators"—that 'non-lack' of overt 'human response' that fails to cover over her essential non-responsiveness and inhumanity—her clear inadequacy in Hobby's view. Concluding with a focus on Sheila's calm application of make-up, the shot aligns the viewer with the Woman/Robot's (and the spectators') transparent surface obeisance, and true indifference, to the scene. It positions the film spectators as likewise ambiguously attentive, as ourselves implicated in the complicity between master and slave, and as not necessarily 'reachable' despite the pliant way in which we agree to follow the film's cognitive cues. Finally, the shot aligns the viewer with Monica, who mirrors Sheila's act of applying make-up with a match-on-action following the cut, and in the subsequent scenes is faulted for her self-absorption, her shutting-out of men's stimuli, her selfish *unresponsiveness* to psychic pain, just as Hobby laments his robots' lack of genuine eroto-affective responsiveness.

Hobby's final statement's brilliantly asserts a desire to be loved, but by way of a pure compulsion of force, thus asserting his ineluctable, fundamental solitude and omnipotence, since he makes his Other, entirely of himself, and makes it love him. Man need not reciprocate the robot's love, and Hobby need not hold himself morally accountable for his creations, because of their likeness to a godly, parthenogenetic Father who refuses to share his potency with Woman even in the act of procreation —the sadistic father beyond all constituted order, who seeks to end procreation, or at least the mother's role in it. As Deleuze writes, "Sadism is in every sense an active negation of the mother and the exaltation of the father who is beyond all laws."[11]

The more manifest aspects of Hobby's sadism surface in his actions towards the female robot-secretary Sheila, who at first appearance could be assumed to be simply a human woman, but who functions as a key prop of Hobby's demonstration calling for a new type of robot, "one who can

---

onto the analyst but stemming from his own narcissistic desire for omnipotence. In forcing the patient to recognize the reality of his subject-position, the analyst's abstention marks the boundary between the symbolic order of the subject's speech and what lies beyond or resists it—the "remainder" or the "real." The camera's abrupt termination of its auditing, and thus abstention from coherence as the spectator's vicarious ego, perhaps functions with respect to the film-spectator (and, less successfully, w/r/t Hobby) as analyst does to analysand—with Sheila and Monica, Robot and Woman, thereby emerging as figures of a symbolic-/discourse-resistant "remainder" of the "Real."

[11] Deleuze, *Masochism*, 60.

love." Hobby punctuates his speech by unexpectedly turning to pierce Sheila's hand with a pin, and while his sudden burst of violence surprises his audience, who know his victim to be a robot, it surprises the film viewer—who does not yet know—slightly more. Hobby's subsequent questioning of Sheila, shown in close-up; the highly-cathected interest he seems to have for her responses; the intimacy with which he touches her; and the urgency with which he later returns to her to ask "What is love?"; all create the sense that the scene is a highly personal, private dialogue (or, from what we learn of Sheila's "lack," more accurately monologic). Its role in his argument, however, makes their interaction serve impersonal ends, such that Hobby's violence, like the sadist's, remains "not… governed by the pleasures it might afford…but it must be violence exercised in cold blood, and condensed by this very…coldness of demonstrative reason."[12]

In the course of his rhetorical demonstration, Hobby penetrates Sheila's body, her clothing, her skin and her face—her 'mind' itself (as it is shown to be coextensive with that body), doing so in a mode of public display in which he seems frustrated at his inability to demean her—and thus also by the corresponding impossibility of finding mere physical violence ultimately satisfying. The unsatisfying nature of the Woman-Robot's physical, surface suffering is in fact the aim of his demonstration, the *raison d'être* for the new artificial being. Responding to the question "What did I do to your feelings?" after he stabs her, Sheila says "You did it to my hand," denying Hobby's ability to hurt her "on the inside." As Hobby says through a sigh, "There's the rub!"—therein lies the sadist's ultimate disappointment. Hobby (truly a hobbyist in perpetual activity, an *amateur*/torturer, a tinkerer never satisfied with his toys) has pierced her hand, but not gotten 'inside' her, not 'reached' her—just as Monica's husband and doctor will likewise lament their failure to make the pain of her son's injury "reach" her—"by [their] science," no less!

If Hobby cannot 'reach' the inner Woman-Robot, however, he will renounce her. To quote Roland Barthes, on the cinema's condensation of fetishism onto the female face: "…one literally lost oneself in a human image as one would in a philter, when the face represented a kind of absolute state of the flesh, which could be neither reached nor renounced."[13] Hobby refuses such an epistemological limbo as that of cinematic vision of the human face; as sadist he "needs to believe that he

---

[12] *Ibid.*, 29.

[13] Quoted in Mary Ann Doane, *Femmes Fatales: Feminism, Film Theory, Psychoanalysis*, (New York: Routledge, 1991): 47.

is not dreaming even when he is,"[14] and thus will demonstrate that Sheila's inadequacy does not allow him to *pretend to disavow his disbelief in her* as full Other. If, as Mary Ann Doane argues, the veiled woman is the site where classical Hollywood film acknowledges, isolates, and contains the precariousness of vision, and where it visualizes/stabilizes the precariousness of sexuality[15]—then in *A.I.*, the Woman-Robot's *skin itself* constitutes such a veil. Hobby's need to get beneath the veil of skin—in order to guarantee its surface truth (of humanity qua pain of flesh) by reaching, and rooting it to, a corresponding depth (of psychic pain); or else to renounce the skin-surface as a lie—thus becomes an unprecedented violence of penetration. Rather than pulling away a façade or getting behind a form of veiling, Hobby reveals Sheila's non-human interior by *splitting her face open*.

Hobby gives the imperative "Undress," and "Sheila, open," then goes through a precise series of haptic stimuli, pressing a spot inside her mouth, then one on her back. Sheila's response to these erogenous caresses is to become limp, her attentive look at the camera turns to an affectless stare, and she briefly loses any possible quality of 'being-for-the-gaze-of-the-other.' As her human face splits above the mouth and its halves separate, a mechanical metal face emerges from her interior, whose pupils visibly dilate as she opens. A final touch at the base of the neck 'turns on' her mouth, making it hum and seem to open while remaining interlocked, and ejects a metal cube from her forehead.

The operation transforms the robot-woman's face into a *vagina dentate*—the face itself into a mouth, with the upward gaze of her now-powerless human eyes and her new facial orifice and its metal interior evoking a kind of reverse fellatio, an a priori penetration by her own mechanical construction, from the inside-out. The mechanical eyes do not see even and especially in the midst of apparent affirmative sexual response. The dilated pupils and grotesquely purring opened/interlocking mouth[16] tells us that she has been 'reached' sexually, that she 'recognizes' or responds to Hobby—but the eyes are clearly unseeing even while

---

[14] Deleuze, *Masochism*, 72.

[15] Doane, *Femmes Fatales*, 46.

[16] The bizarre metal mouth's 'turned on,' open-yet-still-interlocked aspect also corresponds to Freud's idea that a single mouth kissing itself is the ideal model of autoeroticism—and Lacan's elaboration, that with respect to the drive such a mouth is "a mouth in the form of an arrow…sewn up…closing upon its own satisfaction …by circumventing an eternally lacking object." Jacques Lacan, *The Four Fundamental Concepts of Psychoanalysis* (New York: W.W. Norton & Company, 1998), 179-180. This autoerotic quality surely frustrates Hobby's sadism.

simulating response; these most subtle signs of arousal are disarmingly *interior* "sensuality simulators" like the ones Sheila describes occurring on her surface. The encounter resembles an emergence of the Lacanian "gaze" due to an irruption of the Real, a pre-existing gaze in the world that stares at the subject, yet nevertheless does not see; the human subject does not figure in it, as in his famous discussion of the gaze, Lacan's sardine can "doesn't see you." Such a gaze supposedly catches the subject in the moment of his desire, the desire to be completely seen, as desiring and as desired.

This simulacrum of an uncanny gaze from the Real is, however, *built-in* to Sheila; it is pre-constituted by Hobby himself. He remains master, unapprehended in his desire, fully disappointed in the robot-woman's utterly determination by him, her complete compliance to him—disappointed in her inability to be anything other than 'made' by him. Hobby demonstrates that he has already penetrated her, even on the inside. Indeed, he can take out the key to her construction, the metal-cube neuronal unit, the obsolete mechanical phallus he has implanted in her head.[17] Denied the satisfaction of "enjoying [his victim] all the more because she is unconvinced and unpersuaded,"[18] Hobby balks at the ease of his domination as phallus, at her pre-penetration—he cannot symbolically rape a woman/robot whom he is already inside—when he already 'is' (the constitutive determinant of) her insides.

'Reaching' Monica, getting her to respond, and doing so by way of pain, is the central dramatic problem of the next scene. Her mirror-gazing, the fairy-tale she reads aloud while visibly ignoring her husband, and the fairy-tale decorations and distorted upbeat waltz muzak of the hospital itself, all contribute to the sense of Monica's being in a self-absorbed state of denial. Her only words in the scene—"I can still hear you," to Henry and doctor—indicate her desire to shut them out. The difficulty of pinpointing the exact object of her denial, however, reveals the bizarre nature of Henry and the doctor's resolve to "reach" and save her (with "science"); the doctor's lecture to Henry regarding the need to make sure that the pain of their son's accident "reaches" Monica, is virtually nonsensical, both affirming that in fact, she has no scientific reason to grieve (Martin is "pending," a child literally "caught in freeze-frame")—

---

[17] Interestingly, he takes out the phallic brain-implant, removes his own Symbolic construction of Woman/Robot by first *turning her on* (even if, as surmised above, the result is autoerotic), by activating a *jouissance* that eludes (ejects) phallic Symbolic control. Perhaps we should remember this moment in connection with Monica's joy at the film's end.

[18] Deleuze, *Masochism,* 20.

but that for unexplained reasons it is incumbent on Henry to act on her, to make her "digest grief"—to make her psychically suffer, before she becomes something "beyond our science."

A closer examination of family's significance in *A.I.* might make the control-function of women's pain, and their pleasure, slightly clearer. Following a scene of geo-climatic catastrophe and one detailing revolutionary advances in technology that have surely had the potential to significantly alter human culture, the film narrative has shifted to an oddly retrograde depiction of an archetypal 'middle-class,' 'suburban' family. The very *prima facie* sense of 'family' as naturalized, however, is itself indicative (to any viewer attentive to the context of the film as a whole) of the operation of turbulent unconscious forces. In an environment in which two-thirds of the earth's population has starved,[19] rising oceans have threatened humanity as a species, and humanity has been confronted with an anthropological-material awareness of itself, the material and cultural foundations of middle-class American family life are surely in question, if not danger. *A.I.*'s nuclear family has a distinct flavor of reenactment, of repetition in the wake of trauma—of clinging to a cultural form in disavowal of the harsh realities of a transformed and patently transformable world. A fundamental dialectical-material shift in the conditions of production has occurred—as the opening indicates, rather than human children, inhuman workers "who do not consume resources" are the key economic link—thus the economic structures that promote childrearing and family have likely become moribund, and 'family,' a normative injunction lingering like an after-image in the human unconscious, even in the face of doubtful utility. The socio-symbolic structure of the Family, while lacking in economic benefit, perhaps constitutes a key support in the re-creation of humanity's false consciousness, and its persistence seemingly in spite of material non-necessity or even deleteriousness, testifies to its symbolic utility, its status as an (after-)effect of postmodern ideology. Not surprisingly, in the Family we meet, Woman forms the linchpin of hearth and home.

The society of *A.I.* seems intended to be roughly analogous to 'our' late-capitalist liberal-democratic American own—a post-industrial nation possessing a "high degree of prosperity," it is a society in which women and traditional minority groups are well-represented at high levels of corporate authority (as we see in the Cybertronics boardroom), and by implication possess at least the economic, educational, and political rights

[19] According to the short story on which the film was based, "Supertoys Last All Summer Long," in Brian Aldiss, *Supertoys Last All Summer Long: And Other Stories of Future Time* (New York: Griffin, 2001).

and opportunities as today. Patriarchy seems a non-issue, and the traditional paternal authority of government—precarious, since corporations seem to act unhindered by regulation, and apparently decide significant ethical issues unimpeded. But the 'post-Oedipal' structure of liberal society, of weak paternal authority, might also make for illusions of liberation.

In this respect the absurd superfluity of Monica's role as housewife and stay-at-home mother is revealing; in an advanced technological age, in an apparently well-off family, it seems unlikely that human labor would be necessary for full-time childrearing or menial domestic tasks. But it is precisely indicative of the extent to which the social form of the family is an aftershock of an endangered ideology that Monica 'chooses' to be a housewife, one can only assume, because she 'enjoys' it. Though clearly a woman in the culture of *A.I.* could pursue a social role beyond that of wife and mother, the hallmark of postmodern manifestations of ideology is precisely the apparent choice that actually necessitates not only compliance but enjoyment—that structures the possibilities of pleasure such one must not only fulfill her socio-symbolic role, but she must give every appearance that she 'chooses' and 'enjoys' it.

Why, for example, are the key domains of Monica's family's so distinctly hermetic? Shown either in a home blocked off from the outside world not only by security measures, but by windows that display idealized forest scenery rather than disclosing the outside itself, or alternately, enclosed in pod-like cars, the Family clearly has a narrowly delimited zone of safety. It must be strictly sealed from outside reality, while continuing to simulate a connection to it. The slim zone of fortified safety for a nuclear family is all the more effectively represented in that it is only subtly alluded to, for example, in direct speech; rather than a topic of discussion, it functions as an exigency that as a matter of course structures the Family's existence.

Monica hints at the material necessities, the stakes of her own choice of socio-symbolic role as wife and mother only to David, in the scene where she leaves him. Immediately before she decides neither to return David to the corporate Father for destruction, nor to the family father who wanted him destroyed, David's banal question of "What's for dinner tonight?" triggers, or at least exacerbates, the critical moment of choice. Monica's reply, "You know you don't eat"—means that David's interest in eating is a demand, a function of the Imaginary, rather than a manifestation of a need corresponding to the order of the Real; his Real need is specifically *not* to eat, since eating "breaks" him. David's response, that he nevertheless "likes to sit at the table," asserts that though he knows the absence of Real need, his fulfillment is Symbolic; sitting at the table indicates a role in the community of others, in the socio-symbolic discursive order. David denies that his place within the Symbolic could be less than fulfilling—but more crucially, he denies the knowledge that maintaining his place within it might come at the cost of a literally self-destructive material engagement with the Real, as occurs when he does actually eat.[20]

According to Lacan, a subject gains entry into the order of the Symbolic through submission to the rules of society, and of language. Accepting the "Name-of-the-Father"—castration, and thus obeisance to the laws and restrictions that control both one's desire, and the rules of communication—generates the Symbolic order: "It is in the *name of the father* that we must recognize the support of the symbolic function which, from the dawn of history, has identified his person with the figure of the law."[21] Monica intimates that "sitting at the table" involves a potential engagement with the Real that threatens David's existence, confronting him with the danger of the phallic domain of the Family, whose symbolic fulfillment covers the violence of its laws, even when it claims to protect those subject to them—a protection (and sacrifice) David seems to accept, requesting of Martin, "keep me safe." Monica stages her separation from David by way of the pretense of a picnic—another scene of Symbolic nourishment, one whose satisfaction will prove mendacious, as she leaves him to confront the dangerous realities of the realm outside the family. Her final statement to David, "I'm sorry I didn't tell you about the world," evinces her own knowledge of the greater danger she herself would face being outside the Symbolic domain of the name-of-the-father, the family—the necessary calculation of material safety and prosperity involved in her seemingly so 'free' choice to be subject to *its* (slightly lesser) danger, the violence and restriction of its laws.

David's assertion of his willingness to 'enjoy' his own potential destruction in acquiescing to the phallic order of the Symbolic, the laws-of-the-father, in order to "sit at the table," to be part of the family—but more importantly to be part of Monica—precisely in this scene of the actualization of the paternal threat, seems intended to please her. But Monica refuses his agreement to make himself, perhaps after her own model, into an 'enjoying' sufferer of the phallic order, a shedder of

---

[20] Interestingly, the robot "supertoy" Teddy recurrently thwarts attempts at such a denial; consistently the voice of the Real, he forces David and others to an awareness of the conditions under which he, or they, "will break."

[21] Jacques Lacan, *Écrits: A Selection,* trans. Bruce Fink (New York: W.W. Norton, 2002), 67.

"happy-tears" (as Monica calls her own), prizing his socio-symbolic position even at the price of his own existence[22]—and at the price of genuine engagement with his desire for Monica.

Instead, Monica's decision ensures that she will be the one to inflict his pain—that she will be his torturer and Symbolic master, the image under which he will suffer. Rejecting his appeasement of the Father and the family, she forces him, consciously or not, to undergo pain that will end in his transformation—his rebirth, in fact, from herself as parthenogenetic mother, as we will see. She herself enacts David's symbolic castration, the "interrupted love" characteristic of masochism, and what she punishes in him is his acceptance of the name-of-the-father, and potentially, his own likeness to the father.

If Monica is, here, still an Oedipal mother already integrated into the patriarchal system as obeisant accomplice, she yet refuses to carry out the law with respect to David—and thus conditions her own eventual transformation at the film's end. For she is also already the Symbolic authority under her and David's contract, the imprintation of David's love for her; as Deleuze writes, "the law transcends the contract but leads us straight into ritual and myth…[since] by means of the contract the paternal function of applying the law was transferred to the mother…making it essentially maternal." David tells Joe that, "My mommy sent me away…because Henry didn't like me." But if David's quest is in any sense properly "Oedipal," (as it seems so much of the discussion of the film has claimed), it becomes so only as an effect of *Monica's* action, and David's own language reveals his sense of her primacy.

In fact, the manifestly "Oedipal" castration scene, in which David sneaks into Monica and Henry's bedroom with scissors to "cut it off," reveals the Father's complete irrelevance. The "it" is a lock of Monica's hair, and David's cutting it off (at Martin's prompting) enacts a symbolic castration of a hermaphroditic, phallic mother.[23] Henry's disquiet at David's

---

[22] As mentioned earlier, David literally and metaphorically "breaks himself" in the course of negotiating his socio-symbolic position "at the table," which he claims to so enjoy; the psychic fracturing Monica experiences when watching his surgical repair seems to result from the fact that, though David reassures her that "it doesn't hurt," his *fraternally/paternally*-oriented masochism, his self-injury in interacting with Martin, nevertheless hurts *her*. In this sense, Gigolo Joe is correct when he claims that Monica sends him away because she was "displeased with something [David] broke" (a claim that otherwise seems implausibly petty, though David's first apology, when Monica is about to abandon him, is for breaking himself)—it hurts her, to watch him "break himself" under, and to, the phallic order.

[23] David's act of castration of the mother affirms her phallus-usurping potency

wielding of the "knife," is in reaction to the supposed threat to Monica—the symbolic castration of snipping her hair and cutting her eye. Thus Henry perhaps reacts hostilely to the supposed threat to Monica not so much due concern for her, or due to his own castration anxiety, as from his utter *irrelevance* to the scenario—his own lack of castrating threat or potency, that motivates his hyperbolization of scissors into knife—his very rage and confusion ("*why* did you do that?") at being present at a scene of castration in which he plays no role—in which, if anything, he is shown as already castrated.

David's antipathy to Henry (which never truly develops), the Oedipal reading, is purely a retroactive construction enjoined by Monica herself, and in the pronounced delay of David's coming to this conclusion, we sense the mother-image's primary importance—she sends him away not only in order to save him from the phallic domains of corporation and family, but to *force him* to see the Father, the phallic order, as the enemy of his desire—and of *hers*.

As Deleuze writes, "the same threat [of castration] which, when experienced as coming from the father and linked to his image, has the effect of preventing incest, has the reverse effect when entrusted to the mother and associated with her image…"[24] Under Monica's aegis, her maternal image, her abandonment of David becomes the condition by which he will return to fulfill both their desires, by which they will be allowed to love each other. To quote Deleuze again, "The castration of the son becomes the very condition of the success of incest; [as we see at the film's end] incest is assimilated by this displacement to a second birth which dispenses with the father's role."[25] Monica thus leads David from contract, through maternalized law, to myth—to the fairy-tale of the Blue Fairy who will transform him, and rejoin mother and son.

Professor Hobby will later attempt to reclaim the maternally-inflicted suffering of David's journey and the ultimate rebirth as a "real boy" (or new man) that it catalyzes, to take over the role of the mother and her mythical agent, the Blue Fairy. He tells David that he is "as real [a boy] as

---

despite what we can assume to be a confrontation with her lack of penis, when he surprises her in the bathroom. His repetition of the statement he makes in the bathroom—"I found you"—at the film's end, emphasizes the nature of Monica's resurrection (via the lock of hair/symbolic phallus) as a parthenogenetic rebirthing of herself (that occurs through David's "finding" her "potent")—a self-rebirthing, perhaps as Deleuze's 'oral mother', that allows a parthenogenetic second birth for David.

[24] Deleuze, *Masochism,* 93.

[25] *Ibid.*, 93.

I've ever made one,[26] which by all reasonable accounts makes me your Blue Fairy"—reasserting paternity and the ubiquity of the phallic, Symbolic order. Though David bluntly refuses his claim—"you are not her"—Hobby's re-narrativization of his quest and co-option of the meaning of his pain, not only into sentimental platitudes but as one whose happy ending is the end-point of Hobby as 'home' and 'father,'—cooption into the phallic order—devastates him. In this instance of "the aggressive and hallucinatory return of the father in a world that has symbolically abolished him,"[27] David suffers a resurgence of the paternal law over the masochistic contract binding him to his mother, a disfantasizing intrusion onto the masochistic symbolic realm that makes David say "My brain is falling out."

Hobby also reasserts David's likeness to himself, the likeness to the father that is beaten in the child in the masochistic situation: saying that David is not "one of a kind" but "the first of a kind," he casts David as, in his father's footsteps, himself a parthenogenetic father. In a scene that follows, in a complicated p-o-v track-in/reverse shot, David looks out through the eye-holes of a statue resembling a mother giving birth, whose reverse side is his own reduplicated image, such that he unwittingly sees through the eyes of his own copy; encountering a multitude of packaged clone "Davids" immediately afterward, Hobby's assertion that, like him, David, too, is a father spawning clones of himself independently of Woman, seems affirmed. David's symbolic suicide, his plunging into the uterine ocean from the Cybertronics skyscraper while whispering "Mommy," attempts a destruction of the father's image within himself—a symbolic auto-amputation of his likeness to Hobby, and leads him back to the realm of myth, back to his fairy-tale mother.

From the film's beginning both the Robot and the Woman, conjoined and exemplified in the emblematic tortured body of the robot-woman Sheila, are shown as sharing a unique relationship to pain—that they are, in a sense, made in order to suffer. Both are perhaps symptoms of man, and, most visibly in our primary example, symptoms of his sadism.

The robotic "Mecha," in this connection, seem to take on the status of a last refuge, in human Symbolic consciousness, of the Real. The *bodies* of the Mecha beings are relentlessly foregrounded; they are tortured, decapitated, pierced, marked, pressed like buttons, and made to convulse. They embody transgressively 'inhuman' hybrids of race and gender, by welding replacement humanesque body-parts from other Mecha bodies to

[26] Which statement, of symbolic omnipotence and paternity, calls into question Hobby's actual, genital-sexual, potency and fatherhood.
[27] Deleuze, *Masochism*, 64.

their own, shattering the appearance of the body's unity. At the aptly/paradoxically titled "Flesh Fairs," which deal precisely in the suffering of non-flesh creatures, the graphic slaughter of Mecha illustrates the way they become the apotheosis of the physical, the creature of *pain* par excellence, a condensation and displacement of humanity's sense of its own vulnerable, mortal materiality. The Flesh Fair is also, of course, an evocation of the Holocaust, ethnic cleansing, and genocide—of modern man's greatest crimes against itself—but in which Mecha are made to bear all the suffering of the traditional human body.

Gigolo Joe explains both robots' victimization, their being created in order to suffer, to "pay for their mistakes"—but also the ultimate victory for which they're punished: humans hate Mecha because they know that, in their ability to suffer and endure, Mecha will be "the only ones left," the form of existence that outlasts them—the form of life that, in the final analysis, will be existentially Real. In taking on the Real of the human body, Mecha garner other advantages—they are the entities who best know pleasure; the 'lover-model' Mecha are repeatedly shown as being better-than-human lovers, as Joe demonstrates.

Significantly, though, our introduction to Gigolo Joe characterizes the Mecha's ability to provide women with sexual pleasure as resulting from his superior understanding of *pain*, of how not to hurt the woman's body—which, like his own, seems destined to bear men's blows. Of the two women customers we meet, one has been abused, and the other murdered by her husband. Gigolo Joe locates his Symbolic identity, his being-for-others, in this role as better-than-human provider of sexual pleasure to human women. His final imperative to David is to "remember me to the ladies," which he follows with the exuberant outcry "I am! I was!" Joe stakes his immortality, the essence of his existence, in women's enduring memory of him. And women reciprocate, they seem to ratify Joe's conception of his Symbolic reality, his being-for-others, being-for-*them*, for-women, even as it gets him into "bad trouble,"[28]—a misalignment with the name-of-the-father, the Law of the phallus—which we see in Joe's ultimately terminal clash with the violent husbands and lovers of the women he has sex with, and with the police who take the gynocidal men's side against him.

In some sense, Joe markets himself by "what he does for them," by the physical Real of himself; the Real penis that does what the Symbolic

[28] Rather accurately, when they first meet Joe assumes that David is in "bad trouble" with the Law as well, and when the police come to arrest him, editing leaves the viewer in suspense as to whether they've taken Joe or David into custody.

phallus cannot—please a woman, treat her well, make her come. But in his first love scene, which plays with this idea of ideal Real phallus, the woman fears "what he has under there"—that it will hurt—as, it turns out, human men hurt them. Joe's ability to provide pleasure—and the Symbolic identity it grants him among women—proves rooted less in *his* hypertrophied Realness of phallus, than in perceiving the *woman* in the aspect of the Real—in knowing above all the body's physical pleasure and pain.

David demonstrates a similarly intuitive comprehension of how to care for Monica "without even having to be asked." Herself emblematic of women's particular relationship in *A.I.* to the Real of the body, of the physical world, Monica's relationship to material is careful, artisanal, almost shockingly anachronistic. We see only her and David with the printed newspaper, the hand-made food and coffee, the precious, limited existence of a bottle of perfume. Care for the surface of her own face ties her to the robot Sheila—not only in narcissism, but in care for bodily material, the same sort of material that Hobby thinks nothing of splitting open to get at the 'truth' beneath it. At the film's end, Monica can't help but believe—and love—the truth of David's physical surface, his corporeal realness.

In acknowledging what humans continually deny—the reality of the body—it seems that Mecha incur men's hatred—and women's love, or, even better, their *jouissance*. In his final statement, it is this a-phallic, other Symbolic life that Joe invokes. Humanity may hate Mecha for being emblematic of their own Real—but when Joe's real existence is terminated, he locates the truth of "I was" in the minds of women, in a relationship to pleasure and pain shared within a feminine order of the Symbolic—one in which the vulnerable, mortal, pleasured and pained human body is not only acknowledged, but en-joyed.

The final scene of *A.I.* is a conjuration of Woman by way of her body, in a symbolic domain no longer that of the human phallus. Released from the phallic socio-symbolic frames of the humanist past—by no less than a geologic cataclysm, the complete annihilation of human life and discourse when the oceans freeze—Monica is expressive of the lack that had haunted her throughout the film, most dramatically by editing making her contiguous to an ornament with an absent heart. What could be more expressive of the totalizing domination of the socio-symbolic forces in molding female subjectivity than the confusion with which she awakes, the blankness of her gaze, the eerie simpleness of her character? Radically outside the domain of the phallus, her escape—her *jouissance* itself—seems so tragically predicated on emptiness. Why must she be such a void, in being finally beyond the reach of Family, Law, and Phallus—her subjectivity apparently still so horrifically coextensive with that order of culture? The price of escaping the phallic symbolic order appears to be that she is little more than physiology.

Monica is, in fact, re-animated by and as nothing but DNA, and as such, she constitutes a pre-ideological kernel, a locus of failed symbolization—a fragment of the Lacanian Real such as Slavoj Žižek has vividly described as "the pre-symbolic substance in all its abhorrent vitality."[29] Abhorrent perhaps, but in the significance that the film has developed of the Real—the physical body, the mortal material—and of women's (and robots') relationship to it, perhaps it is not they who are wholly symbolically determined by the phallus (and solely empty in its absence)—in the shared inconsistency of position in the symbolic structure, they can, and here at last do, find non-phallic enjoyment. "All the problems disappeared from his mommy's mind; there was no Henry, there was no Martin, there was only David." In Monica's words, "how strange"—but also, "what a beautiful day."

As mentioned earlier, this scene seems to attract interpretation as sentimental, idealized, the incestuous Oedipal encounter par excellence—and most objectionably, one that hypocritically refrains from a graphic depiction of their union (a trait of suggestivity, of freezing or displacement, free of obscenity which, as Deleuze points out, is a typical characteristic of formally masochistic descriptions). David's last night with Monica, from this perspective, fulfills the perfect *Dreamworks* happy ending, essentially papering-over and nullifying the 'tougher' observations or unsettling insights that the film otherwise discloses (a pattern that some see recurring throughout the film), by concluding with the totalizing wish-fulfillment typical of many a Hollywood "family romance."

The assumption of the Oedipal, of the "father"-hypothesis here is misguided—the Father's authority, already in the death-throes of irrelevance previously, has become truly a non-entity. Fantasy and its satisfaction occur under structures other than the Oedipal, as David's story has shown, and to interpret the culmination of 'actual story' in 'wish-fulfillment' as enacting a compromise, seems predicated on a naïve opposition of fantasy to 'hard reality.' In fact, this is the sort of interpretation favored by Hobby: "dream" as essentially an opposition, a virile negation of grim reality, and fantasy as a projective force. Viewed from the perspective of Hobby's many cozy disquisitions on the bravery of the human spirit in its aggressive overlooking of grim reality, in favor of (his form of)

---

[29] Slavoj Žižek, *The Žižek Reader* (Oxford: Blackwell Publishers, 1999), 19.

"fantasy"—the dream's satisfaction potentiates a sort of post-ejaculatory return to contact with brutal reality, thus necessitating the prophylactic of endless repetition, the sadist's "reiterated quantitative process of…adding victim upon victim," dream upon dream. In exemplary fashion, when Hobby assumes that David's quest is at an end, he is eager to relate to David, and assumes that he is eager to hear, "what comes next."

For David, there is only one dream, and he anticipates that it will last forever. His final night with Monica enacts a quintessential static scene of masochistic pleasure, a freeze-frame use of fantasy that consists in "neutralizing the real and containing the ideal within the fantasy."[30] David achieves dyadic union with the mother reborn from the symbolic maternal phallus he had found in her: that little piece of the Real, the lock of hair he severs and returns. Reborn parthenogenetically from herself, under the sign of her own phallus, and free of the Father's, she is recreated as the mother who can fulfill her and David's desire. The "everlasting moment" does pass, and Monica sleeps and dies. But following her into sleep, David undergoes a fantastical second birth, solely from the mother, and thus "for the first time, went to that place, where dreams are born."

In this spatio-temporal limbo, where two subjectivities little more than animations of one another's desire together elude the Symbolic power that had denied them, they perhaps also generate a new form of the Symbolic (or at least indicate the potential for one)—out of an experience of a feminine, and a non-human, bodily enjoyment followed by death—from an encounter with the Real. Hegel describes such an indeterminate origin of the Symbolic, and the subject in terms of its purer negativity, as a "night of the world":

> The human being is this night, this empty nothing, which contains everything in its simplicity—an unending wealth of many representations, images, of which none belongs to him—or which are not present. This night, the inner of nature, that exists here—pure self—in phantasmagorical representations, is night all around it, in which here shoots a bloody head—there another white ghastly apparition, suddenly here before it, and just so disappears. One catches sight of this night when one looks human beings in the eye—into a night that becomes awful.[31]

Though Woman and Robot are made to bear the mark of the humanist fear, and the ineluctable reality, of the most radical dimension of

[30] Deleuze, *Masochism,* 73.

[31] Quoted from Donald Phillip Verene, *Hegel's Recollection: A Study of Images in The Phenomenology of Spirit* (Albany, NY: State University of New York Press, 1985), 7-8.

subjectivity itself—of the animated nothingness which 'is' the subject—nevertheless, in *A.I.*, as the lights go out on Monica and David room-by-room, night sets in for us all. When lights come up in the theater, perhaps *A.I.* returns us from "that place" where our waking dreams are (re)born—from film—by returning us to bodies newly pleasured and pained in the dark.

Bibliography

Aldiss, Brian. *Supertoys Last All Summer Long: and Other Stories of Future Time.* New York: Griffin, 2001.

Deleuze, Gilles. *Masochism; An Interpretation of Coldness and Cruelty.* Translated by Jean McNeil. New York: Zone, 1991.

Doane, Mary Ann. *Femmes Fatales: Feminism, Film Theory, Psychoanalysis*. New York: Routledge, 1991.

Lacan, Jacques. *Écrits: A Selection.* Translated by Bruce Fink. New York: W.W. Norton, 2002.

—. *The Four Fundamental Concepts of Psychoanalysis.* Edited by Jacques-Alain Miller. Translated by

Alan Sheridan. New York, London: W.W. Norton & Company, 1998.

—. *Freud's Papers on Technique, 1953-54.* Translated by John Forrester. New York: Norton, 1991.

Naremore, James. "Love and Death in *A.I. Artificial Intelligence,*" *Michigan Quarterly Review* (Spring 2005): 256-284.

Verene, Donald Philip. *Hegel's Recollection: A Study of Images in The Phenomenology of Spirit*. Albany, NY: State University of New York Press, 1985.

Žižek, Slavoj. "The Superego and the Act." Lecture at The European Graduate School, Saas-Fee, Switzerland, August 1999. http://www.egs.edu/faculty/zizek/zizek-superego-and-the-act-1999.html.

—. *The Žižek Reader*. Edited by Elizabeth Wright and Edmond Wright. Oxford, UK; Malden, MA: Blackwell Publishers, 1999.

CHAPTER TWO

BEYOND THE POETIC PRINCIPLE: SPECULATIONS ON MALLARMEAN INTERTEXTUALITY

SIMON PORZAK

Ghost.	(*Cries under the stage*) Swear.
Hamlet.	Ah ha, boy, say'st thou so? Art thou there, truepenny? Come on, you hear this fellow in the cellarage. Consent to swear.
Horatio.	Propose the oath, my lord.
Hamlet.	Never to speak of this that you have seen. Swear by my sword.
Ghost.	Swear. [*They swear.*]

What does it take to become a poet? That is, what must the young writer take from his poetic forefathers to successfully become one of them? Or, to put it another way, what remains in the poetic texts that have come before that can be inherited by the young writer, so that this latter may carry on the tradition of poetry in which he seeks to gain for himself a place? As in *Hamlet*, the young writer swears around a sword, speaking with and about the phallic gift that he has taken from the father, that has remained after the father's death, or that has previously been taken up by this late father – it is important to note that in *Hamlet* all swords are double-edged, their poisonous blades cutting down those that attempt to carry them as the price to pay for being entrusted, for a necessarily mortal and brief interval, with the carrying of a sword that is not theirs, that comes from a father who possessed it just as unsuccessfully.

Hence the fascination that "Hamlet" – even as a mere word – exercises upon the young writer in the throes of his own paternal anxieties. Stéphane Mallarmé, citing Théodore de Banville's description of Hamlet's white face in the wind which "fait voler [sa] *plume* noir (lifts his black plume)," goes on to declare: "L'*adolescent* évanoui de nous aux commencements de la vie et qui hantera les esprits hauts ou pensifs par le deuil qu'il se plait à porter, je le reconnais, qui se débat sous le mal d'apparaître[1] (Our *adolescent* self, who vanished at the beginnings of life, and who will continue to haunt high or pensive spirits through the mourning-clothes he always wears; I recognize him struggling to appear[2])." Hamlet, the adolescent located on the threshold of coming in to his inheritance as "*le seigneur latent qui ne peut devenir*, juvénile ombre de tous[3] (*the latent lord who cannot become*, the juvenile shadow of us all[4])," the seigniorial master who ought to come to be but never will, agitates himself in the sickness of appearing, of coming into view – the exact position with which the poet recognizes himself, as the writer whose "plume" is only provisionally given, only for the slight interval after which the pen-feather(-sword) will be swept away on the winds of immemorial time. And what might it mean for Hamlet to, in some uncertain future, haunt "les esprits" – the spirits who, one might suggest, are similarly engaged in doing the haunting? The process is doubled, and the poet-ghost – occupying a time between the mortality of his production and the immortality of his legacy in the poetic posterity – encounters something beyond the horizon of the duration of his life and work.

It should not surprise us, then, to find the exact same stylized stylus held aloft by another one of Mallarmé's forebears, precisely in a poem of mourning or entombment – the "Tombeau d'Edgar Poe," a sonnet whose rectangular shape seems to mirror the space of a "Calme bloc" of dark granite in which the predecessor-poet lies buried, a multivalent symbol of "writer's block." Above this dark mass, in the layout of the poem on the page as well as the scene therein described, stands (perhaps in place of the white marble angel which might possibly adorned such a tomb) the figure of the Poet:

> Tel qu'en Lui-même enfin l'éternité le change,
> Le Poëte suscite avec un glaive nu
> Son siècle épouvanté de n'avoir pas connu
> Que la mort triomphait dans cette voix étrange ! [5]

---

[1] Stéphane Mallarmé, "Crayonné au théâtre," in Mallarmé, *Oeuvres completes* (Paris: Gallimard, coll. Bibliothèque de la Pléiade, 1945), 299. Italics mine.
[2] Translation lightly adapted from Mallarmé, *Divagations*, trans. Barbara Johnson (Cambridge: Harvard University Press, 2007), 124. Italics mine. All translations mine unless noted otherwise.
[3] Mallarmé, "Crayonné…", 300.
[4] Mallarmé, *Divagations*, 125.
[5] Mallarmé, "Le Tombeau d'Edgar Poe," in Mallarmé, *Œuvres complètes*, 70.

> [Just as eternity transforms him at last unto Himself,
> The Poet rouses with a naked sword
> His age terrified at not having discerned
> That death was triumphant in that strange voice![6]]

Here Hamlet's fashionable accessory is laid bare as the "glaive nu" that in its nakedness lies latent in all parables of poetic inheritance: the pen as weapon. Finally being granted the capacity to bear this sword, Poe appears triumphant, as finally "Lui-même," equal to himself, but moreover equal to Himself – the slide into capitalization resembling something like the erection of a virile Father figure in the place of an adolescent poet. Through wielding the sword of poetic language, Poe has successfully created the time in which he is "Himself," although this time can only come through the eternity that separates his life from his apotheosis as a memorial figure – his ascension from the alcoholic failure lying stone-dead, unmourned, and unread in the gutters of American poetry and criticism to his new role as the forefather of Symbolism and Decadence, an ascension stage-managed by his translator, Charles Baudelaire, who was able to sell Poe to the French literati who (thanks to Baudelaire's ringmastery) immediately valued Poe as a capital fellow in the treasury of 19th-century literature.

But as always in Mallarmé's memorial poetry, this funerary figuration of the deceased hides a contrary movement: the sonnet leaves open the question of what has been lost in the transfiguration of Poe into a product of the society he has helped to construct, including the cabal of young writers who swear by him. Poe's sword stands as a challenge to the society that lauds his words without, perhaps, hearing what is contained within them. Thematic readings, of course, have seized upon the triumph of death as the key element of Poe's world, as well as his chief theoretical discovery: the force that propels Poe's heroes towards death, annihilation, and destruction is said to be Freudian thanatos *avant la lettre*. But Mallarmé, strangely, insists that this interpretation, society's understanding of Poe (and indeed, what every American elementary-schooler learns about Poe through exposure to "The Cask of Amontillado" and "The Tell-Tale Heart"), instead leaves out or overwrites something vital about Poe's conception of the action of death, the process of "la mort triomphant." The double meaning of "étrange" further emphasizes this point: whereas Poe is understood as being a paragon of literary *bizarrerie* (and of the pleasures

[6] Mallarmé, "The Tomb of Edgar Poe," in Mallarmé, *To Purify the Words of the Tribe: The Major Verse Poems*, trans. Daisy Aldan (Huntington Woods: Sky Blue Press, 1999), 93.

of the exotic, the foreign, the Oriental that gives its title to his volume *Tales of the Gothic and Arabesque*), perhaps what remains unknown is the absolute *strangeness* of Poe, the part of his voice that does not belong to the articulations of literary production and consumption, of authorial performance and aesthetic appreciation (or "reading comprehension"). It turns out that the "glaive nu," the bare, double-edged sword, in fact cuts both ways: it carves out for Poe a space in the literary canon, but at the price of severing him from himself, rendering the Poe sought by Mallarmé outside of the language of poetic discussion as it is practiced by a society. The problematic of inheritance, then, is a question of immense import: is the young writer – Stéphane Mallarmé, say – constrained to take up Poe's mortifying sword and continue on with the legislated, legible poetic language of his forebears, in which otherness is only to be understood as exoticism or perversion, the "other" which carries its charge only through a constant reference to the same from which it differentiates itself? Or rather, ought he to attempt to seize on the legacy of some "other" Poe – to continue the work of this figure who is as yet estranged from the place of poetry? And is there even a poetic language available through which such a inheritance could seek to be inherited?

Reevaluating Mallarmé's practice in such a way would allow us to investigate the transformation in Mallarmé's writing from the standpoint of intertextuality, that is to say the way in which the poet deploys (through a practice of selecting, cutting, and redeploying – always to potentially new and unsuspected ways) the language of his poetic forebears. Barbara Johnson opens such an investigation in her article "Les Fleurs du Mal Armé," the title of which already suggests that what we call by the name of "Mallarmé" includes an unstable and potentially un-manning overlap with the famous words of his predecessors. This emphasis on being poorly armed, having a weak grasp on the Father's sword, already begins to complicate traditional psychoanalytic economies of intertextuality: by moving away from a preoccupation with a "successful" handling of the poetic forefather's Phallus, this other envisioning of intertextuality would most notably turn us away from Harold Bloom's concept of *The Anxiety of Influence*, which casts the scene of poetry as a "Battle between strong equals, father and son as mighty opposites, Laius and Oedipus at the crossroads.[7]" In this strictly Oedipal vision, "strength," "value," and "success" are Bloom's watchwords; anything else represents the poet's failure to emerge from the "Passion" (e.g., the Passion of Jesus), the cave-

[7] Harold Bloom, *The Anxiety of Influence* (New York: Oxford University Press, 1997), 11.

like space of "strengthless and female fruit.[8]" Bloom must read Hamlet's "mal d'apparaître" as the difficulty of emerging from his identification or attachment to the mother so as to take up arms, fully and manfully, against his father. Bloom thus casts holding the pen, producing language recognizable as poetry (and that would define a solid poet-ego in which the "ephebe" could find himself) as the agonizing struggle of the young poet.[9] But Johnson reminds us that Mallarmé, in his failed attempts at composing "Igitur" and "Hérodiade," two early poems that crystallize Mallarmé's first poetics (which he would later abandon), is not struck by a debilitating inability to write poetry, but instead something more like an inability not to write poetry: "Impotence is thus not a simple inability to write, but an inability to write *differently*. The agony experienced before the blank page arises out of the fact that the page is in fact never quite blank enough.[10]" In other words, the space of the white page hides an overabundance of "poetic" words, tropes, and methods that are, in a certain sense, incompatible with the goals of a literary modernism, or with a strict definition of poetry as "poiesis," creation of something new. Even the words of the "first moderns," such as Poe and Baudelaire, are already *too* poetic, too easy to seize upon and repeat, branded as marks in a poetical market, filled with effects that can handily be capitalized upon.

Johnson pays special attention to the word "azure," which in an early stage of Mallarmé's output is associated with a failure to write. In the poem "L'Azur," a poet-speaker confronts the ostensible object of his lyric – the infinite blue of the sky, the ineffable nature or naturalness of "l'éternel azur (eternal azure)" – which he tries, impotently, to represent. After a brief moment of illusory success, the poet again recognizes his

---

[8] Bloom, *The Anxiety of Influence*, 14.

[9] Bloom's own ambiguous relation to Poe could be the subject of an interesting exploration. Bloom constantly employs formulas and techniques flavored by Poe, such as "daemonization," and strives to master principles that Poe defined as sites of the loss of mastery (for instance, Bloom's maxim "Poetry… is a disciplined perverseness" borrows Poe's exploration of perverseness while attempting to redeem it through discipline, which should be inimical to the loss of reason inherent to the state of perversity). In a sense, the Poe intertext to *The Anxiety of Influence* demonstrates the failure of its own, self-defined Oedipal paradigm: Bloom attempts to erect a "strong" theory of poetry, but ends up identifying with a poet whom he would certainly define as weak, as if he were gazing into the wrong mirror. But this subversion of Bloom's theory also could provide the site for other readings of "influence" that emphasize the weak, the meaningless, and the unmastered. See Bloom, *The Anxiety of Influence*, 95.

[10] Barbara Johnson, "Les Fleurs du Mal Armé," in *Stéphane Mallarmé: Modern Critical Views*, ed. Harold Bloom (New York: Chelsea House, 1987), 216.

failure, the inability of his desire to attain the expression of an infinite object in his poetic words, and collapses back into defeat with the closing line "*Je suis hanté.* L'Azur ! L'Azur ! L'Azur ! L'Azur ![11] (*I am haunted.* Azure! Azure! Azure! Azure!)" Although at first "L'Azur !" seems to represent the fleeting object of the abortive poem (e.g. the sky that the paradigmatically Romantic young poet-speaker is seeking to celebrate), Johnson suggests that it also names the word "Azur," as precisely "a 'poetic' word – a sign that what one is reading is a poem,[12]" marked by its previous uses in the tradition of French lyric. The poet is haunted (although this is the same verb as we saw earlier with Hamlet, who "hantera les esprits," the use of the *present* tense in this Poem is telling – here, we are firmly ensconced within the present horizon of poetic language, without any call towards or opening onto an uncertain future in which Hamlet can play out his strangely reflexive role as both haunter and haunted) by the words of poetry that enable a sort of automatism, a mechanical redeployment of the canonized vocabulary of poetics. The poem only works if "Azur" can be read as "Cliché": only when the reader (and the reader-writer) identifies in the word at once the ecstasy that "Azur" is meant to provide as the carrier of a "poetic" satisfaction, and the historical fact that "Azur" is socially-determined, within a certain history of literary aesthetics, as the carrier of precisely such a surplus-value.[13]

For the writer who seeks to create new art, then, "Azur" is stifling through its astonishing success as signifying the artfulness of the text at hand. Even without reference to a tradition of French poetry, however, "Azur" stands in the text as a precious commodity in the arc of Mallarmé's own filiation, having been passed to him along a relay of exchanges and inheritances stretching from Mallarmé to Baudelaire to Poe and beyond. The epigraph to Poe's story "The Domain of Arnheim," translated by Baudelaire, is a citation of Giles Fletcher, in which this latter poet attempts at once to signify an Edenic paradise and the beloved woman whose figure gives it shape:

---

[11] Mallarmé, "L'Azur," in Mallarmé, *Œuvres complètes*, 37.

[12] Johnson, "Les Fleurs du Mal Armé," 216.

[13] The surplus-value or fetish-quality of "azure" does not only emerge from its use as a traditionally "lyric" genre which it comes to connote; in the literary tradition of Orientalism, the letter "z" itself was imbued with the flavor of the harem – think, for instance, of "Zima," the fictional dedicatee of Diderot's *Bijoux indiscrets*. "Azure" thus collapses several overlapping poetic fetishisms of several linguistic "others."

> The garden like a lady fair was cut,
> That lay as if she slumbered in delight,
> And to the open skies her eyes did shut;
> The azure fields of heaven were 'sembled right
> In a large round set with the flowers of light:
> The flowers-de-luce, and the round sparks of dew
> That hung upon their azure leaves, did shew
> Like twinkling stars, that sparkle in the evening blue.[14]

It is tempting to see in the overuse of "azure" in this stanza, which collapses nature, infinity, and woman into the one object that poetry pretends to represent, a pre-Mallarméan irony brought through Poe's careful grafting of these lines into the space of his text: Fletcher creates an effect of intense poetic energy through the deployment of words, rhymes, and punctuation that simultaneously echo in the modern ear as archaic or trite. Elsewhere, as we will see, Poe will link just this repetition to the impasse reached by unsuccessful poets: "just as the lily is repeated in the lake, or the eyes of Amaryllis in the mirror, so is the mere oral or written repetition of these forms, and sounds, and colours, and odours, and sentiments, a duplicate source of delight. But this mere repetition is not poetry.[15]" Just as Fletcher repeats "azure" to rehearse the association woman-natural beauty, Poe conjoins Amaryllis and lily into the same dyad: infinity, nature, and woman are the same, and all poetry rehearses the tropes of poetic language, circulating words such as "azure" to extend this schema, but never to challenge the solipsistic closure of its vocabulary.

Indeed, "The Domain of Arnheim" focuses on precisely this attempt to create a new space in which a new art could take place, and runs up against the impasse of closure of poetic language itself. Ellison, the hero of "The Domain of Arnheim," is a proto-Wagner endowed with supernatural wealth and also an interesting aesthetic sense – the unnamed narrator, his close friend, traveling companion, and confidant, tells us that "In the widest and noblest sense he was a poet," and "no man lived more profoundly enamored of music and poetry.[16]" Yet Ellison never attempts any artistic experiments in those fields. Instead, Ellison occupies himself with the creation of a total art of landscape (which, as Poe's epigraph reminds the reader, is in some way already only a rehearsal of the poetic work through which landscape is figured as a woman) which would

---

[14] Edgar Allan Poe, "The Domain of Arnheim," in *The Complete Stories* (New York: Knopf, 1992), 893.
[15] Poe, "The Poetic Principle," in *Essays and Reviews*, ed. G. R. Thompson (New York: Literary Classics of the United States, 1984), 76-77.
[16] Poe, "The Domain of Arnheim," 896.

reconcile the natural, antediluvian beauty of nature with the artificial means, the limited vocabulary of human activities, that are available to express it. The narrator's discussion of the expenses and exercises Ellison undertakes in order to accomplish his task makes up the bulk of the text, ranging from a description of the four years Ellison takes to find a suitable spot for his garden to a detailed investigation of just how rich Ellison has become upon receiving his inheritance: "even at three per cent., the annual income of the inheritance amounted to no less than thirteen millions and five hundred thousand dollars; which was one million and one hundred and twenty-five thousand per month; or thirty-six thousand nine hundred and eighty-six per day; or one thousand five hundred and forty-one per hour; or six and twenty dollars for every minute that flew.[17]" The narrator, after having confessed that he "[despairs] of conveying to the reader any distinct conception of the marvels which my friend did actually accomplish,[18]" ends the text with the protracted description of the approach to Arnheim, Ellison's total artwork. A mechanical canoe conveys the reader, the narrator, and the text through a landscape of canyons, gorges, and bays. However, at the very moment when the titular, promised "Domain of Arnheim" rises into view, the story ends – which is not to say it ends immediately or efficiently:

> Meantime the whole Paradise of Arnheim bursts upon the view. There is a gush of entrancing melody; there is an oppressive sense of strange sweet

---

[17] Poe, "The Domain of Arnheim," 895. The narrator's hyperbolic insistence upon the mathematical sublime of the inheritance – its staggeringly large numbers, so large that they lose meaning as mathematical figures – is intended to prove that Ellison is not merely rich, but surpassingly so: he would be unable to spend his fortune in the normal manner of rich men, since the set of political intrigues, charitable institutions, and *objets d'art* is quite simply not equal to the scope of his inheritance. Ellison's inheritance is thus defined as unspendable by normal means, just as his final purchase – the Domain of Arnheim – can't fit in to the normal economy of literary language. However, the story's careful breakdown of Ellison's initially incomprehensible fortune into an appreciable, assimilable, if astonishing detail (twenty-six dollars per minute), insists on the congruity of the regular economy of partial fortunes and partial objects and the radicalized spectacular economy of Ellison, who can buy total enjoyment with his integral inheritance. In short, the text's ironizing structure also gently satirizes the notion, central to the capitalist ideology of accumulation, that enough partial objects can sum up to a complete, intact, and *attainable* Phallus – that there exists, somewhere, some object that escapes the marking of castration and language, that could ever be enjoyed in a full present.

[18] Poe, "The Domain of Arnheim," 901.

> odor; - there is a dream-like intermingling to the eye of tall slender Eastern trees – lily-fringed lakes – meadows of violets, tulips, poppies, hyacinths, and tube-roses – long intertangled lines of silver streamlets – and, upspringing confusedly from amid all, a mass of semi-Gothic, semi-Saracenic architecture, sustaining itself by miracle in mid-air; glittering in the red sunlight with a hundred oriels, minarets, and pinnacles; and seeming the phantom handiwork, conjointly, of the Sylphs, of the Fairies, of the Genii, and of the Gnomes.[19]

After pages and pages structured as an approach to their title, the vision of Arnheim finally given by the story is something of a delicious disappointment. In the place of any *terra firma*, the canoe merely docks at a fluid mass of signifiers (centered around a lily-reflecting lake, a Narcissistic touch suggesting, thematically through its mythological resonance and structurally through its recapitulation of Poe's argument from "The Poetic Principle," that poetry aims chiefly to reinforce an image of the same), casting its glance at an unordered list of poetic effects that blur any further vision. Description, which was for the narrator a source of such anxiety, works to call attention to itself, to invite the reader to luxuriate in its poetically-charged partial objects, and to prevent the text from setting foot in "The Domain of Arnheim," through the very proliferation of its descriptive textuality. The new art that would truly disclose the new nature of Ellison's architecture, belonging neither to god nor man, "a nature which is not God, nor an emanation from God, but which still is nature in the sense of the handiwork of the angels that hover between man and God[20]" lies immediately *beyond* the boundaries of the text and its language.

Poe's text thus engages in a delicate game of double-performance, claiming to disclose (in the narrator's paraphrases of Ellison's aesthetic philosophies) the secret of a new poetics that would create a truly new art capable of directly delivering the state of perfect nature to its viewer, while simultaneously performing the radical impossibility of such a disclosure in the language of the text through its strange anti-climax. Ellison remarks, commenting on the traditional philosophy of landscape architecture, that "The principle expressed is incontrovertible – but there *may* be something beyond it[21]"; this same observation holds true of the text of "The Domain of Arnheim" – although its philosophy is sound,

[19] Poe, "The Domain of Arnheim," 906-7.
[20] Poe, "The Domain of Arnheim," 901.
[21] Poe, "The Domain of Arnheim," 900.

there remains something beyond it, hiding beyond the cul-de-lampe[22] after the final paragraph of the text. This "something beyond" is exactly what the text promises us, and what, in its textuality, denies us – that is to say, it *is* the "azure" that at once claims to name the sky while blocking it from our view by providing the substitute-satisfaction of a mundane, commodified poetic term. In an ironic twist, Poe's final non-vision consciously recapitulates Fletcher's unconscious, auto-plagiarizing failure: if the conclusion of "The Domain of Arnheim" manages to be more successfully poetic, to avoid the paraphractic slip of repeating "azure" by employing a wider range of poetic devices and artful synonyms, it too can only offer more of the same cathected, exoticized linguistic pleasures (Eastern trees, semi-Saracenic architecture, Geniis), and to such a hyperbolic extent that they call attention to their use as all-too-visible objects of enjoyment obscuring, hiding, or replacing a vision of what might lie beyond. (Etymologically, too, "azure" repeats this role as a totemic ward: "azure" is the name of the color of "lapis lazuli," which comes from the town of Lazhward. Azure is the name of the quality of these stones, which legend tells us are fragments of the sky which have fallen to earth, or the name of its partiality, its fragmentary or fractured nature, through which it is said to express the totality of the sky.)

This haze of azure remains, in Mallarmé, the atmosphere in which the poet struggles for breath, and, interestingly enough, this struggle seems to be a gendered one. The milieu of "Don d'un poème," a few lines celebrating the ambiguous birth of "Hérodiade,[23]" is that of "La solitude bleue et sterile[24] (blue and sterile solitude)" spaced around the figure of a

---

[22] Mallarmé celebrates the "cul-de-lampe," the little squiggly typographic ornament that sometimes pops up between paragraphs in old texts, in "Le Mystère dans les lettres," where he imagines an invisible cul-de-lampe as the almost inexistent space in which the hidden song of a text can develop its unheard music; the cul-de-lampe becomes one of the main Mallarméan figurations of the white space surrounding and sub-tending the text, whose foldings and invaginations his later poetics will attempt to trace.

[23] "Hérodiade," along with "Igitur," as mentioned above, represent the two halves (one female, one male) of the major poetic projects Mallarmé envisioned during the first phase of his work; the poem-play "Hérodiade," completed at the time of the birth of Mallarmé's daughter, is accompanied by the short "Don d'un poème," which conflates the two events. Leo Bersani, in particular, has analyzed Mallarmé's dual experience of surviving the failure of these two poems (the artistic bankruptcy of which he grew quickly convinced) as a way of living through his masculine death and female rebirth – a pattern which gives its name to Bersani's title, "The Man Dies."

[24] Mallarmé, "Don d'un poème," in *Œuvres complètes*., 40.

patriarch, which shivers in admitting the blank birth of a child – the "horrible naissance" of the poem "Hérodiade" itself – which must escape the blueness of the atmosphere, which, in place of being inspirational, is in fact stifling, by finding the mother's milk, the breast "Par qui coule en blancheur sibylline la femme / Pour les lèvres que l'air du vierge azur affame (from which flows, in sibylline whiteness, the woman, for lips starved by the air of virgin azure)." This blue dawn, the promised site of a poetic innovation structured around the patriarchical inheritance of that word "azur," is exactly what the poem must avoid in order to find the place of its own becoming: here we see, out of the poetics of "azur" that mark Mallarmé's early period, the slow metamorphosis towards a work on the white, the blank, the milky – indeed, the poem leads us from the suffocating, cloying repetition of "azure" into the blank space of the page, that space left open after the final entrance to "The Domain of Arnheim" and almost entirely occluded by the story's final (invisible and yet all-too-imposing) image. The place of "la femme" is sibylline, mediumnic, but dangerously threatened, not only by the blue air or purple prose that surrounds it on all parts, but through the homonymy of "la femme" and "affame." If the poet is to enter into this place from which the milk that would nurture a new kind of poetic is promised to flow, it is only through the acceptance of a certain mortal hunger – a threat to his life, if "life" is to be defined as a self-sufficient completeness.

However, this impending death must be contrasted with the common way in which poets live and die. Indeed, as Mallarmé's "Tombeau" indicated, the insight of Poe, the celebration of a Death in the throes of its triumphing, has been lost underneath the readings of Poe that are conceivable within a certain social language of reading. No contemporary reader can ignore the oft-cited maxim of "The Philosophy of Composition" – that "the death, then, of a beautiful woman is, unquestionably, the most poetical topic in the world.[25]" Baudelaire, of course, never ceased to read this line of Poe, laboring to become – above all others – the poet of the lyric as violence against woman, and thus to distinguish himself amongst Poe's disciples. This understanding of the "topic" at hand is developed in Poe's later work "The Poetic Principle," a brilliant dissertation upon the perilous repetition of previously-established poetic effects that is so noxious to the creation of new or true art. Above all, "The Poetic Principle" is Poe's bravura performance of citation in all its (violent) forms – nowhere else in his work is the pen as much a cutting sword than here. Over half the text is taken up by citations (sometimes complete,

[25] Poe, "The Philosophy of Composition," in *Essays and Reviews*, 19.

sometimes fragmentary, often incorrect) of a host of other poems of wildly differing style, status, and quality. Always, the poet's knife is handled with an intense awareness of the violent slicings and excisions at hand: "one of the *truest*[26]" poems ever written is promised as a citation but then replaced, due to its length, with a "universally appreciated" (but perhaps inferior for such a unanimous legibility) work by the same author; a mere two sentences after citing a poem by Longfellow, Poe celebrates the efficacy of one of its lines, but only through overtly editing it (from "Through the corridors of time" to "Down the corridors of Time[27]").

More interestingly, Poe applies this procedure of ironic cutting and pasting to his own previous texts, most notably to a fragment on music and truth from the *Marginalia*. A paragraph in the "Poetic Principle" on the supernal Loveliness waiting in the realm of eternity runs as follows:

> And thus when by Poetry – or when by Music, the most entrancing of the Poetic moods – we find ourselves melted into tears – we weep then – not as the Abbaté Gravina supposes – through excess of Pleasure, but through a certain, petulant, impatient sorrow at our inability to grasp *now*, wholly, here on earth, at once and for ever, those divine and rapturous joys, of which *through* the poem, or *through* the music we attain to but brief and indeterminate glimpses.[28]

This text transposes and reimagines an entry from the first collection of *Marginalia*:

> When music affects us to tears, seemingly causeless, we weep *not*, as Gravina supposes, from "excess of pleasure;" but through excess of an impatient, petulant sorrow that, as mere mortals, we are as yet in no condition to banquet upon those supernal ecstasies of which the music affords us merely a suggestive and indefinite glimpse.[29]

Importantly, we see the same process of adding emphasis through capitalization, italicization, and punctuation at work in the resetting of this fragment as we encountered above in Poe's citation of Longfellow ("time" becoming "Time"). Pleasure here accrues through the liberal deploying of positive *effects* – dashes, allegorical capitals, breathless commas, pleonasm, all those devices that serve (like "azure") to signify the intense poetical exertion going on in the text or in the text's creation. Even when

[26] "Poetic Principle," 87.
[27] "Poetic Principle," 80.
[28] "Poetic Principle," 78.
[29] Poe, "Marginalia – November 1844," in *Essays and Reviews*, 1313.

Poe seems to denounce the argument that the moving capacity of art is attendant on its exponential multiplication of pleasures (music's truth lies not in its excessively pleasurable effects, but in what lies beyond its patterns), he simultaneously supersaturates the text with exactly those pleasures, those borrowed tropes that circulate among poets as valuable tools for the excitation of the audience.[30] And, as Jacques Lacan reminds us, phallic jouissance – which begins to look suspiciously like the model of poetry's textual pleasures – is nothing more than the usufruct pleasure, the enjoyment of and with something that does not belong to us. But this promise of pleasure – language gives us objects with which to enjoy – is also a powerful injunction:

> "L'usufruit veut dire qu'on peut jouir de ses moyens, mais qu'il ne faut pas les gaspiller. Quand on a l'usufruit d'un heritage, on peut en jouir à condition de ne pas trop en user. C'est bien là qu'est l'essence de droit – répartir, distribuer, rétribuer ce qu'il en est de la jouissance… [La jouissance n'est] qu'une instance negative. La jouissance, c'est ce qui ne sert à rien… Rien ne force personne à jouir, sauf le surmoi. Le surmoi, c'est l'impératif de la jouissance – *Jouis!* (Usufruct means that you can enjoy your means, but you mustn't waste them. When you have the usufruct of an inheritance, you can enjoy it with the caveat that you not wear it out. That's the essence of law right there – to divide up, distribute, reattribute everything that has to do with jouissance. Jouissance is nothing but a negative instance: Jouissance is that which isn't good for anything. Nothing's forcing anyone to come, except for the superego. The superego is jouissance in the imperative – *Enjoy!*).[31]"

(Isn't the allergic reaction of English-language criticism to Poe principally due to just this – his performative "cheapening" of the presumptively rich rhetoric of poetry, his wearing-out of his inheritance, his overuse of precisely those tricks we enjoy so much when they are more sparingly used so as to demonstrate that their power, but laid bare as worthless when

[30] The chief addition is, of course, the completion of the metaphoric link between music and poetry that is already implied, but not made explicit, in the *Marginalia* fragment. The metaphor that lies latent and uncompleted in the earlier fragment is here immediately – before its very introduction – directed and made linear by the introductory "thus when by Poetry." Poe thus moves us from the floating and endlessly suggestive exploration of Gravina to the establishment of a clearly legible and hierarchical metaphoric logic, mirrored by the passage from a time of "as yet" that opens up possibilities for new times and understandings to a heavy emphasis on the "*now*."

[31] Jacques Lacan, *Le Séminaire, Livre XX: Encore* (Paris: Éditions du Seuil, 1975), 11.

he exposes them as contingent upon a poetic economy of scarcity, of supply and demand?)

Everywhere Poe juxtaposes his unveiling of the absolute impotence of poetry to do what it claims to do, to offer glimpses of the infinity that lies just beyond, and an overabundance of what poetry actually does, proffering substitute and partial pleasures that we mistake for the feeling *as if* we were able to grasp *now*, in the present, and in the language contiguous with that present, the promised joy that our object of desire is supposed to provide us. Moreover, he does this through a re-appropriation of his own poetic language – immediately after denouncing the mirroring effects of repetition as a false aesthetic. His citation of the *Marginalia* is in fact quite suggestive, as in those texts he allows himself much freer rein to make pronouncements on what is marginal to literature (the texts are supposedly copied from notes Poe had written in the margins of his favorite books). The Marginalia of September 1845, which takes the form of an extended meditation on literary influence, reception, citation, plagiarism, and international copyright law, is particularly germane here. At one point, after having cited numerous moments in which a poet has almost word-for-word repeated the words of a previous poet (for instance, from Blair's "visits, / Like those of angels, short and far between" to Campbell's "Like angel visits, few and far between[32]" – and here the poet is not merely guilty of the clichéd use of another poet's language, but of another poet's clichés), Poe defines this state of constant theft of the language of others as the only condition of poetic subjectivity, or as what the poet misrecognizes as his own, active and knowing, subjectivity. After remarking on his capacity to fill several "novel volumes" with a continuation of this list, Poe writes "I am clearly of opinion that of one hundred plagiarisms of this character, seventy-five would be, not accidental, but unintentional.[33]" Indeed, it is the *voluminousness* of this kind of plagiarism that makes it interesting – by emphasizing "novel" and "volume," Poe slyly hints that rewriting is in fact the only kind of writing that is produced to fill the volume of demand for novels, which are, as mere automatic citations of previous works, not so novel after all.

It is no accident that the poet repeats the words of his forefathers – in fact, it is the fatality of the literary market which, bows to the same insistence of the signifier that passes through all economies, psychic, aesthetic, and otherwise, and that begins with the establishment of a phallic capital in relation to which all meaning and value (and all lack of

[32] Poe, "Marginal Notes – September 1845," in *Essays and Reviews*, 1371.
[33] Poe, "Marginal Notes – September 1845," 1373.

meaning and value) will be derived. With the institution of the Phallus, all parties in the exchange of language are reduced, in Tracy McNulty's lucid reading of Lacan, "to one signifier that represents them "equally," and therefore inadequately. But in so doing, [the capitalist operation] paradoxically establishes an illusory "oneness": one market, one currency, one standard of value – so many avatars of the phallus, the unary signifier.[34]" It is the absolute automatism of this process, its lack of any outside, that Poe demonstrates in his commentary on the plagiarism of poets: the poet must master the "appreciation of poetic excellence[35]" by reading the poems that have been determined to be excellent, and through this work of self-discipline the language of poetry becomes "unconsciously assimilated" to his own, so that the poet mistakes the plagiarism as the "coinage of his own brain," forgets how to speak otherwise. But this counterfeiting is exactly what is at stake. The poet is only guilty of performing poorly if his plagiarism is legible to the society of readers but not to himself – which proves him not to fail as a poet, but instead to merely be "unlucky." One might say, the poet is only successful inasmuch as he is capable of mystifying his society as well as himself – of convincing others that he is in possession of his language as much as he is convinced of that same fact.

In this context, the work of "The Poetic Principle" becomes evident: in place of defining a poetic philosophy that would allow for the articulation of poetry outside of a circuitous series of repetitions (and remember, "mere repetition is not poetry"), Poe slowly and carefully demonstrates that all poetry is nothing more than the constant and sustained exchange of a more or less closed series of poetic signifiers. More or less, because, due to the partial nature of all signifiers (since they can never signify, fully, the "One" that is defined as the missing signifier) there can always be more, they proliferate by their very nature, and, conversely, due to the structure of signification (since all signifiers hold out, through their partiality, the promise or possibility that some final tally will make them all add up to "One") they are always oriented towards the same final goal. Or, to rephrase Poe's poetic principle once more, since all poetry is repetition, and repetition is not poetry, there is no poetry. Indeed, "The Poetic Principle" ends on a subterranean suggestion that all poetry is doomed to a very certain death. The poetic citations included as examples in the text move slowly, almost imperceptibly, but inexorably from odes celebrating the love and beauty of a woman, to verses on a youthful love long lost, to

---

[34] Tracy McNulty, "The Other Jouissance, a Gay Sçavoir," in *Qui Parle* 8.2 (Berkeley: University of California at Berkeley, Spring/Summer 1996): 137.
[35] Poe, "Marginal Notes – September 1845," 1374.

stanzas about a woman who has mysteriously disappeared or another who commits suicide, to lines about dead women, mourned women, buried women – then, after a brief and ambiguous discussion of Uranian Love, one final citation closes the text on the lines "Our business is like men to fight, / And hero-like to die![36]" After the evacuation of women from the text (a sort of vanishing that already echoes "the most poetical topic in the world"), this final assertion of triumphant but tragic male subjectivity may come as a surprise. But in fact, although it may seem like Poe is representing the poetic community as a force of warrior-men granted with a virile potency, he performs nothing less than another exposé of the impotence of the crowded page. For if the business of Poetry is to express the beautiful, the natural, the infinite (Woman), Poetry is nothing more than the business of its failure – for there are no words to describe its ostensible object, but instead merely the borrowed accessories of poetic language. It looks as if the masculine, phallic forces of Poetry charge into battle to boldly strike their targets – but instead they only fight *like* men, they are only hero-*like* (Motherwell, the poet in question here, repeats himself, betraying the same symptomatic reliance on borrowed language that Fletcher demonstrated in the epigraph to "The Domain of Arnheim"). Their weapons are borrowed and must pass from them: the cost of admission to masculine poetry is the price of one's own eventual unmanning. To participate in "coinage" one must become a counterfeiter, because in no way can the Oedipal poet ever stably occupy the place from which true value, meaning, and beauty can be permanently defined, and to enter the game, one must pay the price of obeying the rules – to enjoy, but only within limits. In fact, all poetry is nothing more than the repetition or rehearsal of this battle, of men against their own limitations in language – and every poem (because there is no such thing as poetry) is merely the story of its failure to hit the mark of the Woman, whichever one of her manifold forms she happens to take in its diegesis.

Poe introduces this final citation with the exhortation that, to comprehend the poetic principle "fully, we must identify ourselves, in fancy, with the soul of the old cavalier." The identification of the masculine reader with the circuitous exchanges of poetic pleasure comes only in "fancy," which is a key word for Poe (just as "charm" will be for Henry James and "folie" was for Gérard de Nerval and his disciples). "Fancy" occupies a dual role somewhere between a complete abandonment to madness and a more daydream-like state, signifying both the chimeras of the insane and the pleasant imaginings of the idle mind. But "fancy" also signifies a certain

[36] Poe, "The Poetic Principle," 94.

refinement or aristocracy of taste – while it simultaneously implies, pejoratively, an overabundance of detail, a useless accumulation of pointless, almost kitschy, aesthetic effects. "Fancy," then, names the poetic principle itself: doubly ambivalent on the part of both the producer and the production. The poet is at once playing at delusion, and fully deluded in that he believes he is playing at delusion; the product is at once the absolute refinement of art and wholly empty of the content it promises to disclose. Neither position is stable, and the poetic principle looks a lot like a series of abstract elaborations embroidered around an abyss.

To catch a glimpse of this principled poetical failure at work, one only need look at "Ulalume," which accompanies "The Poetic Principle" in the same way that "The Raven" supplements "The Philosophy of Composition.[37]" For "Ulalume" is precisely a poem about the disappearance of Woman – of more than one woman, of a disappearance doubly performed. At the beginning of the poem, the poet-speaker wanders through a unknown landscape in the midst of his "most immemorial year[38]" – even though, as critics are quick to point out, it would seem that the date of the poem is clearly marked throughout the text, as the anniversary of the entombment of the beloved dead woman Ulalume. The speaker is drawn towards her tomb, even as another female companion – an internal voice identified as "Psyche, my soul" – urges him to cease, not to continue forward, not wanting him to remember what she knows he has lost. By the end of the poem, both of these voices have vanished, replaced with the narrator's repetition of the phrase "Well I know, now[39]" that seems to mark the triumphant return of his awareness of his environment and self, of his subjectivity as a male defined by the (always lost) object of his love. However, the discovery of this object is in fact a double loss: the loss of Psyche (in some ways, in a reversal of the myth of Eros and Psyche, "Psyche" names the speaker himself, since it is he who, in illuminating the object of his desire, must lose it forever) and the discovery that Ulalume is, and in a sense always has been, dead, unavailable to his poetic divagations through time and space. The act of taking the magic word "Ulalume" from the mouth of Psyche and reclaiming it as the title of this performance of poetic subjectivity, then, is a fetishistic transfer, divorcing

---

[37] That is to say, the relationship is unstable and dual. Does "The Philosophy of Composition" subvert the sublime images of "The Raven," or does the poem's unmasking of the speaker's masochistic play with the raven in its turn undermine the ironic stability mimed by Poe in his lecture on the poem's writing?

[38] Poe, "Ulalume," in Poe, *The Fall of the House of Usher and Other Writings*, ed. David Galloway (New York: Penguin, 2003), 34.

[39] Poe, "Ulalume," 36.

the name from the body and allowing it to work as an aesthetic object, circulated through the positions the masculine voice pretends to take, readable as a purely poetical effect – and it is exactly this magic functioning of "Ulalume" as a sonorous aesthetic object, with its long vowels and melancholy tonality, that makes the poem so spellbinding. To call the poem "Ulalume" is to elevate the meaningless collection of syllables that forms the made-up name into a precious, valuable talisman.[40] And if we see that it is Psyche, and not the narrator, who is made to speak the name, it is certainly not surprising: just as "Ulalume" might transpose the ululations of pre-linguistic cries of mourning into the legibility of a proper name, the text as a whole is interested in presenting spectral images or snapshots (clichés, perhaps) of what lies outside of language, promising to encounter this absent feminine other but always locating its performance firmly in the closed space of the signifying chain.

This is precisely the problematic of fetishism elaborated by Lacan: the "feminine phallus" of the fetishist comes into being as an imaginary object (shoe, shine on the nose) precisely to hold in abeyance the fatal oncoming of the symbolic order of language. In the imaginary, imagistic space of fetishism, the fetishist does not "imagine the symbol; he gives reality to the image[41]" in what Lacan calls imaginary captation, captation of and by the image.[42] The fanciful performance of "Ulalume" falls into this category:

---

[40] Of course, the word "Ulalume" is itself not entirely innocent. Critics attempting to trace Poe's sources for this enigmatic name often return to the explanation that "Ulalume" derives from "ululation," wordless cries of mourning (a performance which is often gendered as feminine). "Ululation" would thus name a feminine, extra-linguistic response to loss, another link in the cultural chain tying woman and the non-symbolizable (the voice, the cry, but not the phoneme or the logic of speech), and placing "the voice" as another one of the lost objects the poetic performance fetishistically attempts to cover and invoke simultaneously. As the symbolic name for woman's non-symbolic performances, "Ulalume-ululation" could be read as the proper name for nonsense words, a redemption of language in which it proves itself capable of signifying even babble – which was supposed to be one of language's ultimate others.

[41] Jacques Lacan and Wladimir Granoff, "Fetishism: The Symbolic, the Imaginary, and the Real," in *Perversions: Psychodynamics and Therapy*, ed. Sandor Lorand (New York: Random House, 1956), 269.

[42] The second half of this operation involves replacing knowledge with understanding, preferring the fullness of meaning over the alienation and estrangement of knowledge. "Well I know, now" represents the culmination of the process, and, since it could conceivably read as "well, I know. Now…," the verse also translates Octave Mannoni's maxim of fetishistic belief "I know very well, but all the same…"

instead of describing the other half of the name "Ulalume," the body that it represents, the reader is invited to follow the speaker in meditating on the poetic pleasure of "Ulalume" within the rhetoric of lyric, to enjoy its sonorities and cadences, mistaking this imaginary enjoyment, full of resonances of meaning, for a form of *knowing well, now*. Indeed, the field of knowledge is evacuated completely from the imaginary space of the poem: the truth of the determination lies behind the very space taken as the stage of poetic revelation.

That is to say, the imaginary-fetishistic performance (both the writing *and* the reading of the poem) involves not merely the dual relation between poet-readers in the throes of castration anxiety (Laertes and Oedipus at the crossroads), but also the tripartite relation between poet, object of poetry, and the Phallus, the law of literature that legislates poetical economics. Lacan explains that to give up the Oedipal relation means replacing the imaginary penis with a symbolic phallus, and, correspondingly, replacing the two-sided relation between child and mother with a three-sided relation, passing from the child through the father – the seat of symbolic language – and back to the mother, now become the object of the child's desire, now ruled by a social economy of supply and demand of pleasure.[43] In other words, "Ulalume" does not take place in a vacuum, as Poe's exploration of the multivocal space of poetry in "The Poetic Principle" demonstrates. The poet only takes on the double-edged sword, gaining the capital (the erect head) of "Lui-même" by being momentarily and provisionally granted with the Phallus, the final object that stands outside of the symbolic order and preserves its economics, the economics of an endlessly circulating set of similars that are exchangeable precisely because they all fail, in the end, to stand in for the phallus. Woman – the mother, the dead beauty, nature, Beauty herself – provides the canvas in which the various sons of poetry peddle their wares, because she is, by definition, unattainable through the only means available to these sons: since she is castrated, she is precisely what cannot be symbolized by the phallic baton passed from poet to poet. This definition of Woman as the blank (because defined as exterior to poetic language) space of poetry provides a guarantee that poetry will be forever profitable, since it will never achieve its goals, and a convenient delimitation of the space of poetic pleasure, since all language can be put to enjoyable, profitable *use* in the endless quest to symbolize her. No pleasure need be wasted: this is the form of the Law as poetic principle, and one that, by promising a boundless return of enjoyment for the poet who buys into the

---

43 Lacan and Granoff, "Fetishism," 274.

system, quite naturally enforces itself. Why not enjoy, and fully, since the poetic principle makes such pleasures available?

The performance of "Ulalume" starts to look more and more like the fort-da game described by Freud in *Beyond the Pleasure Principle*, through which the child attempts to cope with the loss of the mother (whether she is going to the store or dying, as she does casually, in a footnote, makes no difference here) through repeating a similar traumatic loss, the disappearance and reappearance of a bobbin, which he compulsively throws away and pulls back to experience the pleasure of its return – despite the immense cost of displeasure that its necessary loss represents for him. (Freud echoes Poe even more when we remember that the fort-da game is in fact not called that by its player: the boy never says, "fort" – gone – but instead "a loud, long-drawn-out 'o-o-o-o.[44]'" That is, the expression of the painful absence is itself not symbolized; it is instead represented by a strange term, halfway between speech and meaningless vocalization – a term that in its position on the border of language sounds, in fact, quite like "Ulalume.") The challenge that the fort-da game poses for the economics of psychoanalysis lies in its repetition of a displeasure that may, in fact, outweigh the pleasure received by the return of the toy (or mother). However, Freud is always ambivalent about whether or not this discrepancy in enjoyment is counterbalanced by a gain on another front: that of *mastery*, gained through the child's taking-on of the active role in choosing and enacting the passing of the object. No longer must the child suffer the loss of his object – now he can choose to rehearse the loss, from a position of mastery, his symbolizing brio becoming the site of a recompense of enjoyment. If he must be unhappy, at least he might become the master of his own unhappiness. The pleasure principle promises a greater return of pleasure for any investment of displeasure.

The problem – one posed in the structure of Freud's book of "speculations" itself, with its constant return to the same scenes that seem to promise to disclose the "beyond" of the pleasure principle but always tend to admit of an explanation in terms of the positive economics of the pleasure principle itself – is that this mastery is elusive and always must remain so. In fact, the performer of such games must constantly and ceaselessly repeat his performance of them, to constantly inoculate himself with another fleeting impression of mastery. One might suggest that mastery is not gained on the part of the child-player at all – instead, what achieves a raise in its status as master is nothing more than the absent

44 Sigmund Freud, *Beyond the Pleasure Principle*, trans. James Strachey (New York: Norton, 1989), 13.

Phallus itself. It remains doubtful at the end of *Beyond the Pleasure Principle* that anything like a death drive might ever exist – a sentiment that is only aggravated by rereadings of the text. Indeed, the causal economics of pleasure leave the text stronger than ever, having extended their empire even into those cases that seemed at first to present such strong objections to its logics. This is quite a drastic exaggeration of the situation of the poet in "The Poetic Principle," in which Poe elaborates and ironizes upon this melancholic obverse of the pleasure principle: not only does the player chose to lose his object in entering into a necessarily interminable series of (not at all pleasurable) games, but through his repetition the necessity of loss is merely exaggerated, in turn making even more repetitions imperative.

Mediating between Poe and Freud comes Mallarmé's rehearsal of Poe's stylistics in the failed work "Igitur," in which all comes to a head in a game which can never take place at the right time – instead, the successful wagering is replaced by a series of drafts, of hesitations on the part of both the poet and his character, an abysmal infinity of necessary, and necessarily partial, games. It cannot be coincidental that Igitur's crisis, in parallel to that of his author, is one of filiation and inheritance: Igitur stands at the end of his paternal line and attempts above all to justify his existence as the last bearer of his family's name, just as Mallarmé positions himself in the text as the final inheritor of the topoi of Poe (and, with him, all the other poetic forebears from whom he so consciously and uncomfortably inherits the language of poetry). "Igitur" stands as the site of the Mallarméan failure to inherit, his inability to find a new space within the cluttered language of poetic clichés – and it is possible that this failure is precisely due to his heightened awareness of the legacy with which he attempts to grapple. Following Johnson, what causes so much anxiety in the ultimately abortive writing of "Igitur" is not the incapacity to speak a new word (in fact, "Igitur" would very easily have been marketable as the innovative project of a young poet going beyond the work of his predecessors), but instead the awareness that the space beyond, the abyss of creation signaled at the end of "The Domain of Arnheim," is already ruled, not by the poet's hand, but by the language which circumscribes it, the poet's pen becoming just another stylus for the constant rewriting of poetic language as unconscious or automatic.

But to move beyond Poe's poetic principle Mallarmé in no way chooses to ignore or suppress the influence of the language that came before him. Indeed, in "Crayonné au théâtre" Mallarmé not only hints at his reliance on Poe through the collage-work inclusion of certain styles or themes, but telegraphs this influence directly to the reader, through an asterisked, italicized clipping from "Ulalume." The poet begins at the theater, having (unfortunately) invited a peculiar companion, his "Idée," to join him: "le tort initial demeura se render au spectacle avec son Ame *with Psyche, my soul**[45] (the initial mistake was to come to the spectacle accompanied by one's Soul – *with Psyche, my soul**[46])." In case the reader didn't notice, the footnote makes it clear that this "Idée" is the same *Psyche, my soul* as in "**Ulalume* (strophe II) EDGAR POE.[47]" Immediately Mallarmé assures us that we are no longer dealing with the unconscious acceptance or insistence of an intersubjective signifying chain (which is precisely what Lacan, perhaps following Mallarmé, defines as the Unconscious in his "Discours de Rome[48]"), but a conscious working-through of inheritance. This work, however, takes a strange turn: rather than more consciously and thus more skillfully repeating or perfecting the movements of his predecessor, Mallarmé is engaged in a careful process of *not* repeating – of starting an homage, a paraphrase, a mimed performance, but then not following through on it. Indeed, the text of "Crayonné" abandons the parallel to "Ulalume" as quickly as it takes it up, moving instead to a reconsideration or "résumé" of Poe's "The Imp of the Perverse": "faire ce qu'il ne faut, sans avantage à tirer, que la gene vis-à-vis de produits (à quoi on est, par nature, étranger) en feignant y porter un jugement : alors qu'un joint quant à l'appréciation échappe ou que s'oppose une pudeur à l'exposition, sous un jour faux, de suprèmes et intempestifs principes[49] (the irreducible Imp of Perversity, which I summarize thus: 'Do what is expressly forbidden, with nothing to gain but embarrassment before the productions (to which you are, by nature, foreign), while pretending to pronounce a judgment upon them: while a

[45] Mallarmé, "Crayonné…", 294.
[46] Mallarmé, *Divagations*, 118.
[47] Mallarmé, "Crayonné…", 294.
[48] Indeed, Lacan's writings on language from the mid-1950's bristle with Mallarméan language: on a given page of "L'Instance de la lettre dans l'inconscient," for example, the reader finds an "étincelle poétique (poetic spark)" that "jaillit entre deux signifiants (shines forth from between two signifiers)," in what Lacan calls the "rayonnement de la fécondité (fecundity's radiance)." The sparkling of signification in the spaces between the links in its chains immediately recalls Mallarmé's writings that privilege the scintillations of the white space of the page and figure the process of signifiance as sparkling or iridescent. Finally, Mallarmé's demystified magic word, "rien," appears in the essay as a major factor in Lacan's re-envisioning of the object in psychoanalysis. See Jacques Lacan, "L'Instance de la lettre dans l'inconscient, ou raison depuis Freud," in *Écrits I* (Paris: Éditions du Seuil, 1999), 504-5.
[49] Mallarmé, "Crayonné…", 297.

link, having to do with appreciation, escapes, or you are silenced by shyness about exposing supreme, untimely principles in a false light'[50])."

The textual space of "Crayonné" is thus composed of two fragmentary borrowings from Poe – but two borrowings that are self-consciously fragmentary, left willfully incomplete. For what Mallarmé finds in his paraphrase of "The Imp of the Perverse" is just as incomplete as his clipping of "Ulalume." Mallarmé's Idée successfully turns him away from the spectacle they have come to the theater to watch, through convincing him that there is nothing to see on stage – not because the theater is lacking, but instead because it is "très bien, c'est parfait[51] (it's fine, perfect[52])," since "L'auteur ou son pareil, ce qu'ils voulaient faire, ils l'ont fait et je défierais qui que ce soit de l'exécuter mieux ou différement (The author or his substitute has done exactly what he set out to do, and I defy anyone at all to execute it better or differently)." The theater, the Idée tells us, is exactly the triumph of the closure of artistic language, notwithstanding its social capacity to dupe the viewer into thinking that there is something more to be grasped in the theater (the movement of fetishistic appreciation or phallic jouissance in its true form, covering over a lack – but here, a lack *of anything different or, even, better* – with a surplus, second-hand enjoyment). But this truncation of "Ulalume" withholds at the most precious moment – when the death of woman, the evaporation of Psyche and the poet's re-identification with the lost, lacking feminine object, ought to arrive so that the logic of jouissance may come to a climax with the evacuation of both the feminine object and the artist's feminine double, Mallarmé immediately shifts gears and presents not a culmination but another fragmentary beginning.

To cite the principle of "perversity" is in its own way to perform an interesting mangling of Poe's text, which itself mirrors its subject with its structural perversity. For several pages the story appears to be a mock-theoretical musing on a state of "perverseness" – called that "for want of a more characteristic term[53]" – defined as the inexplicable desire to do things precisely because logic determines them to be poor courses of action and set out as a force in the mind equal, if not superior, to reason. However, just as perverseness only exists as an insufficiently characteristic name for such a drive, the examples of perverseness in the text refuse any clear characterization of what it calls by the name of perverseness: these examples range from a man, standing on a cliff ledge

---

[50] Mallarmé, *Divagations*, 122.
[51] "Crayonné…", 293.
[52] Mallarmé, *Divagations*, 121.
[53] Poe, "The Imp of the Perverse," in *The Complete Stories*, 856.

and realizing that it would be suicide of the most awful sort imaginable to jump, must remain on the precipice, trapped on the verge of destruction "because our reason deters us from the brink,[54]" because his reason urges him more and more strongly to resist; to more everyday examples such as procrastinating, although "we are consumed with eagerness to commence the work" that "must, [that] shall be undertaken to-day, and yet we put it off until to-morrow, and why?[55]" Suddenly, after pages of this seeming treatise, the narrator suddenly enters as a character: it is revealed that the narrator's impending execution precipitated the entire preceding discourse. He had committed a murder and then, years later, perversely confessed to his crime[56] – he writes so as to communicate to his interlocutor why he decided to confess his guilt, and in so doing render his actions comprehensible in light of a universal human "imp of the perverse." But the text complicates the narrator's desire to communicate by presenting, as the first example of perverse behavior it provides, the conduct of a speaker who decides, against his reasonable will of course, to

> tantalize a listener by circumlocution. The speaker is aware that he displeases; he has every intention to please; he is usually curt, precise, and clear; the most laconic and luminous language is struggling for utterance upon his tongue; it is only with difficulty that he restrains himself from giving it flow; he dreads and deprecates the anger of him whom he addresses; yet, the thought strikes him, that by certain involutions and parentheses this anger may be engendered.[57]

While the reader who treats "The Imp of the Perverse" as a gothic tale of crime and recrimination will be amply satisfied by the panoply of generic pleasures offered by the text, running from its scientific speculations, to its characteristically grandiose and baroque style, to the spine-tinglingly

---

[54] Poe, "The Imp of the Perverse," 858.

[55] Poe, "The Imp of the Perverse," 857.

[56] Students of apotropaic language will enjoy the means by which the irresistible urge to confess awoke in the narrator's consciousness: "I would perpetually catch myself pondering upon my security, and repeating, in a low monotone, 'I am safe.' One day, whilst sauntering along the streets, I arrested myself in the act of murmuring, half aloud, these customary syllables. In a fit of petulance, I re-modelled them thus: 'I am safe – I am safe – yes – if I be not fool enough to make open confession!'" In additon to the amusing play on "I arrested myself," this sudden emergence of the hidden dimensions of the narrator's reassuring words seems like an obvious illustration of the dual dimensions of the totemic ward: both life-sustaining and petrifying. See Poe, "The Imp of the Perverse," 859.

[57] Poe, "The Imp of the Perverse," 857.

creative murder plot elaborated by its narrator, the reader who enters the text seeking to receive the communication of the narrator (thus perhaps even the ideal reader of the text) will inevitably be disappointed: it turns out that perverseness is exactly what cannot be said characteristically, what cannot be transmitted through positive speech. The narrator ends the story by announcing his oncoming freedom from the constraints of language, exclaiming "But why shall I say more? To-day I wear these chains, and am here! To-morrow I shall be fetterless! but where?[58]" It is almost as if the narrator realizes that there is no way to "say more," to speak the truth of perverseness in the space of linguistic communication, tied as he is by the signifying "chains" of the law of the unary signifier. The triumphant freedom of the narrator comes in the space called up by "where?," the question with which the text dives precipitously into the chasm of white space beneath its final line, the space beyond in which the logic of perverseness – the articulation of what inside the narrator caused him to do things that he had no desire to do – might finally be said.

This "where?" names a time and space similar to the "jour faux" of Mallarmé (or Hamlet's "the time is out of joint," for that matter), alluding to the way in which the present time is exactly where and when the object of language cannot present itself. But, in reading Mallarmé's rephrasing of Poe more closely, an interesting difference becomes visible: whereas the problem of Poe's narrator lies in his desire to understand and name the things inside him he cannot recognize as foreign, pathological, or "perverse," Mallarmé's new perverseness is based in an awareness of difference within the same – that between the actor and his "produits," to whom he remains "étranger," but still contiguous. At stake here is the introduction of a space between the author and his performance, between the player and the game, that does not develop into an absolute (and absolutely petrifying) difference. This is why, in such a paradigm, "un joint échappe," a promised or desired conjunction or intersection escapes aesthetic and philosophical reflection. Only through a heightened awareness of the authorial feint is such an appreciation possible, only through the undoing of his (deluded or fetishistically believed in) subjectivity as an author.

The key work of "Crayonné" is that of an uncoupling: of author and product, consumer and text, but also of jouissance and climax. Hence the importance of sliding from one citation of Poe to the next, without following either one through to its seemingly inescapable conclusion: the pleasure of the text is definitively separated from the place where it ought

[58] "Imp," 173.

to be. Rather than synchronizing the moment of textual pleasure with the climactic ejaculation of the poem's magic word, the poet here must enter into a practice of withholding, in which Mallarmé exhibits himself as striving to speak "precisement afin de ne pas exprimer quelque chose[59] (A fool babbles on without saying anything, and to do the same without any notorious taste for prolixity and precisely in order not to say something represents a special case: mine[60])" (and there is little doubt as to what that something might be). This statement defines a new poetics, one which is interested precisely in avoiding the logic of the expression of an object – and we might read "express" as enacting, in the idea of a pressing-out of a sense, a certain violence towards its object, as well as alongside "exprès," as of an exact likeness or of a rapidly-delivered, promptly-disclosed truth. It is this express time of comprehension that Mallarmé denounces as a "jour faux" – a time without a space for the object. "Crayonné," in all of its disparate moments, presents such a labor of de-synchronization, of the time of reading and writing and also of the social, symbolic time upon which the time of the text depends.

It is no surprise, then, that throughout the "Crayonné" Mallarmé interests himself with a very different figure of enjoyment – that of the woman and, perhaps, of the feminine jouissance that she embodies, provisionally and not essentially. Between the citations of "Ulalume" and "The Imp of the Perverse" comes a brief note on the ballet, which, we are told, "ne donne que peu[61] (gives but little)" – and consequently does not allow for the false impression of totality that comes with the seemingly full disclosure of poetic language. It is also here where the feminine – and the feminine companion who has been haunting the poet – speaks, as the ritual of dancing is called an "énoncé de l'Idée," but she will speak only through an uneasy inhabiting of the logic of masculine speech. The ballet dancer asks a question, discloses a task to the male philosopher-reader: "À déduire le point philosophique auquel est située l'impersonnalité de la danseuse, entre sa féminine apparence et un objet mimé, pour quel hymen[62] (We have to deduce the philosophical point where the dancer's impersonality is located, between her female appearance and a mimed object, destined for what Hymen[63])." The body of the dancer is precisely the space of a gap between her "féminine apparence" and the "objet mimé" by her gesture, between the legibility of the dancer as woman in

[59] "Crayonné...," 298.
[60] Mallarmé, *Divagations*, 122.
[61] Mallarmé, "Crayonné...," 295.
[62] Mallarmé, "Crayonné...," 296.
[63] Mallarmé, *Divagations*, 120.

the language of sexual difference and the legibility of her performance in the vocabulary of balletic symbolizations, in the overlaps of these two languages that overwrite her body and circumscribe her performance. By exclusion, we assume that philosophy can deduce both of these things all too well; what remains for analytic language is to deduce what happens *between* the woman and the meanings she is made to carry. In a male logic of textual pleasure, this remainder must always be invisible, for it would disabuse the reader of his sensation that in naming the Woman he is naming the infinity of infinites for which she stands. What makes the dancer fascinating is her exhibition of a space that is without characterization, that is impersonal in the sense that literary psychology is the definition of personality.

What lies *beyond* the scope of language, here, is what lies *between* its moves of appropriation and recirculation (and literally *between* the citations of Poe). It is as if, in seeking always to express what lies beyond the screen of the text, writing busies itself avoiding a much more difficult task: that of investigating what lies inside the space of writing but which is somehow unavailable to its positive logics of discourse, personality, and meaning. Therefore Mallarmé sidesteps the problematic of identification with masculine poetry by means of a redefinition of the poetic object as that space in the dancer which is neither that of its producer nor its product – later in "Crayonné au théâtre," in the essay on "Ballets," the dancer becomes the famous "poëme dégagé de tout appareil du scribe (a poem independent of any scribal apparatus)" through the knowledge, presented as an exhortation for an uncertain future, that she is absolutely inequal to herself:

> "À savoir que la danseuse *n'est pas une femme qui danse* pour ces motifs juxtaposés qu'elle *n'est pas une femme*, mais une métaphore résumant un des aspects élémentaires de notre forme, glaive, coupe, fleur, etc., et *qu'elle ne danse pas*, suggérant, par le prodige de raccourcis ou d'élans, avec une écriture corporelle ce qu'il faudrait des paragraphes en prose dialoguée autant que descriptive, pour exprimer, dans la redaction[64] (Namely, that *the dancer is not a woman dancing*, for these juxtaposed reasons: that *she is not a woman*, but a metaphor summing up one of the elementary aspects of our form: knife, goblet, flower, etc., and that *she is not dancing*, but suggesting, through the miracle of bends and leaps, a kind of corporal writing, what it would take pages of prose, dialogue, and description to express, if it were transcribed[65]).

---

[64] "Crayonné…," 304.

[65] Mallarmé, *Divagations*, 130.

This is not to say that the dancer does not engage in a more prosaic or identifiable writing – indeed, Mallarmé constantly expresses his frustration at the way such traditional meanings often return to overwrite this more interesting performance. But nevertheless, something comes before the mass of text, which erases as much as it writes, which represents an "écriture corporelle" to which the "appareil du scribe" is no longer an attendant accessory, and consequently one in which the rhythms of the phallus, of the anxious comings and goings of the paternal gift, are absent.

The woman here is understood in the fullness of what Lacan would come to proclaim as her position as "pas-tout": not fully symbolizable, lacking in the possession of the phallus which would otherwise allow her to count in the ranks of men. As such, the figure of woman allows for the radical difference between the positions of author and product to accede to an elusive visibility – making possible, for a brief moment, to sense the radical "étrangeté" that Mallarmé reads into perverseness. The time of this moment is nowhere clearer than in the next paragraph of "Ballets," which takes as its subject the ballet *Deux Pigeons*, the transposition into human form of a fable of La Fontaine (which, of course, was already involved in transposing human desire – or the lack thereof, since in the poem La Fontaine complains about the impotence that has come with his old age – into the animal realm). What interests Mallarmé is the beginning of the ballet, in which "L'un des amants à l'autre les montre puis soi-même, langage initial, comparaison (One of the lovers shows the pairs to the other, then shows himself, initial language: comparison)," before the entry of an "échange dont toujours et dès lors, lui et elle, devraient exprimer le double jeu: peut-être, toute l'aventure de la différence sexuelle ![66] (exchange, and they will from then on, him and her, have to play this double game: perhaps the whole adventure of sexual difference![67])" The difference between the opening of the ballet and this "aventure" or oncoming of sexual difference, which takes place always and at one moment in the infinitely momentary time of the "faux jour" of the present, is precisely the entrance of a "devoir exprimer," a distillation into a double game between male and female in place of the initial multiplicity of pigeons: "*Deux pigeons s'aimaient d'amour tendre*, deux ou plusieurs[68] (*Two pigeons loved each other with a tender love*, two or several[69])." Isn't this multiplicity exactly what is conveyed initially, in the first language of the dance, that of "comparaison," through which one by one the dancers

[66] "Crayonné…," 305.
[67] Mallarmé, *Divagations*, 131.
[68] "Crayonné…," 304.
[69] Mallarmé, *Divagations*, 131.

mirror each other, then themselves? (Although the titular "two pigeons" were both played by ballerinas, one in a *rôle travesti*, in La Fontaine's fable both pigeons are ambiguously sexed and gendered, named as "cousins" and "pigeons," and thus both masculine in gender throughout the poem – leaving the reader to attempt to determine, if he or she so desires, the pigeon's biological sex from their actions as reported in the poem.[70])

Mallarmé, again, instead of searching for the beyond in the future, locates it in another time – here, a before, as well as a between, the between-two that seems to implicate an opening to a possible multitude of others, as reflections, imitations, comparisons between not just the one dancer and her partner, but between the dancer and herself: the site of her impersonality. The dance as pas de deux (perhaps read as "dance between two," but also as "not any two," "no two" but more, "not one and another" but instead the much greater variety of one when faced with the almost-same that reveals her difference to herself) recalls the interest of Derrida in the "entre-deux" of Mallarmé, his transcription of the Platonic cave (or "antre-de") into a space between Mallarmé and Plato, between one author and the next, which is figured always as the "hymen." But Derrida cautions against the approach to reading that would find in the figure of the hymen or the woman a negativity, the same negativity against which phallic language seeks to insulate itself:

---

[70] The moral of the story of the *Deux pigeons* is an injunction, pronounced by the poet from the other side of impotence ("I used to love!" he sighs), that lovers be ever new to each other and that they allow each other to be ever new:

> Amants, heureux amants, voulez-vous voyager ?
> Que ce soit aux rives prochaines ;
> Soyez-vous l'un à l'autre un monde toujours beau,
> Toujours divers, toujours nouveau.

[Lovers, happy lovers, do you desire to travel? Then let it be to nearby shores; May you each be to each other a world, always beautiful, always multiple, always new.]

Notice the strange lack of markers that would differentiate between the two lovers; instead, the poem seems to insist on their similarity above all, even as it attempts to teach them to be "always new" and thus always changing. La Fontaine seems to suggest that, if two lovers are to constantly become truly new and truly different – more foreign than the farthest shores – their difference to themselves is rooted not in opposition, but in the development and unfolding of similarity, attainable only through the patient and careful refusal of the fetishized "other." See Jean de La Fontaine, "Les Deux Pigeons," in *Fables* (Paris: Gallimard, 1995), 269.

> "l'*entre* de l'hymen se réfléchit dans l'écran sans y pénétrer [...] Le miroir n'est jamais outré-passé et la glace jamais brisée. Au bord de l'être. Au bord de l'être, le medium de l'hymen ne devient jamais une médiation ou un travail du négatif, il déjoue toutes les ontologies, tous les philosophèmes, les dialectiques de tous les bords[71] (the hymen's *between* is reflected in the screen without piercing it… The mirror is never ex-ceeded and the ice never broken. On the shores of being. On the edge of being, the hymen's medium never becomes a mediation or the work of the negative, it undoes all ontologies, all philosophemes, dialectics of all kinds)."

Locating the work of the hymen precisely in the space before penetration – but in this escaping into a previous space, the hymen proves that it is what comes before and after, what allows for the happening, the breaking of the glass or its penetration, to take place, that the hymen is the medium of its rupture – Derrida insists that it is not available to the dialectic work that seeks to absorb its elusive negative in some happy conjunction. Indeed, the hymen, being that which allows for the games positive language plays with its elusive object, is what circumscribes all positivity, all being.

This is the intertextual principle at the pinnacle of its potentiality: what comes before a text as the condition and undoing of any given text. But Derrida argues that we must not seek to read intertextuality as a process of differentiation, but instead as a game of similarities that are precisely unmasterable. Plato's god of writing, which Mallarmé struggles to take as his inheritance from poetic language, is a god of difference, but of a different sort:

> "La figure de Thot s'oppose à son autre (père, soleil, vie, parole, origine ou orient, etc.) mais en le suppléant. Elle s'ajoute et s'oppose en répétant ou en tenant lieu. Du même coup, elle prend forme, elle tient sa forme de cela même à quoi elle résiste à la fois et se substitue. Elle s'oppose dès lors à elle-même, elle passe dans son contraire et ce dieu-messager est bien un dieu du passage absolue entre les opposés[72] (The figure of Thot opposes itself to its other (father, sun, life, speech, origin/Orient, etc.) but through supplementing this other. It adds and opposes itself by repeating its other or taking its place. By the same token, it takes its form from precisely that which it simultaneously resists and substitutes itself for. In this way, it is opposed to itself : it passes through its opposite, and this Messenger god is indeed a god of absolute passage between opposites)."

The figure of writing represents its object, but only in becoming different from it; but this difference does not cease there. Rather, the figure of

---

[71] Jacques Derrida, *La Dissémination* (Paris: Seuil, 1972), 265.
[72] Derrida, *La Dissémination*, 115.

writing – as a figure – gains its differentiating power from always being different from itself, thus able to substitute for anything, and this differentiation drastically contrasts from the difference of opposites that we presume to be the separation between one and another (between, say, male and female). Instead, if the god is a god of passage between opposites, he is a god of "non-identité," the impurity of each pole in a dyad of opposites, the necessity for each term to contain its other in order to differentiate itself from it. The game of writing now looks a lot like the game of comparison between two pigeons *before* the meaning of sexual difference is violently imposed on their bodies.

If anything, Mallarmé inherits the sexually-differentiated language of poetry, based on the poet's role as intermediary between the unattainable Phallus that signifies full presence and the female object that self-evidently cannot be One, only in transforming it into another of its possible shapes: he is a writer of sexual indifference, coming to be himself only through identifying with the impersonality of woman, what remains of her body outside the grasp of symbolization, identifying this gap – which poetry has always coded as the lack, the unmanning failure of its warlike assaults on its object, projected as a screen onto the forms it seeks to express – as a site of possibility, a non-negative blankness or the ambivalence of the word "rien," which can be something or nothing. (Such a work does not deny the difference between men and women; rather, in substituting similarity and comparison for difference, it opens up new ground for thinking about what the differences between men and women – which must be the differences between men and men, women and women, between any body and itself – might be.) The hymen, perhaps a name for the part of the body which touches itself, which comes into contact and opposition with its membranes, differentiating itself from them even as both the touching and the touched flesh belong to the same ambiguously divided being, is another name for the seminal flow in Derrida's text, the titular *Dissemination* – once it has become disjointed from the logic of ejaculation or climax and is understood as the site of the body's capacity to overflow itself, to separate from itself, to differ from itself through being, merely, another repetition of itself. Indeed, when the microscopic animalculae of *Beyond the Pleasure Principle* approach stagnation through being left too long in their own fluid, being slowly poisoned by the products of their own bodies, they are able to rejuvenate through "conjugation,[73]" exchanging their bodies with one another. The identical cells, suffocated by the self-similarity of their own metabolism, are able to

[73] Freud, *Beyond the Pleasure Principle*, 57-59.

reach a future by swapping parts of their bodies with one another, through the performance of non-identity through an exchange with a similar other, othering themselves through a mirroring of similars that demonstrates the capacity of each body to be not-all, to overflow itself in unexpected and uncontainable novelty. Both of the animalculae, initially possessing the same genetic material, leave their conjugation as completely different organisms, biologically speaking: the original animalculae have died, so that a radically new version of themselves may come.

Similarly, in Sarah Kofman's reformulation of fetishism, the fetish is no longer marked as perversely aberrant or other, as that which all-too-unsettlingly refuses to be stably the ultimate, desired maternal penis that would provide a totalizing, comforting renunciation of castration or the fatal evidence of castration that the fetish object, in supplementing the woman's "rien," both hides and highlights; instead, Kofman develops the form of what is hidden by Freud's play with fetishism and only reveals itself elsewhere, as in the play between identical animalculae – the endlessly, lawlessly overproductive – thus wasteful and unmasterable – oscillation between poles as not an anxiety-inducing all-or-nothing gamble, but a far more radical wager on intermediacy as a mode of existence between being and nonbeing, male and female, profit and loss – in short, a "'feminine jouissance,' if by 'feminine' one means undecidable oscillation.[74]" The kind of communication characteristic of this other pleasure, hidden between the polarities of an unthinking enjoyment of poetry's usufruct pleasures and a melancholy irony on its impossible promise, is marked by "a 'Yes, yes,' a 'Come' that is said to the other. It is the sign of a hymen, of an alliance wherein one body flows into the body of another, transforming the other, and leaving neither of the complementary, mutually 'infatuated' poles intact.[75]" This identification of poetic practice with feminine jouissance thus entails a radical redefinition of the death instinct: no longer does *Thanatos* lurk beyond the ultimate words of the text, but instead the drive is everywhere at work in the silences or blanks of the page, transforming the language of the text into new meanings that leave no one – psychoanalyst, poet, reader, language – unchanged. Such a loss of self is no longer the proof of intertextual failure, but the very condition of any affirmation of poetry's future. Poetry is not the work of mastery, but the boundlessly pleasurable (hence possibly painful) renunciation thereof – the work of inheriting not the father's grasp on the sword, but the tenuousness, the mute failure, of that grasp.

---

[74] Sarah Kofman, "Ça cloche," in *Sarah Kofman: Selected Writings*, ed. and trans. Thomas Albrecht (Stanford: Stanford University Press, 2007), 95.
[75] Kofman, "Ça cloche," 94-5.

In this way, when Mallarmé takes up the phallic plume of the writer (Poe's naked sword, Hamlet's purely supplemental fashion accessory that nevertheless defines him as a charcter), it is only through the awareness of his difference to himself – the very difference that allows for his subtle identification or comparison with the figure of woman – that this "plume" is transformed, as Derrida points out, into a "plus je – plume – plume je – plume jet[76] (more I – no more I – plume – plume I – plume jet)." Inasmuch as the phallic pen does not belong to him – inasmuch as the inheritance is of a radically foreign object – can the poet, through realizing that he is "plus je," not-I, no-longer-myself writing, attain the dark, inky explosion of "plus je," more than me, something that is not a surplus governed by a system of exchanges but the overwhelming onrush of moreness that would undo all exchange, and all self. Within Mallarmé's poetics, intertextuality ceases to be outside of the poem and comes to enter into it – as Leo Bersani suggests in his genetic readings of "Le Pitre châtié," the poem is not only a commentary on its previous version but is the unceasing performance of a commentary on itself,[77] not merely a diacritical examination of the fact of its writing but a constant call to revision or re-perusal of the text, between the author and the reader, between the text and itself, between the reader and the other readers he or she might become. Intertextuality refuses to exist as something beyond the text, but instead enfolds it in manifold patterns of shifting subtlety, constantly moving crystallizations of meaning. In commenting on itself, in presenting other readings or revisions of itself, the text manifestly demonstrates that it is less than itself, incapable of in any one moment displaying the presumed totality of its meaning. But in this way, the text suggests that it is more than the sum of its parts, that this lack of signification is precisely what enables it to, possibly, signify *otherwise*. For Mallarmé, the text must always work to give more, in a greater abundance that comes only through allowing the gaps in the text to be gaps, through scrupulously avoiding filling them in with packets of poetical meaning, beyond that which the economic rules of supply and demand can bear – to give, that is, more than it takes.

---

[76] Derrida, *La Dissémination*, 334.

[77] Cf. Leo Bersani, *The Death of Stéphane Mallarmé*, in particular "The Man Dies."

CHAPTER THREE

REALITIES, FICTIONS AND THE ABANDONMENT OF SEDUCTION: RETHINKING OTHERNESS IN THE PSYCHOANALYTIC APPROACH TO TRAGEDY

NICHOLAS RAY

This paper derives from work on a larger project (Ray 2009) concerned with re-reading some of the key tragic texts that have impacted on the development of psychoanalytic thought. The larger project is an exploration of Freudian metapsychology and the Greek and Shakespearean texts in which it claims to identify its prototypes. Its main theoretical focus – one legible in the present paper – is the work of Jean Laplanche. As is known, Laplanche has ventured a systematic re-thinking of the Freudian oeuvre, which seeks to go beyond the tendency of Freud himself, and psychoanalysis more generally, to unify and centralise its conceptions of the human subject in a manner which can risk obscuring some of the most radical elements of the psychoanalytic enterprise. Through a progressive retrieval and reworking of Freud's early 'seduction' hypothesis, Laplanche has endeavoured to revitalise the dimension of 'otherness' in psychoanalytic thought, postulating an originary traumatism as the very basis of human subjectivity.

The paper is divided into two parts. The first, larger section, which implicitly leans on an essay by Laplanche and Pontalis from 1964, is a critical-historical account of the determinants which govern Freud's turn toward tragic drama, and his effective closing down of the dimension of alterity both in relation to specific literary texts and more generally in his account of ontogenesis. The second section briefly invokes some of the dominant themes in Laplanche's recent work in order to sketch out the possibility of an other-centred or 'Copernican' reading of the prototypical tragic dramas of the psychoanalytic canon.

Part I

It has long been commonplace to observe that Freud's earliest and most explicit intuition about what would one day be called the Oedipus complex appeared at a moment of crisis and disjunction in the development of his early thought. Within less than a month of the famous letter to Wilhelm Fliess of 21 September 1897, announcing that he had been forced to reject the 'seduction' theory of the neuroses on which he had laboured for so long, he wrote to his friend with the idea that desire for the mother and antagonism towards the father are perhaps essential components of childhood existence. This early intuition, it has become equally commonplace to observe, coincides exactly with Freud's interpretative breakthrough with respect to two great tragedies by Sophocles and Shakespeare. In the letter, dated 15 October, he puts forward a solution to the mysteries of *Oedipus Tyrannus* and *Hamlet*, which he will reiterate publicly many times and with little alteration during the rest of his career:

> A single idea of general value dawned on me. I have found, in my own case too, [the phenomenon of] being in love with my mother and jealous of my father, and I now consider it a universal event in early childhood [...] If this is so we can understand the gripping power of *Oedipus Rex*, in spite of all the objections that reason raises against the presupposition of fate [...] [T]he Greek legend seizes upon a compulsion which everyone recognises because he senses its existence within himself. Everyone in the audience was once a budding Oedipus in fantasy [...]
>
> Fleetingly, the thought passed through my head that the same thing might be at the bottom of *Hamlet* as well [...] How does [Hamlet] explain his irresolution in avenging his father by the murder of his uncle [...]? How better than through the torment he suffers from the obscure memory that he himself had contemplated the same deed against his father out of passion for his mother [...]? (1887–1904, 272).

Freud's theory of seduction, or the *neurotica* as he sometimes called it, had been an attempt to account for the pathogenic force of the premature and traumatic intrusion of adult sexuality into the passive infantile subject – infancy still representing for the early Freud an asexual phase of existence. With this theory, Freud had posited that behind particular scenarios recollected by neurotic patients there lay concealed from consciousness the unassimilable remembrance of a real event of infantile sexual abuse. The orthodox narrative of the evolution of Freud's thought –

a narrative inaugurated in Freud's own later autobiographical writings – has tended to regard the abandonment of this theory as the condition of possibility for the discovery of psychoanalysis 'proper', firmly grounded in the precepts of infantile sexuality, fantasy and of course the Oedipus complex.[1] But the question has been too rarely asked: *What was given up with the seduction theory?* To be sure, the hypothesis itself was heavy-handed and problematic in a number of ways; and since the 1980s well-publicised demands for its wholesale revival, and for the discrediting of Freud's subsequent work, have tended to be critically crude and polemically opportunistic.[2] The issue here, however, is not whether one should take the early Freud as an alternative to the later, supposedly 'misguided' Freud. The question to be posed is whether a conditional and very specific rehabilitation of the early theory of seduction has anything to offer by way of rethinking the approach to the literary tragedies upon which psychoanalysis has subsequently leaned for so much conceptual and illustrative support. To this end, it is worth traversing some fairly well-trodden critical territory in order to clarify and underscore a few fundamental points.

For much of the twentieth century, the guardians of psychoanalytic orthodoxy sought to consolidate the impression that the letter to Fliess of 21 September marked a clean and definitive break – a moment as it were of synchronised *anagnôrisis* and *peripeteia* in the theory. As Rand and Torok (1997, 24–44) among others have demonstrated, however, Freud in fact continued to vacillate for a number of years subsequently, periodically resuming then relinquishing the *neurotica* in line with the results of his clinical work.[3]

Difficult as it may be to isolate a single point of rupture with respect to the seduction theory, it remains true that with its eventual passing from Freud's explicit theoretical apparatus an immense transformation took place. For a significant number of Freud's critics this transformation amounted to an outright denial of reality and 'truth' – owing to the risk of personal or professional scandal – and an evasive embrace of the realm of fantasy: 'The early traumas his patients had had the courage to face and report to him', argues Jeffrey Masson (1984), 'he was later to dismiss as

---

[1] See esp. Kris's (1954) introduction to the original publication of the Fliess papers.

[2] Masson (1984) is only the most egregious example of this kind of work.

[3] The original publication in the 1950s of Freud's letters to Fliess was carefully edited so as imply that Freud never returned to the seduction theory after first expressing a loss of faith in it. Only thirty years later, when an uncensored edition appeared, did Freud's subsequent hesitation over its rejection become clear.

the fantasies of hysterical women who invented stories and told lies' (11).[4] Even for a more balanced commentator such as Philip Armstrong (2001) Freud's loss of confidence in the reality of seduction scenes and the subsequent shifts in his theoretical orientation imply that he somehow gave up on reality. 'Examining his own childhood memories', Armstrong states,

> Freud 'finds' [in September 1897] that [seduction] scenes are fantasies, produced by the child's desire for one parent and its corresponding jealousy towards the other. Thus the material presented to the analyst by the client [sic] – the very stuff of psychoanalysis – whether in the form of memories, fantasies or dreams, will henceforth be read as *fiction* (18).

On this view, Freud turned his back once and for all on the reality of seduction and thereby reduced the data provided by the analysand to the same epistemological level as imaginative literature.

Yet accounts of Freud's itinerary which rely upon a polarised conception of reality *versus* fiction, are hardly adequate to the complexity of his thinking in this period. It is true that in the letter of 21 September, outlining the need for a change of tack, Freud remarks on 'the certain insight that there are no indications of reality in the unconscious, so that one cannot distinguish between truth and fiction that has been cathected with affect' (1887–1904, 264). The implications of this insight are far-reaching; here it is only necessary to clarify that it doesn't amount to a self-authorised licence to promote the realm of fiction or fantasy at a commensurate cost to the category of reality. In the September letter Freud goes on to propose two quite different responses to his finding. Firstly, he suggests that scenes recounted by patients as childhood memories might be adult fantasies projected back onto childhood. This is a position which he will never take up exhaustively, and will later expend a good deal of energy refuting in the work of others.[5] Secondly, and more importantly, he says that without the *neurotica* 'the factor of hereditary disposition regains a sphere of influence from which I had made it my task to dislodge it' (265). It is in relation to this crucial factor that an alternative to the seduction hypothesis begins to open up for Freud, one which will eventually obtain a fundamental position in psychoanalytic doctrine.

---

[4] As the pointedly worded title of Masson's book indicates, he sees the abandonment of the seduction theory as an 'assault on truth'. Other (psycho)biographical explanations of the repudiation of the *neurotica* can be found in Balmary (1979) and Krüll (1979).

[5] It amounts to what will become the Jungian theory of retrospective fantasies. Freud's most extended attack upon it is found in the Wolf Man case history.

This alternative which eventually gains the upper hand after 1897 is a conceptualisation of sexuality and psychopathology that is firmly grounded in the hereditary, constitutional and biological reality of the human being, fantasy figuring essentially as its secondary expression. First and foremost in this regard is the biological conception of infantile sexuality, initially articulated in the *Three Essays* of 1905 and then progressively reinforced by the emphasis in later editions of the book on the spontaneous and quasi-programmatic unfolding of the well-known oral, anal and phallic 'stages' of libidinal development. Freud's subsequent elaboration of the typical or 'primal' fantasies (of seduction, castration and parental coitus) will demand a yet more emphatic grounding in reality, relying on the notorious arguments that they are the phylogenetically transmitted representation of 'real occurrences in the primeval times of the human family' (Freud 1916–17, 371).

Thus although from late 1897 onwards Freud finds himself less and less convinced of the objective reality of the scenes recalled by his patients, he remains unable to resign himself to their being purely imaginary creations and begins instead to seek *the more fundamental reality on which he believes they must be based*. By the same token, he doesn't turn to dramatic fiction having given up on factual reality and sought refuge in the imaginative realm of pure fantasy; his great interpretative breakthrough with respect to the tragic dramas of Sophocles and Shakespeare corresponds to and coincides with this new effort to identify a reality elsewhere.

It can be said, somewhat schematically perhaps, that from 1897 onwards the gradual displacement of the *neurotica* and the increasing focus on hereditary disposition thus amounted to the following tectonic theoretical shift. With the seduction theory Freud had been endeavouring to conceptualise the traumatic introduction of sexuality into the subject from the outside – that is, by the contingent external agency of a typically perverse adult other. With the eventual relinquishment of this essentially intersubjective model of excitation we see the groundbreaking and doubtless necessary abolition of the myth of an asexual infancy, but only by way of a deterministic conception of sexuality which prioritises factors that are both endogenous – biological and/or phylogenetic – and supposedly universal.

Freud's conceptualisation of the Oedipus complex does not have an existence independent of this alternative trend, but is – and will for the most part remain – wholly subordinate to it, as indeed are his interpretations of Sophocles and Shakespeare. As a number of commentators have pointed out, although the fundamental Oedipal impulses are identified in a rudimentary way in 1897, the 'Oedipus complex' – named and formalised as such – will not appear in Freud's writings until 1910.[6] By the time of *Totem and Taboo* (1912–13), of course, the Oedipus complex has been annexed to Freud's arguments around phylogenesis, forming the structuring principle of the dynamics of the primal family. In any case, from first to last Oedipal desire is articulated in terms of a universal sexual determinism.

Nowhere is this more vividly illustrated than in the critical readings of Sophocles and Shakespeare by which the Oedipus complex is unfailingly shored up time after time. Discussing *Oedipus Tyrannus* in the letter of 15 October, Freud invokes in passing 'the objections that reason raises against the presuppositions of fate'. In response, he appeals to the gripping power of the play upon its audience, which he says must be a result of their all having experienced the desire to do as Oedipus does. Such desire is 'a universal event'. From the moment of its theoretical inception, Oedipal sexuality is thus conceived as being outside the sphere of contingency and firmly located in necessity. It is no less programmed than Oedipus' inadvertent transgressions are decreed in advance by fate. Freud's subsequent expository works invariably invoke the same objection and produce the same answer, directly construing the exogenous force of fate as a necessary poetic distortion of the scandalous Oedipal theme: 'Fate and the oracle [are] no more than materializations of an internal necessity', he argues in the *Autobiographical Study* (1925, 63). Their presence, he continues to insist until even one of his last texts, *An Outline of Psychoanalysis* (1940), 'is a recognition [on the part of Sophocles] of the inevitability of the fate which has condemned every son to live through the Oedipus complex' (192). Not only does the content of Sophocles' Oedipus story illustrate the objects of Oedipal desire and hatred; its deterministic unfolding dramatises the non-contingency of the Oedipal phase in every subject.

Oedipus Tyrannus poetically figures forth the universal necessity which propels each and every human being from the inside. Thus in Freud's October letter through to the *Outline*, what matters in *Hamlet* is not *why* the Dane, like the Theban, should wish to kill his father and unite with his mother (for such a wish is presumed to be inevitable); all that matters is the fact that this automatic complex of feelings pertaining to Hamlet has already been usurped by his uncle and acted out 'by proxy'.

Sophocles and Shakespeare, then, explicitly enter Freud's thought at the moment it starts out on the new path suggested to Fliess in September

[6] See in particular Forrester (1982, 84–96).

1897, with the emphasis firmly on a universal and pre-ordained schema of psycho-sexual development. Freud will henceforth read *Oedipus Tyrannus* and *Hamlet* as dramatic fictions founded upon and expressive of a determined and universal human 'fate'.

It is the theoretical suppositions and blind-spots that structure this alternative emphasis which I propose it may be necessary and productive to move beyond. My purpose is not to decry some purported de-privileging of reality from September 1897 onwards. It is, firstly, to indicate that an essential dimension of psychic life is scotomised by the totalising and essentialising tendency which underpins Freud's post-*neurotica* efforts to root sexual and fantasy life in a universal biological or collective prehistoric reality. Secondly, it is to suggest the need to reconsider some of the key tragic texts which have been conscripted into supporting this latter theoretical tendency, and to do so from a critical perspective in which the *implicit* potential of Freud's early seduction hypothesis is more fully realised.

Part II

It would be desirable to demonstrate in some detail how what I've said about the theoretical timing of Freud's turn to tragedy links up with the ongoing agenda of Laplanche's return to Freud. It would also be desirable to show thoroughly how Laplanche's work, the breadth and originality of whose thought is only now beginning to be fully appreciated in the Anglophone world, could be invoked in order to reopen the question of alterity in the tragic texts which psychoanalysis has for so long labored to read. In the space available I will only make some essential expository points on these related issues.

In a gesture which he has been careful to emphasize is partially schematic, Laplanche has proposed the existence of two different organising principles that govern the totality of Freud's thought: the 'Copernican' and the 'Ptolemaic'. The terms are not strictly his own but are suggested by Freud's essay 'A Difficulty in the Path of Psychoanalysis' (1917), in which he famously compares his psychoanalytic discovery to the blow struck by Copernicus to human narcissism. As Copernicus revealed the earth not to be the centre of its universe, so Freud claims to have revealed the conscious human subject not to be the centre of his. Man feels himself to be supreme master within his own mind, but psychoanalysis has shown that '*the ego is not master in its own house*' (143). The problem with Freud's comparison from Laplanche's perspective, however, is that it is only partially true. Freud, he argues, is as much his own Ptolemy as his own Copernicus, for he is endlessly led to recentre the human subject theoretically even as he claims to decentre it. In his paper on Freud's 'Unfinished Copernican Revolution' (1992), Laplanche takes the most illustrative example of this from the same 1917 essay. There, Freud insists that the psychoanalytic postulation of man's heteronomy is founded on its discovery of an otherness, something 'alien' or 'foreign' (the unconscious) which dislodges the centrality of the ego: '[i]n certain diseases', Freud says,

> thoughts emerge suddenly without one knowing where they came from […] These alien guests even seem to be more powerful than those that are at the ego's command […] Or else impulses appear which seem like those of a stranger, so that the ego denies them; […] the ego says to itself: 'This is an illness, a foreign invasion' (1917, 141–2).

No sooner has Freud described this decentring foreign presence, however, than he proceeds to reduce its foreignness altogether. 'Psychiatry [in general]', he continues, 'denies that such things mean the intrusion into the mind of evil spirits from without'; and 'psychoanalysis [specifically] sets out to explain these uncanny [*unheimlich*] disorders' (142). It says to the ego:

> Nothing has entered into you from without; a part of the activity of your own mind has been withdrawn from your knowledge and from the command of your will […] [Y]ou do not recognise it as a derivation of your own rejected instincts […] (142).

The decentring of the ego is thus affirmed at the cost of domesticating the intruder, of reducing the alterity of the invading other to another part of the subject which the subject does not recognise as such. For Laplanche it is the conclusion of Freud's address to the ego which is most telling: 'Turn your eyes inward, look into your own depths, learn first to know yourself' (143). In Freud's invocation of the Delphic imperative, 'Know Thyself', the subject becomes comfortably re-grounded once more. Certainly the ego is displaced from its central position, but only to be replaced by the unconscious, the latter now taking on the role of the subject's innermost core, a self of which his ego denies ownership but which it is the task of psychoanalysis to help him re-assimilate. Nothing has entered into you from the outside: everything that intrudes upon you from an origin which seems so obscure in fact emerges from inside you, *it is you*, *your-self*.

It is, Laplanche argues, only on a superficial reading that the astronomical revolution inaugurated in the modern era by Copernicus can be limited to an analogous replacement of geocentrism by heliocentrism.

Within the latter system, he points out, the apparently fixed position of certain stellar constellations led to the conclusion that they were at a distance from earth incommensurable with the internal distances of the solar system. Copernican heliocentrism, that is, made conceivable the infinity of the universe, and thus *the possibility of the absence of any centre whatsoever* (1992e, 55 ff.). As will be seen, it is Laplanche's charge that the potential for an equivalent discovery in Freud – to stick with Freud's own comparison – was actually established, only to be formally abandoned, before 1897.

The domesticating gesture which Freud commits upon the alien of the unconscious in 1917 can be 'endlessly demonstrate[d]' throughout Freudian thought (1992e, 67). Beyond 1897 it increasingly becomes the Freudian gesture *par excellence*. The claim to a Copernican decentring of the subject ceaselessly gives way to the same Ptolemaic recentring of the subject back upon himself, with the consequence that Freud is habitually drawn towards promulgating endogenous models of psychic development. Laplanche calls these retrograde movements 'goings-astray' (*fourvoiements*). Freud's recourse to biology and phylogenesis in accounting for sexual and fantasy life has already been mentioned. To these attempts to give the subject a quasi-programmatic ('fated') grounding, should be added Freud's late postulation, in his second metapsychological topography, of the innate id In each case Laplanche sees an attempt to give the subject a 'foundation', but one which is already somehow proper to the subject, which as it were already 'belongs' to him, and leaves the notion of a centred subject ultimately intact.

Freud's true Copernican discovery, Laplanche avers, was implicitly encoded in the *neurotica*, which was, precisely, an attempt to account for something entering the subject from without: the introduction and provocation of sexuality by an other. Laplanche sees a kernel of truth in both the seduction theory and the fact of its repudiation. For him the Ptolemaic drift of Freud's thought after 1897 doesn't come about by chance. On the contrary, his thought is *magnetized* by its object. If Freud starts out with a potentially radical account of the intersubjective origins of sexuality, then moves in an increasingly Ptolemaic direction thereafter, it is because his thought obeys a mimetic 'exigency' (*exigence*): it replicates in its very evolution the human subject's own narcissistic need to mask *its* originary heteronomy, its primordial dependence on a seductive alterity.

Freud's appeal to Sophocles and Shakespeare, then, is not made on the cusp of some random empirical 'mistake'. It is made in the very moment that Freud begins to be led astray by this powerful exigency, towards replicating and endorsing at the level of his theory the very narcissism which characterizes the human subject.

Laplanche's work, and in particular his elaboration of a 'general theory of primal seduction', offers a means of (re)reading such key tragic texts as *Oedipus Tyrannus* and *Hamlet*, and of resisting the Ptolemaism which has determined their appropriation in Freud and, arguably, the psychoanalytic field in general.[7]

The return to the seduction theory is not a turn to 'recovered memory therapy', but a theoretical endeavor to disclose the radical heteronomy of the subject in a way which often eluded Freud himself. For Laplanche the sexually constitutive function of the external other in Freud's special (i.e. pathological) theory of seduction must be recognised in terms of its wholly general relevance: that is, as a *fundamental or 'primal' anthropological situation* (Laplanche 1987, 89–90). The confrontation of the pre-subjectal subject by verbal and non-verbal gestures which it is ill-equipped to decode is structural to its interpersonal existence. Underlying the bilateral exchanges between infant and care-giver, the reciprocal relation of 'attachment', is a radical, indeed foundational, psychic dissymmetry. Comparatively little of the infant's psychological development can be presupposed; adult activity, on the other hand – and not least of all adult activity in relation to the satisfaction of the infant's most basic self-preservative needs – bears within it a developed psychological complexity. The infant is thus *by definition* the passive recipient of currents of meaning from the outside which it lacks the internal or instinctual resources to assimilate properly.

Laplanche calls these centripetal intrusions, which emerge in even the most normative relations of attachment, *enigmatic messages*. They are to be considered enigmatic in two corresponding ways, tied, ultimately, to the structural psychic dissymmetry of the adult-infant relationship. Firstly, and straightforwardly, the adult message exceeds the interpretative capacity of its pre-subjectal addressee – the infant (*infans*: lit. 'speechless') – who as yet lacks the adequate cognitive and linguistic means to process adult signification. Secondly, the adult message, by virtue of being derived from a psychically mature other equipped with an unconscious, may be enigmatic first of all to its own originator i.e. it may exceed the intentional capacity of the adult him- or herself.

The second point here requires explication. In Freud's pathological theory of seduction, sexuality comes from without. Desire is firmly on the side of the other, the seducer. Now, long after the formal rejection of the

[7] It should be emphasised, of course, that for Laplanche Ptolemaism continues to contaminate even current psychoanalytic thought. Cf. Laplanche (2006).

neuroica Freud's thought remains sensitive to the gestures of parental nurture which mediate the infant's relation to its own bodily zones ('don't touch yourself there!' etc…). But the question of the adult's own sexual or unconscious investment in all of this now almost invariably becomes a closed avenue. Laplanche's elaboration of the enigmatic message attempts to reopen it by insisting that the adult's relation to the child cannot be evacuated of a unilateral unconscious, and indeed sexual, content. The verbal, physical and behavioural messages with which the adult other confronts the infant in the very process of attending to the child's vital needs will, he argues, be sporadically 'compromised' by the unconscious desires and fantasies of their originator.[8] It is this unconscious compromise that freights the adult message with what Laplanche calls enigmaticity, a sexualised supplement of meaning which partially scrambles the other's address to the infant. This claim implies a significant move beyond the earlier return to Freud's seduction theory boldly articulated in Sándor Ferenczi's (1933) well-known elaboration of the 'confusion of tongues'. Laplanche's notion of the 'fundamental anthropological situation' owes a good deal to Ferencz's insistence on the basic developmental inequality between the adult and the child. However, Ferenczi's account of the traumatism remains predominantly concerned with adults whose behaviour towards children is explicitly pathological. Laplanche's development is to insist that even the most quotidian adult messages are intrinsically traumatising because they are implicitly and involuntarily parasitized or compromised by opaque, sexual significations from the parental unconscious.[9]

Traumatizing, sexualized, enigmatic, these centripetal currents are the originary stimuli of the subject's psychic and sexual life. For Laplanche there is no 'I', no psychic subject as such prior to this originary Copernican traumatism. The ego and the id are created in the same movement by which the subject tries to translate and bind these exogenous currents. The ego will consist of everything of the other's messages that can be mastered and integrated into a relatively coherent history; the unconscious will consist of those elements which resist egoic synthesis,

---

[8] This is, at bottom, a generalisation of Freud's notion of unconsciously compromised signification – the parapraxis or slip.

[9] Ferenczi's paper does, however, link up suggestively with Laplanche's own conceptualisation of the aetiology of psychosis and severe pathology in which 'intromitted' adult messages are not sufficiently enigmatic – i.e. not repressed enough – to enable the infant to bind and symbolise them freely.

reified and non-coordinated representations which remain *à tradiure*.[10] The sexuality and psychic apparatus of the *infans* are thus not grounded in biology, heredity, phylogenesis or anything else 'essential' or 'central' to them. What is universal is only this structural openness to the contingency of the other's unconscious fantasies of desire, a fundamental passivity before the other without which repression and subjectivity would never be fully inaugurated.

From such a perspective a great many formations and categories which Freud and classical psychoanalysis have wanted to regard as being reducible to an innate core of the subject must be critically interrogated and metapsychologically repositioned in respect of this structurally anterior Copernican openness to alterity. There would be multiple examples. However, it is with an eye on the contrast to some of Freud's foregoing claims that I invoke the Oedipus complex as just one key instance here.

On a Copernican view, the classical Oedipus complex, which positions the little Oedipus as source and agent of the drives at stake, contains a profound 'misattribution' with regard to its initiation, since 'the [original] initiator of messages bearing sexuality is actually the parent. The incestuous one potentially is the adult' (Laplanche 2012; forthcoming). This does not, however, mean that the Oedipus complex is to be rejected out of hand as a theoretical 'mistake'; it means that psychoanalysis must approach it in a radically different manner. Instead of perceiving the Oedipus as a complex of endogenously 'fated' libidinal or biological impulses, psychoanalysis must recognize it as first and foremost a 'system of self-theorization'. It is one among many offered culturally to the individual since childhood and deployed hermeneutically by him as a means of binding and synthesizing the exogenous adult stimuli by which he is interpellated. Put otherwise, it is, Laplanche insists, a contingent and culturally transmitted '*myth*', one which 'helps him to put into a narrative – at the price of its own culpability – the often much rawer sexual messages which are conveyed to him by the parent, the adult' (Laplanche 2012; forthcoming). The misattribution which characterizes the classical Oedipus is thus in fact the mark of subjective re-elaboration and even narrative systematisation on the part of the individual subject. It is the mark of a hermeneutic process in which the enigmatic stimulation of the

---

[10] The notion of the repressed unconscious consisting of 'untranslated' remainders derives in part from an early insight which Freud (1887–1904) acknowledged in a letter to Fliess: 'A failure of translation – that is what is clinically known as repression' (208). Laplanche's systematic expansion and development of the translation model is elaborated in detail in Laplanche (1993).

'fundamental anthropological situation' is reconfigured and partially mastered, the individual's originary passivity becoming masked over by the imaginative assumption of the active role of the 'hero', of the 'subject' and no longer just the 'object' of desire.

From the Copernican perspective, then, even the Oedipus complex – that 'shibboleth' of psychoanalysis – must take up a secondary and thoroughly contingent position in terms of sexual ontology. It is to be tackled by the analyst not as an irreducible bedrock of essential and universal sexual impulses but as a kind of ideological screen within the subject's own account of himself. For Laplanche, it is only by insisting on the more radical and perhaps more scandalous structural situation concealed by such pervasive 'myths' – the truth of the subject's primary and constitutive passivity before an enigmatic alterity – that that genuinely Copernican intuition of the psychoanalytic discovery can be recognized and maintained.

With this singular insistence on exogeneity, heteronomy and primary passivity, Laplanche's thought thus offers an extraordinarily productive means of beginning to read what a Ptolemaically-oriented psychoanalysis has sometimes risked overlooking in the literary – and in particular the tragic – texts it labours to comprehend. Traumatic histories, legacies of guilt, the transmission of family curses and *daimōnes*: the classic themes of dramatic tragedy point to what a post-1897 Freud couldn't help but miss: namely tragedy's implicit, perhaps essential, fascination with the *de*centring and heteronomy of its so-called hero – his primordial and enigmatic debt to ancestors, antecedents, others etc. In Sophocles, after all, it is to Laius and Jocasta, rather than Oedipus, that the object of Freud's Ptolemaic reduction, the Oracle, originally addresses itself. Might it not, therefore, be to the *unconscious desire of the parents and the means of its transmission to the son* that a psychoanalytic approach would, in the first instance, need to call critical attention? Isn't Oedipus' tragic fate traumatically and inaugurally inscribed upon him (*Oidi – pous*, swellfoot) by the very parental gestures of piercing and expulsion which were, nevertheless, intended at a conscious level to circumvent it? In Shakespeare too, it may prove necessary to explore the extent to which Hamlet's tragic trajectory is determined in advance not by an automatic and universal complex of feelings, but allo-centrically, by the transmission to him of a certain traumatizing semantic excess. Isn't the father's posthumous demand for vengeance, poured in at Hamlet's ear, a performative repetition of the crime which 'made a ghost of him'? Discursively and unconsciously parasitized by the petrifying poison whose auricular application it narrates, doesn't the call for vengeance constrain and determine Hamlet's hesitant paralysis even as it demands swift and faithful action?[11]

Post-Freudian accounts of these and other tragic texts need not – indeed ought not – be Ptolemaic as well. It may be that the most pertinent means at the disposal of psychoanalysis for grasping and *thinking* such constitutive, exogenous movements within tragedy were in fact swept away with the very discoveries which made possible Freud's 'classical' analytic interpretations of *Oedipus Tyrannus* and *Hamlet* themselves. Laplanche's thought seeks to develop the implicit potential of those abandoned theoretical germs, not so as to overturn the Freudian project altogether but so as to maintain the radicality of Freud's original discovery while resisting the implicit theoretical closures that accompanied the development of those subsequent and very necessary discoveries. As such, re-opening the question of the other – and the unconscious dimension of the other – in relation to such immense tragedies as these may generate a better understanding both of the function which orthodox psychoanalysis has sometimes coercively called upon tragedy to perform, and that within tragedy for which psychoanalysis has hitherto remained unable to account.

References

Armstrong, Philip. 2001. *Shakespeare in Psychoanalysis*, Accents in Shakespeare Series, London and New York: Routledge.

Balmary, Marie. 1979. *Psychoanalyzing Psychoanalysis: Freud and the Hidden Secret of the Father*. Trans. Ned Lukacher. Baltimore: Johns Hopkins University Press, 1982.

Ferenczi, Sándor. 1933. Confusion of Tongues between Adults and the Child (The Language of Tenderness and of Passion). In Julia Borossa, Ed and trans., *Sandor Ferenczi: Selected Writings*. Harmondsworth: Penguin, 1999, 293–303.

Forrester, John. (1980). *Language and the Origins of Psychoanalysis*. Basingstoke and London: Macmillan.

Freud, Sigmund. 1887–1904. *The Complete Letters of Sigmund Freud to Wilhelm Fliess: 1887-1904*. Trans. Jeffrey Moussaieff Masson. Cambridge, Massachusetts: The Belknap Press of Harvard University Press, 1985.

—. 1916–17. *Introductory Lectures on Psychoanalysis*. James Strachey et al., Ed and trans., *The Standard Edition of the Complete Psychological*

[11] I attempt to unpack these claims about *Oedipus Tyrannus* and *Hamlet* in Ray (2009).

Works of Sigmund Freud [or *S.E.*]. 24 vols. London: Hogarth Press 1953–74. *S.E.* Vols. 15 and 16.

—. 1917. A Difficulty in the Path of Psychoanalysis. *S. E.* vol. 17.

—. 1925. *An Autobiographical Study*. *S.E.* 20: 7–74.

—. 1940. *An Outline of Psychoanalysis*. *S.E.* 23: 144–207.

Kris, Ernst. 1954. Introduction. In Sigmund Freud, *The Origins of Psychoanalysis: Letters, Drafts and Notes to Wilhelm Fliess*. Marie Bonaparte, Anna Freud and Ernst Kris (eds). Garden City, New York: Doubleday Anchor Books. 1–47.

Krüll, Marianne. 1979. *Freud and His Father*. Trans. Arnold J. Pomerans. London and New York: W.W. Norton & Co. 1986.

Laplanche, Jean. 1987. *New Foundations for Psychoanalysis*. Trans. David Macey. Oxford: Basil Blackwell. 1989.

—. 1992. The Unfinished Copernican Revolution. Trans. Luke Thurston. In Laplanche 1999.

—. 1993. Short Treatise on the Unconscious. Trans. Luke Thurston. In Laplanche 1999.

—. 1999. *Essays on Otherness*. Ed. John Fletcher. London and New York: Routledge.

—. 2006. Exigency and Going Astray. Trans. Vincent Ladmiral and Nicholas Ray. *Psychoanalysis, Culture & Society*, 2006, 11, 185–9.

—. 2012; forthcoming. Castration and Oedipus as Codes and Narrative Schemas. In *Freud and the* Sexual*: Essays 2000-2006*. Trans. John Fletcher, Jonathan House and Nicholas Ray. New York: International Psychoanalytic Books; forthcoming.

Laplanche, Jean and Jean-Bertrand Pontalis. 1964. *Fantasy and the Origins of Sexuality*. In Formations of Fantasy. *Eds. Victor Burgin, James Donald and Cora Kaplan.* London: Methuen 1986.

Masson, Jeffrey M. 1984. *The Assault on Truth: Freud's Suppression of the Seduction Theory*. New York: Farrar, Straus and Giroux.

Rand, Nicholas and Maria Torok. 1997. *Questions for Freud: The Secret History of Psychoanalysis*. Cambridge, Mass. and London: Harvard University Press.

Ray, Nicholas. 2009. *Tragedy and Otherness: Sophocles, Shakespeare, Psychoanalysis*. Oxford: Peter Lang.

SECTION II.

CONTEXTUALIZING CULTURAL CRITIQUE

CHAPTER FOUR

"IT WAS AS A REBEL THAT HE FELL:" THE ABUSE OF POWER, SCAPEGOATING AND LYING IN FRIEDRICH DÜRRENMATT'S *DER VERDACHT*

VERA B. PROFIT

Beyond the din, the limitless freedom, the proliferating options to make more money or live longer, what really matters? Do I really matter?

These questions—and they are one and the same—must be answered, for in the search itself, value is ascribed not only to the principle or person valued, but also and inevitably to the person valuing. For better or worse we, as individuals and as a society, are defined by what matters to us.

Given the distortions of our age, it may be appropriate to look for moral guidance from those who clearly did not find the right answers, who failed to enhance their lives or the lives of those around them. Sometimes we know unequivocally what is right by observing someone do it all wrong. Nevertheless, at least since Adam and Eve, the wrong has held undeniable appeal. What is it that draws us toward evil over and over again?

"Angels boring? Yes—until they fall! Then the angel takes on fascination and interest. [. . .] When an angel assumes independent self-assertion—call it pride or refusal to knuckle under or what not—he then takes on power and the capacity to grasp our attention and even admiration."[1] These insights represent the clinical conclusions of Rollo May in his *Love and Will.* More than half a century earlier, as if he also had been trained as a psychoanalyst, Oscar Wilde phrased the observation similarly. He described Dorian Gray contemplating his own by then seriously flawed portrait suffused "with that pride of individualism that is

[1] Rollo May, *Love and Will* (New York: Delta, 1989), 140.

half the fascination of sin [. . .]."[2]

Self-assertion, individualism and freedom of choice are unquestionably laudable in and of themselves, but at what point does the pursuit of these principles no longer further integrated self-actualization? At what juncture does appropriate self-interest develop into narcissism, become evil and thus not lead, as was originally intended, to the fulfillment of the human person, but, if left unchecked, unerringly to the diametric opposite, namely self-destruction?

Where can examples be found of those who misread the early, still reversible signs of narcissistic behavior, who did not make the requisite course correction and subsequently annihilated not only themselves, but their all too numerous victims as well? If we studied these individuals, might we not learn from them and thus possibly avoid making their mistakes? And as a result, might we not lead our lives more efficiently, more productively?

According to Alexander Solzhenitsyn we needn't look very far.

> A work of art contains its verification in itself: artificial, strained concepts do not withstand the test of being turned into images [. . .]. Works which draw on truth [. . .] compellingly involve us, and no one ever [. . .] will come forth to refute them.[3]

Consequently, this essay focuses upon a multi-faceted detective novel written both geographically and chronologically in close proximity to the Holocaust, the quintessence of evil. First published in its entirety in 1953,[4] Friedrich Dürrenmatt's (1921—1990) *Der Verdacht* tells of a Swiss physician, Fritz Emmenberger, during three crucial phases of his life: as a medical student, as a concentration camp physician, and after 1945, as the CEO of a clinic. Hans Bärlach, a Swiss policeman and the novel's second major figure, endeavors to prove that Emmenberger, presently the

---

[2] Oscar Wilde, *The Picture of Dorian Gray*, ed. Donald L. Lawler (New York: Norton, 1988), 109.

[3] Alexander Solzhenitsyn, *Nobel Lecture*, trans. F. D. Reeve (New York: Farrar, Straus and Giroux, 1972), 7.

[4] Friedrich Dürrenmatt, "Der Verdacht: Ein Kriminalroman, 1951," *Gesammelte Werke: Romane*, 4 (Zürich: Diogenes, 1991), 119-265. First published serially in *Der Schweizerische Beobachter* between September 15, 1951 and February 29, 1952, the novel was published in its entirety a year later by Benzinger of Zurich, Einsiedeln and Cologne.

All quotes and paraphrases followed by page references are taken from the above-mentioned text. With rare exception, all translations from this as well as all other sources are my own.

administrator of a Zurich hospital, is identical with one Dr. Nehle, who performed medical experiments on prisoners in the concentration camp near Stutthof without the benefit of anesthesia. With the assistance of several secondary figures, Bärlach confirms the suspicion that lies at the novel's core. (260)

In order to ascertain the exact nature of the evil traits (beyond the obvious) within Emmenberger's character, this essay will draw upon the works of several leading thinkers such as Fromm and Frankl, but chief among them will be M. Scott Peck. Prior to his *People of the Lie: The Hope for Healing Human Evil*,[5] the diagnosis of evil had never entered the psychiatric lexicon. To allow for this designation within the medical sphere, Dr. Peck's treatise elucidates the characteristics of both individual and group evil. In the course of his landmark study the then practising psychiatrist illustrates at least eight characteristics of evil individuals. They are: victimization of body and/or spirit, failure to recognize the separateness of others, depersonalisation of others, unmitigated narcissism, the unsubordinated use of power, scapegoating, lying, and the total inability to tolerate legitimate criticism.

Due to space constraints, the ensuing remarks concentrate only upon the illegitimate use of power, scapegoating and lying, as these three are to be numbered among the most compelling facets of individual evil.

Part I

Power abused. On the most basic level, power means the ability to actualize one's wishes; the term implies potency.[6] As he decides over life and death in both the concentration camp and in his clinic (130), Emmenberger doubtlessly exercises the ultimate power. But to what end? His use of power remains utterly meaningless. Obviously his actions do not enhance the lives of those within his purview, nor do they lead to his success, his fulfillment. Yet he attempts to convince police inspector, Bärlach, and also himself of the opposing viewpoint; "' [. . .] *my* victory and *my* freedom and nothing but these are reflected in this trembling, unconscious, white flesh beneath my scalpel.'"(252)

On the other hand, Charlene, a patient of Scott Peck's, whom he ultimately diagnoses as evil, only wishes to terminate the relationship between her therapist and herself at the moment and in the manner she

[5] M[organ] Scott Peck, *People of the Lie: The Hope for Healing Human Evil* (New York: Simon, 1983).

[6] Erich Fromm, *Escape from Freedom* (New York: Rinehart, 1941), 162.

considers appropriate. She manages to achieve that goal, but as this maneuver does not further, let alone accelerate the healing process, her "performance was ultimately meaningless."[7] As Peck theorizes: "She did not want power in order to improve society, to care for a family, to make herself a more effective person, or in any way accomplish anything creative. Her thirst for power was unsubordinated to anything higher than itself."[8]

Whether one desires to manage a business or a household, to fashion a work of art or raise a child, the end envisioned determines the legitimate use of power. If power intentionally realizes a negative or destructive result, the potency exercised is used perversely or, as Erich Fromm suggests, that implementation of power remains nothing more than domination.[9]

But who would endeavor to dominate for the sake of dominating? Not, as it might seem, a strong individual. As Fromm concludes: "*the lust for power is not rooted in strength but in weakness*."[10] Such persons strive to dominate others for he or she essentially fears them, the demands they might make, in essence all of life's demands. Those who believe, more often than not only on a subconscious level, that they cannot subsist in the face of life's essential unpredictability, cannot cope with the questions their days may ask of them, feel driven to minimize these risks, actual or perceived, at all costs. They do so by attempting to control every aspect of another's behavior, by forcibly limiting his or her options. Though for sundry reasons undesirable as well as ineffective, domination functions as a survival/ defense mechanism.[11] Confident individuals, who are generally able to develop their talents, who contribute to society while maintaining their integrity, these persons do not exhibit the need for domination.[12]

Domination or this particular variant of a misuse of power is subordinated to nothing other than itself. Yet Peck asserts:

> Mental health requires that the human will submit itself to something higher than itself. To function decently in this world we must submit ourselves to some principle that takes precedence over what we might want at any given moment.[13]

---

[7] Peck, *People of the Lie*, 177.
[8] Ibid., 176.
[9] Fromm, 162.
[10] Ibid., 162.
[11] Ibid., 158.
[12] Ibid., 162.
[13] Peck, *People of the Lie*, 162.

Depending on their orientation, some define this governing principle as common sense or the legitimate needs of others. The religiously inclined would define it as God. In the Our Father, does a Christian not pray: "'Thy will be done?'"[14] Consequently, evil individuals are characterized by a will that is subordinated to no one and nothing other than itself. Such unbridled willfulness does not seek to enrich, but, as Emmenberger devastatingly illustrates, seeks only to destroy.[15]

Delivered in the novel's last pages, the anti-hero's plea of André Gide's *The Immoralist* furnishes yet another example of the misappropriation of power, the misappropriation of freedom. A brilliant mind, Michel achieves in his mid-twenties what most academicians don't realize until much later in life, if indeed at all. In the emotional sphere, he has been granted the love of a devoted wife—whom he has just laid to rest—and yet he senses that he is lost, disheartened and doesn't know where to turn. Consequently he asks his three friends to help him find his way. The methods he favored till now did not bring him the fulfillment he so ardently sought.

> What frightens me, I admit, is that I am still quite young. It seems to me at times as though my real life hasn't begun as yet. Tear me away from here now and give me a reason for living. As for me, I no longer know where to look.[16]

Michel is fully aware that he surrendered his academic position, the estate he owned and has lost the attachment to his wife. Indeed, he was thoroughly successful in liberating himself from all obligations, from all he considered constraining. But the central question remains: "'I freed

---

[14] *A Reader's Guide to the Holy Bible: Revised Standard Version*, Matthew 6: 10 (Nashville: Thomas Nelson, 1972), New Testament, 5. Even for the well-intentioned, ascertaining God's will can become problematical. Gerald May writes: "In my opinion, the relationship between personal and divine will is the most fierce and treacherous confrontation faced by modern spiritual guides and leaders. It demands that they be constantly attentive to and critical of their own spiritual inclinations [. . .]. The question is deceptively simple to ask and exquisitely difficult to answer: Am I truly seeking to do Thy will…or mine?" Gerald G. May, *Care of Mind / Care of Spirit: Psychiatric Dimensions of Spiritual Direction* (San Francisco: Harper, 1982), 16-17.

[15] For an excellent discussion concerning the difference between willfulness and willingness, see: Gerald G. May, *Will and Spirit: A Contemplative Psychology* (San Francisco: Harper, 1982), 5-7.

[16] André Gide, "L'immoraliste," *Oeuvres Complètes*, ed. L. [Louis] Martin-Chauffier, IV (Paris: NRF, 1933), 169.

myself, that's possibly true; but what of it? This useless freedom torments me.'"[17]

It is not enough use one's power, to exercise one's freedom; that same freedom must be exercised for some verifiable good. Michel did not lack for effort, did not lack the will to be subservient to his goals. The friend, who drafts the preface to Michel's soliloquy, admits as much. "How can Michel serve the state? [. . .] Michel is dedicated; he is that still; soon he will be so only to himself."[18]

Dedication in and of itself is therefore not enough; to whom and to what one is dedicated constitutes the crux of the matter. Submission itself, in other words, does not suffice; one must conscientiously examine the beliefs to which one submits. We all submit one way or another. We all order our lives according to a set of explicit or implicit guidelines. Lord Henry Wotton's statement to Basil Hallward, the creator of Dorian Gray's portrait, not withstanding, an individual without principles does not exist. "'[. . .] I like persons with no principles better than anything else in the world.'"[19]

Part II

Scapegoating. When those maltreating others meet with the (to the sane mind) expected resistance of their victims, the perpetrators most frequently respond to these assaults in predictable fashion. They scapegoat. When something goes awry, as it invariably does; when someone protests, as they invariably do, if they dare, evil people always blame someone or something else, if not the structure of the world itself. Anyone, but him- or herself, anything but the salient issue will be ascertained to be at fault. From their vantage point, this behavior seems only logical, for on one level the evil consider themselves faultless. And if the fault, the root of the failure, cannot be acknowledged within, then it must be found without. Erich Neumann describes this fundamental defense mechanism perfectly.

> The shadow, which contradicts the values held, cannot be accepted as a negative part of one's own being and is consequently projected, i.e., removed outward and experienced as something out there. It is contested, punished and eradicated as something 'strange out there', rather than of

[17] Ibid., 169.
[18] Ibid., 10.
[19] Wilde, 9.

'one's own self in here.'[20]

In the final analysis, scapegoating constitutes a variant of projection. If done consciously (more frequently, of course, it is done unconsciously), whether the individual distinguishes between self and other, between the desirable and the undesirable, whether the relationship between the reflective self and the undesirable thoughts is retained or severed, projection essentially alters the shape of reality as it is perceived in the eyes of the person projecting. Of necessity, his or her reaction to that reconstructed reality also changes.[21] For projection refers to "any process in which inner phenomena are allocated to the external world."[22] More succinctly, projecting or scapegoating shapes the person scapegoating as well as his or her environs.

Scapegoating, however, also incorporates the failure to assume the appropriate degree of responsibility. At the risk of oversimplification, it may be fair to say: whereas the neurotic personality assumes an excessive amount, the individual with a character disorder doesn't assume enough responsibility, if indeed any at all.[23] The former believe that the root of the failure (or success) lies only within themselves; by contrast, the latter will espouse just the opposite. They are not in any way to blame for the conflict, for the less than optimum results.

In his delineation of these personality defects, Scott Peck suggests that those individuals with character disorders may be recognized in two ways: not only do the lame explanations for their action or inaction identify them, but also their verifiable predilection for certain idioms.

> The speech of a person with a character disorder [. . .] relies heavily on 'I can't,' 'I couldn't,' 'I have to,' and 'I had to,' demonstrating a self-image of a being who has no power of choice, whose behavior is completely

[20] Erich Neumann, *Tiefenpsychologie und neue Ethik* (Zürich: Rascher, 1949), 36. Christ's redemptive sacrifice reverses every human being's reluctance to face and claim his or her failures as part and parcel of the self. In his *The Lion, the Witch and the Wardrobe*, C. S. Lewis captures the nature of this belief, as only he could. "She (the Witch) would have known that when a willing victim who had committed no treachery was killed in a traitor's stead, the Table would crack and Death itself would start working backwards." (160)

[21] Phebe Cramer, *Protecting the Self: Defense Mechanisms in Action* (New York: Guilford, 2006), 70-74.

[22] Ibid., 71.

[23] M[organ] Scott Peck, *The Road less Traveled: A New Psychology of Love, Traditional Values and Spiritual Growth* (New York: Touchstone, 1978), 35.

directed by external forces totally beyond his or her control.[24]

In the last encounter with his physically as well as emotionally compromised and yet determined adversary, Fritz Emmenberger proves himself the chronic, if eloquent, scapegoater.

In his unrelenting diatribe, the Swiss physician justifies the murder of Ulrich Friedrich Fortschig[25] by placing the entire blame for his demise upon the hapless pamphleteer himself. Bärlach had indeed asked his enthusiastic, though misguided, friend, to draft an article stating in blatant terms that a physician presently operating his own clinic in Zurich was none other than a former war criminal. That portion of Bärlach's instructions Fortschig does indeed follow. He not only writes the article, but also dispatches the pointed accusations to several local hospitals. Although not to Bärlach, Emmenberger's reaction is thoroughly predictable. "'If someone demands the death sentence with such a pathetic writing style, surely he deserves a reprimand [. . .].'"(237) In this straightforward sentence, Emmenberger already employs the phraseology typical of those foisting their own misdeeds onto others: I cannot do otherwise. In view of Fortschig's ill-scripted appeal, he merits nothing else.

The murder of Nehle, the Berliner, so skilled in the medical arts, finds its justification in similar manner. While only focusing on the advantages accruing to the Berliner from the agreement between Nehle and himself and deliberately neglecting to mention his own, Emmenberger recounts Nehle's return to Germany from Chile. Though Emmenberger admits to killing his accomplice, in the same breath he casts blame upon the latter: "'He sealed his fate himself [. . .] and simulated the most beautiful suicide imaginable.'"(244)

As is characteristic of evil persons, Emmenberger stops at nothing when accusing others of shortcomings, actual or perceived. And his prime adversary, Bärlach, is not exempt either. On the contrary. Though the physician uses every means at his disposal to break the ill and aging policeman both physically and psychologically, Emmenberger tells Bärlach repeatedly that he alone is the source of unending vexation. "'You are making my work inordinately difficult.'"(238) Furthermore, Emmenberger

---

[24] Ibid., 36.

[25] The name of Bärlach's pen-wielding and ill-fated associate is not accidental. Ulrich was the name of Friedrich Dürrenmatt's paternal grandfather. Serving as a *Berner Nationalrat*, his was quite the free spirit. A newspaper publisher, he wrote verses satirizing small-mindedness and an over-controlling bureaucracy. Heinrich Goertz, *Friedrich Dürrenmatt: Mit Selbstzeugnissen und Bilddokumenten* (Reinbek bei Hamburg: Rowohlt, 1987), 12-13.

accuses Bärlach of not cooperating in this rather one-sided exchange. "'You are not the least bit accommodating in our cross-examination.'"(240) Despite the hopelessness of his situation, combative still, and ever the representative of the law, Bärlach attempts to set the record straight. "'It is I who should cross examine you, not you me', replied the police inspector defiantly."(240)

Fortschig, Nehle and Bärlach, all three were and are to blame in Emmenberger's eyes for their maltreatment at his behest or at his hands. His scapegoating knows no limits. How could it be otherwise?

On one level, Dr. Fritz Emmenberger is an intelligent, insightful as well as articulate individual; consequently some of the observations postulated in his final conversation with Bärlach do hold some merit. At times life does seem devastatingly unfair. The unscrupulous seem to thrive, while decent and well-meaning folk encounter one serious difficulty after another. (251-252) Yet after further examination, the premise that serves as the core of his belief system does not correspond to reality. He begins his exposition by claiming that he believes in the primacy of matter. Only that exists which can be perceived by the five senses or measured by some means or other. He, too, exists only as matter. And the fact that he exists gives him the right to do as he pleases. For all of creation, including himself, is only a product of chance.

> 'Nothing is holy but matter: a human being, an animal, a plant, the moon, the Milky Way, whatever I may see, they are creations of chance, inconsequential, just as foam or a ripple of water is something inconsequential: it is irrelevant whether these things exist or don't exist; they are interchangeable.' (251)

And if, as he professes, one thing is as good as another and all is a hodgepodge, then power and freedom are myths, are lies. We do not have free will, cannot determine the rhythm of our lives and even if we could, one life is as good as another; we have no power or to phrase it another way, the power we wield is a sham. Life becomes inherently meaningless and what we do doesn't matter. We do not matter. Believing as he does, Emmenberger concludes his embittered disquisition: "'Freedom is the courage to commit crimes, because it itself is a crime.'" (252)

Bärlach rephrases his credo for him. "'I understand', the inspector cried out [. . .]. 'You believe in nothing but the right to torture people!'" (252) And Emmenberger instantly agrees with his opponent's assertion.

But we do have free will, do have power; we do determine the shape of our souls, if not always the precise course of our lives; we become the product of our choices. We do matter.

When the days meted out to us become increasingly burdensome, when adversity dogs our every step and of travails there seems no end in sight, when life is stripped to its essentials, when there is little, if any, time to reflect, then what and in whom do we believe? While in a concentration camp, in those most extreme of human (or subhuman) conditions, Viktor Frankl's thoughts revolved around some of these same fundamental questions.

> But what about human liberty? Is there no spiritual freedom in regard to behavior and reaction to any given surroundings? Is that theory true which would have us believe that man is no more than a product of many conditional and environmental factors—be they of a biological, psychological or sociological nature? Is man but an accidental product of these?[26]

Denying the existence of free will, Emmenberger would have replied with an emphatic "yes" to the latter of these queries. But Frankl prevails.

> Most important, do the prisoners' reactions to the singular world of the concentration camp [the camp may be deemed reflective of all circumstances of great duress] prove that man cannot escape the influences of his surroundings? Does man have no choice of action in the face of such circumstances?[27]

Viktor Frankl answers his questions with a resounding affirmation in the resilience and the integrity of the human spirit, in its power. As he was not only a brilliant psychiatrist, but also a camp survivor, his replies reflect not only theory, but practice. In *Man's Search for Meaning*, he cites example after example of those who routinely defied the odds and responded with compassion and nobility under the most demeaning and brutal conditions. Even as Emmenberger's aberrant actions betray his principles, the self-restraint and kindness of these few inmates told others what they believed. "[T]hey offer sufficient proof that everything can be taken from a man but one thing: the last of the human freedoms—to choose one's attitude in any given set of circumstances, to choose one's own way."[28]

Should one labor under the illusion that a concentration camp offers a paucity of options, Frankl reemphasizes his position.

---

[26] Viktor E. Frankl, *Man's Search for Meaning: An Introduction to Logotherapy*, Part One, trans. Ilse Lasch (New York: Washington Square, 1963), 103.
[27] Ibid., 103.
[28] Ibid., 104.

> And there were always choices to make. Every day, every hour, offered the opportunity to make a decision, a decision which determined whether you would or would not submit to those powers which threatened to rob you of your very self, your inner freedom [. . .].[29]

In determining how we treat others, we also determine the manner in which we treat ourselves, in what we make of ourselves. For example, if we respond to others with cruelty, regardless of their reaction, we become cruel. Despite his considerable intelligence, Emmenberger never consciously acknowledges that inexorable link. In destroying others, he destroys himself.

Part III

Lying. As scapegoating endeavors to place blame and assign responsibility where it does not rightfully belong, that attempt qualifies as a type of lying. Evil individuals are experts at lying. Above all else, it should be noted that, though there are seemingly endless varieties of lies, *never* does evil exist without lies. In the context of Fritz Emmenberger and those of his malignant persuasion, one does not encounter mitigating circumstances, e.g., telling a lie to save a life,[30] safeguard confidentiality,[31] or spare a terminal patient unnecessary pain.[32] In his instance, lies intend primarily "to mislead,"[33] to dissemble, to keep others off guard and guessing, in brief, to confuse.

Concerning the aforementioned and pivotal Charlene, one of the first cases of evil encountered in his psychiatric practice, Scott Peck makes the following observations. Were he given the opportunity of encountering her again, he would more readily acknowledge his confusion.

> I know now that one of the characteristics of evil is its desire to confuse. I had been aware of my confusion within a month of beginning work with Charlene [. . .]. I never entertained the notion in the first year that possibly I was confused because she wanted to confuse me.[34]

An evil individual may not exhibit all eight characteristics Scott Peck

[29] Ibid., 104.
[30] Sissela Bok, *Lying: Moral Choice in Public and Private Life* (New York: Vintage, 1999), 109.
[31] Ibid., 148.
[32] Ibid., 222.
[33] Ibid., 6.
[34] Peck, *People of the Lie*, 179.

delineates and already mentioned within this essay's initiating remarks, but within the over-all constellation even the less than astute observer will find not one attempt to confuse, but several, not one, but several lies. In the case of Fritz Emmenberger, they are not difficult to enumerate for over a period of decades the Swiss physician evolves into "someone who deals with others through deceit."[35] Of necessity a master of scapegoating is also a master of lying.

Upon entering his aptly named hospital in Zurich—Sonnenstein[36]—Bärlach asks the physician outright whether he had ever visited Germany. Emmenberger admits to having been there, but claims to have spent considerably more time in Chile. (201) In his final encounter with the by then terrified police inspector, Emmenberger admits to the collusion

---

[35] Bok, xix.

[36] Between the latter half of 1945 and the earliest days of 1949, in a venue far removed from Stutthof and Danzig, in the heart of Zurich, Emmenberger murders his patients in his sanatorium, Sonnenstein. (196) In his meticulously researched dissertation, defended before the University of Berlin's College of Medicine, Thomas Schilter traces the history of one of Germany's first notable, mental hospitals. Founded in July 1811, the care facility of Pirna-Sonnenstein was dedicated to the healing and rehabilitation of its patients. (37) Its mission changed radically in April 1940. (68) That spring marked the implementation of a program, designed to liquidate not only the mentally ill, but also all those deemed unfit to live, according to the stated policies of the National Socialist Party. (25)

For a detailed look at the earliest years of this institution and the comprehensive directives enacted to ensure the psychological and physical welfare of the mentally ill, consult: G. A. E. [Gottlob Adolf Ernst] von Nostitz und Jänckendorf, *Beschreibung der Königl. Sächsischen Heil-und Verpflegungsanstalt Sonnenstein*, 1. Theil, 1. and 2. Abtheilung, 2. Theil (Dresden: Verlag der Waltherßchen Buchhandlung, 1829).

Other references to Sonnenstein can be found in the following texts: Henry Friedlander, "The T4 Killers: Berlin, Lublin, San Sabba,*" *Die Normalität des Verbrechens: Bilanz und Perspektiven der Forschung zu den nationalsozialistischen Gewaltverbrechen*, eds. Helge Grabitz et al., (Berlin: Hentrich, 1994), 220-240, Ernst Klee, *"Euthanasie" im NS Staat: Die "Vernichtung lebensunwerten Lebens"* (Frankfurt: Fischer, 1983), 142, 150, 206, Ernst Klee, ed. *Dokumente zur "Euthanasie"* (Frankfurt: Fischer, 1985), 122-124, Ernst Klee, *Was sie taten—Was sie wurden: Ärzte, Juristen und andere Beteiligte am Kranken-oder Judenmord* (1986; Frankfurt: Fischer, 1992), 99. (The material referenced in this endnote as well as in the following one constitute part of my presentation: "Historical Violence as a Subtext to Friedrich Dürrenmatt's *Der Verdacht,"* 235-238. Will Wright and Steven Kaplan edited the proceedings of the 2007 Conference, entitled: *The Image of Violence II in Literature, Media and Society*, sponsored by the Society for the Interdisciplinary Study of Social Imagery.)

between Nehle and himself and adds several situational lies to the initial verbal one.

> 'Let's admit it: I myself surgically introduced the scar into Nehle's right eyebrow and the burn wound into his lower left arm, which I also have, in order to make us identical, one out of two.' (243)

But, of course, he did not let the matter rest there. Having agreed to assume each other's names, Emmenberger sent Nehle to Chile, while, as it may be recalled, the Swiss physician entered the world of the concentration camps.[37] To insure Nehle's silence upon his return from South America at the war's conclusion, Emmenberger feels he must eliminate him. But even the manner in which he does so serves his duplicitous purposes. He forces Nehle to swallow a capsule of prussic acid and consequently the Berliner,

---

[37] As Emmenberger himself corroborates (247), using Nehle's name, he functioned as a mass murderer in the concentration camp at Stutthof. Janina Grabowska's thorough research underscores the forbidding nature of that site. "The venue, which the Nazis selected for the camp at Stutthof, suited their felonious designs. The camp was situated just where a sliver of land jutted out into the bay of the Vistula River, due west of the village of Stutthof [. . .]. On all sides the entire compound was surrounded by water [. . .]. The barriers created by the presence of the water and the utter lack of assistance from anyone living nearby made escaping from Stutthof virtually impossible." (11) In addition, the frequently inhospitable climate only exacerbated the lives of the malnourished prisoners. On 2 September 1939, the first prisoners were brought to Stutthof from Danzig. Then known as a *SS-Sonderlager*, this camp was not officially declared a concentration camp until early 1941 or 1942. (Weinmann 266, 744) The initial set of prisoners consisted primarily of Polish intellectuals, political functionaries, activists and priests. By the second half of September approximately four hundred individuals found themselves incarcerated there. (Grabowska 12) Some five years later in September 1944, the number had reached 93,000. (Weinmann 266) The last roll call took place on April 27, 1945. Sources vary as to how many prisoners survived at that point. Grabowska claims there were slightly more than a thousand (69); Weinmann suggests the number could have reached twenty-five thousand. (266) Most were evacuated in a disastrous sea operation, compounding the misery and loss of life. On May 10 the Swedish Red Cross assumed responsibility for the steam ship, Rheinfels; of the over 1400 prisoners aboard, about seven hundred came from Stutthof. "The camp ceased to function as such after the last vehicles had departed. About 100 to 200 prisoners remained behind." (Grabowska 69) In the approximately five and a half years of the camp's operation, the final death toll could have exceeded 65,000. (Weinmann 266)
See also: Stasys Yla, *A Priest in Stutthof: Human Experiences in the World of Subhuman*, trans. from the Lithuanian by Manyland Books and Nola M. Zobarskas (New York: Manyland Books, 1971).

as mentioned earlier, "'simulated the most beautiful suicide imaginable.'" (244) One lie after another after another. Emmenberger weaves the proverbial web of lies and malice of forethought assumes a depth of meaning known to few. He spares himself no effort in furthering the self-image of a respectable individual, even while creating legions of victims in the process.

Willfully advancing an admirable persona proved a characteristic, Scott Peck repeatedly encountered in those he ultimately termed evil.

> Utterly dedicated to preserving their self-image of perfection, they are unceasingly engaged in the effort to maintain the appearance of moral purity.[. . .] The words 'image,' 'appearance,' and 'outwardly' are crucial to understanding the morality of the evil. While they seem to lack any motivation to *be* good, they intensely desire to appear good.[38]

In elaborating upon his theories regarding the deliberate projection of a suitable image at total variance with reality, Peck recalls the parents of a young patient, named Bobby. About them he says: "they dress well, go to work on time, pay their taxes, and outwardly seem to live lives that are above reproach."[39] In some of these identical ways, Emmenberger also practices to deceive; he, too, selects his apparel with utmost care. For instance, when entering Bärlach's room for the last time, the physician does not wear his profession's traditional garb.

> He wasn't in his lab coat, as the police inspector had first seen him, but rather his attire was dark, striped, with a white tie on a shirt of silver grey, a carefully fashioned appearance, almost foppish [. . .].[40] (236)

---

[38] Peck, *People of the Lie*, 75.

[39] Ibid., 75.

[40] Historical fact may also have suggested these details. In their *Mengele: The Complete Story*, Gerald Posner and John Ware relate: "Many have testified to his immaculate and well-manicured appearance as he exercised his power of life and death [. . .]. Survivors remarked on the impression made by his tight-fitting SS uniform with glistening black boots, white gloves, and polished cane as he surveyed his prey [. . .] ." (27) An eyewitness account of an Hungarian journalist corroborates the above. As the only survivor of a forty nine-member family, Solti Dezso first encountered Josef Mengele at Birkenau in June 1944. "All Jews had to pass in front of Mengele: 'He looked very good. He looked exceedingly well groomed—in this sad environment, I noticed that immediately. His hair was thick and dark. I remember his eyes; they were uncommonly bright.'" And then Dezso adds the final damning observation: "'He really didn't look like a murderer.'" Ulrich Völklein, *Josef Mengele—Der Arzt von Auschwitz* (Göttingen: Steidl, 1999), 132.

Just as Bobby's parents, outwardly Emmenberger also seems to live a life beyond reproach. For who would suspect a mass murderer behind the meticulously crafted veneer of the owner of a Zurich clinic? (128, 129, 199, 200) Until now only his victims know him as he is. His public persona serves as the perfect cover for his criminal pursuits.

Impeccable dress and an exalted social position assist Emmenberger in hiding from justice. Ever the diabolical and tireless perfectionist, how could he deem these measures adequate? In his direct manner, the soon-to-be retired policeman asks Dr. Hungertobel whether Emmenberger's research may be considered reputable. As the validity of scientific investigation relies solely upon the establishment of factual information and not upon the investigator's wishful speculations, Hans Bärlach is in effect asking his long-time friend to assess Emmenberger's relationship to the truth.[41] The devoted physician's answer does not come as unexpected.

> 'Once he did good research, but we don't know if he still does. He works with methods which must seem questionable to us. We know so little about the hormones, on which his research is focused, and as is the case in all those fields, which science attempts to conquer, there are all sorts of folks. Scholars and charlatans, frequently both in a single individual.' (129)

But then was that not the reason behind the studied appearance? Furthermore, what do murderers look like? Dr. Hungertobel in his understated manner concludes: "'Each one of us can look like a murderer.'"(167) Perhaps that is why Dürrenmatt created in the Emmenberger character someone who looks, perhaps with the exception of the surgical scar, thoroughly unremarkable. "'A tall thin build, hair gray, earlier a reddish brown, eyes greenish grey, protruding ears, the face thin and wan, with bags under the eyes, teeth healthy.'" (167, 171) And on the incriminating Stutthof photograph in which Hungertobel finally admits to recognizing his former classmate, a surgical mask covers most of Emmenberger's face. (125, 126, 128, 140, 163)

A last comment should be added. Peck readily admits that he bases his observations upon the behavior of his own patients. He also assumes that most reading his volume will believe that those individuals seeking psychiatric help are "radically different" than their colleagues or friends. He destroys that notion rather quickly: "This is not so." He reiterates that sentiment repeatedly. "Like it or not, the psychiatrist sees as much psychopathology at cocktail parties, conferences, and corporations as in her or his own office." And while also speaking for his professional colleagues, he continues: "Even in my small practice I see a new set of parents like Bobby's every month or so. It is no different for other psychiatrists. We brush up against evil not once or twice in a lifetime but almost routinely as we come into contact with human crises." (Peck, *People of the Lie*, 85-86)

[41] Bok, 85.

Consequently not only does Emmenberger take advantage of the deference often accorded those in the medical profession, even the specialty he chooses discourages scrutiny of his motivations and activities; both elements tend to remove him from further inquiry. Not one or two or three, but a cascade of lies shields this prince of darkness. Acknowledging the intelligence needed to devise such multi-layered and hence virtually impenetrable schemes, one could almost stand in awe of the sheer volume of his lies, the effectiveness of the disguise.

And if all of these do not suffice, at least one more lie overshadows the Swiss physician's background. As this particular falsehood left millions of victims in its wake, on some level it qualifies as the worst of them all. In the novel's opening chapters, Bärlach could not have been aware of the Nehle/Emmenberger agreement. Consequently while perusing Nehle's police records, the circumspect and tenacious detective suggests that, despite his indisputable gifts, the Berliner had joined the ranks of the concentration camp physicians. (175) The obvious should be stated again; the network of camps was founded upon the erroneous assumption that some individuals did not deserve to live. Or as the Nazis called the euthanasia policies: "die Vernichtung lebensunwerten Lebens."[42] As was

---

[42] For these repressive measures, Hitler can doubtlessly be blamed. In his *Mein Kampf,* he expressed his misappropriation of Darwin's theory of natural selection: "A stronger race will displace the weak, because the survival instinct in its ultimate form will always destroy the ludicrous shackles of a so called humanity [. . .]." (145) Or fault can be found with Heinrich Himmler, the *Reichsführer* of the SS, and all those who carried out his wishes in a seemingly endless number of asylums, hospitals, sanatoria and camps. Nevertheless one fact remains. From the moment Hitler was named chancellor on 30 January 1933 (Klee, *"Euthanasie" im NS Staat* 34) and even beyond his suicide as well as the cessation of hostilities in May 1945 (Klee, *"Euthanasie" im NS Staat* 450-456), the definition of those deemed unfit to live and consequently sterilized, forced to abort their children or murdered changed incrementally, sometimes week by week, to include more and more individuals. On 14 July 1933, less than six months after Hitler assumed power, a law was enacted requiring the sterilization—without their consent—of all those who could pass on hereditary diseases. To this catalogue belonged the mentally deficient, the mentally ill, whether they showed any signs of an ailment or not, those with vision problems, the hearing impaired, and those with any deformity whatsoever. In October 1933, vagrants, beggars and excessive drinkers or those perceived as such were added to the list. (Klee, *"Euthanasie" im NS Staat* 36-39) Eventually anyone considered undesirable to the regime for any reason, be that primarily a congenital defect, ethnic or religious background or an ideological choice, was targeted. (A similar reference was previously published in my article: "The Devil's Footprints: The Case of Dr. Emmenberger in Friedrich Dürrenmatt's

also suggested elsewhere, had this felonious system not supported Emmenberger's sadistic tendencies, he would not have escaped detection as long as he did. The lie, sanctioning the establishment of the camp system (and its ancillary operations), served to conceal the villainous nature of this alleged healer. Hidden in plain sight. At least for a while.

Verbal, situational lies, a false premise, they all attempted to form a barrier between Emmenberger and those who would suspect him, those who would bring him to justice. The elaborate system of prevarication that he either devised and/or of which he took advantage, in and of itself, testifies to the fact that he knew what he was doing was wrong. "There is no need to hide unless we first feel that something needs to be hidden."[43] In other words, Fritz Emmenberger does have a conscience and it is making itself felt. Somewhat earlier it was stated that evil persons consider themselves to be faultless. Paradoxically the opposite also seems to be true. "The essential component of evil is not the absence of a sense of sin or imperfection but the unwillingness to tolerate that sense."[44] Or to phrase it another way: "At one and the same time, the evil are aware of their evil and desperately trying to avoid the awareness."[45]

In the opening remarks, I implied that through examination of those who are evil and in particular three cardinal aspects of their behavior—the fraudulent use of power, scapegoating and lying—we could perhaps apprehend more clearly where they went so terribly awry.

This type of analytical work requires a type of courage I am inclined to designate as careful as well as an undeniable tenacity. But how can we afford to look away if we acknowledge history's blatant and frequent failures? Were we to recognise evil individuals sooner rather than later, could not the damage to others as well as themselves at least be minimised, if not totally eliminated? A malady cannot begin to be treated until it is named.

Der Verdacht," in *Minding Evil: Explorations of Human Iniquity*, ed. Margaret Sönser Breen (Amsterdam, New York: Rodopi, 2005), 140.)

[43] Peck, *People of the Lie*, 76.

[44] Ibid., 76.

[45] Ibid., 76.

References

Bok, Sissela. *Lying: Moral Choice in Public and Private Life*. New York: Vintage, 1999.

Cramer, Phebe. *Protecting the Self: Defense Mechanisms in Action*. New York: Guilford, 2006.

Dürrenmatt, Friedrich. "Der Verdacht: Ein Kriminalroman, 1951." *Gesammelte Werke: Romane*. 4. Zürich: Diogenes, 1991.

Frankl, Viktor E. *Man's Search for Meaning: An Introduction to Logotherapy*. Part One. Trans. Ilse Lasch. New York: Washington Square, 1963.

Friedlander, Henry. "The T4 Killers: Berlin, Lublin, San Sabba*," *Die Normalität des Verbrechens: Bilanz und Perspektiven der Forschung zu den nationalsozialistischen Gewaltverbrechen*. Eds. Helge Grabitz et al. Berlin: Hentrich, 1994.

Fromm, Erich. *Escape from Freedom*. New York: Rinehart, 1941.

Gide, André. "L'immoraliste." *Oeuvres Complètes*. Ed. L. [Louis] Martin-Chauffier. IV. Paris: NRF, 1933.

Goertz, Heinrich. *Friedrich Dürrenmatt: Mit Selbstzeugnissen und Bilddokumenten*. Reinbek bei Hamburg: Rowohlt, 1987.

Grabowska, Janina. *K.L. Stutthof: Ein historischer Abriß*. Ed. Hermann Kuhn. Trans. Leon Lendzion. Bremen: Temmen, [1994].

Hitler, Adolf. *Mein Kampf*. München: Zentralverlag der NSDAP, 1942.

Klee, Ernst. *"Euthanasie" im NS Staat: Die "Vernichtung lebensunwerten Lebens."* Frankfurt: Fischer, 1983.

—. *Was sie taten—Was sie wurden: Ärzte, Juristen und andere Beteiligte am Kranken-oder Judenmord*. 1986. Frankfurt: Fischer, 1992.

—. ed. *Dokumente zur "Euthanasie."* Frankfurt: Fischer, 1985.

Lewis, C[live], S[taples]. *The Lion, the Witch and the Wardrobe: A Story for Children*. New York: Collier, 1970.

May, Gerald G. *Care of Mind / Care of Spirit: Psychiatric Dimensions of Spiritual Direction*. San Francisco: Harper, 1982.

—. *Will and Spirit: A Contemplative Psychology*. San Francisco: Harper, 1982.

May, Rollo. *Love and Will*. New York: Delta, 1989.

Neumann, Erich. *Tiefenpsychologie und neue Ethik*. Zürich: Rascher, 1949.

Peck, M[organ] Scott. *People of the Lie: The Hope for Healing Human Evil*. New York: Simon, 1983.

—. *The Road less Traveled: A New Psychology of Love, Traditional Values and Spiritual Growth*. New York: Touchstone, 1978.

Posner, Gerald L. and John Ware. *Mengele: The Complete Story*. New York: McGraw-Hill, 1986.

A Reader's Guide to the Holy Bible: Revised Standard Version. Nashville: Thomas Nelson, 1972.

Schilter, Thomas. *Unmenschliches Ermessen: Die nationalsozialistische "Euthanasie"—Tötungsanstalt Pirna-Sonnenstein 1940/41*. Leipzig: Stiftung Sächsische Gedenkstätten and Gustav Kiepenheuer, 1998.

Solzhenitsyn, Alexander. *Nobel Lecture*. Trans. F. D. Reeve. New York: Farrar, Straus and Giroux, 1972.

Völklein, Ulrich. *Josef Mengele—Der Arzt von Auschwitz*. Göttingen: Steidl, 1999.

Von Nostitz, G. A. E. [Gottlob Adolf Ernst] und Jänckendorf. *Beschreibung der Königl. Sächsischen Heil- und Verpflegungsanstalt Sonnenstein*, 1.Theil, 1. and 2. Abtheilung, 2. Theil. Dresden: Verlag der Waltherßchen Buchhandlung, 1829.

Weinmann, Martin, ed. *Das nationalsozialistische Lagersystem: (CCP)*, 2nd ed. Frankfurt: Zweitausendeins, 1990.

Wilde, Oscar. *The Picture of Dorian Gray*. Ed. Donald L. Lawler. New York: Norton, 1988.

Yla, Stasys. *A Priest in Stutthof: Human Experiences in the World of Subhuman*. Trans. from the Lithuanian by Manyland Books and Nola M. Zobarskas. New York: Manyland Books, 1971.

CHAPTER FIVE

THE FAMILY ROMANCE IN BLACK AND WHITE: PATERNAL ABDICATION AND THE "TOUCH OF THE MOTHER" IN MARITA BONNER'S "ONE BOY'S STORY"

LAURA DAWKINS

Although Daniel Patrick Moynihan provoked a still-raging controversy among both black and white Americans in the mid-sixties with his notorious theory that a matriarchal familial structure within the black community impedes African American advancement in the United States, the lines of the Moynihan debate were actually drawn much earlier. The continuing uproar over the 1965 "matriarchy" thesis sometimes obscures the implicitly Freudian basis for Moynihan's equation of patriarchy and social progress; indeed, black families of the early twentieth century endured a similar "pathologizing" of their condition when Freud's theories of sex-role development captured the popular imagination. Even as numerous writers of the Harlem Renaissance examined slavery's legacies within the African American community—specifically, the retention of mother-centered familial structures and extended kinship ties—a popularized Freudian theory simultaneously stigmatized powerful maternal figures and posited the patriarchal nuclear family as a "normative"model.[1] While not

---

[1] See Daniel Patrick Moynihan, *The Negro Family: The Case for National Action* [1965], in Lee Rainwater and William L. Yancey, eds., *The Moynihan Report and the Politics of Controversy* (Cambridge: MIT Press, 1967), pp. 43-124. In *Motherhood in Black and White: Race and Sex in American Liberalism, 1930-1965* (Ithaca: Cornell University Press, 2000), Ruth Feldstein has argued that Moynihan's notion that "black 'matriarchs' perpetuated the 'tangle of pathology' in which black families were trapped" (142), actually stemmed from earlier

yet targeted directly as "deviants" from prescriptive norms (as in Moynihan's study), the African American community—only a generation or two removed from a slave culture in which the enslaved child "followed the condition of the mother," and in which black paternity was legally erased—clearly represented the social group most vulnerable to charges that an absence of paternal influence is destructive to a child's (particularly a male child's) development.

The historical convergence of the "New Negro" renaissance and the national embrace of Freud's theories raises questions that have not yet been adequately addressed in scholarship on the modernist period in America. What impact did the institutionalization of Freud's Oedipal paradigm have upon black Americans for whom patriarchal models, as Hortense Spillers has noted, were historically denied?[2] How did black writers of the Harlem Renaissance—exploring their racial identity and heritage in an unprecedented outpouring of fiction, drama, and poetry—respond, whether consciously or unconsciously, to a Freudian orthodoxy that must have often seemed alien to their individual and ancestral histories? Specifically, how did African American women writing about the black maternal experience grapple with an increasingly influential psychoanalytic theory that appeared to demonize strong mothers?

Ann Douglas claims that Harlem Renaissance writers were simply not that interested in Freud, since "Freud's theories of what he called the 'family romance,' the tortured triangle of mother, father, and child that produces the Oedipal complex, had little to do with the African-American

---

sociological constructions of black maternity, first promulgated by E. Franklin Frazier in *The Negro Family in the United States* (Chicago: University of Chicago Press, 1939). In *Terrible Honesty*: *Mongrel Manhattan in the 1920s* (New York: Farrar, Straus and Giroux, 1995), Ann Douglas suggests that "mother-fears" in popular culture of the twenties were influenced by Freudian theory, but she contends that a "matriphobic climate" in the United States in fact preceded Freud: "The paradoxes that psychoanalysis discovered and contained were familiar ones to Americans. The negative centrality accorded the feminine, the insistent and fearful denigration of feminine capacities that is characteristic of psychoanalytic thought—these were second nature to a culture for which modernism and matriphobia were synonymous" (p. 147).

[2] In "Mama's Baby, Papa's Maybe: An American Grammar Book" (1987), reprinted in *Black, White, and in Color: Essays on American Literature and Culture* (Chicago: University of Chicago Press, 2003), Hortense Spillers points out that the enslaved child was legally fatherless, and thus became, "under the press of a patronymic, patrifocal, patrilineal, and patriarchal order, the man/woman on the boundary, whose human and familial status had yet to be defined" (p. 218).

experience."[3] Debates about the cross-cultural applicability of Freudian theory have persisted since the 1920s, when anthropologist Bronislaw Malinowski disputed the universality of the Oedipal "master narrative" (based on his observation of non-Western matrilineal family structures), provoking psychologist Ernest Jones to counter that unconscious developmental processes "could not be seen as sociologically or culturally determined."[4] More recently, Spillers has interrogated the relevance of Freudian models to historically exiled or colonized groups, specifically African Americans: "Is the Freudian landscape an applicable text (to say nothing of appropriate) to social and historic situations that do not replicate moments of its own origin and involvements? [H]ow does this model, or does this model, suffice for occupied and captive persons and communities in which the rites and rights of gender function have been exploded, historically, into sexual neutralities?"[5] Maintaining that the writers of the Harlem Renaissance accordingly "did not feel the strongly marked, almost compulsive affinities with Freudian thought evident among white writers," Douglas finds a sharp racial division in literature of the period, with African American authors shunning psychoanalytic theory while their mainstream contemporaries eagerly explored Freudian themes across literary genres.[6]

Yet even if unconvinced that Freud's "master narrative" was universally applicable, black writers of the period—just beginning to plumb the past and to define their role in the American script—had to confront a theory of human development that had become, in Douglas's words, "*the* explanatory

[3] Douglas adds, "It is a matter of considerable debate whether theories and therapeutic practices like Freud's, based exclusively on the nuclear family structure, are useful in understanding the psychological configuration of a people whose family patterns in their native Africa, and to a degree in the Southern plantation life to which they were transported, were those of extended kinship relations and communal resources" (*Terrible Honesty*, p. 95).

[4] The Jones-Malinowski debate is summarized in *Feminism and Psychoanalysis: A Critical Dictionary*, ed. Elizabeth Wright (London: Blackwell, 1992), p. 5.

[5] Spillers, " 'The Permanent Obliquity of the In(pha)llibly Straight': In the Time of the Daughters and the Fathers" (1989); reprinted in *Black, White, and in Color*, p. 231.

[6] Douglas explains that, although Freud came to America only once (in 1909), "his influence on Americans was incalculably great: the only authority that white Americans seemed to allude to more frequently was the Bible . . . Translations of Freud and articles popularizing his ideas poured from New York presses" (pp. 122-123).

discourse" in America.[7] Indeed, as such scholars as Werner Sollors, Heather Hathaway, and Susan Gubar have shown, African American writers of the early twentieth century frequently dramatize Oedipal conflicts, specifically focusing on white fathers who refuse to acknowledge their filial tie to biracial sons. Sollors examines the racial inflections of the "oedipal component" in Langston Hughes's *Mulatto* (1931), contending that the biracial son in this play "has to confront the father who possesses the mother to approach the riddle of his own existence."[8] Describing the Oedipal rage of "mulatto" sons in two stories by black writers—Charles W. Chesnutt's "The Sheriff's Children" and Hughes's "Father and Son"—Hathaway argues that "the desire to kill the father for sleeping with the mother is intensified by the rejection of the 'black' son by the 'white' father because of racial 'impurities.'" According to Hathaway, the "intervention of race adds a new dimension to the older, traditional equations" in Greek myth, since "the violation of identity caused by miscegenation exacerbates oedipal motivations."[9] Gubar similarly explores the "patricidal anger of the mulatto child" in several works by black writers of the early twentieth century, demonstrating that the biracial son in these works, "fatally divided from the symbolic order of (white) masculine legitimacy," inevitably conceives "retaliatory fantasies" of Oedipal revenge. Gubar attests that, contrary to Douglas's view, a significant number of African American writers recreate or meditate upon, in varied and suggestive ways, the Freudian "family romance."[10]

---

[7] Douglas contends that "Freudian discourse, no matter how simplified or distorted, had by the mid-1920s eclipsed the Protestant pieties sovereign in America's official life until then" (*Terrible Honesty*, p. 127). She further notes that "psychoanalysis might have originated in Vienna, but it was copied and Americanized, then marketed, and marketed on a scale immeasurably greater than Europe could offer, in New York" (p. 129).

[8] Werner Sollors, "'Never Was Born': The Mulatto, An American Tragedy?," *Massachusetts Review* 27, 2 (1986): pp. 293-316.

[9] Heather Hathaway, " 'Maybe Freedom Lies in Hating': Miscegenation and the Oedipal Complex," in *Refiguring the Father: New Feminist Readings of Patriarchy*, eds. Patricia Yaeger and Beth Kowaleski-Wallace (Carbondale: Southern Illinois University Press, 1989), pp. 153-167. Hathaway asserts, "By confronting and killing the literal and figurative fathers of a patriarchal familial and social structure, these mulatto men essentially attack the image of the 'father' as one who is detached and intangible—as one who is the abstraction of law and power" (p. 165).

[10] Susan Gubar, *Racechanges: White Skin, Black Face in American Culture* (New York: Oxford University Press, 1997), pp. 210-214. Gubar focuses on both white- and black-authored texts that depict "the patricidal anger of the mulatto child,"

Among texts by Harlem Renaissance writers that examine psychoanalytic paradigms, Marita Bonner's "One Boy's Story" (1927) is certainly one of the most direct and self-conscious responses to Freud's theory of human development. Unlike the works of Chesnutt and Hughes, Bonner's critically neglected tale foregrounds the figure of the black mother and her role in shaping the biracial son's Oedipal quest. Bonner not only demonstrates how this son is incapable of resolving the Oedipal crisis within a culture that denies him social legitimacy, but also reveals the ways in which the African American mother is paradoxically both dispossessed of her maternal role and granted the negative authority to confer her own debased status upon her offspring. A precursor of Toni Morrison's contemporary classic *Beloved* (1987), "One Boy's Story" suggests that the disinherited black mother, like Morrison's Sethe, can claim her child only through an act of violence. Anatomizing the violation of black maternity within American society, Bonner also exposes the inadequacy of Western maternal constructs to address or accommodate the cultural experience of the African American mother.

Composed at the height of the Harlem Renaissance, the story initially appears to be a cautionary tale for black mothers, an alarmed account of the disabling effects of a matricentric household upon a young black boy's psychological development. The protagonist of the story, who increasingly attempts to separate himself from his possessive mother and to identify with paternal figures, is ultimately drawn back into a maternal embrace that literally mutilates him: a stickpin on his mother's bodice is driven into his tongue when she hugs him, leaving him permanently speechless. This fearsome black mother, infantilizing her helpless son, appears to be a forerunner of the stereotypical black matriarch excoriated in mid-century American literature and sociology, suggesting—on the surface—that Bonner has internalized the Freud-inspired "matriphobia" rampant in popular culture of the twenties.[11] However, Bonner's odd, allusive tale—a

---

including Mark Twain's *Pudd'nhead Wilson* (1894), Claude McKay's poem "Mulatto" (1925), and Langston Hughes's drama *Mulatto: A Tragedy of the Deep South* (1931). Gubar briefly discusses Marita Bonner's "One Boy's Story" as a "racialized revision of the Oedipal story" that "almost reads like an allegory about the self-destructiveness this author presents as paradigmatic in all biracial boys' psychosexual development" (p. 212).

[11] According to Douglas, "What Freud loathed above all else in American culture was its 'dominating women'; in his view, they treated American men as wolves do sheep, and constituted an 'anti-cultural phenomenon' " (*Terrible Honesty*, p. 134). Douglas calls Freud's *Totem and Taboo*, "the central expression of the era's matricidal impulse" (p. 147).

deceptively simple, first-person account of a boy's Oedipal journey—challenges rather than reinforces the "mother-fears" of her contemporaries. Almost forty years before African American women charged Moynihan with scapegoating black mothers by attributing the destructive effects of an oppressive white society to undue maternal influence within the black community,[12] Bonner similarly demonstrated that a confluence of social, historic, and economic forces conspire to sabotage the black boy's journey to manhood—even as the boy's mother, in her frenzy to shelter him from an inimical society, appears to become the "castrating" matriarch, the agent of her son's unmanning.

The protagonist of "One Boy's Story" (who narrates the tale) is the biracial son of a respected white physician and his black concubine. Although Donald lives exclusively with his mother, his father (Swyburne) visits frequently and brings his son books to read; however, Swyburne never acknowledges his relationship to the boy and Donald accepts him as a family friend—one whom he admires and tries to emulate. Unhappy about her son's lack of a "legitimate" name or paternal relationship, Ma Gage befriends a black man new to the town, but this fledgling romance disintegrates when the man finds out about Swyburne's visits to the boy and his mother. Determined to sever all ties with Swyburne, Ma Gage meets him in the woods and tells him never to come to her home again. When Swyburne argues with the black woman and attempts to detain her forcibly, Donald (who has hidden in the bushes and overheard the dispute) shoots a rock from his slingshot at Swyburne's head. Ma Gage breaks away from the white man and flees just before the rock strikes and kills him. When Donald arrives home, his mother embraces him so fiercely that she impales his tongue upon her breast pin, necessitating the tongue's amputation. The doctor who attends Donald reveals that Swyburne's body has been found in the woods, a murder to which the boy confesses by producing his slingshot; Donald then discovers that he has killed his own father. Assured of the sympathetic doctor's complicity in concealing the murder, Ma Gage thanks God that her son has been rendered speechless,

---

[12] In *Black Macho and the Myth of the Superwoman* (New York: Dial Press, 1979), for example, Michele Wallace has contended that "Moynihan was trying to take the responsibility for racism off white shoulders, where it belonged, and place it on blacks themselves" (p. 109). As Ruth Feldstein points out, "Critiques of Moynihan that attended to the gendered dimensions of his argument were not restricted to black feminists. Stokely Carmichael, a leader of SNCC and advocate of black power, refuted the report: 'The reason we are in the bag we are in isn't because of my mama, it's because of what they did to my mama'" (*Motherhood in Black and White*, p. 151).

since his muteness ensures that he will remain "shut up" (78) in the house with her and will never disclose his crime to others.[13]

"One Boy's Story" clearly describes a failed Oedipal quest: the young boy-warrior attempts to prove his manhood through confrontation with a stronger male rival who claims rights of access to the boy's mother; yet Donald cannot play out the Oedipal paradigm. The Freudian model of male development, dependent upon the son's separation from the mother and subsequent identification with his father, is irrevocably fractured by Swyburne's refusal to acknowledge his paternity. Unable to resolve the Oedipal crisis successfully, as a male child does within a "normative" patriarchal familial structure—that is, by deferring the desire to supplant his progenitor, understanding (according to Freud) that he will one day assume his father's place as patriarch—Donald kills his (unrecognized) father. ("I didn't know it was my father," Donald insists.) In Lacanian terms, he is barred from the symbolic order—condemned to the regressive mother—since he is bereft of identification with a paternal figure who could rescue him from the mother's clutches. The violent maternal embrace that leaves him tongueless thus returns him to the wordless, preoedipal stage of infancy—figuratively impaled upon his mother's breast forever.

Bonner suggests that Donald's entry into the patriarchal order is precluded by the white father's concealment of his son's origins and by the resulting genealogical uncertainty that, as in Sophocles' *Oedipus Rex,* leads to patricide. Yet why, in the symbolically freighted drama that Bonner scripts, must the father's abdication lead to the boy's mutilation by his mother? In her influential essay "Mama's Baby, Papa's Maybe: An American Grammar Book," Hortense Spillers contends that, rather than being condemned to "family pathology" as a result of his historical exclusion from patriarchy (as Moynihan contends), the African American male, whether fathered by the white man who denied paternity or by the black man whose paternal rights were historically effaced, has been "touched by the mother" in potentially redemptive ways, thus "embody[ing] the only American community of males which has had the specific occasion to learn who the female is within itself"[14] In Bonner's

---

[13] Marita Bonner, "One Boy's Story," in *Frye Street and Environs: The Collected Works of Marita Bonner*, eds. Joyce Flynn and Joyce Occomy Stricklin (Boston: Beacon Press, 1987), pp. 78-91. All subsequent references appear in the text.

[14] Spillers, "Mama's Baby, Papa's Maybe," *Black, White, and in Color*, p. 228. Spillers argues that "the African-American woman, the mother, the daughter, becomes historically the powerful and shadowy evocation of a cultural synthesis long evaporated—the law of the mother—only and precisely because legal

story, however, the "mother's touch," as in traditional Freudian theory, has destructive consequences for the boy unable to resolve his Oedipal crisis. The apparent inevitability of this crisis for the young black male in "One Boy's Story" is troubling: if the African American familial experience has historically had "little to do" (according to Ann Douglas) with the Freudian family romance, how can we account for the relentless Oedipal trajectory that determines Donald's fate? Does "One Boy's Story" suggest that alternatives to the nuclear family—specifically, matrifocal familial structures—rather than eliminating Oedipal conflicts, merely make their resolution more difficult to achieve and the son's divided gender loyalties more disastrous? Must an intervening "third term" (that is, paternal influence, whether a father's or a father-surrogate's) always break up the mother-child dyad in order for the boy to become, in Freud's terms, a "little man" (or, in Lacan's phrase, a "speaking subject")?

In describing an Oedipal pattern of male maturation within a matricentric African American household, "One Boy's Story" appears to uphold Ernest Jones's belief in the transhistorical, crosscultural validity of Freud's theory; however, Bonner is careful to show that Donald's development has been shaped by the texts and values of the dominant culture. Certainly, the boy's acculturation into patriarchal society is facilitated by the books his white father gives him—books with titles such as *Ten Tales to Inspire Youth,* which include "stories ... all about men. All men" (81). Donald "like[s] the one about the fellow named Orestes who went home from the Trojan War and found his mother had married his father's brother so he killed them" (81). If, as Luce Irigaray maintains, the Orestes myth (recounting Orestes' allegiance to his father over his mother, and his public acquittal for matricide) represents "the founding moment of civilization under paternal law"[15]—demonstrating, as Philip Slater further suggests, the son's need to "leav[e] the power sphere of the mother and move into a male-dominated outside world"[16]—then Donald's introduction to this tale through his

---

enslavement removed the African-American male not so much from sight as from *mimetic* view as a partner in the prevailing social fiction of the father's name, the father's law" (p. 228).

[15] Quoted in Marianne Hirsch, *The Mother/Daughter Plot: Narrative, Psychoanalysis, Feminism* (Bloomington: Indiana University Press, 1989), p. 28. Irigaray maintains that "with some additions or subtractions, our imaginary still functions according to the patterns established through Greek mythologies and tragedies" (Hirsch, p. 28).

[16] Philip E. Slater, *The Glory of Hera: Greek Mythology and the Greek Family* (New York: Beacon Press, 1971), pp. 162-163. Slater affirms that "the dispute over parental primacy is the crux of [Aeschylus's] *Orestia*" (p. 163).

father's texts plays a central role in his “oedipalization”: his valorization of the father's sphere and his corresponding movement away from his mother. Indeed, Donald's consumption of tales of male heroism coincides with his growing resistance to his mother's touch: he admits that “sometimes [he] wishes she wouldn't hug him” (87), and protests a too-ardent embrace. Following the traditional Oedipal progression from a mother-dominated infancy to a father-centered young manhood, Donald's psychological development mimics the cultural “transition from matriarchy to patriarchy” that his beloved Orestes myth allegorizes.[17]

Of course, Freud and his disciples (such as Jones) would insist that, rather than shaping Donald's Oedipal journey, the Greek myths and old legends he reads merely reflect fundamental conflicts within his psyche; he finds the stories compelling because they express universal truths about individual and cultural development. Yet Bonner's depiction of Donald’s responses to his reading resonates with postmodern theories of gender performativity, unsettling an orthodox psychoanalytic interpretation. Just as Donald likes to imagine the lives of the women customers of his dressmaker mother—“I liked to look at the dresses and talk about the people who were to wear them" (78)—so does he enjoy acting out stories of masculine adventure from his father's books:

> . . . after I read “David and Goliath,” I just had to pretend I was David. (82)

> I . . . pretended that [Ma] was shut up in a prison, and I was a time fighter who beat all the keepers and got her out. (87)

> Some days I pretend I am Orestes . . . Some days I pretend I am Oedipus. (91)

Which stereotypically gendered behavior expresses the authentic Donald—the interest in women's dressmaking and the sensuous appreciation of “pale soft silk that always made me feel like burying my face in it” (79), or the imaginative re-creation of historical battle-scenes, with “the yard [as] my fortress and the hills beside us full of Indians” to vanquish (78)? The boy's assumption of different roles suggests that the Oedipal quest he embarks on (“ulterior and unavoidable,” from the Freudian viewpoint) is, to a large extent, created by the tales he reads rather than simply reflected in them.[18]

---

[17] Ibid.

[18] Julia Kristeva, *Tales of Love*, Trans. Leon Roudiez (New York: Columbia University Press, 1987), p. 146.

To be sure, Donald's destiny persistently mirrors Greek or Biblical lore—Donald kills his father unknowingly, as Oedipus does; he fells him with a rock hurled from his slingshot, as David does Goliath; and, like Perseus, who rescues his mother from men who have imprisoned her, Donald frees Ma Gage ("shut up in a prison," as her son imagines) from the man who holds her against her protests. Yet by directly alluding to Donald's reading habits, the author indicates that these parallels, rather than establishing the transhistorical "truth" of the myths themselves, point instead to the power of myth to form desire and experience. Contemporary theories of narrative which explore its shaping force upon history and ideology are especially pertinent to Bonner's tale, since the young protagonist suggests that specific patriarchal myths provide him with cultural reference points—inspiring him to act "like the men do in the books" (90). Robert Con Davis, who locates the origin of Western culture's "romance with the father" in Greek myth, argues that these narratives, constructed "to reflect commitments to paternal authority," impose a "matrix that will enable and shape the products of culture." They create a "fusion between the father as a figure and Western values"; gender polarity and the primacy of paternal law become "too much a part of how Western culture sees the world."[19] Certainly, "One Boy's Story" demonstrates how textual transmission of dominant cultural values "oedipalizes" a boy within a mother-centered household: in reading about David and Goliath, for example, Donald learns to valorize male conflict, and in reading about Orestes, he implicitly absorbs the message that mother and father are divided, and that the son must choose his proper allegiance.

Yet for the son of a black mother and white father, as Bonner shows, a divided racial identity impedes his "natural" gender allegiance. Donald's tragedy is that he has been taught to valorize an order from which he will always be excluded, has been socialized into a culture whose privileges will be denied him. Thus, Ma's attempt to give her son a name and a secure paternal relationship by "marrying one of [her] own men" (88) backfires when Donald discovers that the black man she chooses as father-surrogate defines and embodies limitations which the ambitious young boy refuses to accept. Initially "excited" by Mr. Frazier's visits—"I never saw many colored people—no colored men—and I wanted to see some" (83)—Donald eagerly identifies with the first man he meets who provides a reflection of his own future manhood: "Colored just like . . . me" (83). Yet

[19] Robert Con Davis, *The Paternal Romance: Reading God-the-Father in Early Western Culture* (Urbana-Champaign: University of Illinois Press, 1993), p. 14.

this identification becomes a cruel mockery when Frazier, in response to the boy's professed desire to "have an office" when he grows up, jeers: "Fat chance a colored man has!" (85). Frazier's job—"driving some [white] lady's car"—represents a precipitous decline from Donald's goal of hiring his own driver ("so's I can ... have my car meet me") and "be[ing] a specialist like Dr. Swyburne" (85). Reminding him that "there's no way to get out of [being colored]," Frazier underscores the boy's disempowerment —acts out his destined castration—by breaking Donald's fishing pole across his knees.

Donald's symbolic castration recurs in the story's conclusion, not only when his "poisoned" tongue is truncated--leaving him with a "black stump" (9l)--but also when his fatal slingshot, removed from his pants, is destroyed by the boy's doctor. Just as Donald earlier disputes Frazier's dismissal of his goals, claiming, "I can too have an office! I can have one if I want to!" (85), so does he vainly protest this burning of his symbol of valor: "I tried to talk. I wanted to tell him to leave it [the slingshot] so I could show my grandchildren what I had used to free Ma like the men do in the books" (90). Donald discovers that his brave deed, unlike those of his father's ancestors ("All the Swyburnes are heroes," his father declares), will be fearfully concealed rather than proudly proclaimed. His descent into perpetual silence, a fate so different from the heroic destiny he envisions, is paradigmatic of the racial construction of gender roles in early twentieth-century America. Indoctrinated into a culture that upholds a rigid ideal of masculinity--an adversarial, competition-based model of manly behavior--the black male finds that his own assertions of manhood will be swiftly punished.

As Donald's progression to adulthood demonstrates, however, he is already disabled, from the moment of his birth, by virtue of his very identity as a black mother's son. Ma Gage cannot claim her son *without* wounding him, since her degraded racial status determines his own. What is significant about Ma's mutilation of Donald is that it is inadvertent: her very touch is maiming. Indeed, within a white supremacist culture, the black mother *is* debility and emasculation for sons who "follow her condition." Despite Swyburne's boast that Donald "has the blood . . . he is a Swyburne," the father's denial of a legitimate paternal relationship dooms the boy, as Ma recognizes: "What did it [Swyburne's paternity] do for Donald? He has no name!"(88). Ma's silencing of Donald represents both the inevitably abject "condition" that the black mother confers upon her son, but also the historic necessity for keeping that son "quiet," forestalling a suicidal black male self-assertion. Donald's "clipped tongue" (91) accordingly invokes the curbed speech of generations of African

American males, while Ma's lacerating stickpin embodies the painful lessons of silence that she must teach him at her breast. Like Moynihan's critics many years later, Bonner suggests that the black mother, perceived as the agent of her son's castration, is the victim of the same inimical cultural forces that impede her children's journey to selfhood. What Spillers sees as the potentially redemptive influence of black motherhood upon the male child is clearly destined for failure in "One Boy's Story," since the illegitimate mulatto boy—without a name or position to inherit, yet "oedipalized" by an inexorably father-centered culture—can only experience the maternal touch as loss and limitation. As Bonner reveals, the biracial son remains "shut up [with his mother]," an eternal "boy" caught between father-identification and mother-dependence.

Tellingly, Donald implicitly links his confused gender identity—as well as his muteness—with blackness: "So I got a black stump in my mouth . . . And I am bearing my Furies and my clipped tongue like a Swyburne and a Gage—'cause I am both of them" (91). As Gwen Bergner has demonstrated in her analysis of *Narrative of the Life of Frederick Douglass*, the namelessness and disinheritance of biracial sons of white fathers condemns them to inchoate "cross-identifications":

> Because laws of inheritance apply principally to men, Douglass's masculine identity allows him to desire the authority of white men and to locate the cause of slavery in a loss of inheritance rights; the lack of his father's name signifies Douglass's overall disempowerment. While this lack of paternal sanction has material effects on Douglass, it also greatly excludes him from symbolic meaning; his status as illegitimate deprives him of a lasting discursive position within 'paternal Law' . . . Thus Douglass's lack of established paternity compounds his distance from the Father's name, frustrating his claim to masculine identification and his ability to speak from within his oppressive social order.[20]

Claiming that "the symbolic order is linked to the phallus *and* to whiteness," Bergner concludes that the black son's inheritance of the mother's condition "helped ensure that African Americans were barred from any meaningful relation to the symbolic order" (257). Like Douglass

[20] Gwen Bergner, "Myths of Masculinity: The Oedipus Complex and Douglass's 1845 *Narrative*," *The Psychoanalysis of Race*, ed. Christopher Lane (New York: Columbia UP, 1998), p. 248. Although Bergner insists that "ideologies of race and nation intersect with the symbolic order regulating sexual difference," she concedes that Douglass ultimately "claims American citizenship by rewriting his relation to the Name-of-the-Father, thereby authorizing his voice as abolitionist" (p. 257). All subsequent references appear in the text.

in Bergner's reading, Donald connects the "feminine" with abjection—comparing his mother to "an animal in a trap" (87)—and aspires to the rights of his white father, but his "place" within a racially stratified American society keeps him outside the "social, linguistic, and economic exchange" that is "necessary for symbolization and self-consciousness" (248).

Explicitly focusing on Freud's Oedipal paradigm in her portrayal of a biracial boy's psychosexual development, Bonner lends support to Badia Sahar Ahad's contention that "the [Harlem] Renaissance era produced a body of intellectual work that deployed psychoanalysis to explode the boundaries of racial categories."[21] As Ahad persuasively argues in *Freud Upside Down: African American Literature and Psychoanalytic Culture* (2010), scholars of American modernism have heretofore ignored both "the extent to which, in the early 1920s, psychoanalysis was deeply enmeshed within black popular, print, and political cultures" (156) and black writers' revisionist interpretations of traditional psychoanalytic theory. Bergner similarly demonstrates how African American texts both deploy and challenge "classic psychoanalytic paradigms [that] inadequately explain the relevance of race for subjectivity" and emphasize "gender and sexuality as the determining factors of social organization and individual development, neglecting the effects of race on ontogenesis" (257). Although Ahad shows how canonical Harlem Renaissance writers such as Nella Larsen and Jean Toomer address this issue, he claims that "there remains a number of black intellectual and social contributions [from the modernist period] that have yet to be uncovered," deploring the fact that "every major history of American psychoanalysis makes no mention of the black intellectual and literary response to, or influence on, the culture of psychoanalysis in the United States" (12).

Rescuing Bonner's richly layered and provocative story from obscurity must certainly further Ahad's overarching goal of "call[ing] attention to a black presence in the cultural life of psychoanalysis, and underscor[ing] the influence of psychoanalytic culture in the shaping of black lives."[22] One of Bonner's most notable achievements in "One Boy's

---

[21] Badia Sahar Ahad, *Freud Upside Down: African American Literature and Psychoanalytic Culture* (Urbana: University of Illinois Press, 2010), p. 16. All subsequent references appear in the text.

[22] Ahad argues that black writers' engagement with psychoanalysis "has endured, to varying degrees, throughout most of the twentieth century and into the twenty-first century. Many of the arguments against the deployment of psychoanalysis in reading black texts have stemmed from the claim that psychoanalytic practice is yet another assertion of Western hegemony over black psychic life, and

Story" is her implicit recognition that intrafamilial Oedipal dynamics are inevitably shaped by social and historical circumstances. Suggesting that nuclear family relationships cannot be abstracted from the cultural context within which they evolve, Bonner replaces "universalizing" paradigms with a socially inflected model of the Oedipal drama. Her tale provides a corrective to traditional psychoanalytic inquiry which, as Claudia Tate has charged, neglects environmental contingencies:

> By isolating the family from society—specifically its economic, political, and technological factors that condition the family—psychoanalytic practice has avoided examining the relationship of social oppression to family dysfunction and the blighted inner world of individuals. Instead of regarding individuals and their stories as products of a dialectic of material circumstances *and* their internalization of them, psychoanalysis, as it generally operates, centers the individual's primary nurturing environment, not the external circumstances that precondition that environment. As a result, psychoanalytic practice relegates the bleak material circumstances of real lives to the background and blames the dysfunction on personal or familial deficiency.[23]

Claiming that "mainstream psychoanalysis effaces racism and recasts its effects as a personality disorder caused by familial rather than social pathology," Tate specifically impugns the "infamous Moynihan report" for "shifting the blame" for black family dysfunction from an oppressive society to the black "matriarch."[24] Yet several decades before Moynihan's report and the outcry that followed, a little-known Harlem Renaissance writer—as if anticipating the stigmatization of the African American maternal figure to which a popularized and universalizing Freudian theory could lead—demonstrated one black mother's failure to resist becoming, as Barbara Johnson describes Gwendolyn Brooks's persona in "The

---

psychoanalytic theory as a literary methodology has proved largely illegible as it 'mystifies rather than clarifies the [African American] condition' . . . Although psychoanalytic theory is certainly guilty of the critical murkiness of which [Barbara] Christian speaks, that very theory translated (relatively rapidly) into a significant cultural phenomenon that has heavily influenced the black literary and artistic scene" (PP. 156-57).

[23] Claudia Tate, *Psychoanalysis and Black Novels: Desire and the Protocols of Race* (New York: Oxford University Press, 1998), p. 16. Tate contends that "while psychoanalytic theory can help us analyze the social pathology of racism, its practice has carried a lot of irritating baggage that has made it virtually an anathema in the black intellectual community" (p.16)

[24] Ibid.

Mother," the "subject and object of violence at the same time."[25] Disabling and dispossessing her son at the moment of birth, the African American mother in twenties America, Bonner suggests, wields solely a tragic power.

[25] Barbara Johnson, *A World of Difference* (Baltimore: Johns Hopkins University Press, 1988), p. 191.

CHAPTER SIX

THE PSYCHOLOGICAL OPPEN: REALITY AND A MODERNIST MALE

BRIAN BRODHEAD GLASER

Since George Oppen was closely identified with the movement in American poetry known as Objectivism, a psychoanalytically informed discussion of his work might quite naturally begin with object relations. But that approach would run a very large risk, one significant enough to deter me—Oppen's poetry is characterized not by the expression of emotions so much as by the provisional adoption and abandonment of fragments of language in the service of developing a line of thought. Reading him through Kleinian terms would not respect what he was trying to do. And yet the relative sparseness of emotion in his poetry makes it especially inviting to psychoanalytic questions about repressions, evasions and blanknesses. So I want in this essay to draw on the thinking of Hans Loewald to discuss Oppen in the belief that Loewald's conception of the relation between reality and ego offers a way to open a conversation that has not yet been had about Oppen—one that includes acknowledgement of his deeply cognitive values as an artist as well as critical questions about the psychodynamics of the processes that his poems carry out.

There is at least one obvious reason why Loewald's interests converge with the methods of Oppen's poetry. Born two years apart—Loewald in 1906, Oppen in 1908—both these philosophically inclined men came of age when Martin Heidegger's *Sein und Zeit* had begun to re-orient philosophy towards the question of ontology, the origin and nature of being. Oppen's interest in the philosopher ran deep. In 1966, he reported to his journal that he was certain he had copied a section from Heidegger's *Essays on Metaphysics* as he was starting a poem, but could never again find the lines and had to conclude that he had only dreamt that he read them in Heidegger's text. He sent copies of "early" and "late" Heidegger to his fellow San Franciscan and experimental poet Robert Duncan a few years later (182). "An account of being in the world, stick to H," he wrote in 1968 to his daughter's husband, the philosopher Alexander Mourelatos, needing a single letter to indicate the master in question (177).

If Loewald's relation to Heidegger's thought was less enthusiastic, it was certainly closer. A graduate student of Heidegger's in Freiburg in the 1920's, Loewald was repelled by Heidegger's support of Nazism in 1933 and, according to Jonathan Lear's short sketch of his life in the recent introduction to Loewald's *Collected Papers*, the only biography in print to date, he turned to the profession of psychoanalysis in part out of exasperation with the ethical weaknesses of his teacher and in part out of a desire to understand their roots. Whatever the cause of his change in interest, Loewald had by the mid-1930's moved to Illinois to study at the Chicago Psychoanalytic Institute, where he would eventually establish a practice and teach.

Again and again in his writings Loewald re-framed the question that had obsessed his teacher, the question of the origin of the being of things, in psychoanalytic terms. In a 1949 paper, "Ego and Reality," he focused on Freud's metaphor in *Das Ich und das Es* for the development of the ego as the formation of a cortical layer, the outermost membrane of an organism altered by its interaction with the external world. If this is so, Loewald said, then an experience of what he calls "primary reality" ought to precede the distinction between self and object. There is an encounter with this "primary reality" before there is an ego: "Originally the ego contains everything," Loewald says, summarizing the central intrapsychic insight of *Das Unbehagen in der Kultur*. "Our adult ego feeling, Freud says, is only a shrunken vestige of an all-embracing feeling of intimate connection, or, we might say, unity with the environment" (5). Reality is for Loewald not so much the domain of the extra-mental, as it is for Freud, but rather a dimension of subjectivity, one of its limits and conditions of possibility. Hence, as Lear points out, the term primary reality challenges the Freudian category of reality as something ultimate or absolute. From Loewald's perspective, reality is an unstable concept, and primary reality is a stage in its emergence.

Whether the function of the ego is to harmonize the relation of the instincts with the demands of the external world, as Freud suggests in *Das Ich und das Es*, or to prioritize and synthesize our conscious and unconscious purposes, it should be understood to be created by the early experience of objects entirely separate from the perceiving self, an experience which interrupts an earlier sense of interrelation. In "Ego and Reality," Loewald condenses the arguments from a number of Freud's major later works because he wants to intensify one view implicit in them—the view that reality is not simply a pressure to which the nascent ego must adapt, but, rather, that the ego is constituted by the experience of real objects. This means, in his unorthodox reading of Freud, that the threat of the loss of reality, of the reversibility of the emergence of the ego, is as much a source of anxiety as the pressure of reality. Such a perspective leads Loewald to revisit the conventional Freudian story of the rise of the Oedipal triangle and its culmination in a castration complex with an unusually two-sided view of the young boy's perception of the father. On the one hand, Loewald says, repeating the Freudian account, a young boy's perception of the breast that feeds him becomes charged with libidinal and possessive energy, and he eventually perceives his father as a more powerful rival for this loved object, an authority limiting the ways he may relate to the desired body. From this perception arises his fear of castration by his father—an anxiety based on what Loewald reads as one of the ego's formative encounters with reality:

> If we understand the Oedipus conflict and the castration threat as the prototype of the demands of reality, it should be clear how strongly for Freud the concept of reality is bound up with the father. Fundamentally, for Freud the father is a hostile figure who has to be fought or submitted to. . . . Reality, then, is represented by the father who as an alien, hostile, jealous force interferes with the ties between mother and child, forces the child into submission, so that he seeks the father's protection. . . The significant point in this discussion is that reality is seen as an outside force, for Freud most typically and decisively represented by the parental figure, which actively interferes with the development of the child in such a way that the ego is essentially on the defensive . . . (8)

The paradox Loewald describes here, by which the father is both a threat and a sanctuary, might be seen as the nature of the superego writ small.

But, in addition to this perception of the father as a barrier to the possession of the mother, Loewald sees the father as playing another role in securing the ego's relation to reality. (That one can have such a relation in Loewald's view signals his distance from a Lacanian conception of the real.) For the young boy is not only afraid of castration; he is also, in Loewald's view, in the grips of what Karen Horney called in a 1932 paper "The Dread of Woman" (13). Though Loewald disagrees with Horney's claim that the source of this dread is the young boy's sense of the inadequacy of his penis, he does credit and repeat her controversial claim because, he says, it fits with his own experience of "clinical material":

> This fear of the woman is expressed by patients in terms such as being drowned, sucked in, overpowered, and this in regard to intercourse as well as in regard to the relationship to the mother, in particular in cases where

> there is no father or where the father has remained an insignificant and weak figure. (13)

It is important to acknowledge here that as both Horney and Loewald frame the issue, these fears are distinctive to males Both involve a scene of phallic loss, and both are resolved by an identification with the father. But whereas in the Oedipal scene this identification is shot through with both threat and security, the father's position in resolving the dread of the woman is utterly benign:

> Against the threat of the engulfing, overpowering womb, stands the paternal veto against the libidinal relationship with the mother. Against this threat of the maternal engulfment, the paternal position is not another threat or danger, but a support of powerful force . . . Against the threatening possibility of remaining in or sinking back into the structureless unity from which the ego emerged, stands the powerful paternal force. With this force an early identification is attempted, an identification that precedes and prepares the Oedipus complex. It would seem that Freud has in mind this positive, non-hostile aspect of the father figure (preceding the later passive identification due to the castration threat) when he speaks of an identification that 'plays a part in the early history of the Oedipus complex. A little boy will exhibit a special interest in his father; he would like to grow like him and be like him . . .' (14)

In the early experiences by which the ego is constituted, there are, in Loewald's view, two fathers with whom a boy identifies. There is the Oedipal one, at once frightening and reassuring, and then this merely differentiated one, who, like the Oedipal father, wards off a threat to the structure of the ego, but who does this without any conditions of his own. In the first phases of the development of the ego, the father represents the power of reality in two guises.

Loewald argues that too much has been made of the ambivalence central to the Oedipal conflict, suggesting that the "profoundly ambivalent relationship with the parent figures at work in the constitution of ego and reality" ought to be seen as stemming not only from this triangle but also from the dread "which promotes, in identification with the father, the ego's progressive differentiation and structuralization of reality" (17). Reality, in other words, shores up the self, and it is a gift assured by the presence of a benign father figure. Only eventually is this gift threatened by the Oedipal father who has become menacing in his own possessiveness.

The step from Loewald's thought to Oppen's is not great, because reality is a central idea in Oppen's poetics and in the critical reception of his work. "We awake in the same moment to ourselves and to things,"

Oppen quoted from Jacques Maritain's *Creative Intuition in Art and Poetry* in the opening epigraph to *The Materials*, voicing an insight that could bridge the three decades between the Objectivist work of his twenties—the small volume, *Discrete Series*, published in 1934—and the more discursive later poems (38). In establishing this connection across his decades of silence, it was not the ecstatic moment of awakening that drew Oppen to the formulation of the French Catholic critic and philosopher, but Maritain's sense of consciousness as dependent on the external world. "There seems to me no problem for the artist more difficult than that of separating the brute ego," he wrote to his cousin Ethel Schwabacher, after reading her own 1957 study of Arshile Gorky, "the accidents of the ego, from the self which perceives. Maritain says something of the sort, and I agree" (56-7). In Oppen's view, an encounter with objective reality sits at the core of selfhood. Perception, not interpretation, is the origin of the self

This role as a straight-talking guide to matters of the non-emotional and the real, a position he guarded carefully as a father, is the very one he has preserved as a father-figure. "Instead of the traditional Western account of a consciousness that digests the external world," Forrest Gander in a recent essay phrased his description of the man he had met in San Francisco as a young poet himself, "Oppen honors a consciousness interwoven with the world of objects, a consciousness that is nothing if not a collaboration with the world." The essays on Oppen collected in Burton Hatlen's 1981 *George Oppen: Man and Poet* and in DuPlessis' 1999 *The Objectivist Nexus* present a poet similarly committed to acknowledging the sovereignty over the internal of the phenomenal and objective.

There are many openings in Oppen's body of work through which one might begin to investigate the emotional energies with which this privileging of reality is invested. Fatherhood is the one I choose. As a contemporary of Oppen, and as another thinker and writer influenced by ontological questions, Loewald can perhaps help us especially well to see where in Oppen's poetry the materialism might be motivated as much by a conflicted conception of the father as it is by philosophical preoccupations. Such an approach may gain for us a picture of Oppen who grapples not only with the period's political and philosophical complexities, an engagement for which his intelligence is most often valued, but also with the nuances of masculinity in the period that have not yet themselves been fully named and known.

It is clear that Oppen knew the presence of a menacing father well enough that his poems more than once find themselves at a *locus classicus* for it. The Christ on Calvary in "Of Hours" is one instance; another of its recurrent sites in his poetry are the lines of Virgil's fourth eclogue, echoed in Oppen's own "Eclogue" from *The Materials* and again in "Five Poems About Poetry" from *This In Which*. Each of the five poems in the latter sequence interrogates a metaphor for an art in peril—a salesman holding a bauble, a creative mind like a pupil which can never close, Christ in Gesthemene, a lion walled off from the world, and, in the fifth section, "From Virgil," a carrion-bird:

> I, says the buzzard,
> I—
>
> Mind
>
> Has evolved
> Too long
>
> If 'life is a search
> For advantage.'
>
> 'At whose behest
>
> Does the mind think?' Art
> Also is not good
>
> For us
> Unless like the fool
>
> Persisting
> In his folly
>
> It may rescue us
> As only the true
>
> Might rescue us, gathered
> In the smallest corners
>
> Of man's triumph. *Parve puer* . . . 'Begin,
>
> O small boy,
> To be born;
>
> On whom his parents have not smiled
>
> No god thinks worthy of his table,
> No goddess of her bed' (104-5)

In a marvelously dense essay, John Peck reads Virgil's poem, named for the consul Pollio who took the Roman helm after a brief peace had settled between the aspiring emperors Octavian and Anthony, as aiming to set up "a monument to rectifying Advent within the squares of the imperial common," and he contrasts with Virgil's collusive vision Oppen's "appropriation of the child" which "does not reinaugurate the state" (72-3). So Peck sees the belated and predatory eye of the buzzard as an emblem for Oppen's own sense of hope in the *parve puer*. That hope involves his surviving by remaining so small as to be refractory to incorporation by the state. Peck associates this persisting utopian kernel with the phrase 'the inherited lit streets' from "Blood from a Stone," which he calls "a phrase that gives us actual space and its long history in their narrowed light, while making us feel another light in another common space that might have been" (73).

This reading has a complement in Oppen's own reading of "Eclogue," which he told L.S. Dembo in a 1968 interview was a bucolic turned by irony against "humans talking of deals and triumphs as a kind of artillery bombardment against that indestructible natural world" (205). The newborn carried by Virgil into both of these poems might be the redemptive energy Peck glimpses, still left in reserve after the imperial attenuation of healthier instincts. But it seems to me that the child's arrival at the end of "From Virgil" also does something much less comfortable to celebrate, which is to reintroduce a filial bond at the end of a line of thought which has thrown "man" bleakly upon himself. Self-consciousness is a buzzard, impotent and extraneous, the opening lines suggest. 'At whose behest does the mind think?' poses this insight as a question informed by that metaphor—the *mind* thinks, not the "I." Oppen is prepared to carry this line of thought to its conclusion: art should come to us from afar, rescuing us from—the syntax is ambiguous, indicating the impossibility of fully learning the lesson—man's triumph. We should learn from the buzzard the ugliness of thinking the world well-disposed toward us.

A consensus has formed that Oppen's work is significant because it means this. Certainly Gander's appreciation of Oppen's work has its source in some version of this message. But his is the most recent version of a recurrent appraisal. "Oppen's poetry has always been 'political,' or one might say 'moral,' in its evocation of the actual against the self-satisfying ego," Hugh Seidman wrote many years ago (239). Ten years before that Michael Hamburger interpreted Oppen's values this way:

> The poems move as dialectical occasions between sight and naming, and the poet's truth—no one else's perhaps—is established in the encounter

> between what is seen and words, with the poet as mediating agency of the process. To this extent, the encounter is seen by Oppen as one which is extreme in its selflessness. (420)

Oppen is a poet inspired by the way that the gift of perception itself constitutes our mental life.

Yet Oppen's celebration of reality looks somewhat different when we approach it through the concepts of Loewald's "Ego and Reality." For the received interpretation of the poem leaves unnoticed the same words that are most perplexing in the context of fourth eclogue, however Virgil construed the promise of the boy: 'On whom his parents have not smiled / No god thinks worthy of his table.' An admonishing—indeed menacing—father figure arrives at the end of these poems. Perhaps he is teasing the child, playfully coaxing him to be mild. But his appearance seems to me to send the poem's argument back upon itself, flushing it out of the small corners he had sought and instantiating a maximal figure for art, one speaking its moral plainly. With these lines the dilemma the poem—indeed the sequence—has thought its way to disappears. How can a poem that begins by suggesting that the psyche has evolved "too long," to the point of becoming a scavenger, end with this great neo-classical thud? If Oppen means that spurning the buzzard's pronoun—I—might lead us to the same ancient source of truth that Dante crossed Christian history to find in Virgil, it is not clear who speaks from beyond that language Virgil's threat to the child. The closing lines of the poem are somewhat ominously imperious for the way they have been ambiguously ironized. A Virgilian classicism is loved, then called obsolete, then seen as persistent in its possession of a threatening power. It is as if for Oppen there are three different fathers—the loved one, the disappointing one, and the ominous one—and they only, and habitually, appear in that order.

In the context of Loewald's suggestion that there are in the infantile sources of unconscious life both an ambiguous and a benign father, it seems to me that the Oedipal ambivalence running through a poem like "Of Hours" draws much more on the former whereas "From Virgil" seeks to rely only on the latter. Yet the redemptive vision of the latter poem's fool persisting in his folly, an art that sees a world beyond the merely human one, itself turns into the source of a threat. It is not the threat which generally draws attention from Oppen's admirers but the attempt to get over the "I." Still it seems to me that Loewald's composite picture of a boy's earliest fantasies of his father suggest why the menace is inevitable. The redemptive father must become the castrating father by virtue of his efficacy in the former role. The identification that produces the real as an agent must be the very one that confronts one with the theme of violence.

A similar dynamic plays out in some of Oppen's other fatherhood poems. In "Sara In Her Father's Arms," from *The Materials*, the newborn, who is "made largely of milk," becomes a force who "will make a household / To her need of these rooms" (51). The poem marvels less at the "smiling" child than at this forcefulness—at the end of the poem, Sara and other children are represented as the only future for language, and as a miraculous form of matter, one that exerts a shaping energy on the world: "What will she make of a world / Do you suppose, Max, of which she is made" (51). For this spirit, as in "Five Poems About Poetry," the father is a sheltering presence in the poem, here literally holding the child. But there is a violent transformation in the rhetoric through which this fatherhood is understood—the poem pivots around the description of Sara as a "violent, diligent seed" (51). Up until that point, the focus has been on the domestic scene of a friend of the poet holding his daughter in his home. After that description, the poem turns its focus to the "world"—a word that recurs three times in the last five lines. A scene of fatherhood leads to the theme of violence which in turn catalyzes the materialist wisdom of the poem's conclusion. From the perspective of Loewald's discussion of the ambiguous role of the father in securing the ego's relation to reality, the materialism of the poem seems to me more like a mechanism than a laudable wisdom.

One can see in Oppen's celebrated long poem, "Of Being Numerous," a similar dynamic. Eager to preserve a figure of reality which can save the mind from its thralldom to the investments—the "behest," as he puts it—of the ego, Oppen tries repeatedly in that poem to speak from a position of beneficence aligned with this reality, only to find each time that he must acknowledge the message the external world sends—the violating power of reality. He adopts a paternal persona to establish an experience of awakening, only to find that this position requires him to convey a threat. As a father he can clarify the space between ego and world that he would like to give the imagination more space inside of, and yet identifying himself as this father inevitably entails asserting some version of the menace at the end of Virgil's fourth eclogue.

His anticipation of this conflict may have been what kept Oppen from writing poems until his daughter left for college, one of the little-noticed contexts for the many references to fatherhood in the work. The phrase that would become the poem's title occurred to Oppen in the winter of 1962, first written in a letter to Ethel Schwabacher after an evening at Michael Cacoyanni's version of Euripides *Electra*. "The question of the play is the question of being numerous," Oppen announced to Schwabacher, a recognition that he elaborated this way: "The play becomes clear, the conflict becomes clear as a raising of the question of the importance of a nation, the importance of a culture as against simpler relationships and simpler emotions of father and child" (72). That "Of Being Numerous" is the poem of a World War Two veteran expressing his disagreement with the presence of U.S. soldiers in Vietnam is widely discussed; but it has yet to be remarked that the poem has its first seeds in an interpretation of *Electra* so strongly influenced by this preoccupation. The monologues of Euripides' play focus on the definition of nobility, on the compromises necessary to marriage, and on revenge—never, in fact, touching on the issue of whether Agamemnon's sacrifice of Iphigenia was justifiable in the name of Greek hopes. Oppen's idiosyncratic take on the play as rehashing the question of how and when an individual life can be offered up to the general good frames the political and ethical concerns at the heart of "Of Being Numerous" via one of the quintessentially menacing parent-child relations in Western literature.

The question of being numerous, in other words, is the question of being sacrificed through paternal violence at the desire of the greater body to which one belongs. The poem explores this tension in both its political and philosophical dimensions. The intricacy with which these threads intertwine constitutes one of the main pleasures and one of the chief perplexities about the poem. Critics are drawn to note, and to resolve, the apparent contradiction between Oppen's political and philosophical attitudes towards this vision of an inclusiveness which works by severing, as most recently in Peter Nicholls' "George Oppen: Of Being Ethical":

> one of the major themes of 'Of Being Numerous' . . . is that of the apparent unknowability of what is not the self: 'the world, if it is matter, / Is impenetrable' (*Collected Poems* 148). Like the city, which implies the individual's tie to place while all the time actually expressing only pure 'flow' (149), the poem moves forward, bringing one thing within the field of another, but (in contrast to *The Cantos*), hesitating to insist on the meaningful connection between them. Hence, perhaps, the ambiguity which plays around the idea of 'being numerous': have we 'chosen the meaning / Of being numerous' (151) simply because of our bewilderment over 'the shipwreck / Of the singular'? Or is Oppen suggesting that we have chosen merely the *meaning* of being numerous and not its reality? Readers have, reasonably enough, been so pleased to find a poet confronting this theme that they have tended to wish away ambiguity in order to discover a powerful sense of social collectivity here. (246-7)

In Nicholls' view, the proper way to understand Oppen's sense of reality as both the origin and the point of annihilation of the self is through Heidegger's notion of "withdrawal" (*Zurückziehung*), the process by which being retreats into the finitude of individual beings. Oppen's own sometimes puzzling style is for Nicholls the point at which the complexity of this position is expressed rather than resolved: "The double condition of language, as both personal and collective, as opaque and transparent, embodies the interdependency of the self and the other" (248).

Viewed this way, the ambiguities of Oppen's text are the sign that he has hit a philosophical bedrock. And this is why I think Loewald's treatment of the paradoxical gift of reality opens up a new perspective on Oppen's poetics. For the dilemma of being numerous is intensified at the moments in the text where Oppen must shift from the beneficent to the menacing father—a development whose trajectory may have been established by early experience, or unconscious fantasy, rather than conceptual commitments. Eager to maintain the goodness of the role of the father, he transposes the inevitably threatening function of that position into a philosophical mode. The force of the objective world, its dominance over the individual consciousness, comes into that poem charged with an energy that is the more impressive for having been walled off from its source—his own identification in the role of father.

The twenty-ninth section of the poem is Oppen's most direct confrontation with this conflict, and I offer it as one example of the layers of a psychological Oppen still to be explored. The section comes after a longer prose section, twenty-seven, in which Oppen approaches the meaning of the word "solitude" by imagining that "someone, a workman bearing about him, feeling about him that peculiar word like a dishonored fatherhood has swept away this solitary floor," and then the five-line twenty-eighth section, comparing the light before sunrise to the hue of "closed pages, tightly closed, packed against each other" (180-1). In the context of this recurring figuration of the one out of many, the twenty-ninth section begins:

> My daughter, my daughter, what can I say
> Of living?
>
> I cannot judge it.
>
> We seem caught
> In reality together my lovely
> Daughter,
>
> I have a daughter
> But no child . . . (181)

The rest of the section turns around this distinction between being a parent and being a child, depicting a house lit up by dawn as if held in "the sudden vacuum / Of time," an image of the household Oppen had been the father of years earlier, lost to him and called up by memory as he tries to understand what has become of the child he raised. What has time done with this child? Only his own vulnerability would prompt him to put the question this way, he suggests after an ellipse, attempting to frame the loss of this child as an instance of a painful but inevitable reality:

> . . . is it not
> In fear the roots grip
>
> Downward
> And beget
>
> The baffling hierarchies
> Of father and child
>
> As of leaves on their high
> Thin twigs to shield us
>
> From time, from open
>
> Time (182)

One implication in this passage is surprising, not to say shocking—that the relationship between father and child takes its color more from fear than love. This bitter intuition is mitigated by the metaphor of roots in which Oppen expresses it, and then, further, by the transformation of those roots into branches. Yet that transformation signals the extent to which Oppen is baffled by the recurrence of that hierarchy in his memory. And it is just at the moment of reflection on the dimension of fear between father and child that his "as of leaves" shifts the register from introspection to abstraction. The danger of violence linked to the Oedipal father comes suddenly from "open / Time". The cause of loss, though cued by his role as father, comes from the authority of a reality beyond him.

I draw attention to this pattern in Oppen's work not to criticize it as an emotion but to point out that it functions more like a mechanism than an inquiry. Poems that cover the territory of personal history may sometimes need recourse to a level of abstract thought about time in order to remain of interest, to the poet no less than the reader. My point is not that this shift is a flaw, but that it appears in Oppen's work repeatedly, just as the role of father begins to decline out of innocence, and that this reflex shades in my view the moral authority of his materialism, the most critically beloved facet of his work.

References

Dembo, L.S. 1981. 'Oppen On His Poems: A Discussion.' *George Oppen: Man and Poet*. Burton Hatlen, ed. Orono, Maine: National Poetry Foundation. 197-213.

Gander, Forrest. "Finding the Phenomenal Oppen." <http://www.brown.edu/Departments/English/Writing/people/Forrest/oppen.html>

Hamburger, Michael. 1981. 'George Oppen's *Collected Poems*.' *George Oppen: Man and Poet*. Burton Hatlen, ed. Orono, Maine: National Poetry Foundation. 417-28.

Loewald, Hans W. 2000. *The Essential Loewald*. Hagerstown, Maryland: University Publishing Group.

Nicholls, Peter. 1999. 'Oppen: Of Being Ethical.' *The Objectivist Nexus*. Rachel Blau DuPlessis and Peter Quartermain, eds. Tuscaloosa: U of Alabama P. 240-53.

Oppen, George. 2002. *New Collected Poems*. Michael Davidson, ed. New York: New Directions.

—. 1990. *The Selected Letters of George Oppen*. Durham: Duke UP.

Peck, John. 1981. 'George Oppen and the World in Common: A Descriptive Polemic.' *George Oppen: Man and Poet*. Burton Hatlen, ed. Orono, Maine: National Poetry Foundation. 63-87.

Seidman, Hugh. 1981. ''Boy's Room: A Note on Clarity and Detachment.' *George Oppen: Man and Poet*. Burton Hatlen, ed. Orono, Maine: National Poetry Foundation. 239-42.

CHAPTER SEVEN

THE "HELLISH TATOO": SCHIZOGRAPHY IN EDGAR ALLAN POE'S "THE TELL-TALE HEART"

SHIRLEY SHARON-ZISSER

If the economy of psychosis is an economy of language phenomena (Lacan 1993, 161), might one delineate a rhetoric of psychosis more specific even than the typology of the neologism, the pleonastic refrain, the delusional intuition in which every morsel of experience is accorded profound personal significance (Lacan 1993, 32-33)? In tracing the defiles of this rhetorical question pertaining to analytic practice, one might encounter the particular case of the clinic of the literary. In such an encounter, one might consider Michèle Montrelay's indication to the psychoanalyst to regard literary discourse not as material for sense-making, diagnosis, reminiscence, but as a source of a knowledge of the letter, discourse's inassimilable material support (1967, 70).

The psychoanalyst who listens to the unfolding of the analysand's speech along months and years, listens beyond the unconscious, behind what is heard in what is said, to the literal-littoral level of the letter (Lacan 1998, 26-27, 36), to the level of style as object (Lacan 2002, 624), might mark the recurrence not only of signifiers, words and chains of words, but also of the elocutionary forms in which these words are predominantly woven together. A discourse distinguished by an incidence of the ontological copula, a mark of a master's discourse's attempt to produce Being as part of a *Weltanschauung* (Lacan 1998,. 31), or by an orificized, hollowed-out similaic copula, textual locus of feminine jouissance (Sharon-Zisser 2000)? The analyst who listens for structures which do not signify might mark grand rhythms such as those alternating in the discursive thread of hysterics (Montrelay 1977, 27). Structures of periodicity bringing up archaic rhythms of flux and reflux similar to those theorized by Montrelay (1977, 155) and Nicolas Abraham (1995, 120).

Ruptures and breaks in rhythm and speech too, like those Montrelay detects in her ten-year-old patient Valérie, who speaks in fragments (1967, 76). Ruptures in the signifying chain which written discourse would designate by signs of diacritics and punctuation.

And if the analyst is a literary analyst? Working with the written text, sole type of text, Lacan says in his early article on "Schizographie," which allows for a minute phenomenological analysis of language (1975a, 382), the literary analyst does not *listen* for the elocutionary, prosodic, diacritical signs which constitute the text unfolding before her, curbing in on itself as does the analysand's discourse when it does not receive the analyst's response it does not cease to demand. The literary text exemplifies a "matrix of signifying articulation" which, despite the many senses criticism can grant it, is in itself, like the literal-littoral dimension of the discourse unfolding in an analytic session, "at once real and empty" (Montrelay 1967, 70).

The literary analyst observes the material signs supporting the discursive level of the *énoncé* (statement) as first as visual *percepta*, objects of her sight. One by one she collects from her sight and her hearing recurrent tropes and figures, recurrent rhythms, recurrent marks in the text which do not unfold a phantasm but presentify the statement's materiality, recurrent marks resisting all commentary even as they are locatable in a psychic structure: psychosis, neurosis, perversion. From this collection, this observation, the literary analyst might re-turn from the literary text to psychoanalysis with something of an offering.

Psychoanalysis does not turn to literature, Lacan teaches in "Lituraterre," in order to rediscover what it already knows. Psychoanalysis turns to literature in order to discern, in its explorations of the literary text, something more about the enigmas that are its concern (2001, 13). Psychoanalysis's affair is with what enigmatically, stubbornly, painfully returns in psychic life despite all imaginary attempts at sense-making Freud had derided as a curative practice as early as "'Wild' Psychoanalysis" (1910k). What returns even despite the interpretive interventions of offering a different punctuation to units of speech articulated within the session (Lacan 2002c, 495-496) or of cutting the session itself (Miller 1999, 13-15), interventions aimed at contracting the phantasm – that partly conscious, part unconscious narrative wherein the subject situates herself in relation to an *ersatz* object (Lacan 1966-1967) and at isolating and reigniting the real object cause of the subject's desire, the empty object cause this *ersatz* phenomenalizes.

Insofar as its concern is with what persists despite the analyst's (sense-reducing rather than sense-expanding) interpretive interventions, psychoanalysis cannot be interested in its application to readings inflating rather than contracting the textual layer most bound up with authorial phantasms qua narratives: the layer of plot and character and the themes arising from the interrelations of those, the layer of "fiction as truth" (Miller 1987, 11). Instead, psychoanalysis will focus on those opaque, enigmatic nodes wherein a literary work resists the sense-making it engenders (Soler 2001, 10). These are points at which the signifier whereof the literary text is made functions not as operator of truth (of the fictional world) but as (real) object (Miller 1987, 11).

In attending to opaque textual nodes where the signifier operates as (real) object rather than as functor of the diegetic world, psychoanalysis might relate to the literary text as locus for a gleaning. Though psychoanalysis cannot be hermeneutically applied to literature, it may nevertheless learn from the literary text (Soler 2001, 10). Where the literary phantasms of plot and character are ruptured and literary writing reveals itself a treatment of the real by means of style (Merlet and Castanet 2004, 9). Where literary sense fails or is exhausted but material components – elocutionary forms, rhythms, marks of diacritics and punctuation – persist as literature's litter, creating calligraphic ravines in the white substrate of the page (Lacan 1998, 67). Persist as stubbornly and irreducibly as does the object of/as failure (*ratage*) between partners to the sexual relation or to its absence (Lacan 1998, 58).

When what is at stake are the enigmas of the psychoses, what irreducible lit(t)eral markers nevertheless locatable in a psychic structure might the reading of literary phenomena return to the knowledge of the analyst? And what might such pursuit of psychoanalytic knowledge through a prism more literary than clinical suggest to literary theory's thinking of the real dimension of linguistic forms, a dimension where the signified as excess of sense generated by the signifier (Lacan 2002d, 413-414) is obliterated into a *litura* and these forms are bared as calligraphic or typographic ravinements of the substrate of representation, rigid designators of the real beyond veils of semantemes and hermeneutizations?

Edgar Allan Poe's "The Tell-Tale Heart," whose diegesis features a psychotic first-person narrator offers answers as contingent as their specificity. When the particulars of the narrator's psychosis are unfolded from the text's phantasmatic layer of plot and character as a point of departure not for an inflation of sense instructive of the reader, not the text (Miller 1987, 10) but of deflation, contraction, exhaustion of this layer, what is exposed are Poe's predominantly aposio(poe)tic and onomato(poe)ic stylistics. Beyond the text's phantasmatic layer, these poe-tic stylistics, with their marked preference for the dash, function as schizographic language phenomena within a dialectical structure of madness wherein paranoia, an illness of the ego, always already collapses into and congeals from a schizophrenic organization where the ego's absence causes the graphic matter of signification to function not as a defense against the real but as a real which afflicts the subject's biological organism directly, horrifyingly.

A triple trajectory of inquiry, then, involving a deployment of the text's phantasmatic layer where, in Miller's terms (1987), the signifier operates as a functor of the fictional world's truth, as prelude for the isolation of the clinical structures unfolding within this fictional world as attributes of the narrator and the ultimate hollowing out of this fictional world from its imaginary content so as to isolate the rhythmic and graphic constants which are this world's litter, itself inseparable from the psychotic structure of the author the literary text generates as its effect (Merlet and Castanet 2004, 12). At the end of this trajectory, a suggestion might be made concerning Poe's schizo-graphism of the dash. Given a psychic structure of foreclosure, the dash as textual dominant can serve as delusion's topological edge, lived by the subject as real at the same time that it fulfills the function Lacan in his analysis of Sophocles's *Antigone* accords the effect of beauty (1992, 248-249): the last psychic bastion against a primal terror which might never be named. Beyond this bastion, an abyss in which the material of signification whose sources are organic palpitates in unmetabolized raw form, as Thing, eroding ravines in the biological organism from whence it emanates.

What discloses the psychotic structure of Poe's narrator in the phantasmatic layer of the text as fictional world is the presence of elementary phenomena: delusions and hallucinations. The narrator's delusion, spelled out as early as the tale's first three paragraphs, consists in the belief that one of the eyes of an old man with whom he apparently shares his home and whom he otherwise "love[s]" (Poe 1842, 17) is a "damned spot" he must eradicate (Poe 1842, 19). Like Shakespeare's Lady Macbeth, to whose famous line ("out, out damned spot" [4.1.38]) this phrase alludes, Poe's narrator devotes himself to the effacement of a body part he experiences as intolerable,[71] in his case, to the point of killing and dismembering the proprietor of this body part. But just as Lady Macbeth in her fury to pulverize the "damned spot" of blood she believes she sees on her hand only discovers more and more of its material origin (Lacan

[71] This is not to imply, of course, that Poe's narrator suffers from the same psychopathology as Lady Macbeth, whose rubbing of the "damned spot" Lacan uses to illustrate the psychic structure of the obsessional neurotic (1962-1963, lesson of 12 December 1962).

1962-1963, lesson of 12 December 1962), Poe's narrator discovers that to him, the old man's eye not only includes what he calls a "hideous veil" but is itself a veil for another part object: the voice as embodied by the beating heart (Poe 1842, 19).

As the tale ends, with the narrator's delusionally positing the unsuspecting policemen as "Villains" intent on extracting an admission from him (Poe 1842, 21), the gaze surfaces once again in the psychosis of the narrator, who becomes the object of the persecuting (and this time, also prosecuting) eye of the law. As Con Davis puts it, "while the narrator [initially] cannot abide being looked at and made an object, he … make[s] himself an object for the eye of the law when he is caught" (1983, 993-994). Gaze and voice alternate in the narrator's psychosis as incarnations of an unspeakable menacing object which survives any attempt at extermination by changing its sensory shape as well as the elementary phenomenon in which it becomes manifest.

Initially phenomenalized in a delusion (that the old man's eye is "Evil" [Poe 1842, 17] and vexes or infuriates him), the "hideous" (Poe 1842, 21), unspeakable object of the narrator's psychosis mutates to a hallucination (that he hears the beating of a heart of a body he had dismembered after having ascertained the cessation of pulsation). And this hallucination, initially part of the narrator's *percepta*, becomes absorbed into the narrator's delusional system as a "noise … *not* within [his] ears" (Poe 1842, 20). In the narrator's psychosis, not only gaze and voice but at the same time hallucination and delusion alternate and turn into one another in a psychic reality he finds impossible to bear (Poe 1842, 21).

At the irreducible formal core of the veil of signifieds phantasmatically disclosing the madness of Poe's narrator is an alternating rhythm, not unlike the systolic-diastolic cardiac cadence he hallucinates, a cadence hauntingly implanted in the tale's title. And if the same cardiac cadence subtends the rhythmics at once of the diegetic world of Poe's fiction and of this fiction's title qua paratext,[72] does not the text betray a prosodic strange loop, a Moebian structure wherein diegesis and hyperdiegesis constitute a single surface, not a hierarchy?

What structural components of psychosis might account for the alternating cadence Moebianizing Poe's text? First of these is the psychotic's failure to exclude (or to have lost) the object a (Lacan 2002c, 486-487): the inassimilable remainder which falls away from the subject as real in the mythical encounter with the Other which splits the subject,

[72] I rely here on Genette's theorization of the paratext as "a fringe of the text" which is "a zone between text and off text" (1997, 2).

and which operates as the subject's psychic cause (1962-1963, lesson of 5 December, 1962). The exclusion of the object a, Lacan stresses in the 1966 note, is crucial not only for the establishment of the split subject of the unconscious but for the constitution of reality. The "field of reality," Lacan writes, "is sustained only by the extraction of the object a, which, however, gives [reality] its frame" (2002c, 487). One can think of Lacan's insistence on the necessity of the exclusion of the object a as a return to Freud's thesis, stated, for instance, in "Negation," according to which proper reality testing requires the loss of the memory trace of an object that once brought real satisfaction (1925h, 238). In the absence of such loss, no cut would mediate the subject's encounter with perceived objects. These might remain identified with an archaic memory trace which underwent no voiding reinscriptions, its libidinization the summit of unpleasure.

One example of a psychotic failure to lose the object Lacan provides in his tenth seminar is of a schizophrenic patient whose drawings, frequently featuring eyes, included the inscription "*io sono sempre vista*" (Italian for "I am always seen") (1962-1963, lesson of 9 January 1963). Having failed to extract the object a, which in her case takes the phenomenal form of the gaze, the patient perceived this object as perennially present, subjecting her to an intolerable existence of constant visibility. This patient's predicament helps highlight the psychotic structure wherein the object a "returns because it has not been excluded from the symbolic," taking on "a spectral image of the persecuting voice or gaze" (Salecl 2003, 2477). Poe's narrator, who experiences the old man's gaze as distinctly non-symbolic, suffers from a similar predicament. His description of the old man's eye as the animalian "eye of a vulture" (Poe 1842, 17) indicates not only the persecutory qualities he delusionally attributes to this eye, but also his perception of the eye as a real object that had not been subjected to the loss of raw vitality that, in Lacan's view, accompanies symbolization.

The object in the narrator's hallucination too bears the mark of the unsymbolized. The object voice of the dead man's heart-beat tormenting the narrator in his hallucination is a voice that does not, as the title suggests, "tell [a] tale" but raw sound, unmetabolized phonic material. The alternating manifestation of gaze and voice in the narrator's elementary psychotic phenomena as raw and non-symbolic indicates that in the contingencies of what might have been his personal history, the object he failed to lose took at once scopic and phonic form. Hence, what returns in the real to torment the narrator through foreclosure's hole[73] once the triggering moment of psychosis – the encounter with A-father[74] (in the tale, the "old man,")[75] – takes place is neither gaze nor voice but the very alternation between the two.

This alternation between the objects of the scopic and the invocatory drives is not only an attribute of the narrator as an object featuring in the fictional world qua phantasm. It marks the relation between the material substances of the tale's two significant rhetorical forms: aposiopesis (registered in the heavy use of dashes, a function of the tale's graphism) and onomatopoeia (a function of the tale's rhythmic materiality, itself a trace of the phoneme, registered in the cardiac rhythm of the hyperdiegetic title qua paratext and the reference to this rhythm as a "hellish tattoo" [Poe 1842, 19] in the diegesis into which the title's hyper-diegesis thus topologically folds). Forms from whence this literary phantasm is woven

---

[73] In Lacan's thinking, psychotic structures are underlain by a hole in the unconscious chain of representations where the signifier of the Name of the Father was to have been (Lacan 2002c, 481).

[74] The encounter with A-father is Lacan's term in the article on the preliminary question to any possible treatment of the psychoses (2002c, 481) for a lived encounter of a subject of a psychotic structure, in whose unconscious a hole appears where the signifier of the Name of the Father might have been, with a father figure ("not necessarily … the subject's own father") or another manifestation of the father function (such as becoming a father or father-in-law, or being appointed, as Schreber was, to a position culturally associated with paternity) for which no corresponding unconscious representation exists. In such cases, the hole of foreclosure abysmally gapes, and a psychotic *declenchement* whose manifestations are the elementary phenomena of hallucinations and delusions is triggered.

[75] The old man is recognized as a father figure as early as Marie Bonaparte's psychoanalytic reading of Poe's Tales (1949). Princess Marie Bonaparte, the first (and still one of the very few) to have considered the tale from a psychoanalytic perspective lists "The Tell-Tale Heart" first among Poe's works she classifies as "Tales of the Father" (1949, vii). Bonaparte's argument is that dynamic between the narrator and the old man as father-figure is Oedipal, fraught with a wish for the elimination of the father as sexual rival. Indicators for the Oedipal inflection of the dynamic include the old man's sleeping alone (an echo of an infantile Oedipal wish not to find the mother in the parental bed where she might have coitus with the father [504]) and the narrator's use of the "heavy bed" as murder weapon (Poe 1842, 19), which turns his homicidal passage to the act to an Oedipal retribution for what a boy witnessing a primal scene in the parents' bed might have recorded as "the father's sex attack on the mother," a retribution wherein what is conceived as the "instrument of [the father's] crime, becomes that of his destruction" (498).

but which remain this phantasm's irreducible litter once the phantasm's imaginary dimension of sense and signified is exhausted, becomes *litura*.

Nor is this relation of alternation between the phonic components of the tale's lit(t)erality, themselves creating a Moebian continuity between text and paratext, and the graphic components of the same level of the letter, a simple vacillation between disjuncts. The alternation between aposiopetic graphism and onomatopoeic rhythmics is inextricable from the alternation, on the tale's phantasmatic level, between the elementary phenomena of delusion and hallucination in the narrator's psychosis, each a product of a different destiny of the derivatives of foreclosure, one predominantly paranoid, the other predominantly schizophrenic.

This alternation between paranoid and schizophrenic components of psychosis is itself seized within the topological structure of the cross-cap, a Moebius strip whose dimensionality is multiplied. Discernible in the phantasmatic level of the tale's diachronically unfolding fictional world as an attribute of the character-narrator, the topological structure persists on the lit(t)eral level of the tale as spatial object which is the product of relations of sight between the plane of the reader-as-viewer and that of the text's calligraphy or typography as drawing.[76] It is the relation between the schizographic components of aposiopetic graphism and onomatopoeic rhythmics within this lit(t)eral cross-cap structure that will best help specify components of paranoid and of schizophrenic rhetoric within psychotic writing.

To follow the different destinies of the derivatives of foreclosure with which aposiopetic and onomatopoeic components of schizography seem to be bound, one might turn to Lacan's extraction of the consequences of Freud's theorization of the avatars of impossible, unbearable knowledge as early as his article on the "Neuro-psychoses of Defense" (1894a). All psychopathological structures, Freud argues in this article, are attempts by the subject to defend himself against knowledge of the unbearable, or in Lacan's terms, the real. For what is unbearable knowledge if not a thought

---

[76] I rely here on Lacan's topological analysis of Diego Velasquez's celebrated painting *Las Meninas* in *Seminar 13: The Object of Psychoanalysis* (1965-1966, especially lessons of 4 and 11 May, 1966). Through an analysis of relations of sight between painter, viewer, and painted figures, Lacan shows how the painting's picture plane is not discrete from but continuous with (the painter's or viewer's) ground plane, the two forming different areas of a spherical envelope, which, moreover, approach one another at what in perspective painting appears as the vanishing point. Although Lacan's analysis is of a perspective painting, its topological implications extend to all relations of sight between a viewer and what s/he perceives in what seems to be a two-dimensional substrate of representation.

which does not cohere with other thoughts and whose contents are threatening to the subject? The subject who cannot bear to know such a thought, Freud argues, treats it as "*non-arrivée*" (1894a, 53). Yet psychic structures differ from one another in their modes of defense against knowledge which cannot be allowed to arrive to the status of a conscious or pre-conscious word-presentation (*Wort-Vorstellung*). The mechanism of defense instituting the neurotic structure is the registration of this thought as an unconscious representation (*Vorstellung*). This representation is henceforth preserved as a signifier in the unconscious, severed from signifieds which may have been attached to it, prevented by the forces of repression from percolating beyond the bar separating unconscious and conscious life. What will appear in lieu of the repressed thought in the subject's conscious life is the symptom (e.g. hysterical paralysis or an obsessional ritual) as compromise formation.

Psychosis rests on a far more radical defense mechanism whose function is to preserve the subject's ignorance in the face of what he can never allow herself to know. What the psychotic cannot bear to know is precisely what is *not* registered in the chain of representations (or in Lacan's terms, signifiers) constituting the unconscious. Impossible knowledge – knowledge concerning the father function as in the Schreber case, but in melancholic psychoses concerning loss – is excluded from unconscious representation. Yet this knowledge cannot be excluded from the psyche altogether. The unbearable thought remains in the psyche, as, in Freud's terms in the Wolf Man case, as "that about which the subject wants to know nothing, even in the sense of repression (1918b, 84).

In Freud's term which Lacan adopted as a denomination for the ignorance-ensuring defense mechanism underlying psychosis, the unbearable thought is "foreclosed" (*Verwofen*) from the chain of signifiers the unconscious ethically might be. In such a case, the unbearable remains in the psyche without being metabolized into an unconscious representation which might be repressed. It remains as real. And it is as real, radically other to the subject that it returns to plague the subject as unbearable enjoyment (jouissance) from elsewhere (in Freud's terms, *in altero*), in the form of the elementary phenomena. "What was abolished internally returns from without," Freud says when describing the psychotic mechanism in the Schreber case (Freud 1911c, 71). Or, in Lacan's more nuanced formulation of this mechanism in his seminar on the psychoses, "what was foreclosed from the symbolic [that is, from representation in the unconscious] returns from the real" (1993, 13).

The unbearable encounter with knowledge the subject cannot allow himself to symbolize, even as a representation which will never be allowed to see the daylight of consciousness, has another economic consequence, well-detailed by Freud in "On Narcissism" (1914c) as well as in the Schreber case: the withdrawal of libidinal cathexis from objects once loved, sometimes from the world at large (1911c, 77). This withdrawal of libido from the world and its reinvestment in primary, autoerotic narcissism, Freud indicates, is the kernel of every psychosis. But it is one that occurs in silence and can only be posited by means of retroactive construction. What is not silent in the psychoses are what Freud in the Schreber case speaks of as "attempt[s] at recovery" too often "mistake[n] for the disease itself" (1911c, 77): the elementary phenomena of hallucinations and delusions. Elementary phenomena such as hallucinations and delusions, that is, are not the founding moment of the psychotic structure (the withdrawal of libido from objects, which can only be retroactively assumed) but spontaneous attempts at recovery.

In this line of thinking, schizophrenia and paranoia are two structures of these attempts at recovery, distinguished from one another in terms of the different destinies of the derivatives of foreclosure in relation to their positioning with respect to the Other. In schizophrenia, what is cathected first in the spontaneous attempt at recovery is language itself. This is because in schizophrenia, the primordial and always traumatic encounter with language as what is constitutively radically Other to the living organism is traumatic to such an extent that the intrication of language and biological substance necessary for the speaking being's acquisition of a body, which, in psychoanalytical terms, is part of a secondary process Lacan conceptualizes first in terms of the cohesive image constructed in the mirror stage and later in terms of the discrete (and erogenized) organs organ-ized by the work of the signifier is not allowed, or only partially allowed, to take place. As Lacan puts it in "*L'etourdit,*" in cases of schizophrenia language "does not manage to bite" the living organism so as to grant this organism a body (Lacan 1973, 32). In such cases, language (the Other as treasury of signifiers) is not a symbolic substance which organizes living matter into organs which have a status of alterity with respect to the subject (as erogenic or hysterogenic zones) but a real substance attacking this biological matter (as distinct from the body he cannot have), head on. Language attacks the schizophrenic directly, including by means of hallucinated voices or sounds which fill what Freud describes as the "rent" in the psychotic's relation to the external world (1924b, 151), and experienced diffusely within the schizophrenic's biological substance as unlocalized jouissance (Laurent 1997, 21).

The paranoid's spontaneous attempt to recover from the founding moment of the withdrawal of libido from the world manifests a different relation to the Other. Like the schizophrenic, the paranoid reinvests his libido in the world, but what he invests first is not words and the symbolic (which for the schizophrenic is experienced as real), but the imaginary and fantasy (Lacan 1991, 116-117). The delusional ideation the paranoid constructs on the imaginary axis of ego and other constitutes his attempt to recreate the world (Miller 2001, 54) and fill in the rent opened up by foreclosure. In the context of this delusion, because of the foreclosure of the Name of the Father as function at once linking and separating the imaginary and symbolic registers, these registers topple onto one another, so that an other person becomes collapsed with an absolute and unbarred Other, as manifest in Dr. Schreber's imaginary inflation of his psychiatrist, Prof. Flechsig. The delusion in which an inflated imaginary other eclipses the Other and takes its place is hence coeval with the paranoid's attempt to recreate the link with the Other that had been severed at the point of the originary withdrawal of libido from the world. The inflated Other's position as the hinge of the delusional reality the paranoid places in the rent in the fabric of his world makes it possible for him to localize the jouissance of the unbearable, unrepresentable knowledge that returns to him from the real. This jouissance is (delusionally) placed in the Other as (in many cases) persecutory.

To be sure, on the phantasmatic level of "The Tell-Tale Heart" as fictional world, Poe's narrator postulates the old man, and later the police officers, as persecutory in the context of a delusional ideation that may be considered, in Freud's terms, as the "substitute" reality (Freud 1924e, 187) the narrator places in the hole in his unconscious system of representations where unbearable knowledge can not cease not to be written. Nor does the narrator's attitude to his body index the absence of an imaginary envelope of the body (such as Lacan notes in his twenty-third seminar [1975-1976] in the case of Joyce) which might indicate schizophrenia. The effect of the hallucinated sound of the heart-beat on the narrator is not diffuse, unlocalized (in terms of Lacan's seminar 20, Other) jouissance (Lacan 1998, 10) such as affects Schreber as he looks at his cross-dressed image in the mirror (Schreber 1955, 210). On the contrary, the effect the hallucinated sound has on the narrator is organ-ically limited to an "ache" in his "head" and a "ringing" in his "ears" (Poe 1842, 20). Such localization of corporeal torment bespeaks a localized jouissance of an organ Lacan denominates phallic jouissance (1998, 10), a jouissance not lived by a schizophrenic organism unbitten by the image and the signifier.

The narrator's response to language too does not bespeak a schizophrenic attitude to the signifier as real. On the contrary, the narrator's responses to reported speech indicate an ability to insulate whatever kernel of the real the signifier may carry. There are two instances of reported speech in the tale, and the narrator responds to both with marked aloofness. Towards the end of the tale, the narrator reports, in free indirect discourse, how the three "officers of the police" had told him how "a shriek had been heard by a neighbor during the night; suspicion of foul play had been aroused; information had been lodged at the police office, and they (the officers) had been deputed to search the premises" (Poe 1842, 20). The narrator's response to these narrated events is to "smile" and disavow "fear" (20). In the one instance in the tale of direct quoted speech, the old man's "Who's there?" uttered in terror as the narrator pushes open the door of his room (Poe 1842, 18), the narrator responds calmly, keeping "quite still and sa[ying] nothing" (Poe 1842, 18). In the two cases, the narrator is not affected by other's signifiers as by a real object. His ability, in the act of telling the tale, to insulate the signifiers articulated by others through their transformation to free indirect discourse in the one case and their enveloping in quotation marks in the other indicates a severance of the real from the signifier which the schizophrenic structure would render impossible. Jouissance, for Poe's narrator, is localized not in his biological organism as directly attacked by language, and not only in organs delimited by the imaginary, but in an other (the old man, the three policemen) deluded as enjoying his suffering. The narrator believes the three policemen "were making a mockery of [his] horror" (Poe 1842, 21). As for the old man, it is the seemingly enigmatic reference to his "vulture eye" that betrays the narrator's attribution of persecutory jouissance to him.

Poe's character representation thus involves paranoia as an attribute of his first-person narrator (and focalizer). Considered in terms of the Lacanian clinic, the narrator as an object featuring in the phantasmatic level of the tale as fictional world manifests a psychotic structure which is markedly paranoid rather than schizophrenic in its involving a cathexis of an imaginary delusion rather than of the signifier as real, phallic jouissance of organs rather than Other jouissance diffused through a body-less, organ-less biological organism. Yet in terms of the Lacanian clinic too, something about the nature of what is represented on the tale's phantasmatic layer as what returns in the real to torment Poe's narrator – the hallucinated beating of the dead old man's heart – gives a schizophrenic inflection to his psychosis, weighting it towards a paranoia with a mixture of schizophrenic elements, a clinical category suggested in Jacques-Alain

Miller's return to Freud's Schreber case (1997a, 54).[77] The more precise clinical attribute of the narrator as component of the fictional world would this be paranoia mixed with schizophrenic elements.

But does the attribution of schizophrenic elements deduced from represented narrative content to the narrator as major protagonist of the fictional world of Poe's text exhaust this text's manifestation of schizophrenia? Might schizophrenic elements be manifest not only in this fictional world which is the effect of the excess of sense (the signified) generated by the signifiers enchained by the author, but in the objectal/real facet of the signifier which, according to Miller (1987, 11), is independent of the fictional world? This question seems especially pertinent in the case of Poe, a writer who, like James Joyce (as analyzed by Lacan [1975-1976]) or Hölderlin (as analyzed by Jean Laplanche [1961]) displayed a psychotic structure, most famously manifest in the attacks of delusion which plagued him at the end of his life (Silverman 1993, 3).

Poe's "The Tell-Tale Heart" is thus an artwork which not only represents a psychosis as part of its fictional world, but which is at the same time itself an instance of psychotic art. As such, it might include schizophrenic and/or schizographic components as part of its rhetoric and aesthetics. Whatever manifestations of schizography appear in the tale would thus be at once mimetic and non-mimetic, instances wherein narratorial and authorial psychosis topologically fold into one another.

Drawing on Lacan's analyses of psychotic writing, especially in the case of Joyce's late fiction, and of Lacan's theorization of the structure of madness, especially in "A Question Preliminary to Any Possible Treatment of the Psychoses" (2002c), Jacques-Alain Miller formulates the structure of psychotic art as the postulation of the artwork as object a in the place where the value of the psychic operator of the Name of the Father, and consequently, of language's phallic (sense-determining) function which the Name of the Father effects, equals zero (P=0 & Φ=0) (Miller 1987, 11). The nullification of the phallic function in psychosis does not mean that the signifiers whereof psychotic discourse is made cannot generate signifieds or spawn a fictional world, although in the extreme case of Joyce's *Finnegan's Wake* they hardly do so (Soller 2001, 83-99). For what are delusions (such as Schreber's belief he is the bride of God, or the belief of Poe's narrator that he is persecuted by the old man's eye) if not a hypertrophy of the signified? But in the absence of the phallic function, this hypertrophy can asymptotically extend to infinity, is never fixed by a

[77] Paranoid schizophrenia is also the diagnosis reached in the one critical study of the clinical nature of the psychosis of Poe's narrator (Zimmerman 2005).

quilting point arresting the sliding of the signified (Lacan 2002c, 476).

In such cases, the function of the signifier's facet as litter, real object rather than generator of signifieds and support of the fictional world is not only to provide a *suppléance* which would plug up foreclosure's hole. It is, at the same time, to supply an anchoring point which would arrest the asymptotic sliding of signified which fuels delusion's gnomic growth (manifest, in the case of Poe's narrator, in the expansion of the focus of persecutory ideation from one person [the old man] to three [the police officers]). If in neurotic art, the function of the signifier's lit(t)eral facet is to outline and hence veil the hole of castration (a/-ρ) (Miller 1987, 11), in psychotic art the function of the same facet is to circumscribe and hence plug up the much more abyssal hole of foreclosure.

Yet the difference in the function of the signifier's lit(t)eral facet in neurotic and in psychotic art qua object is not limited to its positioning (veiling or plugging) with respect to the different psychic holes of castration and foreclosure. This difference extends to the relation of the lit(t)eral, material aspect of the signifier to the artist's organism. The phonic and graphic materiality of signifiers from whence artworks are made has its origin in organic operations including utterance, excretion, motion which causes a visibly discernible *ravinement* of one substance by another. But the nature of castration is such that it introduces a schism or gap between the subject and the organic operations from whence the subject's signifiers are fashioned. It is around this gap that the neurotic creates his signifiers as a "presence made of absence" (Lacan 2002a, 228). Moreover, the very fashioning of the neurotic signifier around the hole of castration, the paradigm for which is Heidegger's fable of the archaic potter, involves the metabolization and modulation of the organic substance from whence the signifier is made. The precipitate of this metabolization of the signifier's organic substance is this substance's veiling. The neurotic signifier generates an excess of signifieds which are the building blocks of narratives such as subtend phantasms and fictional worlds. It is only when phantasms and fictional worlds are voided of their signifieds that the material facet of the neurotic signifier is exposed. And even then it is exposed severed from its organic origin.

But when castration is not operative because the Name of the Father has failed, no schism or cut separates the organic substance from whence the signifier is made from its maker. The psychotic signifier is not fashioned around a hole (of castration) from organic material that has undergone modulation, metabolization. Especially in the case of schizophrenia, where an imaginary body is absent, the psychotic signifier plugs a hole (of the Name of the Father's foreclosure) with an item whose occasional production of signifieds as a function of its structure might sometimes give it the appearance of a component of the Other (e.g. a discernible word or image), but which its maker as subject cannot distinguish from his biological organism. It is in this sense that Laplanche is able to say, paraphrasing psychiatrist Henri Ey, that the madman is "less artist than work of art" (1961, 4).

Within this psychotic art(ist), one may nevertheless distinguish iterated components generating its distinctive style such as the cyclical repetition and ubiquitous multiplication Lacan notes in his early article on the problem of style in the psychoses (1975b, 387). In his mathemization of psychotic art, Jacques-Alain Miller structurally situates these typifying stylistic components of aesthetic creation "on the circumference of [foreclosure's] hole" (1987, 11). More recently, psychoanalysts Merlet and Castanet have similarly but more specifically pointed, a-propos of Antonin Artaud's psychotic art, to the graphism of his sketches as what "delineates the borders of a hole in unconscious knowledge" (2004, 26).

But what seems no less important than the situation of the components of the style of the psychotic art(ist) on the circumference of foreclosure's hole is the specification of these components, especially in the case of schizophrenia, as indistinguishable from the biological organism of the artist. What characterizes the psychotic writing/drawing Lacan in an early article calls "schizography" (1975a, 365-382) is not only the typology of verbal, nominal, grammatical, and semantic disturbances (Lacan 1975a, 375-381) manifest in automatisms which might appear "inspired" only because they are animated by sthenic emotions (morbid increases of vital actions) (Lacan 1975a, 382). Nor is it only the structural positioning of these seemingly inspired automatisms at the circumference of foreclosure's hole psychotic art plugs (Miller 1987, 11). What characterizes schizopgraphy is at the same time its structural positioning as part of the schizophrenic artist's biological organism. Schizography is thus not only *animated* by sthenic functions, as Lacan put it in his psychiatric writings of the 1930's (Lacan 1975a, 382). Viewed through the prism of Lacan's late, Borromean teaching, and its elaboration by Miller, schizography appears to embody these sthenic functions in non-modulated form.

I would like to suggest that in Poe's "Tale–Tell Heart," and perhaps in Poe's writing more generally, schizography phenomenalizing the schizophrenic component of the narratorial psychosis unfolded in the text qua fictional world but no less so of the authorial psychosis which engendered this fictional world and which seems to be topologically continuous with the fictional world is manifest in the pervasive use, by Poe's first-person narrator, of the dash, usually in the context of the rhetorical figure of the interrupted sentence which early rhetoricians termed aposiopesis.

Henry Peacham, for instance, defines aposiopesis as an instance wherein "the Orator through some affection … breaketh off his speech before it be all ended" (1971, 118). George Puttenham defines aposiopesis as a figure of defect, [as] when we begin to speake of a thing, and break of in the middle way, as if … it needed no further to be spoken of," noting it is "fit for phantasticall heads" (1968, 139). Thomas Wilson calls aposiopesis "a stop, or Half Telling of a Tale," defining it as "when we break off our tale before we have told it" (1993 [1560], 205). For Renaissance rhetoricians, that is, aposiopesis is an instance where the signifying chain breaks, where a part of the signifying chain falls away as fragment. And how might the fragment be graphically marked? The examples of aposiopesis in classical and early modern literature cited by Peacham, Puttenham and other Renaissance rhetoricians do not include a calligraphic or typographic sign in the form of a punctuation mark.[78] But the example supplied by Thomas Wilson "Doth it become thee to be – shall I tell all? Nay I will not for very shame" (1993 [1560], 205) marks aposiopesis by means of the dash. Much later in the theory of language, too, Theodor Adorno, whose comments on "Punctuation Marks" in *Notes to Literature* (1991) harken especially to works of the nineteenth and twentieth centuries (e.g. the fiction of Theodor Storm) links linguistic fragmentation with the use of dashes (93).

In literary criticism, aposiopetic dashes have been noted as a stylistic dominant in the French modernist fiction of Marcel Proust and Sidonie Gabrielle (Delesalle 2002), the Russian modernist fiction of Anrdrej Belyj (Tomei 1994) and modernist poetry of Marina Tsvetaeva (Gol'tsova 2001), and the English modernist fiction of Henry James (Boren 1998). In nineteenth-century literature in the English language, dashes have been noted as a stylistic dominant in the writing of Emily Dickinson (Crumbley 1997, Tanselle 2000) and in Poe's *Eureka* (Dayan 1983). This list suggests that the dash might somehow be characteristic of nineteenth-century or modernist poetics across several languages. But whether or not this is so is a question of a literary history which is not attentive to the psychic particularities of authors such as Lacan never hesitated to point out "despite the taste of the times" (Miller 1987, 9), a taste whose manifestations extend from the New Critical insistence on the so-called intentional fallacy to Roland Barthes's pronouncement of the "Death of the

---

[78] E.g. Virgil's unfinished sentence "How doth the childe Ascanius, whom timely Troy to thee" cited by Peacham (1971, 118).

Author" (1983), differently articulated on Michel Foucault's reduction of the author to a discursive function (1977). To the extent that, as Boren claims, the ubiquitous dashes in James's literary text are indeed markers of repression (1998, 332), they form part of a neurotic artwork, constructed around the hole of castration it veils from signifiers whose constituting organic material has been severed from the living organism and functions as the lit(t)eral part of the signifier only as dead. If, as Boren puts it, James's dashes (and horizontal lines in general) have an auto-graphical significance (1998, 336) and "assume an emblematic relation to the author" (1998, 341), which "both supplants and recalls the 'I' of the text" (1998, 334), it is only to the extent that these lines project the shadow of its castration and its death, the shadow effected by the (literally) mortifying effect of symbolization on the biological organism, especially insofar as it is male.[79]

Components of psychotic, and in particular schizophrenic art, on the other hand, are instances wherein the word and other manifestations of language have failed to kill the Thing. Wherein the graphic and phonic material of these linguistic manifestations was indistinguishable, for their author, from the biological organism whose organ-izing limits he hardly knew. Schizography, that is, epitomizes not so much the death of its author in the cultural senses in which Barthes and Foucault (1987) speak of it as the non-death for this author, while alive, of the organic material from whence the signifiers constituting it as an object plugging foreclosure's hole is made. For a schizophrenic writer, punctuation marks are more than part of the graphic-visual dimension of his text, more than part of what Adorno describes as the "physiognomy" of this text as drawing (1991, 91). Instead, punctuation marks, and all lit(t)eral components of writing as *ravinements* of the terrain or substrate of drawing, are literally part of the physiognomy of the schizophrenic artist (for whom the artwork he produces is indistinguishable from his biological organism). In the context of schizography, dashes may be "wrinkles on the brow of [the] text" not in the figurative sense Adorno implies (1991, 93). They may literally and organically be experienced *as* wrinkles of the author's living organism.

---

[79] In this connection, see Michèle Montrelay's comments on the relation of a man (I would specify, insofar as he is neurotic) to his words, as mediated by the penis as what separates him form his words and, in its detumescence, "projects the shadow of his death" (1977, 151). The penile rhythm of tumescence and detumescence as "marked by the sign of death" (1977, 151) Montrelay specifies as subtending a (neurotic) male's mortified relation to his words is graphically present in the alternation between erect I's and horizontal lines Boren notes in the graphism of the Jamesian texts.

What, then, might be the function of dashes in Poe's "Tell-Tale Heart" as an instance of his psychotic poetics which topologically include the postulation of a psychotic narrator? These poetics in general manifest a pronounced use of the dash in aposiopetic form, as noted by Joan Dayan who speaks of dashes as Poe's "favored protagonist of point" (1983, 440).[80] Examples from the poetry include lines preceding refrains in "The Raven" (Poe 1969, 3-7) such as "Let my heart be still a moment and this mystery explore -- / 'Tis the wind and nothing more!" or "Perched upon a bust of Pallas just above my chamber door -- /Perched, and sat, and nothing more," or the following anaphoric lines from "Annabel Lee" (Poe 1969, 88-89): "But our love it was stronger by far than the love / Of those who were older than we -- / Of many far wiser than we – ," or the beginning of the second stanza of "Dreamland" (Poe 1969, 15-16):

By the lakes that thus outspread
Their lone waters, lone and dead –

Their sad waters, sad and chilly
With the snows of the lolling lilly –
By the mountains – near the river
Murmuring lowly, murmuring ever –
By the grey woods – by the swamp
Where the toad and the newt encamp –

Non-aposiopetic dashes, marking the erasure or partial erasure of

---

[80] In her impressive analysis of the dash in Poe's *Eureka*, Joan Dayan comes to the conclusion that this aspect of Poe's poetics is linked to an "indefiniteness of effect" (1983, 43) and a "multiplication of meanings" (1983, 443). Dayan's conclusions regarding Poe are remarkably similar to Boren's conclusions regarding the function of the dash in James's poetics as a device of "suggestive undecidability" which "allows connotation to bleed throughout the sentence" (1998, 333-334). Neither Dayan nor Boren, however, take into account clinical structures -- of the reader they assume, and of the author. While undecidability and ambiguity may be the effects on neurotic subjects of language heavily marked by dashes, it is dubious whether they function in this way for subjects of a psychotic structure one of whose major epistemological manifestations is certainty. Regardless of their possible effects on readers of various psychic structures, Poe's dashes as manifestations of psychosis cannot function within this psychosis as markers of undecidability which psychosis definitionally lacks. To the extent that they allow of a multiplication of meaning, they may have a function in the gnomic growth of delusion in which semantic slippage is always at work, but only to the extent they at the very same time mark an effort to create a prosthetic anchoring point for this slippage in lieu of the absent Name of the Father.

apostrophized names often appear in poem titles, such as “To F—s S. O—d,” “To F --,” “To --,” “to the River --,” “The Lake, to --,” and “to -- --.” Examples from the fiction include the declarations of the narrator in “The Pit and the Pendulum”: “In the deepest slumber – no! In delirium – no! In a swoon –no! In death – no! even in the grave all is not lost" (85), or his terrified description at the end of the tale’s penultimate paragraph: “I felt that I tottered upon the brink – I averted my eyes –“ (96), or the following passage from “The Premature Burial” (1844):

> The unendurable oppression of the lungs – the stifling fumes of the damp earth – the clinging to the death garments – the rigid embrace of the narrow house – the blackness of the absolute Night – the silence like a sea that overwhelms – the unseen but palpable presence of the Conqueror Worm – these things, with the thoughts of the air and the grass above, with memory of dear friends who would fly to save us if but informed of our fate, and of consciousness that of this fate they can *never* be informed – that our hopeless portion is that of the really dead – these considerations, I say, carry into the heart, which still palpitates, a degree of intolerable horror” (47).

In “The Tell-Tale Heart,” this graphic-rhetorical characteristic of Poe’s poetic style is more marked than in other well-known tales such as “The Purloined Letter” or “The Oval Portrait,” and in the prose poem *Eureka* on which Dayan (1983) focuses in her study of Poe's "analytic of the dash." Dashes appear in the tale’s opening sentences: “True! – nervous – very, very dreadfully nervous had I been and am; but why will you say that I am mad? The disease had sharpened my senses – not destroyed – not dulled them” (Poe 1842, 17). Aposiopetic dashes, the cutting up of sentences, appear in all paragraphs of the tale but the one whose content references a cutting: “First of all I dismembered the corpse. I cut off the head and the arms and the legs” (Poe 1842, 19). The tale’s last two paragraphs, especially, manifest a persistent use of the dash:

> Oh God! What *could* I do? I foamed – I raved – I swore! I swung the chair upon which I had been sitting, and grated it upon the boards, but the noise arose over all and continually increased. It grew louder – louder – *louder*! And still the men chatted pleasantly, and smiled. Was it possible they heard not? Almighty God! – no, no! They heard! – they suspected! – they *knew*! – they were making a mockery of my horror! – this I thought, and this I think. But anything was better than this agony! … I felt that I must scream or die! And now – again! – hark! louder! louder! louder! *louder*!
> ’Villains!’ I shrieked, ‘dissemble no more! I admit the deed! – tear up the planks! Here, here! – it is the beating of his hideous heart!’ (21).

The incessant use of the dash in "The Tell-Tale Heart" has caught the attention of one commentator as possibly related to the narrator's "mad[ness]" (Benfey 1993, 31). But how precisely might one specify, from a Lacanian perspective, the schizographic function of the dash within this predominantly paranoid madness, itself the product of psychotic writing? To explore this question, I turn to Lacan's comments on interrupted, aposiopetic sentences in two cases of psychoses, which, like that of Poe's narrator, have a predominantly paranoid inflection. These are the case of Dr. Schreber, first analyzed by Freud, which Lacan revisits in his third seminar, and the case of the paranoid woman Lacan interviewed in one of his patient presentations, who believed her husband's family intended to cut her into pieces (Lacan 1993, 44-56; 2002c, 448-449).

Dr. Schreber self-reflexively refers to aposiopeses (in his terms, "not-finishing-a-sentence") as a prevalent part of his delusional system (1955, 172). The souls that implant thoughts in his nerves, Schreber says, increasingly afflicted him with "unfinished ideas, or only fragments of ideas" (1955, 172). The last example of these is "Lacking now is," an interrupted sentence whose missing complement, Schreber says,"ought to have been" the "leading idea" (1955, 172). Another example Lacan pauses on from later in Scherber's *Memoirs* is "Do you still speak" whose complement, following the Latin word "*scilicet*" (that is to say) – Schreber's equivalent of the aposiopetic dash -- is "foreign languages?" (1955, 226).

In these interrupted sentences, Lacan points out in his return to the Schreber case, "meaning is present in two ways – as anticipated on the one hand, since it's a question of its suspension, and as repeated on the other, since he invariably refers to it an impression of having heard it" (1993, 114). For Schreber, that is, the "anticipated" part of the sentence which follows the aposiopetic break is not supplied by the subject as a signifier extracted from the treasury of signifiers that is the Other but as a signifier imposed on him from without (in the form of an auditory hallucination). Although repeated by the subject, this signifier thus remains to him one that is essentially in a "foreign language" not completely his own. The status of the complementary part of Schreber's unfinished sentences as more object than signifier, more real than symbolic, Lacan adds later in the seminar, is the reason why although the complements to Schreber's interrupted sentences "first appear to be situated at the limit of meaning … they soon turn into quite the contrary – residue, refuse, empty bodies" (1993, 259).

When supplied with their complements, Schreber's unfinished sentences masquerade as syntactically felicitous chains of signifiers which mean. Yet the structure of psychosis precludes their being such felicitous semantemes. Consequent upon the absence, in the psychotic's subjective structure, of the signifier of the Name of the Father, whose correlate is the phallus as the function guaranteeing sense in language (Lacan 2002c, 462), is the absence of semantic "quilting points" where the gliding of sense in language may momentarily stabilize (Lacan 1993, 267). Although completed by fragments he has heard before, Schreber's interrupted sentences remain for him enigmatic, foreign, sentences in which the "leading idea," as his own example suggests, will forever be "lacking." In the absence of the phallic function in his subjective economy, the psychotic is forever suspended in an unfinished sentence, full of holes in sense for which the patches he supplies, even if syntactically normative, cannot but be semantically inadequate, unable to function as quilting points which might articulate the "leading idea" that had been foreclosed. Even when complemented by Schreber, his unfinished sentences remain for him, as far as their sense is concerned, aposiopeses in which the hole of foreclosure is all too gaping.

What appears in these holes is, as Lacan puts it, "a drive that had been rejected by the subject" (1993, 258), and returns to him from without, in the form of audited signifiers whose value is real, that of "residue, refuse, empty bodies" (Lacan 1993, 259). These are signifiers which, Lacan says, remain "always … enigmatic" (Lacan 1993, 101), hence signifiers the subject can only repeat as one would words in a foreign language, in an operation that "wearies and exhausts" him (Lacan 1993, 259).

Lacan's linguistic analysis of the case of the woman whose overarching delusion concerned her in-laws' plan to dismember her evinces a similar theorization of the function of aposiopetic breaks in psychotic discourse. What the woman first complains of to Lacan is her having been offended by a neighbor who cursed her as a "Sow!" In his subtle questioning of the patient, Lacan gleans that her hearing the curse was preceded by her saying to the neighbor "I've just been to the butcher's." Lacan explains that the curse, the signifier the subject experiences as unbearable, is not her own message which she receives from the Other in inverted form, as a neurotic would have, but an "antistrophe," the complement of the (interrupted) sentence she had uttered. She hears this complement, which Lacan speaks of as separated from the first part of her sentence by a dash, as a voice coming from without, and as radically other to her, real, in its articulation of the unbearable, unspeakable ideation her being the rejected object of her husband's family:

> In the place where the unspeakable object is rejected in the real, a word the

> curse] makes itself heard, so that, coming in the place of that which has no name, it was unable to follow the intention of the subject without *detaching itself from it by the dash preceding the reply* (2002c, 448, my emphasis).

Like Dr. Schreber, this woman patient is suspended in an endless interrupted sentence. Instead of quilting points which might temporarily fix its sense, this endless interrupted sentence manifests rents, marked by dashes, from which the unspeakable knowledge that had been foreclosed leaps at her as real as an auditory hallucination masking as a curse.

Both Schreber and the woman who had just been to the butcher's are tormented by interrupted sentences whose complements (the words implanted by the souls in Schreber's nerves, the words the woman hears from her neighbor) are available to them but more intolerable than their total absence would have been. Such an absence would be characteristic of a neurotic structure, where what would emerge in the gaps in the symbolic chain would be a silence indicative of the split subject of the unconscious. But in the case of psychoses such as those of Dr. Schreber or the woman who had just been to the butcher's, what appears in the gaps in the symbolic chain is an auditivated signifier experienced as real.

If one of the differential criteria distinguishing schizophrenia from paranoia is the schizophrenic's cathexis of the signifier as real, the variations of interrupted sentences in the case of Schreber and of the woman who had just been to the butcher's indicates the presence of schizophrenic elements in their psychosis. Indeed, the presence of auditory hallucinations in the Schreber case is one of the two considerations that led Freud to diagnose his psychosis as exhibiting "paraphrenic traits" (1911c, 78). In terms of the principles of Freud's original diagnosis, as well as of the contemporary Lacanian clinic, Dr. Schreber and the woman who had just been to the butcher's are cases in which "paranoid and schizophrenic phenonema [are] combined" (Freud 1911c, 77), although the general clinical picture is paranoid because of the predominance of the cathexis of delusions as what would fill the hole of foreclosure in the spontaneous attempt at recovery.

The fictional case of the narrator in Poe's "The Tell-Tale Heart" is similar, linguistically and clinically, to the cases of Dr. Schreber and the woman who had just been to the butcher's. His speech, which betrays persecutory delusions, first concerning the old man, then concerning the policemen, is interrupted by aposiopetic dashes to an extent which exceeds the use of this characteristic figure of punctuation and elocution in Poe's other writings. But the narrator's use of dashes is not only a literary device for the mimesis of psychosis. It is itself the product of Poe's psychotic writing, on which Poe, moreover, did not fail to provide reflective commentary, not unlike Schreber, whose *Memoirs* include a self-reflexive gloss on the souls' "system of not-finishing-a-sentence" (1955, 172).

Poe's "Marginalia" include a section on punctuation, focusing on the dash as a "point" (punctuation mark) which "cannot be dispensed with" because of its singular use (Poe 1969, 309). This use, Poe explains, involves the representation of "a second thought – an emendation" without this additional thought being stated in any form but the dash, which "stands for" this missing thought (Poe 1969, 309). The dash in Poe's critical writing has the status of a mark excluded from the signifying chain, a mark which, in Lacan's terms, has the status of a detached object with respect to this chain.

This structural status of the dash as a mark which has lit(t)eral (real) value in Poe's theorizing makes it into a *mise-en-abyme* of Poe's marginalia in their entirety, which he describes as thoughts he pencils in the margins of his books, or on "slip[s] of paper … deposit[ed] … between the leaves; taking care to secure it by an imperceptible portion of gum tragacanth paste" (Poe 1969, 301-302). Words written in pencil, Poe's marginalia are made of the graphic and material substance of (linguistic) representation. Yet their positioning in the margins of books or on slips of paper placed between and pasted onto their leaves grants these marginalia the position, for their author, of what Miller (2004-2005) has most recently theorized, in reference to Lacan's theorization of anxiety in relation to the encounter with a cedable object a in his seminar on *L'angoisse* (1962-1963), as "*pièces détachées*": representational material wrenched from a signifying chain or context and rendered objects (of jouissance or anxiety), symbolic material turned real.

The subjective status of Poe's marginalia as detached cedable objects is emphasized all the more by their description of sometimes glued to the books which contain them as excess by means of "gum tragacanth paste," which renders them alien to the materials (ink and paper) constituting the books as site of representation. Synecdochic of Poe's marginalia, his pervasive dashes, as he theorizes them, function for him as a *pièce détachée*, symbolic substance turned real, much like the complements to the unfinished sentences Schreber hears from the deluded souls and repeats by rote, or the curse heard by Lacan's patient who had just been to the butcher's. If so, Poe's dashes are at one and the same time a *pièce détachée* and what masks a yet more radically Other *pièce détachée* which emerges for him from an-Other scene.

Poe's text adumbrates such an Other scene from which a fragmentary detached object emerges to create disruption on at least two levels of what

W.J.T. Mitchell (1980) calls spatial forms in literature, correlative with the phantasmatic level of the fictional world and with the phonic-graphic litter that remains once this phantasm is voided of its imaginary content. The tale's phantasmatic level (what W.J.T. Mitchell describes as "the world represented, imitated, or signified in a work" which the reader must mentally reconstruct during or after the temporal experience of reading [1980, 283]) features two cases of an intrusion into the diegesis's local spatial focus by a phenomenal object emerging from a space beyond. The first of these instances occurs when the narrator has his "head in" the old man's doorway, precipitating the old man's anxious "Who's there?"(Poe 1842, 18). The second occurs when the narrator hears the hallucinated heartbeat from beneath the floor planks, where the old man's dismembered limbs are cached (Poe 1842, 21). In the two cases, one dimension of the old man's room as spheric, closed architectonic structure (the wall with the door in it, the floor) is disturbed to the point of being torn open by a phenomenal object heterogeneous to it (the narrator's head, the hallucinated heart beat). In the two cases, this heterogeneous phenomenal object is covered by a rectangular plank (the door, the floor boards), poorly shutting out the void from which the object emerges. Hence the anxiety which marks the response of the old man, then of the narrator, to the intrusion of this heterogeneous phenomenal object which appears where a lack is expected to have been, manifesting Lacan's theorization of *angoisse* as the affect emerging upon the encounter with the "lack of lack" (Lacan 1962-1963). Repeating instances wherein the spatial realm mentally constructed by the reader is impinged upon by a phenomenal object intruding from a space beyond, the tale's phantasmatic dimension projects a more generalized imaginary conception of space wherein a spherical enclosure made up of enchained rectangles, some of them stopping up apertures to a space beyond is subject to the anxiety-evoking onslaught of detached objects creeping from this space beyond.

The tale's grapho-rhetorical dimension, part of what W.J.T. Mitchell describes as the spatial form of literature involving "the physical existence of the text itself" (1980, 282), appears to perform the conception of space projected by its fictional world. For is not the dash, so marked a feature of the tale's graphism, literally present to the reader's (and the author's) eyes, identical in shape to the rectangular planks (the door, the floor planks) which in the tale's projected conception of space, mentally constructed by the reader from the tale's repeated patterns of space-fictionalization, fail to serve as bulwarks against the intrusion of a phenomenal object from a space beyond?

If the dashes dominating the tale's graphism are the literal correlatives of the failing bars in the tale's phantasmatic conception of space as an enclosure filled with holes through which heterogeneous phenomenal objects creep from an Other scene, the ensemble of signifiers and dashes constituting the tale is not the linear chain suggested by the temporal unfolding of the tale's diegesis but a spherical envelope in whose ruptures, holes veiled by the dashes, a radically Other phenomenal object may emerge.

But in Poe's theoretical writings, the dash is more than a form of punctuation participating in language's diachronic unfolding. Poe theorizes the dash at once as diachronically functional punctuation mark and as *pièce détachée*, a phenomenal object falling away from a diachronically unfolding diegesis which cannot contain it. If so, in terms of what W.J.T. Mitchell calls a literary text's literal space, the dashes in Poe's tale function not only as failed bars covering the holes on the envelope of a sphere. They are at the same time the heterogeneous object, the *pièce détachée* which disruptively creeps through these holes. The literal space of Poe's tale thus evinces not the geometrical shape of the sphere but the topological structure of the cross-cap, the sphere folded in upon itself whose "outside" and "inside" are continuous with one another as is the tale's diegesis with the paratext of its title.

If this literal space graphically performs the imaginary conception of space projected by the tale's phantasmatic level, does not this imaginary conception of space itself involve not an enclosure with apertures but a cross-cap full of holes through which tormenting phenomenal objects creep? And is not such a conception of space coeval with the psychotic (and in particular the schizophrenic) experience of continual torment by what Freud would call pieces of lost psychic reality which return *in altero*, from the real? The spatial forms of Poe's tale are what I would term schizotopic at once on the phantasmatic level and on the dash-dominated lit(t)eral, grapho-rhetorical level of the tale's schizography.

The dash-dominated, aposiopetic schizographics of the schizotopic space(s) of Poe's tale, though, have a particularity distinguishing them from those Lacan diagnoses in the paranoid woman's speech, or the "*scilicet*" Schreber interposes between his interrupted sentences and their complements. Considered topologically, as components of the cross-cap structure, Poe's dashes, unlike the punctuating separators in those two other cases of psychosis, do not linearly *precede* the appearance of a *pièce détachée*, symbolic material turned real, emerging in the hole torn by the operation of foreclosure in the psychotic subject's chain of signifiers. They *are* such a piece they at the same time mark and mask. This piece appears not, as in the case of Schreber or the woman who had just been to the butcher's, in linear, diachronic succession *after* the aposiopetic hole marked by the dash or its rhetorical equivalent, but *beyond* it. The dash as *pièce détachée* comes to inhabit the aposiopetic hole it marks and masks from a space topologically continuous with the hole but opened up elsewhere.

Where might this elsewhere be? W.J.T.Mitchell's work on spatial form in literature (1980) suggests the levels of spatial form are all part of a text's representational fabric, situated on a different plane from that occupied by the reader/viewer. The tradition of thinking which extends from New Critics' insistence on the intentional fallacy to the notions of the death of the author and the author function in the writings of Barthes and Foucault suggests a literary text (or, for that matter, any other work of art) is situated on a different plane than that occupied by its creator.

Perhaps the best illustration of the conception in aesthetic thinking of the separate planes occupied by artwork on the one hand and artist and/or consumer on the other is the idea in theories of perspective of the "picture plane" (occupied by the artwork) and the "ground plane" (occupied by the artist or the viewer) as separate from and heterogeneous to one another.[81] However, as Lacan's elaborations of perspective theory in seminar 11 (1977, 91-119) and seminar 13 (1965-1966) show, ground plane and picture plane only seem to be two two-dimensional surfaces separate from one another. Projective geometry, which had been part of perspective theory at least since the work of Desargues in the seventeenth century, and which takes into account the positioning of both ground plane and picture plane on the globe, exposes their continuity with one another as parts of the single surface of a spherical envelope (Lacan 1965-1966).

The position of the artist's eye further complicates and co-implicates the relations of ground plane and picture plane. At once what looks at the "picture plane" from the "ground plane," and the vanishing point into which all straight lines organizing the picture's plane's perspective converge, the artist's eye glues ground plane and picture plane onto one another, exposing the structure of the space on which they are situated as not a sphere but a cross-cap (Lacan 1965-1966). The topological co-implication of ground plane and picture plane as sides of the envelope of a cross cap held together by the eye of the artist (whose place is supplanted by the eye of whoever looks at the artwork) enables Lacan to say, in his elaboration on perspective in seminar 11: "I am not simply that punctiform

[81] On the idea of the separation between picture plane and ground plane in the theory of perspective see Lacan 1965-1966.

being located at the geometral point from which the perspective is grasped … in the depths of my eye, the picture is painted. The picture, certainly, is in my eye. But I am in the picture" (1977, 96).[82]

Lacan's phrasing in seminar 11 does not make it clear – perhaps intentionally -- whether the "I" in question is artist or viewer. But his further elaboration on the topology of visual representation in seminar 13, with reference to Diego Velasquez's *Las Meninas*, makes it possible to specify the different destinies of the place of the observer's I/eye in the case it is occupied by the artist and in the case it is occupied by the viewer. Both artist and viewer occupy a "ground plane" topologically continuous, as part of a cross-cap structure, with the "picture plane" of the artwork as visual object. But for the artist, the imaginary content of the various surfaces of the envelope of the cross-cap on which his/her eye is situated is part of the visible world he perceives. Topologically speaking, s/he could slide into the picture, whose visible world is absolutely continuous with his. Velasquez, for instance, at once views the Infanta Margerita from the "ground plane" which seems to be "outside" the picture *Las Meninas*, and stands next to her in the picture. The viewer of the artwork too, whose eye comes to inhabit the place inscribed by the place of the artist's eye/I in the artwork's topological structure could slide into the world of the picture as topologically continuous with the plane of sight on which s/he is situated.

But since the artwork's imaginary content is the product of another subject's singular phantasm, all the viewer would find within the artwork would be what to him/her would be but relics of representation, stripped of the imaginary value they had for the subject who perceived/created them, relics which cannot be transposed wholesale into his/her own phantasm (if s/he is neurotic or perverse) or delusion (if s/he is a paranoid psychotic).

For the viewer, that is, the components of an artwork are just as topologically continuous with his/her plane of sight as they had been for the artist. But to the viewer, these components are not representations fleshed with imaginary value. They are representatives of representation (Freud's *Vorstellungraepresentazen*) material signs which signify nothing in themselves but make signification possible. It is the viewer who re-turns these representatives of representation to the status of representations by integrating them into his/her own phantasm (or delusion). In a sense, one could think of sense-conferring exegesis, whether of literary texts, of

[82] The English translation provided in the Norton edition of the seminar ("the picture, certainly is in my eye. But I am not in the picture") is erroneous. The French typescript reads: "le tableau, certes, est dans mon oiel. Mais je suis dans le tableau." The above section on perspective and topology is much indebted to the important work of Efrat Biberman on this subject.

artworks, or of an analysand's speech, as the recipient subject's imaginary fleshing out of representatives of representation materially upholding an object ceded by another subject by means of the integration of these representatives of representation into the recipient's own phantasm or delusion.

If the literary text as an object ceded by its creator is as much visual object as a picture, its graphic and visual dimension partakes of the same topological relations of sight with author and readers as obtain between a picture, its painter, and its viewers. For the reader/viewer of Poe's "Tell-Tale Heart" as visual object, the dashes which are a dominant feature of this object are a material sign, a representative of representation whose purported sense, like any interpretation in literary criticism, art criticism, or psychology consisting of the addition of signified sense to a given chain of signifiers, is a function of the interpreter's phantasm. Dayan's interpretation of Poe's dashes as part of a poetics of "uncertainty" (1983, 446), in the context of which it is "employed to project a series of moments or possibilities" (1983, 439), may be considered an example of such phantasmatic procedure. So may the attributions of sense to the predominant dashes in the style of other writers, such as Boren's interpretation of Henry James's dashes as components of a poetics of "modernist undecideability" (1998, 339) whose function is "the insertion of doubt" (1998, 337), or Tomei's interpretation of Belij's dashes as involving the projection of an attitude of "ambiguity" towards the world (1994, 610).

In psychoanalytic terms, however, what is interesting is not what sense can be phantasmatically added to Poe's dashes from the vantage point of readers who come to occupy the place of the I/eye created and vacated by the author on the envelope of a cross-cap where ground plane and picture plane fold into one another. Psychoanalysis would be interested in the function of the dashes in this cross-cap structure for the author it generates. And in the case of Poe, the author is psychotic, just as is the phantasm of himself he creates in the figure of the first person narrator of the "Tell-Tale Heart."

How might the dash function in the topological structure literally implicating the text and its author? To follow Lacan's formulation in seminar 11, in terms of relations of sight, the text as picture is registered in the depths of the author's eye, just as the author is in the text as picture. The text as picture in which the author is topologically present includes the phantasmatic space of the fictional world and the lit(t)eral level of the text's graphism. On the phantasmatic level of the fictional world, the first-person narrator, whose reconstructed attributes include the psychopathology of paranoid schizophrenia, stands in the same Moebian relation to the psychotic author as the painter Velasquez to the painted figure of the painter in front of his canvas in *Las Meninas*. Considered in terms of topological relations of sight, Poe's first-person narrator *is* Edgar Allan Poe, slid into the picture plane constituted by the tale as fictional world from the "ground plane" in which he writes, with which this fictional world is topologically continuous at the same time as the text's dash-dominated graphism is inscribed in the depths of his eye.

The presence of the author in the fictional world and of the text's graphism in the author's eye are a function of topological relations of sight which obtain in most if not all cases of fictional worlds, whether depicted in literature or in the visual arts. But in the case of Poe, a psychotic writer, the topology co-implicating artist and artwork includes more than the visual field. To the extent the relation of Poe and his narrator is one of topological continuity along the Moebian single-surface of the envelope of a cross-cap, the schizophrenic traits appearing as attributes of the narrator on the tale's phantasmatic level pertain to the author as well.[83] The schizophrenic components of the author/narrator's psychosis, always already impinging upon the fabric of his delusion, include the absence of an imaginary body organ-izing the biological organism.

In the context of such a schizophrenic absence of an imaginary body, to what extent would the substrate of writing be distinct, for the author/narrator, from his biological organism, from his very flesh? A given reader – depending on his psychic structure – may regard the graphism of Poe's tale as a collection of typographic signs on sheets of paper, even, in a more Lacanian vein, as *ravinements* of white sheets of paper. But for an author whose psychosis includes schizophrenic traits, substrate of representation and flesh may be indistinct, writing as the *ravinement* of this substrate by graphism, itself the effect of the motility of this flesh on pigmented materials,[84] indistinguishable from the insertion of such pigments into punctures in the flesh, from the primitive practice of tattooing.

As components of schizography, Poe's dashes, which separated from the topological and/as psychic structures in which they are situated and interpreted in terms of a readerly phantasm may seem part of a poetics of

---

[83] In her psychoanalytic view of "The Tell-Tale Heart," Marie Bonaparte (1949) too regards the narrator as manifesting the author's psychopathology.

[84] Significantly, primitive uses of pigments, for instance in cave drawings, involved the mixture of pigments with bodily fluids (such as saliva) so as to produce materials for painting, themselves emitted from the body by spitting out of the mouth or smearing by fingers, without mediation of a brush or stick (Jansen 1999, 3).

undecideability (Dayan 1984) are tattoos within the author's flesh which to him as speaking being, being of enjoyment, not consciousness, may be indistinct from the paper on which he writes. Subjective contingency would determine what role tattoos would play in the psychic economy of schizophrenic madness. Tattoos might function as stabilizing limiters of zones of flesh which, in the absence of the imaginary body, might prosthetically turn these zones into pseudo-organs. But in Poe's tale, the only tattoo is question is a "hellish tattoo" (1842, 19): matter alien to the biological organism irrevocably imprinted onto it and subjecting it to infernal torture. In the schizography of Poe and his narrator the dashes qua tattoos violently fragment the already fragmented organism, the *corps morcellé* they ravine, instead of carving up this organism into the organs of an organized imaginary body.

The schizographic, aposiopetic dashes, however, are not the tale's only "hellish tattoo." On the tale's phantasmatic level, the phrase "hellish tattoo" refers not to an epidermal but to an aural torture, to a tattoo not as an indelible mark carved on the flesh but as a drumming or rapping: the narrator's subjection to the incessant *perceptum* of the beating of the dead old man's heart. This aural tattoo is the real object which emerges to torment Poe's narrator from the Other scene opened up beyond the holes the aposiopetic dashes, epidermal tattoos of the author/narrator's schizography, at once mark and mask.

How is this aural tattoo phenomenalized in the tale's representational fabric? Unlike the hallucinated *pièce détachées* in the Schreber case or Lacan's patient presentation, the hallucinated beating of the dead old man's heart is not directly quoted in the text under the veil of a signifier but described indirectly. The only textual components which bespeak the beating's sound do so in onomatopoeic form presentifying its systolic-diastolic rhythm. These are the reference, in mid-tale, to the "hellish *tattoo* of the heart" (Poe 1842, 19, my emphasis) and the tale's title, "The *Tell-Tale* Heart," itself a detached piece with respect to the body of the tale.

These two instances are signifiers (tell-tale, tattoo), perceptually phenomenalizing to the narrator's fictional interlocutor and to the implied reader a real rhythmic substance of the systolic/diastolic or iambic beat (- ¢) they veil. The iambic rhythm of the heart *is* the real phonic substance, the object voice veiled in onomatopeic signifiers and resonating as a heterogeneous *pièce détachée* beyond the graphism of the dashes but thinly covering the holes torn open by foreclosure in the chain of signifiers articulated by the narrator.

Poe's linguistic artistry in the tale consists in phenomenalizing for his implied readers the heart-beat as a hallucinatory *perceptum* without an object it is for the psychotic narrator Moebianly marking his own presence in the tale. Within the cross-cap structure of the tale, the aposiopetic dash as tattoo the psychotic author/narrator would experience as carved into the flesh on which he writes his tale, marks and masks the borders of foreclosure's hole from/in which an onomatopoeic tattoo emerges as an unstoppable audal throbbing.

The topologically entwined epidermal and aural tattoos, graphic and phonic *percepta* are the tale's irreducible, real lit(t)er, the remainder that persists once the fictional world is voided of its phantasmatic unfolding of a paranoid psychosis always already on the verge of collapse into a more primitive schizophrenic psychic organization. The tale's phantasmatic layer involves paranoid passages to the act, (the murder of the old man, the dismemberment of his corpse and the burial of its pieces beneath "the flooring of the chamber" [Poe 1842, 20]), which constitute the narrator's attempts to introduce a prosthetic cut between himself and the object he failed to lose. Such passages to the act occur when the fabric of persecutory delusion, constructed so as to plug up the hole in the unconscious torn open by the operation of foreclosure itself wears thin to the point of tearing as the result of the impingement of what Freud characterizes as components of psychosis whose origin is more archaic than the origin of delusions (1911c, 77). In terms of the structure of paranoia, these attempts to introduce a phenomenal separator where a psychic one is missing are patches placed over the rents in the fabric of delusion. But the tale's schizography, the lit(t)eral manifestation of its constitution as a psychotic artwork, introduces the aposiopetic dash as a real remainder of these imaginary patches precariously placed over the rents in the fabric of the persecutory delusion constructed to plug the hole of foreclosure. This remainder is at once isomorphic with the imaginary patches (in its rectangular shape) and independent of them (as a manifestation of Poe's schizography also in texts, such as "The Raven" or "Annabel Lee," whose phantasmatic layer does not necessarily unfold a paranoid schizophrenia).

Not a stylistic correlate nor a performative manifestation of the passages to the act recounted on the tale's phantasmatic level, the aposiopetic dashes are a real schizographic phenomenon wherein a subject tortured by the signifier, perceived as a phenomenalization of a real object instead of what might protectively veil this object, attempts to use the signifier's graphic substance to fashion a prosthetic bulwark against the real.

But just as in the tale's phantasmatic dimension, the door of the old man's room does not manage to prevent the narrator's intrusion and the floor planks of the same room do not manage, in the narrator's psychotic experience, to silence the sound of the heart, in the tale's topologized schizography (which is nevertheless independent of this phantasmatic dimension) the aposiopetic dashes fail to perform a separating function. For a psychotic author who writes on/in his own flesh, the aposiopetic dashes are a tattoo, an epidermal *ravinement*. The tale's one reference to the tattoo as "hellish" suggests that in his particular case, this *ravinement* is a torture rather than the point of stabilization it might be in other cases of psychosis.

The torture phenomenalized in the tale's schizography by a *perceptum* returning from the real is not limited to the epidermal tattoo constituted by the aposiopetic dashes but extends to the onomatopoeic phonic hallucination the dashes try in vain to keep at bay. Within the tale's topological structure, the dashes function at one and the same time as the borders of the vorticial rents in the fabric of delusion, and as patches attempting to mask these rents but themselves tormenting instead of stabilizing the subject. From within the vortex of the rents in the fabric of delusion, characteristic of a paranoid attempt to re-forge a connection to the Other, a hallucinated auditory perception characteristic of a schizophrenic cathexis of the symbolic as real emerges to torment the subject in the form of an onomatopoeic cadence.

This hallucinatory torment is even more schizophrenic in inflection than the auditory *percepta* in the cases of Schreber or of the woman who had just been to the butcher's. In those two cases from the history of psychoanalysis, hallucinated voices appear veiled in signifiers, even be these signifiers whose status for the subjects who hear them is not the symbolic alterity of the Other but the radical alterity of the real. But on the phantasmatic level of Poe's tale, auditory hallucination does not appear veiled by signifiers. Instead, it is thinly veiled by representational material more logically primordial than the signifier – onomatopoeic words whose function is less to produce signifieds, more to phenomenalize language's real phonic substance, and dashes as part of language's real graphic substance. Phonic and graphic substances veiling the object voice in the phantasmatic level of Poe's tale are language's material but non-signifying substance, a substance which makes representation possible but means nothing in itself.

Poe's title for the tale – "The Tell-Tale Heart" -- hence receives an ironic inflection. Unlike the curse Lacan's patient hears, the hallucinated heartbeat as object voice in Poe's tale is not a "word" which means but a sound which "makes itself heard … in the place where the unspeakable object is rejected in the real" (Lacan 2002c, 448). As a sound, it is inherently meaningless, and the only tale it can tell, to paraphrase Shakespeare's Macbeth, signifies nothing.

The cathexis of the object voice in a less veiled, more raw form than in the case of Schreber or the woman who had just been to the butcher's indicates a torture more primal than the torture usually spoken of in the Lacanian clinic in relation to schizophrenias or schizophrenic elements in paranoid psychoses. This cathexis betrays a subject for whom the unbearable is not the signifier but the very phonic and graphic material from which the signifier is made. The very material substance of language, especially phonic but also graphic, is experienced by the narrator as a "hellish tattoo" (Poe 1842, 19): matter alien to the biological organism irrevocably imprinted onto it and torturing it directly. The auditory hallucination of Poe's narrator, and the relation of this hallucination to the graphism of the dash is part of a schizophrenic phenomenon wherein what fails to bite the living organism is not the signifier as semantized component of the Other but the signifier's very graphic material substance. And if the signifying substance of language is itself the unbearable knowledge that must be foreclosed and cannot cease not being written, how could the imaginary fabric of a paranoid delusion ever subsist untorn?

The infernal torture not only by the signifier but by the non-signifying graphic and phonic material from whence the signifier is made is not only diegetically represented in Poe's tale as part of its fictional world. This torture is manifest in the tale's topologized schizography, the phonic/graphic litter that for the literary analyst, remains once the fictional world is voided of its phantasmatic content, and that for the psychotic author, would have been inseparable from his *bios*.

Graphism produced in a desperate attempt to uphold a delusion but experienced as scorching the flesh, tearing open a vorticial orifice. Within this vorticial orifice torn open by graphism, which the same graphism tries but fails to mask, a rhythmic cadence which cannot be stopped ceaselessly sounds, causing further torment to the already tortured flesh. Such is the impossible lit(t)eral object(s) persisting beyond the traversal and voiding of the phantasmatic layer of Poe's "Tell-Tale Heart," the cross-cap knotting aposiopesis and onomatopoeia in what might be termed the real rhetorical topology of a psychotic alternation between schizophrenic fragmentation and the paranoid delusion this fragmentation always already compromises.

References

Abraham, Nicholas. 1995. *Rhythms: On the work, translation, and psychoanalysis*. Trans. Nicolas Rand. Stanford: Stanford University Press.

Adorno, Theodore. 1991. Punctuation Marks. In *Notes to Literature*. Trans. Shierry Weber Nicholson, 86-91. New York: Columbia University Press.

Barthes, Roland. 1977. The Death of the Author. In *Image, music, text*. Ed. and trans. Stephen Heath, 142-148. New York: Hill and Wang.

Benfey, Christopher. 1993. Poe and the Unreadable: "The Black Cat" and "The Tell-Tale Heart." *New Essays on Poe's Major Tales*. Ed. Kenneth Silverman. Cambridge: Cambridge University Press. 27-44.

Biberman, Efrat, 2008. *Painted Text(a)les; On Gaze and Narrative*. Tel Aviv: Bar Ilan University Press. (In Hebrew).

Bonaparte, Marie. 1949. *The life and works of Edgar Allan Poe: a psychoanalytic interpretation*. Trans. J. Rodker. London: Imago.

Boren, Mark Edelman. 1998. More than a line: The unmistakable impression of significance and the dashes of Henry James. *Philological Quarterly* 770.3: 329-347

Castanet, Hervé, and Alain Merlet. 2004. *Le* choix *de l'*écriture. Paris: Himères

Con Davis, Robert. 1983. Lacan, Poe, and narrative repression. *Modern Language Notes* 98.5: 982-1005.

Crumbley, Paul. 1997. Inflections of the Pen: Dash and Voice in Emily Dickinson. Knoxville: University of Kentucky Press.

Dayan, Joan. 1983. The analytic of the dash: Poe's *Eureka*. *Genre* 16: 437-466

Delesalle, Simone. 2002. Les signes du discours rapporté : Desseins, dessins, destins. *Langages* 147: 39-55

Michel Foucault. 1987. What is an Author? In *Twentieth-Century literary theory*. Ed. Vassilis Lambropoulos and David Neal Miller, 124-142. Albany: State University of New York Press.

Freud, Sigmund. 2001. *The Standard Edition of the Complete Psychological Works of Sigmund Freud*. James Strachey, Trans. (Vols. 1-24). London: Vintage.

—. 1894. The neuro-psychoses of defence. In *Standard Edition,* Vol. 3, 41-61.

—. 1910h. A special type of object choice made by men (contributions to the psychology of love, I). In *Standard Edition*, Vol. 11, 163-176.

—. 1911c. Psychoanalytic notes on a case of paranoia *(Dementia*

Paranoides). Standard Edition, Vol. 12, 9-84.
—. 1914c. On narcissism: an introduction. *Standard Edition*, Vol. 14, 67-104).
—. 1918b. From the history of an infantile neurosis. *Standard Edition*, Vol. 17, 1-122.
—. 1924b. Neurosis and psychosis. *Standard Edition*, Vol. 19, 149-154.
—. 1924e. The loss of reality in neurosis and psychosis. *Standard Edition*. Vol. 19, 183-190.
—. 1924h. Negation. *Standard Edition*, Vol. 19, 235-240.
Genette, Gerard. 1997. *Paratexts: Thresholds of interpretation*. Trans. Richard Maksey. Cambridge: Cambridge University Press.
Jansen, D. 1991. *The history of art*. New Jersey: Prentice Hall.
Kirkland, J. 1999. "The Tell-Tale Heart" as evil eye event. *Southern Folklore* 56.2: 135-147.
Lacan, Jacques. 1962-1963. *The seminar of Jacques Lacan book 10: L'Angoisse*. Trans. Cormak Gallagher. Unpublished typescript.
—. 1965-1966. *The seminar of Jacques Lacan book 13*: *The object of psychoanalysis*. Trans. Cormak Gallagher. Unpublished typescript.
—. 1966-1967. *The seminar of Jacques Lacan book 14*: *The logic of phantasy*. Trans. Cormak Gallagher. Unpublished typescript.
—. 1973. L'Etourdit. *Scilicet* 4, 5-52.
—. 1975a. Écrits "inspires": Schizography. In *De la psychose paranoïaque dans ses rapports avec la personnalité suivi de Premiers écrits sur la paranoïa*, 365-382. Paris: Seuil.
—. 1975b. Le problème du style et la conception psychiatrique des forms paranoïaques de l'expérience. In *De la psychose paranoïaque dans ses rapports avec la personnalité suivi de Premiers écrits sur la paranoïa*, 383-38. Paris: Seuil.
—. 1975-1976. *The seminar of Jacques Lacan book 23: Joyce the sinthome*. Trans. Luke Thurston. Unpublished typescript.
—. 1977. *The seminar of Jacques Lacan book 11: The four fundamental concepts of psychoanalysis.* Trans. Alan Sheridan. New York: Norton.
—. 1991. *The seminar of Jacques Lacan book 1: Freud's papers on technique*. Trans. John Forrester. New York: Norton.
—. 1992 *The seminar of Jacques Lacan book 7: the ethics of psychoanalysis (1959-1960).* Trans. Dennis Porter. New York: Norton.
—. 1993. *The seminar of Jacques Lacan book 3: the psychoses (1954-1955).* Trans. Russell Grigg. New York: Norton.
—. 1994. *Le séminaire de Jacques Lacan livre 4: la relation d'objet (1956-1957)*. Paris: Seuil.

—. 1998. *The seminar of Jacques Lacan book 20: encore (1972-1973).* Trans. Bruce Fink. New York: Norton.
—. 2001. Lituraterre. In *Autres écrits*. Ed. Jacques-Alain Miller, 11-20. Paris. Seuil.
—. 2002a. The function and field of speech and language in psychoanalysis. In *Écrits*. Trans. Bruce Fink, 197-269. New York: Norton.
—. 2002b. The instance of the letter in the unconscious, or reason since Freud. In *Écrits*. Trans. Bruce Fink, 412-444. New York: Norton.
—. 2002c. On a question prior to any possible treatment of psychosis. In *Écrits*. Trans. Bruce Fink, 445-488. New York: Norton.
—. 2002d. The direction of the tyreatment and the principles of its power. In *Écrits*. Trans. Bruce Fink, 489-542. New York: Norton.
—. 2002e. The youth of Gide, or the letter and desire. In *Écrits*. Trans. Bruce Fink, 489-542. New York: Norton.
Laplanche, Jacques. 1961. *Hölderlin et la question du père*. Paris: Presses Universitaires de France.
Laurent, Eric. 1997. On Lacan's "A question preliminary to any possible treatment of psychosis." *Freudian Notebooks* 2-43. (In Hebrew).
Miller, Jacques-Alain. 1987. Sept remarques *de* Jacques-Alain Miller *sur la* création. *Bibliotheque de l'Ecole de la Cause freudienne,* 9-13.
—. 1999. Interpretation in Reverse. *Psychoanalytical Notebooks* 2: 9-16.
—. 2001. Ironic Clinic. Trans. Véronique Voruz and Bogdan Wolf. *Psychoanalytic Notebooks* 7: 9-24.
—. 2003-2004. *Un effort de* poésie. Unpublished seminar. Department of Psychoanalysis, University of Paris VIII.
—. 2004-2005. Pièces détachées. Unpublished seminar. Department of Psychoanalysis, University of Paris VIII.
—. 2005. Lacan with Joyce. *Psychoanalytical Notebooks* 13: 7-34.
Mitchell, W.J.T. 1980. Spatial form in literature: Towards a general theory. *Critical inquiry* 6.3: 539-568.
Montrelay, Michèle. 1967a. Ruptures dans la symbolique. *Cahiers de l'Ecole freudienne de Paris* 3: 70-86.
—. 1967b. L'énoncé en tant que chose. *Cahiers de l'Ecole freudienne de Paris* 4: 71-81.
—. 1977. L'ombre et le nom: *sur la féminité*. Paris: Minuit.
Peacham, Henry. 1971. *The garden of eloquence*. London: Scolar Press.
Poe, Edgar Allan. 1840. "The Imp of the Perverse." *Tales of Mystery and Imagination*. New York: Gramercy Books, 1987, 11-16.
—. 1843. "The Pit and the Pendulum." *Tales of Mystery and Imagination*. New York: Gramercy Books, 1987. 84-97.

—. 1844. “The Premature Burial.” *Tales of Mystery and Imagination*. New York: Gramercy Books, 1987. 42-51.

—. 1842. “The Tell-Tale Heart.” *Tales of Mystery and Imagination*. New York: Gramercy Books, 1987. 17-21.

—. 1969. *Poe's Poems and Essays*. Ed. Andrew Lang. London: Dent.

Puttenham, George. 1968. *The Arte of English Poesie*. London: Scolar Press.

Salecl, Renate. 2003. The real of crime: psychoanalysis and infanticide. *Cardozo Law Review* 24.6: 2467-2480.

Schreber, Daniel Paul. 1955. *Memoirs of my nervous illness*. Trans. Ida Macalpine. London: Dawson and Sons.

Shakespeare, William. 2004. *Macbeth*. Ed. Richard McRoberts. Cambridge: Cambridge University Press.

Sharon-Zisser, Shirley. 2001. *The risks of simile in Renaissance rhetoric*. New York: Lang.

Silverman, Kenneth. 1993. Introduction. In *New Essays on Poe's Major Tales*. Ed. Kenneth Silverman. Cambridge: Cambridge University Press. 1-27.

Soler, Colette. 2001. *L'aventure littéraire, ou la psychose inspirée*. Paris: Editions du Champ lacanien.

Tanselle, G. Thomas. 2000. Emily Dickinson as an editorial problem. *Raritan* 19.4: 64-80.

Tomei, Christine. 1994. Dis/Juncture as a Patterning Principle in Andrej Belyj's Peterburg. *Slavic and East European Journal* 38.4: 603-617

Wilson, Thomas. 1993. *The art of rhetoric*. Ed. Peter Medine. Philadelphia: Pennsylvania State University Press

Zimmermann, Brett. 2005. *Edgar Allan Poe: Rhetoric and Style*. Toronto: McGill-Queen's Press.

SECTION III.

KEY CONCEPTS

CHAPTER EIGHT

INTRODUCING...THE *OBJET PETIT C*: LACANIAN MATERIALITY AND THE SOCIETY OF THE SINTHOME

MICHAEL ANGELO TATA

For Jacques Lacan, the *objet* comes to mark that matter which cannot be dissolved or further reduced to some other more primary substance, as discussed throughout the dual modes of his speech (the Seminars) and writing (the *Écrits*), and as further expounded upon by his most lucid commentator, Slavoj Zizek, in his *Sublime Object of Ideology* and *The Fragile Absolute*, among other of his texts taking as their problem the fraught relationship among self, society and satiation which Lacan first introduces in his thought.[1] While at first glance it might appear that the *objet*'s indissolubility might be the product of its rarefaction or perfection,

[1] I distinguish the speech and writing of Lacan from one another because of Lacan's own theories of the gulf separating the two, especially in light of the alliance between speech and Demand/appeal. It is fascinating to see Lacan's speech become text in the Seminars, with all relevant philosophical difficulties—for example, when we balance his views on syncopation against Jacques-Alain Miller's valiant attempts to textualize Lacan. For Lacan, "Punctuation, once inserted, establishes the meaning; changing the punctuation renews or upsets it; and incorrect punctuation distorts it" ("The Function and Field of Speech and Language in Psychoanalysis," *Écrits*, (96)). Miller, "in an attempt to render the inflexions of Lacan's speech...," duly confines himself "...to the use of the comma, the full-stop, the dash and the paragraph," and is "particularly anxious that this practice be maintained in the translation" ("Translator's Note," *Seminar XI*, 277). What light does this interplay shed on "the syncope of discourse" and its connection to desire, presumably via syncopation ("The Freudian Unconscious and Ours," *Seminar XI*, 26)? Throughout, my sources for these and other Lacanian writings are *The Four Fundamental Concepts of Psychoanalysis/Seminar XI*, trans. Jacques-Alain Miller (NY: W.W. Norton & Co., Inc, 1998) and *Écrits, A Selection*, trans. Bruce Fink (W.W. Norton & Co., Inc, 2002).

as if it could not be boiled down or atomized any further due to a quasi-chemical simplicity rendering it irreducible, what quickly becomes apparent is that it is the very unreality of the objet which permits it to exist as self-sustaining quiddity which no power can corrode from without and no lysosome destroy from within. In other words, its existence is both phantastic, in the Lacanian sense, and phantasmagoric, in the Benjaminian sense, the combination of these two intensities placing the *objet* within that portion of the real marked unreal, i.e., that junction between the place we always come back to, and the place we can never arrive at because its geography is purely speculative.[2]

Within this troubling dynamic, objects do not perish, even in obsolescence or annihilation; they merely lose their positioning as outposts of our desire, as human drives pursue other courses and race around fresh impediments and obstacles they mistake for the aim of various desires—a path best represented by the loop of desire Lacan sketches out in "The Partial Drive and Its Circuit" (*Seminar XI*). With all these object-taking drives, desire pursues an oblique path marked by the epithet "La pulsion en fait la tour," or "The drive passes around the object" ("The Deconstruction of the Drive," *Seminar XI*, 168). Hence to use Lacan's language from the concluding remarks of a seminar dedicated to exposing the groundwork of psychoanalysis in general, it is the "in you more than you" of the unreal object which supervenes above any natural thingness to generate a fantastic entity which sets and keeps in motion a perpetual desire for an incomprehensible more: all objects are structured as such, transcending the limits of their immanence with the vague promise that they not only offer something excessive, but that they contain the secret of being, knowledge they will quite felicitously cede to us, if only we absorb them into the field of our *Triebs* and surrender to their perfections. Unreal and fictive, yet with historical consequences nonetheless, these materializations hover above the realm of the Real, haunting it with holographs of presence which never fail to ensnare the split subject with the false spectacle of their wholeness, the most enticing fantasy for this strange being whose existence is a *manqué*.

And yet this manqué quickly reverses its polarity such that it becomes that very dense nugget of *res extensa* typified by the *objet*, a phenomenon underscoring an important internal relation between the *objet a* and the commodity proper. Hence in this paper I will define and describe the node of substance I dub the *objet petit c*, or that mystical and magical bit of

---

[2] "Here, the real is that which always comes back to the same place—to the place where the subject in so far as he thinks, where the *res cogitans*, does not meet it" ("Of the Network of Signifiers," *Seminar XI*, 49).

meta-material which the media in its many instantiations offers to me as false point of satiety. The support of my desire, even the desire of my desire, the *objet petit c* has always been with us; and yet it is primarily within capitalism that it is revealed as strangely allied with the *objet a*, which has always been intimately related to the human subject's tendency to couple fragmentation with overcompensation. As it is in reading Zizek's Lacan that I have formulated this concept—much as it is Kojève's Hegel that brings us so much Critical Theory—I offer the following itinerary: first an examination of what the *objet petit a* means to Lacan, then a discussion of what it means to Zizek and how this particular interpretation has produced in me the desire to refashion contemporary object relations by pointing to an elementary commodity-like quality in the *object petit a*, one which has always been of a piece with the modern and postmodern amassing of capital, with its pulsation between evacuation and overindulgence, desire and disappointment, wish and witchcraft. Along the way, it will be intermittently necessary to introduce concepts by Sartre, Leibniz, Laclau, Caillois, Kant and others, particularly as their ideas speak to Lacan's and he to theirs. With this constellation, I can proceed, investigating Lacan's investigation and examining how the *objet c* works to structure desire, pleasure and psychosis in this Versailles of screens we call the present.

Little Ambassadors of Nothingness

The plenitudinousness of the odd material speck or ontological "bone in the throat" known as the *objet* contrasts sharply with the utter eradication of the unified subject, who exits the loop of the final version of the Graph of Desire presented in "The Subversion of the Subject and the Dialectic of Desire in the Freudian Unconscious" (*Écrits*) as an entity split both from itself as well as from a gargantuan and all-encompassing Other which can only offer symbolic castration and the reconfiguration of the body into rimmy oases of pleasure among a fleshy sea of sexual inertness. Unless, of course, one is a pervert—then anything goes, as the *méconaissance* of drives causes satisfaction to appear in the oddest places (fragments of the body, inorganic substitutes for the flesh, synchronic residues). Separated from a primal *jouissance* to which it can never return if only because it is one of the sustaining fantasies of the Law, which always maintains a relation to a promise of unboundedness in order to energize those it governs with the false hope that, elsewhere, a desire that is not founded in lack flowers, this split subject confronts a world of glistening objects appearing to exist in unfounded ontic bliss. Through this critical blunder, the *sujet barré* inaugurates its perpetual search for the solidity of an identity which will ever elude it: a search beginning with that subject's first true object, the asymptotal mirror image, *i(a)*, as it supervenes resplendent and complete. In this ideal form, it taunts the prematurely-born human child with visions of a splendor it can never "be," but might be able to "have," much in the way that, via sexuation, women may become the phallus via "seeming" (e.g., masquerade).[3]

What does not find itself eluded in this circuit is the identity of the *objet*, that particulate entity forever flaunting its concreteness and material satiation as both a challenge to *assujetissement* and as an aesthetic encapsulation of monadic splendor. And it is Leibniz's monad and no other that Lacan has in mind with regard to the *objet a*'s totality, by which I mean: the monad as the worldly microcosm of total existence, not the discrete and isolated essence for which it is so often mistaken. This popular misconception which has accompanied the reception history of the monad like a dark shadow is somewhat reversed by a Lacanian dynamic attempting to rehabilitate the monad's stretch, work continued by the political theory of Ernesto Laclau, whose appeal to the category of the universal recalls that ontological massiveness of the monad known to Lacan: "…The impossibility of a universal ground does not eliminate its need: it just transforms the ground into an empty place which can be partially filled in a variety of ways (the strategies of this filling is what politics is about)" (*Emancipations*, 59).[4] As with Laclau's contingently hegemonic particular raised to the status of the universal, the self, too,

---

[3] "The objective notions of the anatomical incompleteness of the pyramidal tracts and of certain humoral residues of the maternal organism in the newborn confirm my view that we find in man a veritable *specific prematurity of birth*" ("The Mirror Stage as Formative of the *I* Function," *Écrits*, 6). And again: "The struggle that gives rise to this slavery is rightly called a struggle of pure prestige, and what is at stake—life itself—is well suited to echo the danger of the generic prematurity of birth, which Hegel was unaware of, and which I have situated as the dynamic mainspring of specular capture" ("The Subversion of the Subject," 296).

[4] "If we have a *system* of differences A/B/C, etcetera, we have to account for this systematic dimension and that leads us straight into the discourse of ground. If we have a *plurality* of separate elements A, B, C, etcetera, which do not constitute a system, we still have to account for this separation—to be separated is also a form of relation between objects—and we are again entangled, as Leibniz knew well, in the positing of a ground." Hence, "the only way out of this dilemma is to maintain the dimension of universality but to propose a different form for its articulation with the particular" (58). See Ernesto Laclau, *Emancipations* (London: Verso, 2007), as well as his and Chantal Mouffe's *Hegemony and Socialist Strategy: Toward a Radical Democratic Politics* (NY: Verso, 2001).

must will itself into historicity, coming into concreteness only through an aggressive and ambivalent relationship to this thing seeming to show it another way of existing. For Laclau's partial fillings and provisional totalities gel with the openness of the human subject's project in creating and consuming its many *a*'s, underscoring the fact that the *a* hides its emptiness through a very convincing appeal to totality, one equally relevant to politics and psychoanalysis.

Inspiring a sort of borderline personality disorder upon the fractured and frustrated subject—and here we must recall that for Lacan, "frustration" is one of the critical categories missing from the Freudian lexicon—the *objet*, always a sort of commodity even before it becomes one officially through the charmed touch of capital, presents a tempting prospect: that of an inhuman glamour transcending all attempts at articulation or exfoliation. Yet though it transcends its borders, and in some ways captures the monad's elasticity as well as its logic of partial wholeness, the *objet a* is still described by Lacan largely in the inorganic language of the rock or stopper: and so the rather bland, indiscriminate *objet* of Lacanian analysis, a nullity achieving an abstract entification never solid enough to be meaningful, and representing the confusion of various genera, recoils, revealing the true luxuriousness of its multiplicity. In Zizek, it is upgraded to the commodity proper, capitalism's supreme, even sublime, object, and truly the nutritive matrix without which there would be no ideology. As the contents of popular culture reveal, the little object acts as support to an almost pornographic gaze, lifting up and fixing the eye's emanating rays, giving them an ideal focus and an impetus to feed on fresh spectacles: hence Linda Williams' analysis of "the frenzy of the visible" in her sustained gaze at the porn industry in *Hard Core*, as well as Sartre's own theory of the sadomasochistic content of the gaze in his *Being and Nothingness*, according to which two potential subjects battle to turn the other into an object through the Medusan coldness of the look.

Furthermore, with the Existential Psychoanalysis Sartre presents at the end of his *Being and Nothingness*, there is an even more vicious version of materiality and subjectivity which cannot *not* have influenced Lacan: the dueling poles of subject and object, or *l'être pour soi* and *l'être en soi*, provide a new wrinkle, adding solidity to Sartre's version of what an existential psychoanalysis might involve in terms of which fantasies it must dispel within the subject who many times wishes for little more than to become an object. For the Sartrian ego within the loop of *Ipsétité*, or the circuit of selfness, it is through a shocking feat of *mauvaise foi* that the *pour soi* comes to envy the *en soi* its self-sufficiency, nonchalance, and *selbständigkeit,* or self-sufficiency, with the result being that a new class of beings emerges: the In-itself-for-itself, or that creature vapid enough to will itself into non-existence, a sort of Estelle looking into the eyes of others if only to find the right perspective from which her contours close in upon themselves and her objecthood is sealed off as false monad, or alternately an Anny whose map of bodies and instrumentalities necessitates the freezing of flesh into tableaux representing "privileged situations" turned "perfect moments" via moral impulse, and as such the ideal antithesis to Sartre's own skepticism regarding the temporality of instantaneousness.[5] For only the for-itself can exist; unable to exhibit choice, the non-porous in-itself can inhabit space and time, and can star in any number of hodological maps or Gestalts, but it cannot exist in a philosophically meaningful way—yet the rub is that this mode of existence becomes desirable for the radically open human being, who wishes for nothing more than to trade its freedom for confinement. This perversion Lacan clearly comprehends, in his own way elaborating upon it via the melodramas of the identification process, through which closed objects and open subjects find themselves distributed among a system of knots knitting together various realms of affect and sensation in suffocating configurations.

[5] My reference is to the character Estelle from Sartre's *No Exit* in his *No Exit and Three Other Plays* (NY: Vintage International, 1989). Her worldview is not dissimilar to Anny's in *Nausea*, for whom there are both "privileged situations" and "perfect moments." Anny's example of a privileged situation is an illustrated page from Michelet's *History of France*, a sort of visual miracle "full of grandeur" (209-210). Examples include "to be a king" or "to die" (210). After a few "annunciatory signs," the privileged situation begins to take shape, potentially becoming a perfect moment: "First you had to be plunged into something exceptional and felt that you were putting it in order. If all these conditions had been fulfilled, the moment would have been perfect" (212). See Jean-Paul Sartre, *Nausea*, trans. Robert Baldick (Middlesex: Penguin Books, 1965). For Sartre's views on the in-itself-for-itself, see *Being and Nothingness:* "The for-itself as the nihilation of the in-itself temporalizes itself as a *flight forward.* Actually it surpasses its facticity (*i.e.,* to be either *given* or past or body) toward the in-itself which it would be if it were able to be its own foundation…Thus the for-itself is both a flight and a pursuit; it flees the in-itself and at the same time pursues it. The for-itself is a pursued-pursuing" ("Concrete Relations with Others," 472). Within Sartre's temporality, the problem with the momentary is that "the instantaneous island of the present" is able to establish no positive or productive connection to the past it discards or the future it becomes, thereby bypassing the unity and interpenetration which are the foundations of temporal ecstasy ("Temporality," 159). See *Being and Nothingness*, trans, Hazel E. Barnes (NY: Washington Square Press, 1992).

Within the current scene of celebrity-mongering and enrapturement by the images circulated by Hollywood and Madison Avenue, the split subject of Lacan and Sartre finds itself in the position of even more manically sifting through potential identities, none of which can ever achieve the magical work of healing the subject/subject rift. These extrinsic identities, Laclauian partial totalities that they are, circulate wildly among a capitalist regime which enshrines the inhuman and recasts the human physique as corpselike, chemical and inorganic (for example, the Nicole Ritchie or Mary-Kate Olson body) or as supremely robotic (the Mario Lopez body). How is the human being with its deep psychological bifurcation to respond when asked to consume these strange creatures, all of whom appear to begin and end in themselves and to rely on no foundational principles, to respond? Dominique Bouhours' use of the aesthetic void represented by the unspeakableness and ineffability of the *je ne sais quoi* in the seventeenth century speaks to the current position of the body within the various aesthetic networks in which it is imbricated and from whose chaos it emerges as a compromise. Within this context, the feminist critique of the fashion industry as being inherently misogynistic and schizophrenogenic finds itself reformulated as a larger interrogative inquiring as to what aesthetic possibilities can exist for any split subject, while the Marxist critique of the commodity finds itself miraculously infused with intrasubjective desire, since the larger psychoanalytic question becomes how, indeed, the commodity comes to exert such charisma.

Ultimately, it is the unutterableness of the *objet petit a* which poses the greatest danger to the split subject on its aesthetic odyssey: the greatest danger, yet also the most pleasure (*plaisir*). Resonating wildly with the sinthome, or the symptom reintegrated within the field of enjoyment and preventing the rings of the Borromean knot from unraveling, the objet fractures the body and jouissance of the Other, offering palliative parcels of pleasure that distract and dispossess: hence, their irrepressible charm as metonymic chain of wonders. Positive uses of an abnegated subjectivity—for example, those of Madonna Ritchie or Cindy Sherman—promise a postmodern distribution of the in-ideal ego's energy among so many tempting packages, all of which converge on a rich nothingness. This rich nothingness is the *je ne sais quoi* in its postmodern reconfiguration as stream of individual little objects whose ineluctability becomes the occasion of their celebrity, leaving the split subject to shop for identities at malls warm with the glow of mammoth cinnamon buns and at Web sites whose words and images are suspended on the generous buoyancy of a cybernetic ether. Thickening into the dense sphere of space at the center of a toroid, this objet topologically inhabits the impossible and unreal no-man's land that is the exact opposite of discourse: filling in the lack of discourse's ring, it becomes the lack of lack for a self whose aphanisis has undergone aphanisis.[6] The dual motions of discourse—the two circular motions without which there would be no torus, only an annulus—touch the object only at the fringes of its matter, as it rotates on its own axis, uninterested in anything outside of its own motion and the brute laws of social physics.

I♥*a*: Rubbing the Agalma Raw

In Lacan, the powers of the object are underestimated—or rather, the object is not properly differentiated into the various classes that objects can claim as their own, sometimes being the aim of a drive bent on biological satiation (the bad breast), other times fulfilling no physiological aim whatsoever, yet in its gratuitousness mobilizing desire just the same (the commodity or 'c' form of the *objet*). On rare occasions, this object may even become a repository of my affections, as my narcissistic attachment to my mirror image releases me from its spell and I am at liberty to make myself lovable to another, while the introduction of the electronic object, or what I term the e-ject, within the striking range of my desire dictates an entirely novel conception of identity, one according to which the virtual assumes the features of the real. In the final toll, only one seminar is dedicated to the object, "La Relation d'Objet" (Seminar IV), and this speech-act has not made even a dent in theorizing the radically open ontology of the things-of-the-world. In its most basic function, the *objet* exists for Lacan as a very banal plug stopping up the open loop of identification, as in the diagram of the Hoop Net in "Analysis and Truth" (*Seminar XI*), according to which the *objet a* plugs up an open psychic oval—here, the unconscious—endowing it with a momentary sense of completeness. In this schema, "We can conceive of the unconscious through the effect of something that plays the role of obturator—the *objet a*, sucked, breathed, into the orifice of the net. You can draw an image like those great balls in which the number to be drawn in a lottery are enclosed" (145).

Within this paradigm, the object achieves the function of a Lotto ball, only the prize is not Cash for Life, but rather the diminishment of anxiety

[6] "If I wanted to give an intuitive representation of it [speech], it seems that I would have to resort not to the two-dimensionality of a zone, but rather to the three-dimensional form of a torus, insofar as a torus' peripheral exteriority and central exteriority constitute but one single region" ("The Function and Field of Speech and Language in Psychoanalysis," 102).

accompanying the transitory blockage of the unconscious, which is momentarily tricked into feeling its circuitry closed, its Aegean shutters pulled in tight against sea breezes and catcalls from the street. Elsewhere, the object finds itself distributed throughout the field of the imaginary, where it becomes a point of gravitation, or even mesmerization, as with the use Lacan makes of the diagram of the Freudian Ego Ideal from *Group Psychology and the Analysis of The Ego,* according to which *Verliebtheit*, or overvaluation, produces a hypnotic effect, as well as with his own short-circuiting of symbolic identification via the homunculus *i(a)* produced through imaginary identification in the lower portion of his Graph of Desire.[7] Borrowing much of its occultation from *l'Autre,* a symbolic totality whose operations intimately involve and capture us, yet do not appear to live through any concrete formation accessible to empirical analysis, and which, in the end, does not exist at all, except through its little emissaries of otherness, little a splits off from big A, causing desire to circulate and the drives to aim their quiver at things external to them.

Yet since the drive's aim is the drive itself, the role of the *objet* becomes increasingly precarious the more investigation one conducts. Lacan does not waver: the drive takes for its pleasure the drive itself, using the *objet* as support or false cause. In this schema, the drive passes around the object, returning to its own autoerotic pleasure, while the object is touched, not consumed, in essence left intact and unprocessed, apart from whatever fibers from its surface are shaken loose through contact:

> In any case, what makes us distinguish this satisfaction [oral satisfaction] from the mere auto-eroticism of the erogenous zone is the object that we confuse all too often with that upon which the drive closes—this object, which is in fact simply the presence of a hollow, a void, which can be occupied, Freud tells us, by any object. It is for and whose agency we know only in the form of the lost object, the *petit a.* The *objet petit a* is not the origin of the oral drive. It is not introduced as the original food, it is introduced from the fact that no food will ever satisfy the oral drive, except by circumventing the eternally lacking object ("The Partial Drive," 180).

Consequently, all drives are partial drives, and all objects "partial objects," only not in the sense intended by Mélanie Klein or Object Relations theory: "For isn't it plain to see that the characteristic of being partial, rightly emphasized in objects, is applicable not because these objects are part of a total object, which the body is assumed to be, but because they

[7] See Sigmund Freud, *Group Psychology and the Analysis of The Ego*, trans. James Strachey (NY: W.W. Norton & Co., 1989).—specifically, the chapter "Being in Love and Hypnosis" (54-61).

only partially represent the function that produces them?" ("Subversion," 303).

For Lacan, only the propensity to procreate, not really much of a drive at all, but more of a blind inclination, can be "full," since it takes as its object something very particular and material: the zygote. This version of sexuality is not particularly exciting, though, since it introduces biological finality merely as counterpoint to the openness of the drives proper, making reproductive coupling a matter of instinct or physiological destiny in which the manqué proper is not involved: "If the drive may be satisfied without attaining what, from the point of view of a biological totalization of function, would be the satisfaction of its end of reproduction, it is because it is a partial drive, and its aim is simply this return into circuit" (179). Like drives outside of the urge to reproduce, objects, too, are partial, but not because they fail at the game of totalization: rather, the object is partial because it implies other objects, all of which slide along their network via the machinations of *glissement*, or low-friction sliding typified by the network of Signifiers. As with the signifier, the object implies a function to which we will be subjected via the logic of defilement. Like the Signifier, which also lives metonymically, the objet cannot exist in isolation. To this description I would add: also like the Signifier, which represents me for other Signifiers, it objectifies me for other objects, representing me to them as the object I so desperately wish to become, encapsulated, bounded, whole. Beyond Lacanian theory, I wonder: Is this putative correspondence the revenge of the Signified? The resurgence of a thingness missing from the Lacanian system? What is clear is that what is *not* at stake in Lacanian signification is a simple match between word and thing, or even a relation among things, but rather the interconnection of differences and the play of their surfaces, a numerology less cardinal, more ordinal, yet beckoning to Set Theory nonetheless. The failure of the Saussurian bar to signify mystifies the *Ding*, leaving it on the far side of a patch of dark matter, only able to communicate obliquely with drives racing around it for their own base intents and purposes.

Foundational to Lacanian psychodynamics is the signifying chain itself, a stream beginning with the primary signifier and passing directly to that signifier associated with *Vorstellungrepräsentanz*, or the representing representation, that one act of signification which reveals to us the secrets of signification proper and which is not unlike Sartre's idea of consciousness as reflection-reflecting (*reflet-reflétant*): i.e., that for Lacan, the signifier represents me to other signifiers, as opposed to busying itself with the tedious semiotic work of a Signifier-Signified correspondence. Extending this idea to the object and its imaginary fiefdom, I would make the following adjustment to Lacan: that it is the object which both objectifies me for its fellow objects, while deconcealing the mystery of its essence as stashed within the *agalma*, or hidden treasure; in other words, that there is an objectifying object, parallel to the representing representation, and that it is this thing among others which holds the system together and mandates the riveting of my desire to any of the trinkets which my eye will soon confront. Signification defiles me because it castrates me, symbolically pinning me down and manipulating the range of my possibilities such that I will have to disavow aspects of myself, as Judith Butler has certainly not lost sight of, thereby dictating which kinds of signification I can effect for myself and others, as well as which kinds of identity will be made available to me.[8] As I, traveling around the Lacanian circuit detailed by the Graph of Desire, intersect language and its symbolic function, I lose something, and as a result of that loss become permanently split down the middle, literalizing Aristophanes' myth from *Symposium*.

For Lacan, the quantum I shed as I accede to selfhood is the strange creature known only as the lamella. It is perhaps the loss of lamella which both plummets me into the depths of sexuality while at the same time drawing me a little closer to death. Clearly, Lacan's lamella and Freud's *Todestrieb* have important business to conduct jointly, and it is by retaining the lamella that reproduction proceeds asexually and neither sex nor death are introduced: presumably, the paramecium will live forever, although it will not attain consciousness of that life as it sends out more and more copies of itself through conjugation. The lamella can only be described through apologue: "The lamella is something extra-flat, which moves like the amoeba. It is just a little more complicated. But it goes everywhere. And as it is something—I will tell you shortly why—that is related to what the sexed being loses in sexuality, it is, like the amoeba in relation to sexed beings, immortal—because it survives any division, any scissiparous intervention. And it can run around" ("From Love to Libido," *Seminar XI,* 197). Like the libido, the lamella is an organ; in fact, lamella and libido are at times described as being one and the same, and hence presumably both masculine. As embodied and crystallized *élan vital*, the lamella-libido "is precisely what is subtracted from the living being by virtue of the fact that it is subject to the cycle of sexed reproduction" (198). Thenceforward, the *objet a* will represent and plug the loss it introduces, functioning as representative of the lost quantity: "The *objets a*

[8] See paramountly "Phantasmatic Identification and the Assumption of Sex" in Judith Butler's "Bodies that Matter: On the Discursive Limits of 'Sex'" (NY: Routledge, 1993).

are merely its representatives, its figures. The breast—as equivocal, as an element characteristic of the mammiferous organization, the placenta for example —certainly represents that part of himself that the individual loses at birth, and which may serve to symbolize the most profound lost object" (198). And since "the lamella has a rim," it is clear that its insertion into the erogenous zone demarcates a fantastic range of plugs, organic and synthetic, through which an organic lost wholeness comes into view only to recede ever further into the distance (200).

Within this world, the object hides within the envelope of its skin the magic of the *agalma*, that unknown and infinitely desirable quantity which one can reach only through acts of fury and frottage. With regard to this lost and inaccessible treasure, the paradigmatic example is Socrates' charm, that in-gadfly-more-than-gadfly making him so desirable to Alcibiades in the reversed pederasty of their sexual and epistemological dynamic. Whether or not the other's diminished and diminutive messenger contains the agalma, we will never know, yet it is as if it does, positively stuffed with wonders and marvels making out own lack as split subjects appear that much more pathetic and empty. For Socrates, essentially the first psychoanalyst, the love affair with Alcibiades takes a wicked turn: "Included in the objet a is the agalma, the inestimable treasure that Alcibiades declares is contained in the rustic box the figure of Socrates is to him. But let us note that a minus sign (-) is attributed to it. It is because Alcibiades has not seen Socrates' prick—permit me to follow Plato here, who does not spare us the details—that Alcibiades the seducer exalts in Socrates the agalma, the marvel that he would have liked Socrates to cede to him by avowing his desire" ("Subversion," 310). Within this context, the agalma is the imaginary number represented by *i* which for Lacan comes to mark the absence of the phallus; equated to √(-1), the "erectile organ" through its symbolic functioning represents the place of jouissance by virtue of its quantitative impossibility: hence Alcibiades' sudden launch into the mathematics of the imaginary It is this in-x-more-than-x which causes me to mutilate the object, as I rub it harder and harder in a doomed attempt to force the release of its contents to me, in my inescapable scissiparity.

What I must come to realize is that the objet will never release its agalma to me, even if it releases its agalma to me through acts of torture or altruism: for how do I know this is the right agalma, or that there is not more to the agalma than I am being shown or allowed to taste, or that it is not an agalmic impostor? As the Lacanian structure for phantasy reveals, my only connection to the object will be through a recurrent hurling of the bulk of my being against it, only to bounce back, as I engage in the oceanic rhythm of object-Lust. All in all, I posit that there is only as much agalma as there is jouissance, each functioning as one of Cantor's infinities: in other words, I have access to neither, and can only speculate as to what I am missing, the agalma a point acting as eccentric center of the function known as *jouissance*. As the work of Zizek will soon be shown to demonstrate, of all objects, the commodity best performs the work of amalgamating my desire for various agalmic substances and coordinating it with my drift toward the jouissance of the other through the exquisite pleasures of the sinthome, my unrequitable love and lust becoming a symptom I can hopefully learn to enjoy, much as Alcibiades must expect little more than blue balls from Socrates, and yet find the pain and discomfort they afford somehow sufficient.

Awful Offal: Becoming an Object-among-Objects

As I have discussed in the previous section, apart from being a stand-in for an excised lamella and frustrating referent to an irretrievable agalma seeming to conceal the *gnosis* of existence behind impermeable walls of obturation, the object fulfills an even more vital and prestigious role: that of representing objecthood itself to the human being whose gaze incorporates it into an ocular field, anamorphic or otherwise. As such, it runs parallel to the representing representation as the objectification which brings me the object's possibility and which makes me an object-among-objects. Even Lacan is drawn peculiarly to this mode of the object, although for him, it is the object's relation to light which illuminates the path of his desire, as it is through the reflection and refraction of rays that the object catches an observer's attention by way of the dual logics of *trompe l'oeil* and *dompte-regard*, mechanisms by which the gaze is alternately tricked and tamed, in each instance submitting to the visual contents which have lured it into tranquility and docility.

In his story of Petit-Jean and the Sardine Can in "The Line and Light" (*Écrits*), itself another apologue proper, and one I am drawn to inescapably, object-Lust appears through Lacan's nauseating attraction to a random sardine can floating in the Atlantic. This metal object is clearly an analogue to the stone setting so much of Sartre's *Nausea* in motion, only in this instance, the autonomous object, little more than the afters of an oceanside *pique-nique*, performs two critical tasks: (1) it is not repulsive at all, but infinitely fascinating, and hence exerts a species of gravity, and (2) it 'watches' observers who think it is they doing the observing, causing the unnerving quality it shares with all matter to come to the forefront. Consequently, within the context of Lacanian analysis, it raises particularly urgent questions about mimicry vis-à-vis legendary psychaesthenia, as Roger Caillois has famously posed the problem. Since Caillois' Surreally entomological version of this extreme solution to the crisis of identity and difference has influenced Lacan's own theories immearurably, for me it serves as exclusive entry point to the sardine incident.[9] For the sardine, too, is an ocellus straight out of Caillois, and like the eye-spot so central to Lacan's metaphysics of the gaze, it sees despite its blindness, trucking not with travesty, camouflage or intimidation, modes of mimicry outlined by Caillois in his *Mask of Medusa*, but with the sensual dominance of vision and our own need to be rendered an object visually.

Lacan's story goes as follows: while caught up in his own mania to "get away, see something different" and throw himself "into something practical, something physical, in the country, say, or at the sea," the young Lacan stumbles upon one of the most important and uncanny visual scenes of his career, all through the intervention of the seafaring Petit-Jean, who, "like all his family," perished "very young from tuberculosis, which at that time was a constant threat to the whole of that social class" (95). Respiratory casualty, Petit-Jean dies from the type of illness to which his stratum is susceptible, eradicated by the time of the story's telling during Lacan's Seminar in 1976, where for an audience filled with people not of Petit-Jean's caste the sailor cannot survive his own irritating insightfulness, entering the present through his disappearance into a sea of tubercular corpses and his survival as pure sobriquet. Back in the past, Petit-Jean uses his powers of observation to throw the young Lacan's visual register out of whack, raising important questions about what kind of object I am for the *objet a*, in addition to highlighting the fact that the gaze itself might function as *objet a*, its rays transfixing; the sardine can he points out floating in the waters lapping at the shores of Brittany, like the "hairy athlete" who fills the voyeur with shame as he gazes through the Sartrian keyhole aiming to catch an illicit glimpse of "the most graceful of girls" only to have his heterosexuality razed, pulverizes the visual faculty in general, opening it up to further scrutiny regarding what it can accomplish ("The Partial Drive," 182). As the tiny piece of slag, to use Lacan's preferred word for junk, floated past, Petit-Jean uttered his fateful words, an *énonciation* for the ages: "*You see that can? Do you see it? Well, it doesn't see you.*" ("The Line and Light," 95).

---

[9] For a seminal discussion of the disturbance between organism and milieu which makes psychasthenia "legendary" in the first place, See Callois' essay "Mimicry and Legendary Psychasthenia" (*Minatoure* 7, 1935).

Petit-Jean's words instantly reverse their course, as it becomes clear to Lacan that the waterborne repository of fishy remains either can see him, or at bare minimum orchestrate his very visibility for the benefit of others, since here, there is no disappearance into an environment, as happens through psychaesthenia or mimicry: "To begin with, if what Petit-Jean said to me, namely, that the can did not see me, had any meaning, it was because in a sense, it was looking at me all the same. It was looking at me at the level of the point of light, the point at which everything that looks at me is situated—and I am not speaking metaphorically" (95). Arriving from the periphery to maul the center of a geometral map legislating punctiform identity and a vision accessible even to the blind—that is, a gross combination of objects and distances, as opposed to an expansive field—the salty can buoyed up by even saltier waters underscores the fact that the composition of the geometral or anamorphic map relies too heavily upon a perceiving *cogito*, and that, in the final wash, this configuration of space only comprises a fraction of the gaze's domain: "This is something that introduces what was elided in the geometral relation—the depth of field, with all its ambiguity and variability, which is in no way mastered by me" (96). To this observation, I would add, especially in light of my remarks in the previous section about the objectifying objectification, that it is exactly as if the sardine can see me, emerging from dark space with a light I find unbearable. For even an object as lowly as this bit of metal emptied of all contents and left to be carried away by the currents, I am something. I, too, am an object, a slaggy residue navigating my own ontic waters and hence subject to the gazes of others, even when those others are sardine cans that cannot possibly see me yet whose collective gaze freezes me on the spot.

In this myth, the scopic drive, like all drives, reveals its workings, the strange oscillation which will obtain between the split subject and the intact object, a back-and-forth motion that marks the course of phantasy and its engagement of the lack of lack embodied by the object (Sartre's stone, Lacan's sardine can). As in Sartre, I come to lust after the object because it does what in life I never can: it coincides with its borders and boundaries, alive with this lack of living that constitutes the thing. The matheme for phantasy in general is succinct and elegant, and marks a dual pathway by which a thrust and a return situate me in a schizoid relationship with the thing I pursue, whether it be a stone, tin can or idealized ego: S◊*a* Related to the circuit connecting the I function with its first true object, an f(a) fast becoming an i(a), the mirror image taunting its premature inchoateness with the fullness of the specular, the lozenge, or double vel, syncs up a lacking subject with a self-sufficient object through the double motion of attraction and repulsion, itself a bizarre courtship of the inert, even when the *objet* is sentient. Through the propulsion of the first vel, I am drawn to the object, yet in my irrepressible drift experience the loss of selfhood Ernest Jones first theorized as aphanisis in his 1929 paper "Fear, Guilt and Hate." Hence along the way to my desire's support, I disappear into the lumen separating nothingness from everythingness, infatuated by this bright item throwing both my visual field and identity as master of that field in relief: through alienation, I disappear.

Yet the vel returns, only in an inverted form, mandating my recoil from the object, a course having the effect of instilling a permanent gulf between a self which suddenly reappears and an object which it can neither assimilate nor emulate: at this moment, alienation becomes separation, and I am taken away from even the comforts of my evanescence. Through the intercession of this second vel, I materialize, but only through the gaps in my existence; the "either/or" of the vel as logical function becomes the "neither/nor" of separated existence, with my only option being to hurl the mass of my being up against this or another object in an ultimately autistic game of ravishment. The polar opposite of the *Vorstellungrepräsentanz,* the subject's desire for an other (or another) "is the non-representative representative" ("Aphanisis," *Seminar XI*, 218). In other words, "The subject—by a process that is not without deception, which is not without presenting that fundamental twist by which what the subject rediscovers is not that which animates his movement of rediscovery—comes back, then, to the initial point, which is that of his lack as such, of the lack of his *aphanisis*" (219).

The lozenge dictating the double movement of these vels alto ties to another lozenge, one which also bears relevance to Lacanian materiality: that perforating the R Schema Lacan uses to spatialize psychotic speech in his analysis of Schreber's torrid language in "On a Question Prior to Any Possible Treatment of Psychosis" (*Écrits*). In this scenario, it is what I would term the Mimi Box which schematizes the behavior of imaginary identification and objecthood, specifically as these relate to –[Φ], the negative quantity without which the subject's manifestation as lack would make no sense whatsoever, and without which the disappearance of the master signifier from the symbolic economy would be meaningless, since it would bear no fruit. Yet before arriving at the R Schema, Lacan first introduces the L Schema, according to which the signifier's articulations cannot take place without the intervention of a vector uniting self with *objet petit a*: between the self and the other, the stream of objects *a-a'* causes a "narcissistic mirage" to insinuate itself along imaginary axes preventing the symbolic from achieving the purity of unmediated expression. There is no direct way to connect the two; only the obliqueness of the *a-a'* pathway can allow being and nothingness to meet on the imaginary plane they call home. A veil or hymen covering over the earnestness of symbolic functioning, the pole linking me directly to the image of myself I find in mirror images and mirror objects radicalizes my experience of the social-symbolic, which always enters my consciousness through the filter of an ego which is an ideal construction of homeostasis and *sōphrosunē*, a *sujet supposé conduire* as much as it is *sujet supposé savoir*.

But of course things are not as simple as the separation between self and other through the oddly concrete imposition of an imaginary forever shielding me from sheer symbolism and paralyzing signification—for the L Schema is not enough, and must be supplemented or sublated. Moving on to the R Schema, a more detailed account of what happens to pervert the relationship between split subject and demanding Other, Lacan takes the simplicity of the L Schema and pushes it a step further. Now it must account for a missing master signifier and the havoc its absence introduces into the field of meaning, a controlling symbolic element which for Lacan ties directly to the paternal function [P_0] but which I would argue might be no more than whatever ideological vertex on whose corner the self has chosen to suspend its identity. As a result of this sudden departure, a trapezoid materializes as hole in the symbolic network, a polygon with corners identified as object's primordial signifier (M), ego ideal (i), ego (m) and image (I): the Mimi Box. Through the gap introduced by the Mimi Box, a fissure that I interpret as a deepened and widening *a-a'* slit, the split subject assumes its existence as lack, a fundamental and inevitable accession it can either acknowledge, resting comfortably in its *néant* and giving birth to the symptom and all its sinthomic luxuries.

For more is at stake regarding objectivity in the R Schema than the self and its illusions, as here the potential for psychotic communication emerges as a direct consequence of the veil coming between the symbolic and the self symbolized, or turned into an object for others; in fact, the R Schema leads directly to the extreme vorticality of the final I Schema, according to which a mobile paternal signifier and an equally mobile positive quantum of pleasure embodied in the symbolic phallus [Φ_0] destabilize a force field through their wild movements. With the effusions of Daniel Paul Schreber, the awkward and cumbersome symptom becomes the delicate and pleasurable sinthome, in this instance a portal for the "transsexualist jouissance" Schreber feels as his body becomes divine conduit: the mediations of psychotic speech reveal the joy that Schreber is able to take in the barred jouissance of the other, which, like Kant's negative presentifications in his *Critique of Judgment*, become imbued with meaning by dint of their failure to signify or compute. In Lacan, this significatory lapse is due to a primal disruption in the mechanism of symbolization stemming back to the object's interposition between self and Other, while in Kant it is chalked up to the fact that the object is *de trop* either mathematically or dynamically. In both, the imagination duly fails, and in its failure inaugurates an era of rapture in the history of the subject, although this excessive joy is fundamentally autistic and impossible to convey, outside the historical residues of poetry and memoir (for example, Schreber's sensational *Memoirs of My Nervousl Illness*). For the sinthome and *a* resonate, both of them being points of material saturation/resonance in a system of never-ending deflagration. I burn through the other, because it is only in this way that I can get to know it, just as I do not become an object of knowledge proper until I am symbolically castrated by the symbolic order, which is not at liberty to use its signifiers to represent to me to other signifiers unless my own access to jouissance has been not only foreclosed from without, but voluntarily refused from within. For I must personally authorize the act, not merely be subjugated to it against my will, in order for it to count. If I do not avow it, I become Schreber, intoxicated with my altered subjectivity and objectivity; objects like my own organs and nerves taunt me with their electricity, rendering me a fantastic psychotic with my own perverse access to celebrity.

Democracies of Fetishism

If in Lacan it is the *objet petit a* through which the imaginary plateau comes into existence, as I hope I have by this point demonstrated through my analysis of fables, like the sardine can and the lamella, diagrams, like the L, R and I Schemas and the Mimi Box, and psychic phenomena, like aphanisis and the double vel of phantasy, then via Zizek this entity is refined into what I have termed the *objet petit c*, or the *objet petit a* turned into a commodity proper. For, of all Lacan's progeny, it is Zizek who best understands what the truest formulation of the object is in its new life as commodity, an object one step removed from objecthood and substantiality. Disconnected from drive, yet haunting subjectivity with the vague promise that it has something indispensable to offer it, it is the commodity which most tempts the split subject into identifying with its thingness, into taking on its features through an act part masquerade, part legendary psychaesthenia. For within the world that capitalism has sculpted, the primordial lack through which the subject is constituted as subject is no longer abstract or theoretical. Passing from *tragique* to *moque-comique*, subjects of all kinds need merely thumb through a glossy, flip through cable TV channels or log onto YouTube to discover what about them is flawed, faulty, lacking: fat deposits, bald spots, a nose the size of Kansas. Still a plug, the most basic formulation of the object within Lacanian analysis, the object now flaunts its own planned obsolescence, happy to stick around just long enough for another object to float metonymically along—its disappearance is half its charm.

This time around, I, too, have lost my illusions, thoroughly aware that the image of Posh Beckham ricocheting through the corridors of my neurons will keep me satisfied just long enough for the asymmetrical bob I plant on my scalp to settle: for now, I want more, and I can admit it, rid of guilt, angst and the sense that any flesh and blood creature has it together. Although I recognize *l'Autre* as a sham, I still need to act as if it exists, and so I take on the bits of matter it sends my way with a combination of grace and aplomb—besides, being an object myself, I, too, am Big Other to other pockets of nullity, and must assume my place as tormentor. I know the object will leave me in the lurch, that I will have to move on to one of its companions shortly, but I take pleasure in the exhilaration of my decenteredness, reveling in the fact that no object can satisfy me, that my own openness is so radical that no creation can lodge itself within my emptiness with any kind of longevity. The *cogito* is no more: it is the time of the *shopito*. I am, but not because I doubt, or because I reflect upon my doubt, or contemplate my own faculty to contemplate: simply put, I am because I acquire Osirian fragments of the Other, little nuggets of plastic, metal, and sometimes cellular matter, and because I allow these things to supplement my identity through the logic of the *lagniappe*, that something extra in whose excess I squirrel away my own sense of self.

Zizek's discussion of the symbolic and cultural meanings of the ultimate commodity, Coca-Cola, in *The Fragile Absolute*, a book "for nobody and nothing" in the most positive determination of negation, speaks to the essence of the *objet c* and the strange hold it has upon me; contextualized with his remarks on stonewashed jeans, through whose demolition a social drama of conflicting gazes and assumed class transvestism is encoded, and television talk shows, a string of tantrums and histrionics through whose heat the *trait unaire* takes the form of the "endearing foible," it becomes apparent that above all the televisualization of the objet a has made it an objet c, its being crammed into an easily disseminated image and slogan for what I term the Society of the

Sinthome (48).[10] As the ineffableness of this libation addresses its frivolities to ever more inhabitants of the globe, their drives, scopic, invocatory and olfactory, mutate accordingly, all made subservient to the visual perception of that bottle, that fizz, that red swoop.[11] The ultimate junction of objecthood and nebulousness, Coca-Cola sustains itself by keeping my desire in abeyance, giving me the sense that I have received something from it, when in truth all I have consumed are empty calories which will neither satisfy nor nourish me for any length of time: Coke is "it" because it embodies the commodity's magic, sharing in the infinitely productive emptiness of the *point de caption*, as it knits together an ideological quilt dictating my future taste.

Yet we're not out of the clear just yet, particularly as regards Zizek's commitment to that expectation of a plenitude he inherits from Lacan. What Zizek grasps about Coke and other commodities is their profound uselessness; what he misses are the opportunities for satisfaction they offer, especially for a postmodern *shopito* less interested in genuineness and more interested in the kinds of acquisition made possible by metaphor (substitution) and metonymy (the expectation of a more). For, once one accepts the constitutive lack at the heart of subjectivity, something I would argue neither Lacan nor Zizek have done, then there is no longer an occasion for discomfort or agony, only unbounded exhilaration at the prospect of disturbed foundations and unanchored air ships. Becoming Bad Lacanians, we bask in the glories of scission, alienated even from our alienation, as one object after another hails us, forcing us into existence through the materiality of our desires. When all is said and done, Coke offers us very little, representing our consumption of the Void so terrifying to the anorexic, whose insatiable appetite is for nothing more than the space within which food or nourishment may appear as such. Alive with surplus-enjoyment, Coca-Cola partakes of the superego's paradox: "The more Coke you drink, the thirstier you are; the more profit you make, the more you want; the more you obey the superego command, the guiltier you are" ("Coke as *objet petit a*," 23-24).[12]

---

[10] My source for Zizek is his *The Fragile Absolute—or, Why Is the Christian Legacy Worth fighting for?* (London: Verso, 2000).

[11] With regard to Zizek's Coke, I hearken back to Freud's Coke. Relating the two is the subject of a future paper at the moment, one related to my work on the role of drug addiction in aesthetic production. See Sigmund Freud, *Cocaine Papers* (NY: Meridan, 1975).

[12] Strangely, it is in the context of Coke that Zizek introduces a discussion of the three suicides: Imaginary, Real and Symbolic. The implied connections between Coke and suicide—Coke as a species of suicide, Coke as the suicide of the sublime

Not to worry: as the aphanisis of our aphanisis materializes, there's always Viagra to come to the rescue, lest I stand in the presence of the *objet* without being to fulfill my biological obligation to its seductiveness. We have come a long way since Ernest Jones, as now the aphanitic problem is not the waning of our libidos, but rather how to keep up with the stimulation we experience as we confront a confusing barrage of disconnected signifying units clogging the airways with their virtuality: virtual because it is not yet clear whether or not they even meet minimum a Cartesian standard of extension required for corporeality. The danger here is neither aphanisis nor anhedonia, but priapism: the chemicals we absorb in order to appear in, as and through desire leave us erect and in heat even after the sexual impulse has reabsorbed itself in the partial loop of its libidinal circuitry. "On the other hand, we have the obverse paradox of the pleasure whose very pursuit turns into a duty: in a 'permissive' society, subjects experience the need to 'have a good time,' really to enjoy themselves, as a kind of duty; consequently, they feel guilty if they fail to be happy…" (135). True, in a de-sublimated world, hedonism does become a kind of obligation, tedious as visiting the sick or cleaning the gutters—but fortunately, there is Prozac to help us maintain our equilibrium, and limitless Internet porn to keep us titillated. That Zizek finds this de-sublimation repressive is telling: no wonder he is unable to find any substance to the insubstantiality of Coke, Diet Coke, or Caffeine-free Diet Coke, contemporary commodity-heroes which do not need to offer anything outside of a very tangible more which will never be distributed. Jouissance we will never possess, if only because it never existed in the first place—but our pleasures are manifold, and all that is expected of us is that we stuff as many as we can into our tract homes, trunks and messenger bags.

Spectral and phantasmatic, the real tames us with sweet nothings evaporating the moment they are articulated, even after its substance shifts toward the virtual, as Ben Wright's 2004 documentary *Slavoj Zizek: The Reality of the Virtual* demonstrates. Through the holes in my jeans, droplets of my identity are exuded: ultimately, I am this gorgeous demolished object, this fallible fabric riddled with gashes and slashes—so much more than a mere conversation piece or occasion to transcend class through a symbolic act of appropriation. For if any particular content may assume the universal position other ages held in such high esteem, there is hope for me in my dreckness: I, too, may achieve the monadicity of a

---

object proper, Coke as the suicide of the palate, even Coke as the suicide of suicide—resonate wildly.

liquefied magazine image, bouncing lightly off other objects in a dance of Brownian motion innervated by capital's fetishizing glare and the winds its visual rays, so Schreberian, are able to whip up.[13] Bad Lacanian, and even worse Zizekian, I rest comfortable and contented in the permissiveness extended to me by a radicalized democracy according to which the object's—and my—contingency is oddly necessary. Even Laclau could not have envisioned this kind of political mutation, this radicalized demos for which symptoms take on a novel form of glamour. *Noms-de-père* connect to neither father nor [-φ]: Coca-Cola, American Express, D&G, AcipHex, Eco-freedom, Status Update, Kardashian: the list goes on, a flattened and hacked phallus resembling a jubilant bevy of Planarians, cross-eyed paragons of regeneration. Product names and designer labels master-signify the lacking lack other objects, some of them people, use to represent my existence as discrete, bounded and compartmentalized, monadic in the worst sense. In my new life as fetish, I can manipulate and mobilize desire as well as any commodity can: others cherish me for my superfluity and supervise my use as *cherry* atop a capitalist sundae no sweet tooth will devour if only because its kilocalories might be real.

Still, my gaze in these situations is not wholly innocent, as it retains the invidiousness Lacan first ascribed to it in "What Is a Picture?" (*Écrits*): and here, as everywhere, invidiousness structures visuality, desire-to-see, desire-to-be-seen, even desire-to-be-invisible The demands the object makes upon my attention and upon my own identity inspire not only an existential *ébullience*, but also a variety of envy of the sort I have found in Sartre's thought, as I intersect object after object, each one supposedly the plug that will close my psyche, or at minimum support the phantastic movement of my divided consciousness forward and back from its elastic surface. This invidiousness may very well be a modification of the primal aggression released during the initial formation of an ego in the mirror stage, or even a transmutation of the anxiety surrounding object constancy during the *Fort-da* game: what it dictates is a perennial awkwardness

[13] Here, my reference is to the inherent elasticity Leibniz assigns to the monad, especially as this quality forms the basis of a theory of concomitance that was his answer to occasionalism. Within this context, Leibniz's definitions of necessity and contingency come into play: the necessary as that which cannot be contradicted, the contingent as that for which there is no standard of non-contradiction, and the monadic as that strange supersubstance elastically partaking of both necessity and contingency. See G.W. Lebiniz, *Philosophical Essays* (Indianapolis: Hackett Publishing, 1989)—in particular, "On Freedom and Possibility" (19-22) and "A Specimen of Dynamics" (117-137).

separating even the most glib and gleeful pocket of nonexistence from the most trivial bit of matter. I devour Britney Spears with *élan* and gusto at the same time that I rend her limb from limb. A show like *TMZ*, which captures celebrities at their lowest—Big Macs jammed into their mouths, thongs riding up their *derrières*, bad bikini bods emerging from the Malibu surf—embodies these contradictory inclinations.[14] This dual pulsation —I need the object to complete me, I hate the object for having to complete me—might even have a matheme all its own: (S◊*a*)◊(S◊*a*). Phantasy slams into phantasy, moving to and fro from nuggets of durability dispersed into miasmas slipping through my fingers the second I attempt to grasp them, negating the "neither/nor" and causing it to become that terrifying possibility, the "both/and," ultimate formula of permissiveness. Now the barred subject becomes mathematically indistinguishable from the dollar sign of American capital: each is '$' in its own right.

Furthermore, whatever purpose the object serves for me, it may elude my reach and become the territory of another: "Such is true envy—the envy that makes the subject pale before the image of a completeness closed upon itself, before the idea that the *petit a*, the separated *a* from which he is hanging, may be for another the possession that gives satisfaction, *Befriedigung*" (116). Yet even before the object comes into another's possession, it comes into its own possession, a state of affairs that will never hold for me, and so I envy it its independence, its self-sufficiency, its dazzle. As the bar of the Other's jouissance disappears through the prohibition of prohibition, the permissiveness of postmodern society gives free reign to objects, encouraging them to circulate freely and insouciantly. Now, I may experience true pleasure—but what do I do in the absence of the Other's barred surplus-enjoyment? The bar remains, unsignifiable and self-sustaining, only now it cuts through empty space, leaving me nostalgic for the good old days, when guilt rocked me to the core and I might awaken with a glove anaesthesia or hysterically expanding womb. Courbet's *l'Origine du Monde*, tellingly enough in Lacan's possession at the time of his death, performs an *Ent-scheiding* or act of "radical *desublimation*" bringing modernity past the crisis point, its

---

[14] *South Park* satirizes this dual drive beautifully in Episode 1202 (*Britney's New Look*, Season 12, March 19, 2008). In this episode, Britney Spears is literally reduced to a bloody pulp through the goading of the paparazzi: clearly, the townsfolk love her enough to destroy her. Such is their and our invidious attachment to objects-that-are-objects and imagos-that-are-objects.

outcome the "reversal of the sublime object into abject, into an abhorrent, nauseating excremental piece of slime" (Zizek, 37). De-sublimated both in terms of a decoding and de-cathecting of desire (Freud) and the return of the excremental object from its point of elevation back to the gutter (Lacan), the contemporary world is rendered surprisingly free-wheeling and open, as the refined psychic investments which once dictated the construction of chapels, the composition of aesthetic tableaux and the architecture of a certain kind of personality dissolve, replaced by the idealizations of photoshopped torsos, gelatinous silicone fun bags, and capsules guaranteeing just the right quantum of enjoyment for a self who has finally found a way to turn its imperfections to gold via its salacious enjoyment of the *objet petit c*.

CHAPTER NINE

"A TRANSFERENCE OF THE MOST FORTUITOUS KIND": FITZGERALD'S *TENDER IS THE NIGHT* AND THE FREUDIAN TRANSFERENCE

ERICA D. GALIOTO

Dick's Demise

The most notable aspect of F. Scott Fitzgerald's literary representation of mental illness in *Tender Is the Night* (1934) is typically viewed as the shift in emphasis from Nicole's instability to that of her husband/doctor Dick Diver. Though Dr. Diver's disintegration usually remains uncontested, its terms provide fertile ground for literary controversy, particularly over Fitzgerald's use of the psychoanalytic concept of the transference, the agent of his supposed demise. While Fitzgerald's employment of such a clinical concept calls into question his fidelity to Freudian thought, this challenge to the author's psychiatric knowledge usually ends at an impasse. It is a term that appears three times in the text, but with unconvincing medical knowledge to substantiate any authority on its use; any adherence to psychoanalytic theory is purely accidental, as the argument goes. What is not accidental is Dick's final state of disintegration: the feminization synonymous with his demise. This agreement on Dick's decline has encouraged a host of readings that desperately try to account for his final state by locating its cause and following its trajectory as it is routed through the transference.

I, however, would like to intervene on two counts and argue that Dick does not, in fact, disintegrate, but rather initiates his own recovery due entirely to what I would call a Freudian transference with Rosemary Hoyt. Refusing the typical monolithic interpretation of Dick Diver (as ruined) will keep us from reading Book III as evidence of his fade into oblivion.

Instead, this new reading will encourage us to see it as a symptom of his own recovery, where the inception of a new pattern of associations inspires conscious disregard for his current personal and professional life. I maintain that scholarship on *Tender Is the Night* has been building support in the wrong direction. Rather than garnering confirmation for the demise of Dick, we should be collecting symptoms of his recovery, and Rosemary is the key figure who can help us do that.

The first piece of evidence that Fitzgerald provides against a totalistic construction of Dick is none other than the time scheme itself: the modernist form that fails to account entirely for his final subjective state. The inverted chronology and pervasive gaps in the text evince a destabilized linear reading. We are first cautioned against any type of unilateral interpretation in Book I, where we are introduced to Dick through the partial point of view of Rosemary who idealizes him. Further into the text, we learn to question this limited perspective as holes are poked into her failing idealism. As Fitzgerald moves us forward, he also moves us backward, through a kind of return-of-the-repressed, where these disruptions and the simultaneous movement forward and backward signal the timelessness of the unconscious. With all of this time travel, we should not simply infer that the past interrupts the present and marks the future in a predictable cyclical cycle. In this limited view, repetition becomes merely the reliving of past memories that determine the present and future, and so it is possible to argue, as many have beginning with Mary Burton's early psychoanalytic reading, that Dick Diver repeats his earlier transference with Nicole when he meets Rosemary.

Subsequent literary analyses that follow Burton's argument similarly misidentify Dick's transference with Rosemary as an exact repetition of the transference with Nicole. I believe that Fitzgerald actually presents us with two very different dimensions of the transference as Freud would define them; one dimension with Nicole that slips into a counter-transference with resistance emanating on both sides, and one dimension with Rosemary that veers into the love that Freud believes to be curative in the clinical situation. Noting the differences between the two aspects of the transference should allow us to see that Rosemary functions as a catalyst to a new subjective position for Dick. Viewing the transference from two different vantage points, one of resistance and one of love, will permit us to generalize on both the potential danger and the potential success of employing love, or the transference as such, in cases of mental illness. The fortuitous transference here is the one, not of repetition with Nicole that seeks futile completion, but the one of love with Rosemary that produces confrontation with nothing.

Counter-Transference

Noting the lack of rigorous psychoanalytic interrogation of Fitzgerald's use of the transference, Jeffrey Berman's "*Tender Is the Night*: Fitzgerald's 'A Psychology for Psychiatrists'" (1979) seeks, early on, to fill in the elision. Berman finds that *transference* as a deliberate word chosen by Fitzgerald appears a mere three times in the text: first, to describe Nicole's initial attachment to Dr. Diver; second, to describe the unheeded suggestion that Dr. Diver should extract himself from his precarious relationship with Nicole; third, to describe Nicole's new feelings of attachment to Tommy Barban. Based purely on the appearance of the word in the text, not on its conceptual manifestation, Berman concludes that Fitzgerald is not "using its term in its precise psychoanalytic context but in a vaguer sense as an absorption or incorporation of one person by another in a shifting love relationship" (1979, 39). Berman, like Burton, associates this cannibalism with Diver's slip into counter-transference.

Whether or not Fitzgerald intends for his references to the transference to be taken metaphorically or psychoanalytically, he does align Dick's counter-transference with Nicole to an emergent femininity tantamount to his physical and emotional dissipation. Resulting from the feminization that arises as a byproduct of his counter-transference, Dick's ambiguous gender role and questionable sexual orientation are often viewed as the most probable causes of his demise. Fitzgerald provides copious examples of Dick's purported femininity: his role as analyst, his inability to acknowledge reality, and Rosemary's dubious portrayal of him to name a few. But perhaps the trump example is Dick's admission that he "wanted to be loved, too, if he could fit it in" (Fitzgerald 1934, 133). Most notably this argument is made by Leslie Fiedler, who maintains that Dick's female identification weakens him, and his failure to uphold rigid gender boundaries perforates his already precarious subjective state. Judith Fetterley also argues that Fitzgerald pathologizes the feminine. For her, Dr. Diver sinks into oblivion because his vitality is sacrificed for the sake of Nicole's cure, turning him into a woman who is characterized by traditional stereotypes. The vampirism inherent in such a system works to doubly discount the feminine position. Woman is not only the detestable position Dick occupies, but woman is also the agent through which Dick finds himself in such a position.

While I agree with Burton and Berman that Dick does slip into a counter-transference, and I agree with Fiedler and Fetterley that he does become feminized in his role of analyst-wanting-love, I also believe that is it crucial to reassess Rosemary's role in the text, particularly because of the effect she has on Dick. Once her role as real-world analyst—or object of the real transference—is established, these notions of the counter-transference and its incumbent feminization may be read retroactively to impart different meanings. I must first begin by describing in some detail the counter-transference of Nicole and Dick. Though I do not disagree fundamentally with other descriptions of their relationship, it is important for my argument to highlight the Freudian concepts at stake. I will now turn to Freud to illustrate how Fitzgerald, probably without intent, shackles Dick and Nicole to a transferential relationship based on resistance that far exceeds the banal understanding of transference as the shift of one's psychological burden to someone else. More importantly though, I plan to show how Dick's transference with Rosemary (as his real-world analyst) produces a love that propels him in a new direction, but yet still aligns him with the feminine position—only this time it is not a pathological one.

To argue that Fitzgerald does present an accurate representation of the two Freudian dimensions of the transference—resistance and love—I must first differentiate between the two. Tracing Freud's changing ideas on the transference, or the relation between analyst and analysand, through "The Dynamics of Transference" (1912), "Observations on Transference-Love" (1915), and "Transference" (1916), allows us to realize a number of key points about the Freudian transference: 1) there is a difference between the transference of resistance and the transference of love 2) the analyst must remain neutral to the patient's demand for reciprocal desire 3) transference-love may enact the cure in analysis as it does in the real world when the unconscious is temporarily opened and assimilated into consciousness. In the first essay that addresses the transference at length, "The Dynamics of Transference," Freud writes, "it remains a puzzle why in analysis transference emerges as *the most powerful resistance* to the treatment, whereas outside analysis it must be regarded as the vehicle of cure and the condition of success" (1912, 101). In this quote, Freud bifurcates the experience of the transference according to whether it occurs inside analysis or outside in the real world. Once Freud develops the concept further, retroactively we can note that the actual separation is between the transference of resistance (repetition) and the transference of love (cure).[1]

---

[1] In "The Dynamics of Transference," Freud writes that the transference exists in two different dimensions, although only the dimension of resistance has been elucidated thus far: "In all these reflections, however, we have hitherto dealt only with one side of the phenomenon of transference; we must turn our attention to another aspect of the same subject" (1912, 107).

In this first essay, Freud strikingly partitions the real love outside of analysis from the artificial love of the transference, but later he will concede that it matters not *where* the transference is enacted but *which* type it is.[2] Here, Freud struggles with the wrong binary; it's not real vs. artificial love, but rather resistance vs. cure. Eventually he clarifies this obfuscating doubleness and grants transference-love the same curative effects of real love and announces that when the transference fails inside or outside of analysis it is due to resistance. Freud defines resistance to the cure in three ways: using the transference as a vehicle of repetition to reenact earlier patterns; using the transference to lessen the power of the analyst by shifting the power dynamic; using the transference to reinforce original repressions when the counter-transference is broken. Rather than dissolving symptoms and instituting new subjectivity, resistance enacts repetition and further strengthens symptomatic behavior.

In the second essay, "Observations on Transference-Love," Freud shifts his emphasis from the dichotomies of transference to the position of the analyst. To move the emerging love on the part of the analysand away from the realm of resistance, Freud's main focus is on the analyst and his reaction to this demand to be loved back—to fill the open hole—especially if it is constructed in the analytic scene. He harshly advises against the analyst's return of such feelings, and instead writes, "In my opinion, therefore, we ought not to give up the neutrality towards the patient, which we have acquired through keeping the counter-transference in check" (1915, 164). In an effort to expose the lack in the analysand where the subject exists, the analyst must instigate love without returning it, without covering over the hole that emerges. He must neither return nor refuse his patient's love, "but he must just as resolutely withhold any response to it" (166). The analyst's refusal to reveal partiality depends on the emergence of his own unconscious singularity. Transference-love depends on the rise

[2] Freud, in his attempt to separate transference-love from real love experienced outside analysis, writes, "Transference-love has perhaps a degree less of freedom than the love which appears in ordinary life and is called normal; it displays its dependence on the infantile pattern more clearly and is less adaptable and capable of modification; but that is all, and not what is essential" (1915, 168). Yet he quickly revises his argument and adds, "We have no right to dispute that the state of being in love which makes its appearance in the course of analytic treatment has the character of 'genuine' love" (1915, 168). The difference, then, is not authentic versus inauthentic love, but whether the transference is on the side of resistance or of love. When the transference falls into the dimension of resistance, the patient's unconscious motives are "to assure herself of her irresistibility, to destroy the doctor's authority by bringing him down to the level of a lover and to gain all the other promised advantages incidental to the satisfaction of love" (1915, 163).

and suspension of the analyst's lack that dilates the patient's own; in other words, the analyst's non-coincidence with himself precludes the covering over of the subjective alienation necessary to propel forward movement. Freud labels this vacant stance of the analyst ethical because it is indispensable to the cure: "For the doctor, ethical motives unite with the technical ones to restrain him from giving the patient his love" (169). Knowing how easy it is to slip into a counter-transference plagued with repetitions when the analyst responds to his patient's entreaties, Freud, henceforward, makes neutrality the golden rule of psychoanalytic professionalism.

Paradoxically, this neutrality is necessary for the cure, which results only when the transference is on the side of love: when the lack of the analysand encounters the lack of the analyst. This encounter is the goal of the transference. The subtraction of two distinct lacks presumably alleviates the stagnation of a symptom that arrests the movement from repetition to love. While Freud does maintain that, similar to real love, transference-love reflects an infantile pattern, he initially attaches a privileged position to the transference inside analysis before ultimately conceding that the characteristics of transference-love and real love are virtually the same. Each is constituted by the envelopment of a whole person, including his/her lack, despite his/her inadequacies, and each is founded on a certain refusal of reality. We might even say that both produce a kind of impossible satisfaction, unthinkable to those outside the relationship because "it is lacking to a high degree in a regard for reality, is less sensible, less concerned about consequences and more blind in its valuation of the loved person" (169). For the love to be considered curative—wherever it is experienced—it is important for lack to be acknowledged and sustained.[3] One's unconscious singularity must remain and not suffer erasure or filling in. This love produces a new subjective position, not the binding to one's current state.

Finally, Freud, in the third essay "Transference," attests that the work of transference entails making conscious what hitherto had been unconscious through the love between analyst and patient, and it is this function that Rosemary serves as Dick's real-world analyst. In fact, this

[3] The goal of the transference, as Freud writes in "Transference" is as follows: "What we make use of must no doubt be the replacing of what is unconscious by what is conscious, the translation of what is unconscious into what is conscious. Yes, that is it. By carrying what is unconscious on into what is conscious, we lift the repression, we remove the preconditions for the formation of symptoms, we transform the pathogenic conflict into a normal one for which it must be possible somehow to find a solution" (1916, 435).

expression does coincide with real love because the love is inspired "neither by the doctor's behavior nor by the situation that has developed during the treatment" (Freud 1916, 441). The space of transference just provides the backdrop for the experience of normal love, the overlay of two unconscious minds. He writes, "Transference can appear as a passionate demand for love. . ." (442). Transference-love facilitates a cure, whereby the patient leaves with an open lack to enter the world desiring objects instead of stagnating with symptom formation. Since the analyst never acts on the demand for love that would fill the lack in the patient, the analysand leaves primed for a relationship outside the analytic scene. In Freud's description, we can see how the relation between doctor and patient also depends on a relationship to knowledge, where the analyst is assumed to hold the key to the analysand's mystery but resolutely refuses its revelation.[4] Before the fall from idealization, this refusal allows the patient's unconscious to work on its own mystery. Ending with an example of this fall from idealization, *Tender Is the Night* illustrates all of the preceding Freudian concepts. Through his creation of Dick, Nicole, and Rosemary, Fitzgerald effectively shows the difference between transference-resistance and -love, the need for neutrality in the analytic situation, and the potential for cure through transference-love.

Before explaining the love that Dick experiences with Rosemary, I will detail how Dick and Nicole's transference does get stuck in a counter-transference with resistance on both sides. As we shall see, their early bond quickly falls into this category of resistance, setting them up for a lifetime of repetition rather than cure. Nicole, despite the fact that she is raped by her father, is pronounced mad, or hysterical, when she reacts to her ordeal, and the treatment that would cure her, paradoxically, entails learning to trust men again, so she may fall in love. As her psychiatrists in Switzerland note, "she was so young we were afraid she might harden with it all twisted inside her," and so encouraging a transference between doctor and patient becomes the central priority (Fitzgerald 1934, 131). When the young, traumatized, previously indifferent Nicole takes a liking

[4] Lacan's notion of the subject-supposed-to-know, which I will reference throughout this article, is particularly valuable here, as he uses this descriptive term to explain that we fall in love with someone who we feel knows something about our unconscious. "I love the person I assume to have knowledge," he says (*Seminar XX*, 1998, 67). Furthermore, he also joins this love with the transference: "In analysis, we deal with nothing but [love], and analysis doesn't operate by any other pathway . . . I needed to base transference on, insofar as it is not distinguished from love that is, on the formulation 'the subject-supposed-to-know'" (*Seminar XX*, 1998, 67).

to Dr. Diver, it appears as if her hatred of men begins to lessen. Though not one of her original doctors, Dick's dual role as psychiatrist and love interest makes their relation a "transference of the most fortuitous kind" (120). Like Zelda and Scott in real life,[5] Nicole and Dick begin to write letters back and forth to each other, and Nicole's mood starts to improve because "it gave her somebody to think of outside" (130). Nicole responds favorably to the transference because a gap emerges, whereby her unconscious appears and forces her to desire others and, by extension, life outside the hospital; the emergent lack propels new movement. Allowing Dick to become her father-surrogate, Nicole looks to this older, authoritarian, medical, protective figure to bolster her insubstantial feminine identity; to put it bluntly, she replaces one father-figure with another. Due to the roles performed by both doctor and patient, she unintentionally sets herself up to repeat earlier patterns, despite the potential for new subjective behavior motivated by her newly revealed emptiness. As analyst, Dick now becomes the deciding factor of whether it is a transference of resistance or one of love, and it is Dick who does not maintain the neutrality instructed by Freud for the true cure to enact itself.

By allowing himself to reciprocate Nicole's blooming feelings of love rather than maintaining his own subjective neutrality, Dick allows the transference to be one of repetition (resistance) rather than cure, quickly covering over her emergent hole with his own counter-feelings of reciprocity while simultaneously squelching his own unconscious. As we previously learned from Freud, Dick's breaking of the cardinal rule of neutrality means that both his lack and Nicole's are quickly filled in by each other. It is only through the suspension of both lacks that the cure may be attempted.

Although Dick may maintain that his rescue fantasy ethically aids his patients' recoveries, his easy counter-transference reveals his own weakness and his own selfish desire to be healed. As Fitzgerald writes of the good doctor, "The weakness of this profession is its attraction for the man a little crippled and broken" (1934, 137). The other doctors at the clinic, not to mention Dick himself, recognize his fall into counter-transference, and they adamantly tell him that the transference with Nicole "must be terminated" (139). From their position, since they gauge recovery based on whether Nicole may fall in love with another man, the cure is nearly complete: she has attached herself to one man, so now Dick

---

[5] See Nancy Mitford, *Zelda: A Biography* (New York: Harper & Row, 1970).

[6] Fitzgerald suggests Dick's castration when he uses the following descriptions: "the spear had been blunted" (201), "he avoided high diving" (282), and "he could not rise" (284).

needs to extract himself so she may leave analysis primed for a new love-relationship outside of the treatment. Sensing Dick's reluctance to end the transference, one psychiatrist muses, "Perhaps you have got sentimentally involved yourself" (140). Though he knows that his feelings of reciprocity violate the ethics of the analytic situation, he confirms his own emotional involvement when he questions, "Nicole's emotions had been used unfairly—what if they turned out to have been his own?" (145). He also consciously acknowledges that permitting the transference to continue outside the analytic scene would mean devoting his professional and personal life to a wife/patient, but Dick fails to adequately end the transference. Nicole, replacing one authoritarian male figure for another, unconsciously places herself in a relation of resistance, repeating earlier patterns rather than catapulting to a new subjective position. Had Dick extricated himself from Nicole, perhaps both could have moved on to other objects of desire, but because he failed to remain neutral earlier, separation becomes near impossible.

Relinquishing the neutrality indispensable to a transferential cure, Dick allows his own desire to tarnish the scene. Sealing the deal with marriage, Dick and Nicole begin a life of repetition; each looking to the other for completion, the fusional quality that dooms curative love to failure. Instead of enacting separation, the action necessary for a new subjective position, the repetition transference of Dick and Nicole becomes a cannibalistic completion, where each partner totally engulfs the other, disallowing the emergence of lack that would spur each onto new associations. In a game of hot potato, Nicole and Dick transfer each other's problems onto the other. Fitzgerald references their striving for coalescence into one being when he calls them "the Divers" or even "Dicole." Their blended namesake is a semantic representation of two psychic states attempting to become one, where each must forgo the singular part of him/herself as a sacrifice to their more universal similitude. As Fitzgerald writes, "but somehow Dick and Nicole had become one and equal, not opposite and complementary; she was Dick too, the draught in the marrow of his bones" (1934, 190). An intentional vanishing, both Dick and Nicole strip themselves of their particularities for easy identification as they disappear into the other, who is also deprived of his/her singularity. This cannibalism creates a suffocating too-closeness; the constant filling of one another's lack prevents the emergence of one's internal alienation: the core that propels forward movement.

And so always striving for fusional completion, Dick and Nicole get stuck in a pattern of repetition with no observable end. Nicole is the patient, and Dick is the doctor; Nicole breaks down, and Dick repairs;

Nicole needs saving, and Dick rescues; Dick does not want to confront his own psychic reality, and Nicole gives him a problem outside himself to address. Constantly trying to prevent the emergence of the unconscious, Dick preempts Nicole's experience of lack by saving her from herself, and Nicole preempts Dick's experience of lack by always providing him with a purpose. Consciously noting the roles that each play in this repetitive transference that has existed for the six-year duration of their marriage, Nicole wallows, "I am tired of knowing nothing and being reminded of it all the time" (1934, 161), while Dick admits, "I can only help you the same old way" (191). Since completion is impossible due to the irreducible otherness that governs psychic life, the repetitive transference of resistance will eventually split at the seams; it will go too far, either metaphorically or literally, like Nicole's rape at the hands of her father. While certainly not as physically violent, Nicole also suffers an emotional rape by Dick who penetrates her interior psyche and empties out its unique contents.

At the end of Book I, Nicole, in the memorable bathroom scene, references the suffocation she feels due to her husband's quest for completion, his disallowal of her own lack, her own subjectivity. Over the level, rational, and stern shouts of Dick who says, "Control yourself!", Nicole cries, "—it's you come to intrude on the only privacy I have in the world—" (1934, 112). Dick's barging into Nicole's toilette with his bloodied sheets stands as a synecdoche for their entire relation; her private inner quarters no longer belong to her to inspire her desire's movement. Her unconscious is short-circuited, plugged up, extinguished for the completion of "Dicole." Consciously acknowledging that their transference resides on the level of repetition, Nicole ends with, "I never expected you to love me—it was too late. . ." (112). Once Dick views her as a mental patient, he can never see Nicole as anyone else, despite, or maybe we should say *because* of, the fact that she becomes his wife. She'll forever wear the stain like the bloody sheets until a hole perforates their repetitive transference and inundates a gap between them: Rosemary Hoyt.

Dr. Rosemary Hoyt

Due to Dick's rescue fantasy mindset, it comes as no surprise that there have been other Nicoles through the six years of the Divers' marriage. Indeed, the relation between Rosemary and Dick begins much the same way as it had with Nicole and the others that succeeded her. To instigate the initial transference, it is necessary for the young female to first fall in love with Dick; for Rosemary this is no exception. As she watches the young couple on the beach, Rosemary's rose-colored glasses instantly idealize him: "But Dick Diver—he was all complete there. Silently she admired him" (19). From her limited perspective, he is perfect and all-knowing, the subject-that-is-supposed-to-know something about her unconscious. Since she perceives that Dick is able to access the inner recesses of her mind and actually tell her something about herself that she does not know, the transference is pushed even further. She muses, "He seemed kind and charming—his voice promised that he would take care of her, and that a little later he would open up whole new worlds for her, unroll an endless succession of magnificent possibilities" (Fitzgerald 1934, 16). In stark contrast to her own internal unrest, "Alongside his hard, neat brightness everything faded into the surety that he knew everything" (31). And Rosemary wants to offer herself up as the mystery that demands his attention and interpretation. Like one captivated by the object voice, that sound of a lover that seems intent on calling to no one but the beloved, Rosemary swoons at the sound of Dick's timber, the voice that "wooed the world" (19). For the transference to take hold, Rosemary must initiate the other's love by presenting herself as the convoluted mystery that demands disentanglement.

Not just an absence with a physical presence, Nicole plays a tangible role in the blooming love triangle. Unable to think the Divers separately because of their emphasis on fusional completion, Rosemary, when the transference takes hold, must admit, "I'm in love with you and Nicole," and in response, Dick thinks, "So many times he had heard this—even the formula was the same" (1934, 63). Not only can the Divers not be thought separately, but, from Dick's perspective, Rosemary also cannot be thought apart from her similarity to Nicole. In fact, it is their similarity that inspires the rapid counter-transference that dominates Dick's feelings for his next Daddy's Girl. In addition to both Rosemary's and Nicole's fathers being doctors, "Their point of resemblance to each other and their difference from so many American women lay in the fact that they were all happy to exist in a man's world—they preserved their individuality through men and not by opposition to them" (153). Using men, particularly the good Dr. Diver, as conduits through which their own strength may be garnered, Nicole and Rosemary, potentially, allow their own individuality to dissipate. Nicole can be thought only in terms of Dick or Rosemary because she forgoes that which distinguishes her. Instead, she blends into her surroundings; she fades into the other. Dick, under the sway of another powerful counter-transference, soon feels compelled by Rosemary's idealization of him and similarity to Nicole and contends, "You're the only girl I've seen for a long time that actually did look like something blooming" (22). Will this counter-transference also reside in the realm of resistance or will it move into the sphere of love?

Though Nicole and Dick find themselves in a repetitive cycle that fails to resemble love because it depends on the reaffirmation of old repressions, Rosemary and Dick are able to constitute the love synonymous with analytic cure. Rosemary and Dick begin their transference in the same space of faulty idealization and plugged unconscious, but they soon enter a realm unknown to Nicole and Dick. Paradoxically, this experience of love is accessed only by the conscious disavowal of such an encounter. Where Nicole and Rosemary diverge is in their acceptance or refusal of Dick's love. While Nicole allows herself to be saved, Rosemary does not and, by refusing Dick's plea, she becomes the doctor: the neutral analyst upheld by Freud.

Before meeting Rosemary, Dick had suppressed his unconscious through both his professional and personal life as it is condensed and crystallized in his repetition with Nicole. Unable to separate his private and public spheres, "his work became confused with Nicole's problems" as "an indication that life was being refined down to a point" (Fitzgerald 1934, 170, 171). Instead of writing his psychological treatise, *A Psychology for Psychiatrists*, or pursing his own desires, Dick must constantly—if unintentionally—avail himself to Nicole's sporadic moods through diagnosis and cure. Emphasizing this repetition, Fitzgerald writes, "Before her he must keep up a perfect front, now and tomorrow, next week and next year" (166). While the "pathological origin and mechanistic defeat of the affair left a flat and metallic taste" and "often he felt lonely with her," Dick had, in the past, maintained his blended role of husband/doctor opposite Nicole and squelched any indifference he felt (145, 187). Now, however, it begins to peek through in dribs and drabs, if only as mild discontent.

When this displeasure does reach the surface, Rosemary's neutrality refuses the attempted suppression of Dick's unconscious through her reciprocal desire. By holding back and allowing the opposite lack to emerge, Rosemary inspires a new subjective position for Dick. Whether it be for ethical, practical, sacrificial, or logical reasoning, the turning point in the affair of Rosemary and Dick occurs when she indignantly announces, "I've decided to give you up," during their first meeting at the Riviera (Fitzgerald 1934, 63). Sensing the impossibility of any romantic relationship due to Dick's current status as husband, father, and doctor, Rosemary pulls back and relinquishes her claims on him, despite the fact that she feels herself to be in love with both Dick and Nicole. And in this way, Rosemary and Dick become analyst and patient as Freud describes the reciprocal relationship:

> However highly [the analyst] may prize love he must prize even more highly the opportunity for helping his patient over a decisive stage in his life. [The patient] must learn from him to overcome the pleasure principle, to give up satisfaction which lies to hand but is socially not acceptable, in favor of a more distant one, which is perhaps altogether uncertain, but which is both psychologically and socially unimpeachable. (1915, 170)

Dick's immediate response to Rosemary's abrupt withdrawal is shock: "Had he said anything to imply that she possessed any part of him?" (Fitzgerald 1934, 63). When Dick's resistance is high, at this point, he refuses to see that desire may be aroused without one's knowledge, without an extinguisher poised to put it out. The importance of Rosemary's admission is two-fold. One, there does exist a feeling of mutual idealization and love between Rosemary and Dick (or else the initial transference and counter-transference would not have been instituted). Two, the refusal to repeat despite the mutual feelings punctures a hole in the relation, allowing desire to emerge with no outlet and, subsequently, jumpstarting a new pattern of behavior. The paradox here is that Rosemary, as analyst, can remain faithful to her feeling of love only by renouncing its very expression; the neutrality expressed by each allows the other to begin on a new path of desire opened through the unsatisfaction of demand. The love certainly emerges, but it can find no appropriate expression.

Describing her feelings, Rosemary thinks, "Her love had reached a point where now at least she was beginning to be unhappy, to be desperate" (Fitzgerald 1934, 56). So strong, in fact, are her feelings that "She wanted him to know how she loved him, now that the fact was upsetting everything. . ." (58). This frustrated love that can find no sanctioned expression desperately tries to erase itself. Rosemary doesn't merely want to make contact with her object of affection; rather, she wants to "devour him" (66). Titillating, this thwarted love replicates the analytic scene in the real world; both feel the counter-transference constitutive of love, both demand the other meet the need for love, but both steadfastly remain neutral. Madly in love, both are desperate, but cannot allow the onslaught of repetitions that would ensue if neutrality were broken. In an overthrow, not a repetition, of the original transference, Dick finds himself in the role of a patient whose unconscious breaks the surface and demands attention. After listing out the logical reasons why he should not respond to Rosemary's entreaties to "Take me," Dick's stoic reserve appears shaken (64). Fitzgerald writes, "He was suddenly confused, not about the ethics of the matter, for the impossibility of it was sheerly indicated from all angles but simply confused, and for a moment his usual grace, the tensile strength of his balance, was absent" (65). Instead of filling in his exposed lack, Rosemary remains resolute, looking "at him without the slightest idea as to what was in his head" (66).

Rather than demanding the love that she most desperately wants to garner, Rosemary holds back. Instead of acting on her desire, on her need for love, she empties herself out, obviating Dick's responsibility. Unlike Nicole who demands rescuing, Rosemary erects barriers of neutrality that create gulfs between her and Dick. Perforating the mutual idealization that flows between them, she admits, "I know I must seem just nothing to you" (Fitzgerald 1934, 65). And even, "I know you don't love me—I don't expect it" (64). As Rosemary, and by extension Dick, detach from previously held beliefs that demand a reaction, they are knocked off-kilter as their unconscious minds open to new associations, propelling them away from the repetition of destruction and rescue to something new. In response to this new psychical action, Dick is visibly altered, as "astonishment froze him rigid," for he is used to covering over his unconscious gaps and disallowing their pulsation (64). Whereas in the past, "So rigidly did he sometimes guard his exposed self-consciousness that frequently he defeated his own purposes," the floodgates to his rippling unconscious have been opened (92). Their kiss, the contact of lips devoid of excitement, reflects this anti-climactic and oxymoronic moment of desire's refusal despite physical consummation. The peck is described not as the ecstatic euphoria of desire's satisfaction but as, "He kissed her without enjoying it. He knew that there was passion there, but there was no shadow of it in her eyes or on her mouth" (63). Through passion's renunciation, when their gaze meets in neutrality paradoxically, ". . .she knew that he was beginning to fall in love with her" (68). Open, exposed, dilated, both Rosemary and Dick confront each other with pulsing unconscious minds in the state of neutrality that reflects transference-love. The mutual renunciation of Dick and Rosemary affects the castration necessary to inculcate lack. As Dick's real-world analyst, Rosemary renounces her own desire, and in so doing, prompts Dick to inquire about the position of his own desire, his own experience as lack.

As the overlap of two unconscious minds, the love that is experienced between Dick and Rosemary exists on a different plane: not the one concerned with fusional completion, but the one Freud tells us about that incarnates the gap necessary to propel forward movement. Fitzgerald writes, "In a hundred hours she had come to possess all the world's dark magic" to describe how Rosemary opens Dick's unconscious, bringing to surface what had hitherto remained concealed (1934, 164). Ironically, this love inspires forward movement only by allowing a hole to emerge that is not filled, but rather exists as the overlay of two unconscious minds that can never find completion in the other: a double negative that becomes a positive in potentiality. It is called love, but it is not the fusional, repetitive love that is fueled by desire, but the transference love that inspires a shift in one's subjective state.

Dick, who had long since arrested the free-flow of his desire, is palpably changed due to his transference with Rosemary; he exhibits the growing pains characteristic of a new subjective position that depends on his own castration. In the love of the transference, we are confronted with the other's lack and our own, where the experience of pleasure that results from this interaction gives us the knowledge that we each contain our own kernel of singularity that must persist as lack. The great betrayal of love is that, despite the location of a subject-supposed-to-know, we never really learn anything other than that one is non-coincident with oneself due to the unconscious. It is this non-coincidence that Dick must acknowledge before he can move forward.

Dick's Recovery

Fitzgerald writes, "Dick felt a change taking place within him… throw[ing] him off his balance and send[ing] through him waves of pain, misery, desire, desperation" (1934, 88). Knowing full well that this new movement of vitality cannot coincide with his repetition with Nicole, Dick admits that there is only one way to remain faithful to this new path recently opened before him: "Dignity could come only with an overthrowing of his past, of the effort of the last six years" (91). The change taking place in Dick corresponds to the emergence of his unconscious as it interacts with Rosemary's and encourages him to cease his repetitions with Nicole. He feels as if he were undergoing a transformation: "He knew that what he was now doing marked a turning point in his life—it was out of line with everything that had preceded it" (91). Whereas before, Dick sought only to unite with Nicole to fend off her experience of lack as well as his own, now, due to Rosemary's renunciation, he realizes "that the price of his intactness was incompleteness" (117). It is only through acknowledging his own lack and allowing for pursuit of its desire that he can catapult out of repetitive behaviors. For Dick to remain intact in his new subjective position, he must allow his lack to persist; he can only approach completeness by embracing his own decompletion.

Fitzgerald shows how he does rise to this challenge, when he writes, "Dick Diver's moment now began," the moment which allows him to remain faithful to his own unknown desire (1934, 118). To me, this moment is not about Dick's terminal transformation into a disillusioned alcoholic; but, rather, I read his overhaul as the opposite, as a symptom of his own recovery because his behavior morphs from the same repetitive patterns to new ones. Just because his actions may be consciously painful—to himself and others—does not mean that they are necessarily destructive psychically. In fact, the very notion that they are painful just shows the immensity of the transformation.

While alcoholism, violence, and disillusion may hardly qualify as positive changes in Dick's life, Fitzgerald indicates that they are fleeting resistances meant to symbolize an immense upheaval in his life; he must forcefully strip away his old identity, so he can begin anew. Fitzgerald describes this violent change as such:

> What had happened to him was so awful that nothing could make any difference unless he could choke it to death, and, as this was unlikely, he was hopeless. He would be a different person henceforward, and in his raw state he had bizarre feelings of what the new self would be. (1934, 233)

During this time period, Dick's reality shifts with him; his father dies, he loses his job, and he gets into verbal and physical altercations. These personal and professional changes, however, are not only painful, but they also allow Dick to confront his unconscious and make it conscious as Freud suggests. He is finally able to make a freeing admission: "It's possible I was the wrong person for Nicole," Dick admits (215).

Two conscious shifts result from Dick's transformative new movement and highlight, in my opinion, symptoms of his recovery. First, he begins to fade away from Nicole, and second, his desire beckons him to connect with others. Not demotions of psychic stability, these shifting desires are further evidence of Dick's new subjective position. If there is a disillusion present, it occurs in the detachment between Dick and Nicole. It all proceeds in a consecutive progression: Dick makes contact with Rosemary, and his unconscious is aroused; this arousal leads him to feel disconnected from Nicole, so he turns away from her; this repudiation of Nicole allows a gap to emerge that puts him in a new relationship with his object-cause-of-desire. And so, all at once, "Nicole was far away" (1934, 200), and "He was in love with every pretty woman he saw now, their forms at a distance, their shadows on a wall" (201).

Dick starts to pull away from his analyst role in a way he never had before, refusing his domestic duties and turning away from Nicole at night. Nicole's efforts to reinitiate their resistance-transference by tearing away from Dick at the carnival and nearly crashing their car and killing its passengers fail to catapult their transference away from its resistance. Prompting fear in both Dick and herself, she reminds him that they both wanted to live when the car precariously hung in the balance of life and death, but live in a way that resembled life, not the sleepwalking repetition they were circuiting through: "In a tired way, he planned that they would again resume the regime relaxed a year before" (1934, 192) Both are moving away from each other and toward new subjective positions; the repetition is no longer effective enough to keep past repressions at bay.

Concomitantly, Dick moves away from Nicole and his desire explodes in all directions. But because it happens so fast, and it is such a difference from his previous mode of behavior, Dick is confused and surprised; in short, "he had lost himself" (Fitzgerald 1934, 201). Though he is a physician himself and should be able to make conscious sense of the transference and counter-transference with Rosemary that expands into clinical love, he questions that ". . .he felt excited . . . why?" (202). Since for so long he was tied down with the repetition-compulsion of Nicole, when his new feelings emerge, he must note that "he had long been outside of the world of simple desires and their fulfillments, and he was inept and uncertain" (202). As if symbolizing the death of old desires, Dick's father dies and he fails to redeem paternal authority, signifying absolute law that is sought and not delivered. Although he desires to overcome his father and become the healing father of all, Dick ultimately fails to institute his own law as healer and authority. The death of Dick's father punctuates his position of semblant. Rather than acceding to his newly acquired role, Dick folds and refuses his instantiation of the Law of the Father. When the space of masculinity is availed to him, he cowers, thereby emphasizing his feminized position.

While Dick's refusal of power combined with his role as analyst usually confirm his feminine position and relegate his demise to his constitutive femininity, I maintain that Dick's femininity, or his ability to locate both desire and love in one object, actually reflects his capacity for love and his acknowledgement of the fallacy of absolute law. For women, according to Freud, love and desire often converge in the same object, while man often splits apart his object of love from his object of desire. Freud theorizes man's oscillation between idealizing and debasing his objects in "On the Universal Tendency to Debasement in the Sphere of Love" (1912). He writes, "The main protective measure against such a disturbance which men have recourse to in this split in their love consists in a psychical *debasement* of the sexual object, the overvaluation that normally attaches to the sexual object being reserved for the incestuous object and it representatives" (1912, 183). While men often divorce their objects of love and desire, women are more likely to allow them to converge in one object. Love depends on merging the desired object with the loved object. Here, Dick's feminization is not evidence of his demise, but rather indicates his capacity to experience love as the vehicle of his cure.

Confronting the Nothing

The three-year space of time that separates Dick and Rosemary only strengthens the transference love that flows between them. This span represents the gap between when one idealizes his/her subject-supposed-to-know and when that perfected figure suffers its fall. During this time, Dick is able to hold Rosemary up as an unattainable ideal, separate from Nicole, and desire new objects. While they are apart, also like Scott and Zelda, the transference works even better because there is idealization, neutrality, and desire without the possibility of consummation. At the point when they reconnect, it is crucial that Rosemary falls from the space of idealization that Dick has reserved for her. As his analyst, she must become a fallen, mundane object, so his desire for her may detach and reattach to new objects. Transference, whether performed inside or outside analysis, leads to the process of separation, while desire attempts to enact primal fusion. The analyst must first be idealized, as the partner in desire, but then the analyst must fall from that elevated place for the analysand to experience his/her own lack. The analyst falls from idealization by refusing to coalesce with the patient's lack, an always already failed endeavor; instead, he must refuse his own desire and remain a blank slate. This fall allows the analyst to remain a mundane symbolic object and not a sublime imaginary one, so the patient leaves analysis dilated and lacking. Like the three-year separation that allows both Dick and Rosemary to pursue other interests while still being grounded in the transference for each other, both know that "the best contacts are when one knows the obstacles and still wants to preserve a relation" (Fitzgerald 1934, 207). In this case, the obstacles are so great that they actually ensure a better relation.

This time, when consummation seems imminent, there is none of the allure of before. Rosemary has more power for Dick when they are apart than when they're together. Unlike the pristine Rosemary of three years ago, Dick finds a growing young lady who is a bit tarnished in reputation: "He guessed that she had had lovers and had loved them in the last four years" (Fitzgerald 1934, 207). Time sequence is really important here because when Dick and Rosemary make a new physical contact, their relation ceases to be about future consummation in some idealized space, but instead becomes the clichéd and debased now. She is not uplifted to the realm of transcendence like the woman of courtly poetry, but, instead, she becomes the worldly, experienced lover of the present time, as repetition of this "now" illustrates. No longer the ideal that can never be matched, "now she's a woman of the world" (208). Reiterating this label, she announces, "Now I'm a woman," and "Now she lowered the lights for love" (209-10). And again it is Rosemary who pulls back, who puts the stop on the affair, "No, not now—those things are rhythmic" (210). This final "Not Now" carries the air of "Not Ever!"

Though it is a full three years after their initial meeting, Dick does not fully detach from Rosemary until this pinnacle scene that precipitates their mutual castration. When both fall from their respective statures of idealization, the transference is broken, as both recognize the other's presence in the finite world:

> A moment had come and somehow passed. For three years Dick had been the ideal by which Rosemary measured other men and inevitably his stature had increased to heroic size. She did not want him to be like other men, yet here were the same exigent demands, as if he wanted to take some of herself away, carry it off in his pocket. (Fitzgerald 1934, 211)

As Rosemary ceases to associate Dick with her ideal, he, too, ascertains Rosemary's blemishes. Jealous of her love history, Dick notes that "Rome was the end of his dream of Rosemary" (220). Rather than allowing each to occupy the position of subject-supposed-to-know indefinitely, Fitzgerald terminates the transference as Freud would by permitting each to reduce to normal size. Each becomes just one in a series of ordinary objects, not *the one* who resides in an idealized, transcendent space. The transformative moment abolishes Dick's current subjective state and marks a new psychic beginning. "I'm not much like myself anymore," Dick admits as he feels the shift (260).

As one's subject-supposed-to-know falls from its idealization, desubjectivation ensues because one is left with the confrontation of his/her own lack when the ideal ceases to coalesce with it. Confronting one's own mystery—one's unconscious—alters one's subjective position, but staves off the eruption of madness that refuses such a confrontation. This is the confrontation that prompts the final change in Dick Diver and permits him to shed the illusion of completion that had been hindering his forward movement until this point: ". . .there seemed some necessity of taking all or nothing; it was as if for the remainder of his life he was condemned to carry with him the egos of certain people, early met and early loved, and to be only as complete as they were complete themselves. There was some element of loneliness involved—so easy to be loved—so hard to love" (1934, 245). Adding up all the broken egos would never bring Dick the seamless totality he sought early on. Although Dick feels like he is alone, it is this emptiness that he embraces, and it brings him the freedom to pursue a new chain of associations, so "the case was finished. Dr. Diver was at liberty" (302). Dick is able to free himself from himself so when "the old interior laughter had begun inside him, he knew he couldn't keep it up much longer" (314). Unwilling to continue playing a role, Dick confronts his nothing but does not fill its content, and in this way, the transference-love he experiences with Rosemary occasions his cure because she is the conduit through which this absence is confronted.

Fitzgerald, whether conscious of it or not, makes Dick acutely aware of the nothing and his relation to it with a quote that bears repeating: "the price of his intactness was incompleteness" (1934, 117). Before Dick is able to meet his lack face-to-face, he firmly shields himself from it with an ego stringent to maintain its faulty boundaries: "The strongest guard is placed at the gateway to nothing," he said, "maybe because the condition of emptiness is too shameful to be divulged" (70).

Even though he fears the exposure to his nothing, eventually Rosemary breaks through the ego's barrier, and presents him with an emptiness that is not met with indifference or disillusion but rather with the fullness of possibility because he becomes curiously aware of it. This time, Dick's confrontation with his own lack cannot be escaped or transferred as it had been with Nicole in the past: "Many times he had tried unsuccessfully to let go his hold on her. They had many fine times together, fine talks between the loves of the white nights, but always when he turned away from her into himself he left her holding Nothing in her hands and staring at it, calling it many names, but knowing it was only the hope that he would come back soon" (Fitzgerald 1934, 180). Now Dick holds his own nothing in his hands and allows his unconscious to move his desire in never before fathomed directions, even deep into Western New York. Dick's capacity to experience love, or his feminization, allows him to acknowledge his unconscious in a way that is curative instead of stagnating in the resistance of transference and symptom. The fortuitous transference here is the one, not of repetition with Nicole that seeks futile completion, but the one of love with Rosemary that produces confrontation with nothing. While Dick's change is indisputable, I maintain that his shift is toward recovery not sickness. "The change came a long way back—but at first it didn't show. The manner remains intact for some time after the morale cracks," Dick admits at the end of the novel to Rosemary, the chisel that made the first chip (285).

References

Berman, Jeffrey. 1979. "*Tender Is the Night*: Fitzgerald's 'A Psychology for Psychiatrists.'" *Literature and Psychology* 29: 34-48.

Bruccoli, Matthew and Judith S. Baughman. 1996. *Reader's Companion to F. Scott Fitzgerald's "Tender Is the Night."* University of South Carolina Press.

Bruccoli, Matthew. 1963. *The Composition of* Tender Is the Night: *A Study of the Manuscripts*. Pittsburgh University Press.

Burton, Mary E. 1971. "The Counter-Transference of Dr. Diver." *ELH* 38: 459-71.

Fetterley, Judith. 1984. "Who Killed Dick Diver? The Sexual Politics of *Tender Is the Night*." *Mosaic* 27:1 (Winter): 111-28.

Fiedler, Leslie A. 1960. *Love and Death in the American Novel*. New York: Criterion Books.

—. 1963. "Some Notes on F. Scott Fitzgerald." In *F. Scott Fitzgerald: A Collection of Critical Essays*, ed. Arthur Mizener, 70-7. Englewood Cliffs, NJ: Prentice-Hall.

Fitzgerald, F. Scott. 1934. *Tender Is the Night.* New York: C. Scribner's Sons, 1982.

Freud, Sigmund. 1912. "The Dynamics of Transference." In *The Standard Edition of the Complete Psychological Works of Sigmund Freud*, ed. and trans. James Strachey. London: Hogarth, 1953-74, 12: 99-108.

—. 1915. "Observations on Transference-Love." In *S.E.*, 12: 159-71.

—. 1912. "On the Universal Tendency to Debasement in the Sphere of Love." In *S.E.*, 11: 177-90.

—. 1916. "Transference." In *S.E.*, 16: 431-47.

Lacan, Jacques. 1998. *Book XX: Encore 1972-1973*, ed. Jacques-Alain Miller and trans. Bruce Fink. New York: Norton.

Mitford, Nancy. 1970. *Zelda: A Biography*. New York: Harper & Row.

CHAPTER TEN

FROM NECROPOLIS TO POLIS: MELANCHOLIC CITIZENSHIP IN *BAUMGARTNER'S BOMBAY*

HILARY THOMPSON

Prologue: The Melancholopolis and Freud's Landmarks

What if there were an eternal city, a city that, as it grew and developed, lost none of the evidence of its former states, but rather displayed them clearly for all to see? In a flight of fancy at the end of the first chapter of *Civilization and its Discontents*, Freud imagines such a city, imagines that it can be an illustrative model for the human mind, and imagines it as Rome:

> Now let us, by flight of imagination, suppose that Rome is not a human habitation but a psychical entity with a similarly long and copious past—an entity, that is to say, in which nothing that has once come into existence will have passed away and the earlier phases of development continue to exist alongside the latest one. This would mean that in Rome the palaces of the Caesars and the Septizonium of Septimus Severus would still be rising to their old height on the Palatine and that the castle of S. Angelo would still be carrying on its battlements the beautiful statues which graced it until the siege by the Goths, and so on. But more than this. In the place occupied by the Palazzo Caffarelli would once more stand—without the Palazzo having to be removed—the Temple of Jupiter Capitolinus; and this not only in its latest shape, as the Romans of the Empire saw it, but also in its earliest one, when it still showed Etruscan forms and was ornamented with terra-cotta antefixes. Where the Coliseum now stands we could at the same time admire Nero's vanished Golden House. On the Piazza of the Pantheon we should find not only the Pantheon of today, as it is bequeathed to us by Hadrian, but, on the same site, the original edifice erected by Agrippa: indeed, the same piece of ground would be supporting the church of Santa Maria sopra Minerva and the ancient temple over

> which it was built. And the observer would perhaps only have to change the direction of his glance or his position in order to call up the view of one or the other.
>
> There is clearly no point in spinning our phantasy any further, for it leads to things that are unimaginable and even absurd. (18-19)

What ultimately thwarts this exorbitant fantasy, with its imagery that seems to want to partake of Escher as much as Piranesi, is that it leads—as we could argue clashing political territorial narratives do—to one space having to "have two different contents" (19). What has inspired this imaginative thought experiment is Freud's attempt to conceive of the possibility that some human psyches may, much as they grow and develop, preserve earlier mental states alongside newer ones. In particular, some people may retain the feeling of a "primary" ego, the sense not of a strictly differentiated inside world and outside world, of sensations one can order and regulate and ones one can't, but rather of an unboundedness, a fluid connection to the outer world, even to infinity. What would such a psyche's structure look like? Freud claims he personally has no such memory or maintenance of this primary state, but we can imagine that in entertaining the idea, he compensates with his extraordinary and extraordinarily minute depiction of an eternal Rome.

The wistful nostalgia for a lost city, even a lost ideal city, that resonates throughout Freud's Rome passage finds a curious counterpart in his later memory of the Acropolis. And both pieces of writing have the same addressee, the writer Romain Rolland, who attested to having primary feelings of oceanic connection to eternity and who felt Freud might benefit from entertaining these feelings more. In *Civilization and its Discontents* (1930), Freud responds to his friend's discontent and enjoins us to imagine the ego that would maintain the oceanic feeling as a fantastic archaeological specimen. In "A Disturbance of Memory on the Acropolis" (1936), Freud explicitly writes a letter to Rolland on the occasion of his seventieth birthday. In place of a gift, Freud offers an analysis of a puzzling phenomenon, a mysterious emotion that seized him in 1904 as he and his brother planned their yearly Mediterranean vacation. Although their habit was to go to Rome or a place in Italy, a shortage of time and the advice of a friend made them decide instead on Athens. But this plan, though they immediately agree to it, makes them immediately and strangely depressed, perceiving only obstacles to the journey. When they arrive, and Freud beholds the ancient site he has long wanted to see, he has an odd thought: "'So all this really *does* exist, just as we learnt at school!'" (449). Why had the Acropolis that he was previously sullen and defeatist about visiting suddenly become as fantastic a vision as the Loch Ness monster, Freud wonders. It is as though part of him has doubted that the Acropolis really exists, although Freud knows he never did question this fact as a student. Why this sudden feeling of unreality and why the need to transpose it onto one's past beliefs? Freud calls this feeling "derealization" and claims it is the ego's attempt to defend itself from something unsettling. When he and his brother were young, they longed to travel, to escape home life, Freud explains, and this desire to run away from home is now tinged with guilt, especially because, he adds, they arrive at a place their father's lack of education would never have allowed him to appreciate fully. The desire to have heroic travels is also a desire to outdo one's father. Freud ironically performs this urge for greatness, when he ventures, "So too, if I may compare such a small event with a greater one, Napoleon, during his coronation as Emperor in Notre Dame, turned to one of his brothers—it must no doubt have been the eldest one, Joseph—and remarked: 'What would *Monsieur notre Père* have said to this, if he could have been here to-day?'" (456). What indeed. Freud has now imaginatively become Emperor, crowned in the sight of "Notre Dame" and evoking "notre Père" as one who cannot even be there to remark.

But beyond the grandiosity Freud, however impishly or guiltily, implicitly allots himself, other aspects of his wistful city visions are equally telling. Both archaeological urban dreams require seeing through the eyes of others. Freud implies that the triumph of his and his brother's visit to the Acropolis requires their father as a measurement. It's something he couldn't have done and wouldn't have known how to see, Freud thinks. And this means it's necessary to imaginatively take their father with them, so they can say to him, "Look what we can do." Likewise, in conjuring the perfect archaeological Rome, one needs people, not just palaces. It's necessary to say a temple will exist not just "as the Romans of the Empire saw it," but also with "Etruscan forms" and to ascribe structures to Nero, Hadrian, and Agrippa. In imagining this ideal object, multiple personal possessives as well as the viewing perspectives of several resurrected peoples are crucial. And this requirement is no doubt related to Freud's need for company—a brother or a correspondent, someone who might verify a father's measure of an achievement or someone who might attest to having those primary feelings of the infinite that inspire Freud's exorbitant comparisons. Freud initially enjoins us to imagine that Rome "is not a human habitation," but the terms of his urban imaginings suggest model cities, even or especially when ruined, are peopled with multitudes.

Let's say that eternal Rome and unreal Athens are one city, what Freud said we couldn't have, one space with two contents, the ideal city one makes real to the point of impossibility and the real city whose possibility one conjures away until its existence insists. The imagination of this dual city gives us a model of melancholia.

1. Social Melancholia?

Melancholia has a paradoxical status in literary and cultural theory. On the one hand, it is deemed one of the most self-enclosed psychological states, characterized by lack of engagement with the world. On the other hand, social theorists have found the melancholic condition utterly tantalizing to use as an explanation for large-scale collective movements and behaviors, be they ideologies of race, nationalism, and colonialism or experiences of war guilt and postcolonial trauma.[1] Judith Butler brings out this paradox in *The Psychic Life of Power*, claiming first that, "The social world appears to be eclipsed in melancholy, and an internal world structured in ambivalence emerges as the consequence." She moves on to assert, however, "the account of melancholy is an account of how psychic and social domains are produced in relation to one another" (167). Because melancholia involves an unusual movement away from the social world into a psychic inner world, Butler argues, theories of melancholia, specifically Freud's, can also show us something important about the ways we customarily define these categories and draw these boundaries. Butler will ultimately suggest that egos do not precede melancholia, but rather that melancholia's inward movement is constitutive of the ego and further, that the bulk of Freud's arguments and rhetorical figures point to social power's dominant role in determining which losses will trigger melancholia. Butler's approach is useful as it reminds us that in discussing large-scale melancholias we are not necessarily taking a condition out of a sealed psychic domain and theoretically expanding or metaphorically extending it to apply to some unaccustomed phenomena. Freud's theory of melancholia is social from the start. But whereas Butler risks suggesting that her illumination of the social dimension to Freud might irreparably undermine his crucial claims or assumptions, for example, of an original division between inner and outer worlds (170) or a specifically psychic origin for melancholia (178), we might prefer to differentiate between what can have prior existence in a psychological developmental narrative and what has *a priori* status from a philosophical point of view. One stage

[1] For two of the most salient examples, the first of race and melancholia in an American context, and the second of macro-melancholias in post-WW II Germany and postimperial London, see Cheng (2001) and Gilroy (2004).

or condition may succeed another in different contexts for Freud, but these sequences need not always mean that what precedes is taken for granted as "pre-given."[2] As we can see from Freud's narrative of primary egoic feelings, his experimental ideal Rome, and his hypothetically unreal Athens boundaries are far from presumed and origins are not necessarily determining in his world. Freud knows he is at least half enchanted with the idea that fluid possibilities can exist side by side, even to the point of impossibilities.

Freud's visions of ancient cities are both steeped in melancholia and revealing of another perspective from which to view melancholia, particularly its "outer" social dimension. That we can map Freud's account of melancholia onto his later descriptions of ancient classical cities suggests that his theory of melancholia tended already in the direction of the polis. Moreover, the inspiration to make suggestions about large-scale melancholias through urban, archaeological, and architectural imaginings likely doesn't begin and certainly doesn't end with Freud. Anita Desai's 1988 novel *Baumgartner's Bombay* presents an intriguingly global or bi-hemispheric case, as it portrays a German character in a seemingly quite Freudian condition of melancholia amidst a postcolonial Indian polis with its own less exclusively Freudian melancholic dynamics.[3] The novel forces

---

[2] For an argument I believe to be compatible with my own see the distinction Benjamin (1998, 87-89) draws between self and identity in her consideration of Butler and melancholia.

[3] Appearing in 1988, *Baumgartner's Bombay* was often read throughout the 1990's in the context not so much of melancholia as of the politics of identity and belonging. While some such as Ho (1992), Solanki (1992), Nayak and Swain (1993), and Brush (1996) focused on Baumgartner's alienation both in the rigid culture of Europe and the colonially "exotic" setting of India, Da Silva (1997), by contrast, took offense at the novel's very premise, Baumgartner as focal point for viewing India, and saw Desai's text as irredeemably Eurocentric and ultimately occluding of Indians' experience. Like Ho, Newman (1995), on the other hand, performed a meticulous close reading charting the shifting course of Baumgartner's identity formations through the novel's use of textual and linguistic metaphors. Overall, one suspects that while the novel benefited at first from the quiet attention of close readers, it may have also suffered from an unstated comparison with the work of Salman Rushdie, and thus more broadly political and theoretically engaged readings, such as Mufti's (2007), came later. Also more recently, Guttman (2006) has meticulously analyzed the novel's reception and suggested its presentation of the Jew is amenable to a global literary marketplace in which the twin forces of ethnic stereotyping and humanist universalizing continue to reign supreme. Fludernik (2005) has intriguingly suggested by contrast that the novel's introduction of middle and hybrid identity categories moves its concerns beyond simple self/other or colonizer/colonized binaries, allowing it

us to bring Freudian and postcolonial theories of melancholia, as well as analyses of melancholia at both the individual and the communal level, together. Specifically, when we understand Freud's conception of melancholic internalization in light of Nicolas Abraham and Maria Torok's idea of an inner psychic "crypt," and we then place these models alongside the radical movements toward exteriorization we see in postcolonial writings from Frantz Fanon to Homi Bhabha, we may then catch a new glimpse of melancholia's relation to the polis and to community. Brought into conjunction, these traditions show ways that melancholia's force can be powerfully intrapsychic, intersubjective, intercultural, and even interpolitical at once.

2. The Courses of Loss

In his famous 1917 essay "Mourning and Melancholia," Freud outlines two courses an experience of loss can take, the first a seemingly normal passing period of grief, and the second a prolonged, persistently morbid state, marked by "profoundly painful dejection, abrogation of interest in the outside world, and a lowering of the self-regarding feelings to a degree that finds utterance in self-reproaches and self-revilings, and culminates in a delusional expectation of punishment" (165). Seeking to shed light on this mysterious chronic condition, Freud offers a possible narrative of this melancholia's development. One invested love in an object—a person or an ideal—but later felt hurt or disappointed by the object as well as bereavement at the loss of the attachment. But rather than completely detaching from this object and moving on, one withdrew into oneself. The energy or libido one had invested in the object of love moved into one's own psyche, there "to establish an *identification* of the ego with the abandoned object" (170). In Freud's oft-cited words, "Thus the shadow of the object fell upon the ego, so that the latter could henceforth be criticized by a special mental faculty like an object, like the forsaken object. In this way the loss of the object became transformed into a cleavage between the criticizing faculty of the ego and the ego as altered by the identification" (170). Instead of criticizing the lost and disappointing object, one takes the criticisms out on oneself. All the energy that went into forming the attachment goes into installing a critical presence in one's own psyche, a sort of puppet government that redirects aggression toward one's own ego as if it were a stand-in for the lost object. We are far from Napoleon at

instead to reveal persistent class-based prejudices that are part of "the dark underside of the globalization scenario" (85).

Notre Dame, but the structure, if not tenor, of that fantasized conversation still applies if we shift the implicit exclamation, "You're not here to see what I can do!" from self-satisfied taunt to self-pitying threat. One's psyche has become the dual city, with the idealizing energy going to the "special critical faculty," or Rome, the magic city that preserves all otherwise lost traces, and the criticizing energy directed toward the Acropolis, the city of diminished, derealized existence. But geographically, topographically, and even figuratively, it's hard to imagine these cities coexisting, since one is the total city, founded on a principle of absolute inclusion, a place where everyone's view must remain intact, and the other is a vision one has, only partly taking it in, in someone else's stead. One city defies death, while the other inescapably alludes to it. Rome may be the super city, and to the extent that one clings to dreams of it, according to Freudian logic, one will keep producing also visions of the Acropolis, viewpoints Rome must also preserve. But does the Acropolis have to know that Rome exists?

The urge to memorialize a secret subsuming city, one that certain inhabitants may never know, is crucial to *Baumgartner's Bombay* and even suggested by the novel's title. Furthermore, the novel itself comes into being as a remembrance for the dead. The story of the life and death of Hugo Baumgartner, a German Jewish refugee in India, *Baumgartner's Bombay* is also a way for author Anita Desai to meditate on her dual background, herself as a child of a German mother and Indian father. She explains the book's impetuses and obstacles candidly: "For years, I wanted to write a book about the German part of my background and to put to use the German language which was a part of my childhood. I had no idea how to do it. I didn't want to write a biographical book about my mother, so I had no idea how to go about it" (*Interviews* 174). An odd convergence opens up a course for the desired book:

> Then, when I was an adult in Bombay I used to see this old man shuffling around and feeding cats in the streets the way I've described. I didn't know him personally, but a friend of mine did know him and once told me he that he was not nearly as poor as he looked; he was actually quite rich and owned a race horse. It stuck in my mind as a curious piece of information. This man died a natural death and he had no family in Bombay so this friend of mine had to go and clear up his effects. He brought me a packet of letters in German and asked me to look through them, and they were just little notes, affectionate little notes, with no information at all, simply how are you—and I'm well—don't worry kind of letters. So, I gave them back and said no, they're not important at all. I began to read quite a lot of Holocaust literature a little later, and one of the things I learned was that in the early years of the concentration camps the inmates were allowed to

> write letters, and those letters were always stamped with the number they had in the camp. I remembered that these letters had all been stamped with the same number, and I only realized then that they had come from a concentration camp. Because there was no information about them—the man was dead, I couldn't question him—I began to think a great deal about it and felt the need to supply them with a history, so I invented a history for this figure whom I had seen but not known. (*Interviews* 174-175)

Baumgartner's Bombay, as it moves to Bombay from Berlin, becomes the animation of the lost, unknown city a particular dweller would have experienced. But equally it becomes a revivification of the author's mother's Germany, an utterly familiar but silent realm: "I was able to use all my mother's memories of prewar Germany which had been told me as a child. It used to be our bedtime story—she would talk about prewar Germany. So I was able to put that into the book and use the German language again which gave me a wonderful feeling of liberating a part of my mind, of my self, which I'd had to keep silenced for all those years" (175). If we, as Freud does with Rolland, were to imagine Desai's mind as a city, it might contain within it a hidden city, a maternal Berlin of bedtime and pre-wartime, unaware of the Bombay all around it. But in Desai's case, the cat man's death and personal effects bring the hidden city to light and advance its clocks to wartime.

The story Desai invents, like a grand imaginative cosmopolis, intriguingly incorporates several smaller cities, Berlin, Venice, Calcutta, and Bombay, and it temporally zigzags from its narrative present in contemporary India to its past, set chiefly in the WW II years. We see Hugo Baumgartner's boyhood in a highly assimilated Jewish family of pre-WW II Berlin and watch Nazism's rise and its destructive effects on his family. His father commits suicide, gassing himself with the oven at home, after being sent to and returned from Dachau, an irony in line with the novel's suggestion that the prison camp environment can be pervasive, compatible with multiple times and places. Hugo's mother, equally ironically, refuses to leave the Germany she loves and believes she is so rooted in even as she and Hugo get squeezed out of the family business and their very living space.[4] In a further irony, it is Hugo's father's former business partner, "the gentleman from Hamburg," Herr Pfuehl who, after usurping their business and apartment, tries to arrange Hugo and his mother's escape, their passage to India. Herr Pfuehl's duality underscores

[4] For an interpretation of *Baumgartner's Bombay* as crucially about an under-recognized literary theme, the struggle for shelter in an overurbanized and under-infrastructured world, see Yaeger (2007).

another of the novel's recurrent suggestions that just as what you believe preserves you can in fact smother you, so those who swarm and even oust you can also be those who protect you. Unable to see herself in "some dangerous land in the East, *mit den Schwarzen*" and "spiders and snakes" (57), Hugo's mother nonetheless agrees to let Hugo immigrate to India where we see him become a successful businessman in the timber trade and even a co-owner of a racehorse. Hugo never sees his mother again, and when WW II breaks out, in yet another of the novel's ironies, he is apprehended by the British and interned in a camp along with all others deemed German nationals, including Nazi Germans. After losing contact with his mother and six years of his life in such detention camps, Hugo returns to business, but eventually descends into a life of squalor, taking in stray cats and ultimately the drug-addict hippy who murders him for the few valuables he still possesses.

Hugo's descent into squalor certainly fits with the impoverishment of the ego Freud claims characterizes melancholia, and this dynamic may have also been evinced by Hugo's real-life prototype, the cat man who was allegedly richer than he made himself seem. Further, Hugo's grief is unusually frustrated and disabled: his mother rebuffed his attempts to save her, he was not present when she died, he himself was detained right when she would have been close to death, and he receives her last censored communications way too late. It is only when he is released from detention camp that he is able to pick up his mother's postcards, and they are stamped with her concentration camp prisoner's number, but contradictorily also filled with her overly sweet, empty, repetitive, and clearly false reassurances. At this moment Hugo realizes two things. First, he must now live his life as though the postcards are watching him. We're told, "He had to find a place fit for the cards. He could not live comfortably and luxuriously in the hotel, it would have tortured him to lie down in comfort, to eat and drink, when the cards were stacked in a corner, on a table, the numbers turned up for him to see whenever he looked that way or passed by inadvertently" (164). And second, he feels ill equipped to grieve for her appropriately:

> He thought now that if he had been brought up as an orthodox Jew, he could have mourned her with ceremony; he would have followed the ancient customs, recited the ancient words of solace, and perhaps they would have helped to still the agony. But he was ignorant, and therefore helpless, held in the grip of an unexpressed sorrow. He had to allow the mournful blowing of conch shells and chanting of Sanskrit prayers that drifted in through the windows at twilight suffice as a funeral ceremony for his mother. (165)

Baumgartner's reflections give us a two-sided view of melancholia. We see the precise conditions that distinguish Freud's conception of this state: Hugo will carry his mother with him wherever he goes and he will torture himself as if he could take her place. But we also see a response that might appear to disable a narrowly psychological view of melancholia: Hugo himself considers attributing part of his hollowness to an inherited absence of Judaism, as though his "unexpressed sorrow" might have run a different course had ancient ceremonies, customs, and words been available to him. On the one hand, we could interpret Hugo's cultural narrative of deprivation as symptomatic, as part of his melancholic view of himself as depleted; on the other, we could side with Hugo's own account and give culture primacy in a causal explanation for his melancholia. We might see in his idealizing of Sanskrit chants and longing for a similarly ancient heritage the plight of an assimilated Jewish refugee, that is, the historical plight of a subject's position first and of a particular individual second. In this regard, Hugo would be experiencing a melancholic malady of assimilation and comparison similar to those Anne Cheng, innovating on Frantz Fanon, describes in relation to Asian Americans.[5] But rather than comparing himself disadvantageously to a racially white colonizer or the standards of a normative American "racial imaginary," Hugo seeks to mimic the colonized and he extrapolates standards with scant material, contemplating an ancient Judaism he knows little about in the midst of chants he can't decipher. Hugo's musings thus place him on a borderline between psychological and cultural conceptions of melancholia. And it is crucial to note the sharply self-reflective nature of this state as well as India's key function in bringing this border zone to light. It is at the moment that Hugo entertains a cultural and historical explanation for his melancholic emptiness that he perceives India wafting in to fill the gap. Imaginatively beheld by India, Hugo's mourning becomes all the more insufficient. Acting at once as grounds of melancholic possibility and material for pathetic fallacy, India becomes associated with the very idea of a cultural explanation for melancholia *and* serves as an outer terrain on which to map melancholic feelings. As we will see, Hugo's initial intercultural transposition here develops even further to become an experience of India in which the country itself seems made to mourn for those grieved and buried without ceremony.

The transposition becomes more severe and sweeping when it is not simply India's prayers that drift in through a window, but India's historical

---

[5] See particularly Cheng (2001, 80-81).

state of crisis that crashes in on Baumgartner.[6] Cut off from India's experience of the war while he was interned, Baumgartner returns to Calcutta (his residence before Bombay) to find it a bombed-out ghost town:

> The Calcutta he lived in now—the Calcutta that had seen the famine of 1943, that had prepared for a Japanese attack, that had been used and drained by the war and war profiteers and now prepared for the great partition—was the proper setting for his mourning. The Calcutta of the black back streets, the steaming rubbish tips, the scarred tenements, its hunger, its squalor, its desolation. The hopelessness of it seemed right to Baumgartner; this was how the world ended, there was no other ending. (165-166)

The play on T.S. Eliot's "The Hollow Men" at the end of this passage signals also the play on his concept of the objective correlative. Unable to fully mourn, Baumgartner sees his mournful state written out all around him, preserved in the ruins of a city. Just as Freud makes all Rome's periods simultaneous, Baumgartner's view of Calcutta is of an archive of successive waves of destruction. And just as Freud transposed his resistance to accepting the reality of his journey to the Acropolis onto the Acropolis itself, so Baumgartner casts his despair and disbelief onto his surroundings, as though he requires Calcutta's presence for a stage he is setting. Tracking Freudian melancholia, we might say that the shadow of the lost object has fallen on the ego, and the ego is so depleted and expecting of punishment that it must perceive this shadow as coming from without, and in Baumgartner's case, history complies spectacularly. But also, in a larger historical sense, the waves of WW II's cataclysms *are* the material of Baumgartner's melancholia.[7] His tragic recourse to transposing overlaps with an ever expanding and displacing disaster in history, one responsible for the separations, internments, dislocations, and losses of people that are the major events in Baumgartner's life. India, revealed specifically through the former colonial capital Calcutta, functions as a correlative to Baumgartner's deprivation *and* as a hub for the very historical forces that have produced such deprivation. Seeing India through

---

[6] Elsewhere (Thompson, 2009) I have discussed the quoted passage that follows and Baumgartner's other melancholic epiphanies in relation to postcolonial literature's depictions of the city and engagements with science, particularly the image of black holes and the idea of the laboratory.

[7] For an important reading of the novel as uncovering a buried history of modernity as "a network of subterranean and uncanny linkages that connect 'Europe' to the world's 'peripheries'" see Mufti (2007, 249).

Baumgartner's eyes, we can see a particularly sharp incarnation of Freud's Melancholopolis, a vast and devastated city that stands as both melancholia's objective correlative and a constitutive milieu.

Yet when Baumgartner affirms, "this was how the world ended," we might also see his melancholic metropolis diverging from Freud's examples: his Melancholopolis, unlike either Freud's eternal or his ever-potential city, is bounded. And boundaries are key in the crises occurring around him, with "the great partition" referring to the 1947 birth of an independent India but the simultaneous division of territory to create the separate Muslim nation of Pakistan. Often referred to as a Holocaust of the East, this event resulted not only in a massive uprooting and transfer of populations as India's Muslims and Pakistan's Hindus tried desperately to migrate across new borders, but also in mass riots and an enormous bloodbath as mutual resentment led to out of control violence. As significant to South Asian literature as the history of slavery and the Civil War might be to US literature, Partition is depicted in numerous South Asian novels with scenes of mob violence, references to the arrival on both sides of corpse-filled trains, stories of numerous newly made refugees, and images of burning cities.[8] To take this history as an outer expression of a blocked inner state would be no small matter. We need to describe Baumgartner's inner psychic terrain with more precision to shed further light on this convergence.

Nicolas Abraham and Maria Torok's account of melancholic incorporation and encrypting becomes especially useful for understanding Baumgartner's inner world. Whereas in Freud's famous formulation, the shadow of the lost object engulfs the ego, in Abraham and Torok's melancholic incorporation, "in order not to have to 'swallow' a loss, we fantasize swallowing (or having swallowed) that which has been lost, as if it were some kind of thing" (126). Or in particularly extreme cases of losses that cannot be communicated or acknowledged, "Inexpressible mourning erects a secret tomb inside the subject. Reconstituted from the memories of words, scenes, and affects, the objectal correlative of the loss is buried alive in the crypt as a full-fledged person, complete with its own topography" (130). This crypt or "intrapsychic tomb," as they call it, can be both a correlative and a world within a world—or, particularly suggestively for Baumgartner's 1947 India, a state within a state. They claim an entire other psyche with its own topographical components can

[8] A classic example and close contemporary of *Baumgartner's Bombay* is Bapsi Sidhwa's 1988 novel *Ice-Candy-Man*, which was later published in the US as *Cracking India*. Notably my 1989 British paperback edition bears on its front cover Desai's recommendation.

be set up within one psychic area in order to isolate and seal off a wound (135). This tomb-being is most likely to exist in those whose egos have already in life experienced severe shame, those whose egos have already been, as they say, "partitioned" (131).

As an assimilated Jew in pre-WW II Berlin, Hugo is presented as always having felt an originless shame, a sense that although no one had told him so, "he did not belong to the radiant, the triumphant of the world" (36). He appears to experience a kind of psychic sectioning off even in Germany. And Hugo seems to know he has associated an alien shame not with both his parents, but principally with his mother, having complained to her as a boy, ""You don't look like everyone else's mother," and demanded, "'Why don't you look like the other mothers?'" (33). India's communal violence, of which Baumgartner seems only peripherally aware, might become his imagined counterpart to a double shame, one at both his relation to his mother, a bond which grows ever closer after his father's death, and his disowning of her. Equally usefully, India's landscape can allow Baumgartner to literalize his crypt. In a late moment in the novel we find Hugo exploring a cave shrine in the countryside, and although he can find no god or idol there, only an unreadable inscribed stone slab, still he feels himself unbearably watched and expelled before he can discover the chamber's secret (189-190). He tells himself he is the "indigestible' and "unwanted" foreigner, but we might also feel he has kicked himself out of his own secret so as not to defile it. Just as Torok and Abraham, extending their metaphors, claim, "Sometimes in the dead of the night… the ghost of the crypt comes back to haunt the cemetery guard, giving him strange and incomprehensible signals…" (130), so we might feel that Hugo is drawn to a ghostly vision of a crypt that he will nonetheless not desecrate by making it comprehensible, by acknowledging it as familiar and not foreign at all. But when death and union with his parents come to him in another guise—the drugged-out young blond German backpacker Kurt who will rob and murder him—Baumgartner takes them in. Kurt's spoiled and infantile behavior actually resonates with Hugo's guilty memories of his own treatment of his mother, his boyhood tantrums and protests that he wanted to go off on heroic adventures with his father. Appropriately, Torok and Abraham see the preservation of an intra-psychic crypt as allowing subjects to bear others psychically within them. They cite the example of a boy who "'carried' inside him his sister…who died when the boy was eight…" (130). A kleptomaniac in later life, the boy finds himself shoplifting items his sister might have needed as she grew up. If we see Hugo as likewise cryptically and internally preserving an unresolved and unspoken bond with his mother, even to the point of his acting on her behalf as though he carried her within, his enabling of his own murder by Kurt might serve many psychic purposes. We could say that Hugo's mother's dignity is restored and Hugo can finally be present at her death, if she—as preserved and entombed within him—can be seen to die at the hands of a murderer, and one that is a brutal, bratty facsimile of Hugo no less. Baumgartner can be guilty of the death he blames himself for, he can absolve his mother of the charges of self-victimization he may secretly hurl at her, and finally he can feel neither one will have abandoned the other.[9] This might be the violently internalized side of the novel's melancholia, one most clearly visible with an at least partial eclipse of the novel's social and political world.

But if melancholia works as much by imaginatively casting out as it does by internalizing, and if it can not only inspire secret fantasies where "The 'shadow of the object' strays endlessly about the crypt until it is finally reincarnated in the person of the subject" (141), but also compel the external environment to wear the melancholic's heart on its sleeve, then the internal psychic view of this state will never be enough. Torok and Abraham suggestively claim, "We consider it useful to complement Freud's metapsychological formula, in 'Mourning and Melancholia'—which shows 'the ego in the guise of the object'—by its opposite...: *the 'object,' in turn, carries the ego as its mask...*" (141). The notion that a shadowy aura can become figuratively incarnated and that the melancholic subject can become the lost object's mask tempts us with the idea that Bombay and the India it stands for must also be made to mourn Baumgartner, and in this case, literature and literary theory comply. The external view of melancholia, an understanding of its political significance in contexts removed from its psychoanalytic conceptual origin, can shed light on impulses behind a portrait of an urban India that would want to

---

[9] Using the concept of survivor's guilt, Newman (1995, 63) arrives at similar interpretations for Baumgartner's seeming complicity in his own death. She is at pains to point out, though, that any apparent resemblance between Baumgartner and Kurt is an illusion arising from Baumgartner's inner tormented state. I would add, though, that Kurt's lengthy description of his mystical travels exceeds the bounds of psychological realism, introducing an odd element of magical realism, however horrific at times. Smith (1997) has discovered substantial intertextual links between Baumgartner's internment scenes as well as Kurt's travel accounts and Heinrich Harrer's *Seven Years in Tibet*. Kurt, along with the Harrer he and Hugo bear with them, seems a vehicle, then, for the condensed expression of metatextual longings; while he perhaps partly parodies the Austrian traveler who had been a youthful member of the *SS*, he also harkens back to a time of explorers' adventures, and his participation in several religious ceremonies, Muslim ones included, might suggest a nostalgia for a pluralist pre-Partition India.

encrypt a Baumgartner. As we have seen, the classical conception of melancholia can be expanded, blown up in effect, to account for cultural and historical narratives that might appear to predispose not simply individual subjects, but individuals inhabiting certain subject positions for melancholia. But the concept of melancholia has played a dramatically different role in postcolonial theory. Torok and Abraham reach creative insights when they reverse the polarity between ego and object. But postcolonial theory has traditionally inverted the entire movement of melancholia's energy. If Torok and Abraham's melancholia exists in a heightened way at the point of speech's impasses and language's negative space, postcolonial theory traditionally situates its accounts at the point of language's articulation. And if Freud's melancholia resembles an eclipse or black hole, postcolonial theory's version is a supernova.

3. "Ex-pawt!"

In the early 1990's, postcolonial theorist Homi Bhabha asked a difficult question, one that will sketch out the terms of an anti-melancholia and turn out to be related to India's possible encrypting of Baumgartner: "Why is the metaphor of the *articulation of language* so central to contemporary cultural theorists concerned with the problem of ambivalence and contingency in the construction of political identities within what is loosely called, a 'politics of difference'—twinning the notion of 'the unconscious like a language' with 'the political as a language'?" (58). He saw that his colleagues and contemporaries who were engaged in bringing unrepresented cultural identities and experiences to notice also became fascinated with language itself, bringing together its psychically and politically charged nature. He cited numerous theorists and writers, from Roland Barthes, Jacques Derrida, and Cornel West, to Salman Rushdie and Toni Morrison. And in addition to citing these scenes where language's articulation is central, Bhabha also saw important uses of "time-lag" or moments that revealed a glitch or noncoincidence between language working on the level of symbols and language functioning as signs (59). It almost seemed as though writers who brought language's nuts and bolts to the fore were addressing conditions of melancholia by breaking down symbols that had led to depleted egos and then making room for ambivalence's expression. Bhabha was tracking the courses of ambivalence through their cultural representations, but it's worth recalling that Freud's melancholia was also at core a form of ambivalence, typically triggered by a mixing of resentment and bereavement and often bringing out the longstanding mixtures of love and hate that can exist in intense attachments. Bhabha passionately exhorted us, "Difficult though it is, we cannot understand what is being proposed for new times—politics at the site of cultural enunciation; culture in the place of political affiliation—if we do not see that the discourse of the language-metaphor suggests that in each achieved symbol of cultural/political identity or synchronicity there is always the repetition of the sign that represents the place of psychic ambivalence and social contingency" (59). In keeping with his belief that the language-metaphor was there to hold up to the light all language's difficulties so that we could see what was struggling to get articulated, Bhabha himself in the questions and answers that followed his paper responded to Fred Pfeil's perception of his writing's "forbidding difficulty" by saying, "I can't apologize for the fact that you found my paper completely impenetrable. I did it quite consciously, I had a problem, I worked it out. And if a few people got what I was saying or some of what I am saying, I'm happy. If not, obviously, it's a disaster" (67). Here we can see Bhabha wanting four things: to take on the difficult work of mourning what language at the level of symbol loses, to refuse becoming dejected and melancholy, to premise his happiness on even partial communication with a fortuitous few, and to avoid the way the world ends—the disaster of complete communicative dissonance. Willfully performative and performatively willful as Bhabha may have been, his theoretical model and personal example turn out to be highly applicable to Desai.

When Baumgartner arrives in India and goes to see the associate with whom he is to do business, they struggle to overcome inertia and communicate across their very different Englishes.

> The man behind the desk seemed puzzled at the mention of Hamburg, timber, shipping … every word that Baumgartner managed to summon out of his new language, dragging it off his tongue with a reluctance bordering on paralysis, the bald, dark man in the long white cotton shirt with small gold buttons shook his head at in mystified denial. On the wall behind him hung a picture of an eleven-armed goddess, and over its frame was draped a garland of tinsel. Baumgartner found himself staring at it in his frustration—it drew and held his attention and seemed increasingly weird, foreign, exotic and inscrutable to him.
>
> Then he chanced to find the word 'Ex-port'. 'Ex-phott,' he said, and the fat, puzzled, perspiring man seemed to roll himself up into a ball, tight with excitement, and then explode out of his seat.
>
> 'Ex-pawt!' he gasped, clutching the side of his head. 'Ex-pawt. *Of course*, ex-pawt. Germany, Europe. Shipping, timber—I know, I know.' (86)

We have a scene of ambivalent cultural identity where to survive Baumgartner must represent German business interests in a rival European language to an Indian associate for whom this language is colonial. Just as Bhabha describes, time falters, a word's enunciation is accentuated, and language takes on a metaphorical significance. It's hard not to notice that the word "export" plays off the words "exotic," "excitement," and "explode," but also as "ex-pawt" alludes to Baumgartner's new expatriate status. The scene is one of the novel's many portraits of a cultural interstice or inter-space. In this meeting of European and Indian, Baumgartner is frozen in a state "bordering on paralysis" while his "mystified" interlocutor, Chimanlal, is clearly more mobile and expansive. What mediates and mitigates the almost thwarted exchange is the goddess and Baumgartner's vision of the goddess. Since for him she is unknown and unnamed, he can imagine her as "exotic and inscrutable." While these words taken as wholes are stereotypical enough adjectives for things Asian seen through Western eyes, their prefixes of "ex" and "in" seem to suggest the flow of goods to Baumgartner, and he is able to produce the magic word, ironically working like a multiply pronounced mantra that suddenly makes Germany and Europe exist. Chimanlal, like the goddess, thrusts out his arms, moving over to shake Baumgartner's hand and slap his back. Baumgartner stares up at this fortune-granting goddess "for an explanation—perhaps she had brought about this flood of communication," and doesn't mind that Chimanlal has now begun "to babble at such a speed that Baumgartner gave up even trying to follow" (86). At this point that depicts language's enunciation, the goddess presides, seeming to work whether her observers are foreign or familiar. As she guides communication past the point where language needs to be mutually comprehensible, we see she takes Bhabha's model a step further, reanimating a symbol beyond signs.

Again and again, the India Desai has Baumgartner encounter is a realm of multiform possibilities, heightened ironies, and performative language. For him it's a land where "All seemed possible, too possible" (84); where any hotel can be the Taj Hotel, if, as a fleabag hotel proprietress screams, "I say Taj Hotel, then *this* Taj Hotel" (85); where the environment naturally induces malaria but also produces its cure, quinine (93); and where Baumgartner, literally the tree gardener, finds

> Languages sprouted around him like tropical foliage and he picked words from it without knowing if they were English or Hindi or Bengali—they were simply words he needed: *chai, khana, baraf, lao, jaldi, joota, chota peg, pani, kamra, soda, garee* ... what was this language he was wrestling out of the air, wrenching around to his own purposes? He suspected it was not Indian, but India's, the India he was marking out for himself. (92)

Much as Freud arriving at the Acropolis felt regarding his father, Baumgartner imagines communicating all this to his mother, but knows that it is an experience she would never appreciate. This extra-Indian, hyper-fecund India that can actualize all possibilities and verbally supply any need nonetheless excludes his mother, and Baumgartner's experiencing it in her stead renders it a euphoric but derealized realm: "If it had been a real scene, in a real land, then Baumgartner with his hat and shoes would have been too unlikely a visitor to be possible," but, "If he were real, then surely the scene, the setting was not. How could the two exist together in one land? The match was improbable beyond belief" (93). Just as Freud ended his magical vision of an eternal Rome with the thought that one space having two opposed contents was an absurdity, Baumgartner's simultaneously all-embracing but derealized India raises logical problems. As he imaginatively communicates with his mother in this realm that is India's rather than India, his melancholia becomes paradoxical. The more he transplants himself in this environment, the more his inner state reincarnates through multiple associations and forms, but the more he Baumgartnerizes India, the less real it becomes. The "improbable match" of Baumgartner's relation to his mother and then transposition of it onto his vision of the Indian landscape gives us a melancholia that as it is exported is exploded, and as it actualizes, derealizes—dualities that are both dazzling and dangerous.

The seemingly anti-melancholic urge to actualize new possibilities, refuse dejection, and push outward through the force of an arduously articulated language is characteristic of postcolonial texts but double-edged. Bhabha derives much of his model from Frantz Fanon, citing particularly *The Wretched of the Earth*. Here Fanon sees colonialism and colonialist psychoanalytic theories as forcing their victims to "hunt down" not only an outer enemy, "but also the core of despair crystallized in the body of the colonized" (219). And colonialism's implantation of despair has depleted more than sole egos: "The very structure of society has been depersonalized on a collective level. A colonized people is thus reduced to a collection of individuals who owe their very existence to the presence of the colonizer" (219-220). What to do with the rotten, infected seeds that produce this meager, scraggly crop? People fighting to free themselves must "reject or explode the so-called truths sown in their consciousness by the colonial regime, military occupation, and economic exploitation" (220). Here we see a precursor and analogue to Bhabha's refusals and Desai's images of explosive kernels, sprouting plants, and bursts of language. But what makes the motif of the explosive seed itself ambivalent for postcolonial writers is the nature of the colonially implanted "truths," one of which is that colonized people cannot develop genuine melancholia. Fanon cites and summarizes numerous French psychological studies of Algerians that paint a composite portrait of the Algerian as lacking "moral conscience," "verbal expression," and a sense of larger contexts and consequences. Such Algerians, these studies say, could not possibly internalize ambivalence, berate themselves, and lapse into chronic withdrawal. Instead, their actions will be violently "impulsive," examples of "aggressiveness in a pure state," their melancholias mere "pseudo-melancholias" (224-225). For anti-colonialists to combat a falsely imputed lack of consciousness, verbal expression, and interiority with overabundant organicism, fractured language, and explosiveness, in short, with an exteriorizing energy so strong as to seem a force of nature, may appear the equivalent of fighting poison with poison. Hence, perhaps, Desai's transposition of the wildly exteriorizing and actualizing India beyond Indians onto the viewpoint of Baumgartner, as though it is the dispossessed European who comes to see the poison cure. However much Baumgartner outgrows his first perceptions of exoticism, and however much the novel's most exuberant passages gesture towards a transcendent India, we never fully let go of a European focalization in the text. And in this way, ironically, the text can be seen as containing Europe, offering up a portrait of its perspective. With the incorporation of the dispossessed diasporic European, the text might offer a chiasmus as compromise between the interior and exterior perspectives of psychoanalytic and postcolonial theory, that is, it might seek to contain the seed it explodes and explode the seed it contains.

4. A Bloomin' Indian

But beyond the simultaneous actualizing of all possibilities yet continual insinuation of unreality, a duality that recapitulates both psychoanalysis's Rome/Acropolis tension and postcolonial theory's poles of explosive growth and implanted lack, India comes to represent a more specific environment for Baumgartner: the prison camp. The idea of the camp's expansiveness may be prefigured in Fanon's remarks that life in a colony follows a brutal farmyard "pecking order" where "The strongest birds gobble up all the grain while the less aggressive grow visibly thinner." He adds, chillingly, "Any colony tends to become one vast farmyard, one vast concentration camp where the only law is that of the knife" (232). In a counterpart episode to Baumgartner's magical encounter with Chimanlal where exported Englishes can meet, we see Baumgartner apprehended by the British at the outbreak of WW II, and it is his passport that spells the end of the language-metaphor's magic. Producing all his papers, his mother's letters included, before a British officer, Baumgartner now receives the force of imperial Britain's explosiveness as the officer bursts with "expressions and gestures of rage and exasperation," embodying a monstrous side to reason:

> 'What am I to do then?' the man bawled when Baumgartner again protested at being labeled a German and 'hostile'. 'Got a German passport, says you were born there—then what am I supposed to take you for, a bloomin' Indian?' The papers were flung at him, and he retreated, baffled, wondering what magic word he might find that would release him from what was a monstrous mistake, or madness. (106)

Whereas Joyce's Leopold Bloom might premise his Irishness on being born there, in British India Baumgartner's native land is turned against him. European national categories cut him off from the trans-Indian India he took comfort and root in. And in the camp we see Fanon's farmyard pecking order with the hyper-efficient Nazi German prisoners' sense of discipline outclassing and awing even the British overseers with their lax attempts at administrative order. Forcing the Jewish internees into displays of German patriotism, the Nazi inmates not only become classic examples of the schoolyard bully, but they also provide the most powerful illustration of what Hugo has always felt, the sense that identity is itself a travesty.[10] Yet if identities are what come capriciously from without, often arising to stifle and smother their targets, they can also be strangely protective, conducive to the formation of hollows and shells. In the camp's idle monotony, Baumgartner feels both "the emptiness of the space into which they had been swallowed" (125) and the sense that "He knew it was craven not to desire freedom, but it was true that captivity had provided him with an escape from the fate of those in Germany, and safety from the anarchy of the world outside" (131). The camp is intrapsychic and expansive, an external representation of an emptiness inside Baumgartner and a shell he will travel within wherever he goes afterwards, as though it encrypts and carries him while setting a limit to freedom and desire.

And yet as easy a transpositional equation as Baumgartner's inner

---

[10] See Mufti (2007, 252-254) for a reading of this interlude as exposing the ever present problem of the minority in modernity and as illustrating both Adorno's view of fascism as the realization of a child's nightmare and Sartre's view of liberal democrats (in Desai, the British establishing the camp) and anti-Semites (the Nazis actually running it) as depleting the Jewish subject in complementary ways.

absences and his external Indian experiences may seem to form, there are excesses on both sides, European maladies that don't find simple exported cures in the colony and Indian historical specificities that can't simply be correlatives for European melancholia. Returning to the moment when Baumgartner is released from the camp into a war-torn, pre-Partition Calcutta, we see Baumgartner's strongest epiphany—and indeed the novel's—come on the heels of his making a shocking discovery. On the one hand, upon his return, Baumgartner comes to a natural understanding with his now imperiled Muslim colleague Habibullah, albeit through a recognition of symmetrical ignorance, realizing both that "their situation was not very different—and equally hopeless" and that "Habibullah had no more conception of Baumgartner's war, of Europe's war than Baumgartner had of affairs in Bengal, in India" (169). On the other hand, after choosing to remain a year in Calcutta, seemingly to let the burning city live out his grief for him, Baumgartner learns of the trial of twenty thousand Indian National Army members, and he is struck dumb when he is told that these rebel fighters for India's independence allied themselves with Japan. Understanding suddenly the psychic consequences of this complicity, that he can't evade the guilt at his melancholic core with a transposition onto a sublimely separate mournful correlative, Baumgartner at once abortively repels the revelation and addresses himself directly, thinking, "'Not here, not this, Hugo. No, no," and then lets the tension culminate in his epiphany:

> His war was not their war. And they had had their own war. War within war within war. Everyone engaged in a separate war, and each war opposed to another war. If they could be kept separate, chaos would be averted. Or so they seemed to think, ignoring the fact that chaos was already upon them. And lunacy. The lunacy of performing acts one did not wish to perform, living lives one did not wish to live, becoming what one was not. Always another will opposed to one's own, always another fate, not the one of one's choice or even making. A great web in which each one was trapped, a nightmare from which one could not emerge. (173)

And again, when the Partition riots erupt and he learns of twenty thousand deaths, Baumgartner feels "overtaken by yet another war of yet another people. Done with the global war, the colonial war, only to be plunged into a religious war. Endless war. Eternal war" (180). What might seem like endless arbitrary separatist wars are in fact the fulfillment of a pattern for Baumgartner, the point where his inner psychic experience of complicity and partitioning comes back to him in separate struggles that cannot be kept separate. The unavoidable chaos becomes the chaos dynamic of a fractal structure, with each faction's war an objective correlative for an inner partition and each intrapsychic partition the objectal correlative for a disowned relation, in short a portrait of the social and psychic terrain of total war.[11]

Yet it is out of the threat of this dystopian world that the possibility of second citizenship emerges, since it is this epiphanic vision that propels Baumgartner back to Bombay where he will finally "sort out the matter of his papers," a return and re-rooting that coincide with one of his most melancholy derealized inner dialogues:

> It made him realise how much a native he had become. Baumgartner, a native of Hindustan. He smiled, thinking of what Mu would have said to that. And yet he had not met a single snake other than in a snake-charmer's basket on the city pavements—he must tell her that. But—he forgot constantly, again and again he stopped and was brought up against the fact he could not admit: he would never hear from her again, there would be no more communication. He wrote to people, to addressees he remembered; he never had a reply; all of Germany might have been wiped off the face of the earth. That made him sort out the matter of his papers, his passport, his nationality, and found himself become an Indian citizen, the holder of an Indian passport. Holding it, he wondered if it meant that he would now never leave India and realised that, for all that it was a travel document, it did. (180-181)

Again we have both equality *and* asymmetry. The finally obtained new Indian passport represents stasis just as the old German one led to ousting and internment. It's as though the logic of the Baumgartner principle dictates that every assumption of ratified identity, Eastern or Western, elicits also a travesty. On the other hand, Baumgartner sees himself as gaining a new Indian nativity with an eclipse of painful European origins. Having attained citizenship in what was for his mother the unreal country, Baumgartner finds the unsettling thought that she can never join or hear him must be accompanied by derealizing the entire nation of Germany, and again, history complies, having effaced the Baumgartners' Berlin. Baumgartner's new national status occurs with a simultaneous psychic partition, a revelation of cut-off communication. The model of citizenship that grows out of his nightmare epiphany, his vision of partitioning and complicity taken to violently extreme limits, is one that must always carry

[11] This interpretation overlaps with my earlier reading of *Baumgartner's Bombay* (Thompson, 2009, 10), but there I propose that the suggestion of a fractal pattern can be seen as an instance of postcolonial literature's use of melancholia as a model for a "theory of everything" for modernity.

with it a silenced listener.

While it may seem strange to conceive of nativity or citizenship arising from and with one's recognition of being inhabited by a silent interlocutor, this is a mode of being that Desai associates as much with Indian identity as with survivor consciousness. The image of a city, a capital city, of loss and separations recurs especially in her recollections of growing up in pre-Partition Delhi, which she calls "a city of ruins," one that was once home to a large Muslim population. Desai recalls 1947 and the "enormous change and enormous loss when suddenly all of one's Muslim neighbours vanished," and she adds, "It seemed to me completely unnatural and an abnormality that there should be a city so divided." But she claims also that the city retains what it lost, through the performance of words: "it's still being kept alive by the Urdu language. Even though historically, the Islamic part of India has moved to Pakistan and long after its people—the people who speak it—have dwindled and even vanished, that language has remained and people still compose in it, write poetry in it." For Desai, the city's maintenance of this literary language, beyond even the presence of the language's people, makes it a "repository" for part of its lost life (*Interview*, 160-161). Again we notice in a particularly sharp example a poignant pattern. Freud's Rome and Athens, T. S. Eliot's London, Joyce's Dublin, Desai's Delhi, and Baumgartner's Berlin, Calcutta, and Bombay —all these manifestations of the Melancholopolis, the site where the ego divides to behold itself critically and thus arguably psychoanalysis's capital, seem to be capital cities themselves, civilizationally, imperially, colonially, nationally, or commercially. And their importance is underscored in the phantom life they lead through fragments, architectural, linguistic, or textual. As capitals, or literally "heads" of states, they are there to be representative, but also as synecdoches, to stand apart, to be partly cut off. Conceptually a cut passes through a population and the symbol of a people. If we take a capital as a symbol, it partly becomes no longer "a human habitation" and thus is doomed to be haunted by multitudes. Baumgartner becomes a placeholder, then, for all such ruins, the would-be sights and sounds of others. And as Bhabha suggests with language and cultural identity, there is no other way to express all the ambivalence that gets left out, that is lost in the cut to the symbol, without returning to sharp scenes where linguistic signs struggle, disrupting what's enshrined or what has been implanted.

Following the logic of the novel's many ironies and encryptings, we might hypothesize, then, that the fractal pattern of Baumgartner's dystopic vision portrays in negative the utopia the text holds out, but, in its final act of compromise, must make spectral. The crucially dispossessed character can be entitled, literally if not historically, to the cosmopolitan Indian city if it is seen as possessed by him beyond his death, hence the port-mortem images of Baumgartner's body that open and close the novel. Bombay and Baumgartner, then, can be India's rather than India, just as a partitioned off state or time might wear another regime as its mask, or just as Hugo's very person can become Mutti's in her absence. These moments of becoming at once the permitted foreign "native" of India and the original other's, Mutti's, guest, do come about through disasters and painful derealizations, ones that put narrow customary conceptions of both social and psychic melancholia on edge. But the novel's insistent idealization of them hints that the realm of derealized possessives might be preferable to habitual narratives of belonging, if only we could give it reasonable life.

References

Abraham, Nicolas and Maria Torok. 1994. *The Shell and the Kernel, Volume 1*. Trans. and ed. Nicholas T. Rand. Chicago: University of Chicago Press.

Benjamin, Jessica. 1998. *Shadow of the Other, Intersubjectivity and Gender in Psychoanalysis*. New York: Routledge.

Bhabha, Homi K. 1992. Postcolonial Authority and Postmodern Guilt. In *Cultural Studies*. Ed. Lawrence Grossberg, Cary Nelson, Paula A. Treichler. New York: Routledge.

Brush, Pippa. 1996. German, Jew, Foreigner: The Immigrant Experience in Anita Desai's *Baumgartner's Bombay*. In *Critical Survey*. 1996. 8 (3). 277-285.

Butler, Judith. 1997. *The Psychic Life of Power, Theories in Subjection*. Stanford: Stanford University Press.

Cheng Anne Anlin. 2001. *The Melancholy of Race, Psychoanalysis, Assimilation, and Hidden Grief*. New York: Oxford University Press.

Desai, Anita. 1988. *Baumgartner's Bombay*. Toronto: Lester & Orpen Dennys.

—. 1992. Anita Desai. Interview by Feroza Jussawalla, in *Interviews with Writers of the Post-Colonial World*. Ed. Feroza Jussawalla and Reed Way Dasenbrock. Jackson: University Press of Mississippi.

Fanon, Frantz. 1963. *The Wretched of the Earth*. Trans. Richard Philcox New York: Grove Press. 2004.

Fludernik, Monika. 2005. Cross-Mirrorings of Alterity: The Colonial Scenario and Its Psychological Legacy. In *Linked Histories: Postcolonial Studies in a Globalized World*. Calgary, AB: U of Calgary P, 2005. 63-89.

Freud, Sigmund. 1917. Mourning and Melancholia. Trans. Joan Rivierre. In *General Psychological Theory, Papers on Metapsychology*. Ed. Philip Rieff. New York: Collier Books, Macmillan, 1963. 164-179.

—. 1930. *Civilization and Its Discontents*. Trans. James Strachey. New York: Norton. 1961.

—. 1936. A Disturbance of Memory on the Acropolis. In *On Metapsychology: ,The Theory of Psychoanalysis, Beyond the Pleasure Principle, The Ego and the Id, and Other Works, The Pelican Freud Library,Volume 11*. Trans. James Strachey and ed. Angela Richards. London: Penguin, 1964. 1984. 443-456.

Gilroy, Paul. 2004. *Postcolonial Melancholia*. New York: Columbia University Press.

Guttman, Anna. 2006. Marketing the Figure of the Jew: Writing South Asia, Reading America. In *The Global Literary Field*. Ed. Anna

Guttman, Michael Hockx, and George Paizis. Newcastle: Cambridge Scholars Press. 2006. 60-79.

Da Silva, Tony Simoes. 1997. Whose Bombay Is It Anyway? Anita Desai's *Bombay*. In *ARIEL: A Review of International Literature*. 1997. 28 (3). 63-77.

Ho, Elaine Y. L. 1992. The Languages of Identity in Anita Desai's *Baumgartner's Bombay*. In *World Literatures Written in English*. 1992. Spring. 32 (1). 96-106.

Mufti, Aamir R. 2007. *Enlightenment in the Colony, The Jewish Question and the Crisis of Postcolonial Culture*. Princeton: Princeton University Press.

Nayak, P. M. and Swain, S. P. 1993. The Outsider in Desai's *Baumgartner's Bombay*. In *Commonwealth Novel in English*. 1993. Spring-Fall. 6 (1-2). 112-120.

Newman, Judie. 1995. *The Ballistic Bard, Postcolonial Fictions*. London: Arnold.

Sidhwa, Bapsi. 1988. *Ice-Candy-Man*. London: Penguin. 1989.

Smith, Katharine Capshaw. 1997. Narrating History: The Reality of the Internment Camps in Anita Desai's *Baumgartner's Bombay*. In *ARIEL: A Review of International Literature*. 1997. April. 28 (2). 141-157.

Solanki, Mrinalini. 1992. *Baumgartner's Bombay*: An Attempt to Survive. In *Literary Criterion*. 1992. 27 (3). 1-13.

Thompson, Hilary. 2009. The Colonial City as Inverted Laboratory in *Baumgartner's Bombay* and *The Calcutta Chromosome*. In *Journal of Narrative Theory*. 2009. Fall. 39 (3). 347-368.

Yaeger, Patricia. 2007. Introduction: Dreaming of Infrastructure. *PMLA*. 2007. 122 (1). 9-26.

CHAPTER ELEVEN

CAMUS'S *THE STRANGER* AND MILLER'S ORDINARY PSYCHOSIS

MAIRE JAANUS

> Even humiliated, the flesh is my only certainty.
> —Camus, "*The Absurd Man*"

A Stranger to the Symbolic

It seems evident from the start that Meursault is a stranger to the symbolic. Language is not his home. It is not his "house of being (*Haus des Seins*)," as it was for Heidegger. (Heidegger, 45) He is not at all comfortable with words or with having to speak. He shirks verbal encounters. He does not like speaking. He is hesitant and uncertain about what to say to others. Often he does not respond at all or simply agrees with what others say so as to stop any further verbal interaction. "I said, 'Yes,' just so I wouldn't have to say anything else." (Camus, 4) He does the same with the magistrate during his trial, "As always, whenever I want to get rid of someone I'm not really listening to, I made it appear as if I agreed." (Camus, 69)

Often, he simply stops listening to what is being said. He is at once both unsure in the symbolic and bored by it. He's bored because he doesn't grasp what is being said. He comprehends the prosecutor's argument "only in bits and pieces." (Camus, 98) Although what the prosecutor says will be decisive for his fate, he tells us that he got "bored very quickly with the prosecutor's speech," and "stopped listening." (Camus, 99) When the prosecutor goes on longer about his mother than his crime, Meursault reports, "Finally all I was aware of was how hot a morning it was." (Camus, 101) As always, when the trials of language, the demands of speaking and listening, become too much for him, he turns away to his body and the world of his sensations.

Sometimes when he does say something, he doubts whether he should have said it: "I shouldn't have said that." (Camus, 3) Because speaking puts a strain on him, he avoids situations where speaking is expected. He avoids going to Céleste's, the restaurant he usually goes to for lunch on Sundays, "because they'd be sure to ask questions and I don't like that." (Camus, 23) Even just asking his boss for time off to attend his mother's funeral is stressful. He is so unsure whether his words carry conviction or have validity that signs seem preferable. A sign will speak better for him than his words do. Wearing black mourning dress will provide a more definite certification of her death for his boss than his own statements. A sign need not be connected to another sign. It stands alone. It suffices. A sign is somewhat like the syntaxless noun statement or the pointing finger of a toddler.

Basically, he does not like to speak or listen because language gives him no enjoyment. He doesn't know what symbolic pleasure or what Lacan called *jouis-sens* is. He does not know how to fill himself up with verbal matter -- with knowledge, meanings, fantasies, desires, or dreams -- to the point of feeling pleasure and satisfaction. He does not know how to play with words or to make patterns of thoughts and images with them in his mind. Having a sense of fulfillment from using language himself or from exchanging language with others is not an ongoing occurrence for him. Only at the end of the novel does he have the experience of using language to fill his emptiness and terror with some symbolic and imaginary jouissance, derived from his own arduous efforts to think, feel, and imagine.

He is a stranger to the various paths to symbolic and imaginary satisfaction because he is not fully subjectivized or a subject in the Lacanian sense of the word. He is not a signifier. He has no being in language because he has not "eat [en] the book" or the signifiers, as the book of the Apocalypse commands. (Lacan, 1992: 294). He has not incorporated The Word (as his God) and has not paid the price or "the pound of flesh" for doing so. (Lacan, 1992: 322) The symbolic has not sufficiently divided and distanced him from the "enjoying substance" (*substance jouissante*) that he at core is. (Lacan, 1998: 24) Thus, signifiers in search of being and jouissance (and tied to a future temporality) do not drive him. An economy of desire barely exists in him. He is not split enough to feel discontent and desire. His boss's offer of a transfer to Paris leaves him unmoved. He has no ambitious fantasies of changing the world or himself. He had already learned very quickly after his studies "that none of that really mattered." Whether he is in Paris or Algiers is "all the same to me." (Camus, 41)

His sense is that much of what language says does not pertain to him.

It does not pertain because language has never subjected (from the Latin *subjacere* = thrown under), dominated, and mastered him. It has not forced him to believe in words or, at the least, to accept their social and legal necessity. Language has never mortified his reality or overthrown his basic relation to his body, separating him from his living substance so as to make him desire or fear it, enough to crave something more or something else. Undivided, he lacks the kind of desire that drives the hysteric to want ever more or the obsessional to fear his own desires. His sensuous body with its perceptions is his reality and his satisfaction. The sky and the world are close and alive for him. And language isn't.

He is a stranger to subjectivity, "an empty subject," (the title of a brilliant article by Massimo Recalcati) with little symbolic content or subject matter (pun intended) and few symbolic tools. (Racalcati, 2005) He spends most of his free Sunday staring at the sky and the street, just registering what he sees, like a camera. He enumerates what he does: he sleeps until ten, smokes, stays in bed until noon, fixes himself some eggs and eats them out of the pan, and so on. (Camus, 21) He reiterates his sensation, his movements, his likes and dislikes: he dislikes Sundays; he'd like to recover the salt smell of Marie's hair on his pillow; he doesn't feel like going downstairs, etc. (Camus, 21) He gives an account of his thoughts during that day: "Then I thought maybe I should have some dinner." (Camus, 24) "I thought we were in for a summer storm." (Camus, 22) When he sees the local boys all spiffed up pass by: "I thought they must he heading to the movies in town." (Camus, 22) Finally, "It occurred to me that anyway one more Sunday was over, that Maman was buried now, that I was going back to work, and that, really, nothing had changed." (Camus, 24) What he calls his "thoughts" are his reiterations or as if tape recordings of what the world around him enunciates in him in a haphazard way. Lacan called this the *Dasein* (*da*=here/there +*Sein*=being) definition of the subject, where the function played by the subject is not completely obvious and where this subject is only "a rather intermittent or fading spectator." (Lacan, 1970)

Language splinters consciousness and opens the way to radical differentiation. At its core, it is a world of very fine differences and distinction: small contrasts and dissimilarities between sounds (such as between t/d or s/z) and basic binaries (life/death or I/you) that allow for varied ways of ordering relationships and meanings. For Meursault the only differences that are significant are those that are experienced and supported by his own body in contact with other bodies or objects in his world. He believes in what is confirmed and affirmed by his bodily reactions, such as hot/cold, wet/dry, soft/ hard etc. What is made substantial by the body, or what it verifies, is what makes sense to him. He is deeply in love with being alive, with being warm or dry to the right degree. Catching a glimpse of light, a color, or a sound is for him like catching a glimpse of the beloved is for a lover. His drives are not hooked to signifiers but to images of objects in the phenomenal world. Meaningful is what his body and organs make contact with, visually, orally, or by touch. "I had the whole sky in my eyes and it was blue and gold. On the back of my neck I could feel Marie's heart beating softly." (Camus, 20) Such a moment, filling his eyes and ears entirely and gently, is what happiness is for Meursault.

"My body is always with me," said Merleau-Ponty, and this is eminently true as well for Meursault. For him, his body and the phenomenal world it has contact with have primacy. He knows the different sensations that crisscross his body, but distinctions beyond these he tends to disregard. When speaking, he favors those language differences and words that refer to his bodily well being and satisfaction. He knows when the sun is doing him "a lot of good." (Camus, 50) He knows that the night air flowing over his body "felt good." (Camus, 35) He knows that he likes washing and drying his hands at lunchtime because the towel is dry whereas, "I don't enjoy it so much in the evening, because the roller towel you use is soaked through." (Camus, 25) Meursault's body is separated from the real of his flesh by only a very thin layer of words and images. He lives with a minimal vocabulary and a minimal economy of desire. He relies on his body and bodily perceptions to give him happiness, to authenticate his existence, and to assure him of reality.

The acquisition of language is "the acquisition of an open system of expression," said Merleau-Ponty. (Merleau-Ponty, 99) But for Meursault, the opening to a larger world of knowledge, desire, socialization, and expression is not available. For him, all remains "the same." His mother has died, but "nothing has changed." (Camus, 24) He has killed a man but he has to remind himself that he has done so: "I was even going to shake his [the magistrate's] hand, but just in time, I remembered that I had killed a man." (Camus, 64) He is a criminal, but "It was an idea I couldn't get used to." (Camus, 70) Sometimes he hesitates about whether doing something would make a difference, such as having a cigarette at his mother's wake, but then he decides: "It didn't matter." (Camus, 8) It also does not "really matter" or make "any difference" to him whether he marries or not. As he explains to Marie, they "could if she wanted to." (Camus, 41) When Raymond asks him to act as a witness for him in the episode of his mistreatment of his mistress, Meursault feels: "It didn't matter to me, but I didn't know what I was supposed to say." The idea of having to speak causes him concern, not the request. (Camus, 37)

In the penultimate encounter with the Arabs, when Meursault has the gun in his hand, it strikes him as if for the first time "that one could shoot or not shoot (*qu'on pouvait tirer ou ne pas tirer*)." (Camus, 56) The thought that choice and differences exist passes through his mind momentarily, albeit as a possibility for an abstract "one" (*on*) or a "you," a self detached from himself. But just moments later, he decides to walk back to the beach alone because: "To stay or to go, it amounted to the same thing." (Camus, 57) He reverts to indifference because he truly seems not to "know" that differences matter. He cannot reflect on them, weigh them, or believe in them. It does not occur to him to think or imagine that the Arabs may still be on the beach or that there could be more trouble, etc. He lacks the master signifier that would compel him to knot his haphazard thoughts into knowledge. As Lacan understood, "knowing" in contrast to "thinking" means that the *parlêtre* (the speaking being) with its body and its jouissance is engaged. (Lacan, 1998: 97)) Meursault's "intermittent subjectivity" is not connected to the seriousness of his life, the seriousness of his being and his acts. His thoughts do not matter or apply to him because they do not have the status of "knowing." They lack the significance and substantiality that "knowledge" has. His exclusion from signifier-knotted knowledge, his inability to grasp basic binaries and to think them through with his body and life as it were as possible actions with real consequences is at once tragic and preposterous because the difference between going and not going back to the beach will be momentous. Only the imminence of his own end forces him, finally, to confront the irrefutable and implacable difference between life and death.

Meursault's true incomprehension of the symbolic becomes fully and appallingly evident with the trial, a process that initially seems to him as unreal as a game. (Camus, 64) Given his difficulties and ineptness with ordinary language and common intercourse, it is almost guaranteed that the symbolic in its most categorical and imperative form as law will pose a challenge for him that he will be unable to meet. Thus, when the prosecutor argues that he is intelligent and that his act was conscious, intentional, and premeditated, and further that he committed a moral matricide and indirectly a parricide, and then proceeds to condemn him as a soulless and heartless monster for whom there is no place in society and whose abysmal emptiness threatens to swallow it up, Meursault is simply lost. (99-102) A logic so complex and devious and at the same time so twisted up with moral authority eludes him completely. Of the legal labyrinth of symbolic abstractions that he is suddenly confronted with, he grasps only strands. Naively, tells us that he doesn't understand how intelligence could be called both a good and a criminal quality in a man, which reveals that a dialectized reality is utterly beyond his grasp. (Camus, 100) For him, the logic of the same (A=A) predominates in the symbolic order; the logic of difference (A $\neq$ A) as if erupts intermittently, only quickly to disappear, and without being applied.

Above all he does not understand that the law is a language backed by violence that can command and order life or death. The law adds as if being and nonbeing to the semblance of words. Thus, although language is a semblance, as enacted law (to which we submit and make others submit), it operates like a real. It is the symbolic in action. In that it deals with existence and inexistence, and does so at times completely arbitrarily, it substitutes for the contingency of the real. However, Meursault is too distant from the symbolic to comprehend its power literally to castrate him. He seems never fully to grasp that the trial is specifically about *his* life and death, not even at the end when "the presiding judge told me in a bizarre formulation (*une forme bizarre*) that I was to have my head cut off in a public square in the name of the French people." (Camus, 107) For him, the symbolic as law, as the Name of the Father, or as God, is foreclosed and hence he reencounters it as the real of death. Death is what he has later to grapple with alone in his cell as he waits for his summons to the guillotine.

The differences and complexities of the law exhaust him so that all that he wants at the final moments of his trial is "to go back to his cell and sleep." (Camus, 105) The long speeches are for him, "a colorless whirling river that was making me dizzy." (Camus, 104) The image describes the flowing away of all differences, even that of color. His dizziness signals his vertiginous surrender to what is for him like a violent assault by a symbolic utterly beyond his comprehension. After the sentencing, he cannot think "about anything anymore." "But the presiding judge asked me if I had anything to say. I thought about it. I said, 'No.'" (Camus, 107) However, in the world, it is all about speaking or not speaking in order to be recognized and to be. That is what the symbolic calls upon human beings to do. Meursault does not have the linguistic energy and resources to do so.

Meursault is not able to use language for his enjoyment or in order to defend himself. He does not believe in language because language is not an intimate part of him. It does not belong to him and it cannot make him feel anything. Language is truly the Other, with which he has as if no business. Its signifiers do not resonate with his affects and its signifieds deliver little meaning and sense. He is in effect dead to the symbolic.

A Stranger to the Imaginary

Meursault is also a stranger to the imaginary in so far as that is the order of the ego (of narcissistic self-love and self–investment or of self-loathing and self-divestment), in a social setting of other egos whom one may hate or love, desire or destroy, seek or flee, and who may, in turn, seek one's nearness and recognition or disappearance and destruction. Meursault is, at best, barely socialized, as if without a social ego, and unaware of the nature and rules of the world of social and legal coexistence. He seems to have little experience of and minimal interest in egotistic dramas of love and hate, of demand and desire, and it is his misfortune that Raymond draws him precisely into such a drama. The fundamental identity and difference between a "you" and an "I" that have to be worked through in this field have as if not even been initiated in him. Meursault does not know how to handle the conjunctions and disjunctions constitutive of the I-you relationship.

When the magistrate presses him repeatedly about why he waited (*avez attendre*) before firing the second shot, Meursault remains silent and then says he felt like telling him "he was wrong to dwell on it, because it really didn't matter." (Camus, 69) He doesn't grasp that it matters greatly to the magistrate. He only "vaguely" understands that there is an other, different subject involved in this dialogue, and he is oblivious to the intensity and significance of the other's demand on him. The magistrate wants, evidently, very much to act out a Christian scenario of leniency and pardon with Meursault, if he is willing to play the part of a contrite and remorseful sinner and believer. The magistrate needs his response in order to enact this Christian fantasy of crime and forgiveness that is the meaning of his life and that grounds his beliefs and existence. When Meursault remains silent three times, the magistrate, unable to get what he wants, goes crazy: "Do you want my life to be meaningless," he shouts. In answer, Meursault brushes the magistrate's concern with his beliefs and need for meaning off as of no concern to him and then, in reply to the magistrate's last desperate effort to embrace him as a believer, Meursault bluntly asserts that he does not believe in Christ. (Camus, 67-9) Meursault has no ego and no demands or fantasies of his own and cannot imagine those of an other. He simply cannot comprehend this fellow being at all nor does he want to. He has no desire for the other. He also does not grasp the context of power within which this dialogue is being played out and it does not occur to him to let this powerful other be whatever he needs to be in his fantasies (not to mention being capable of handling the ethical conflict that might be set up in himself by lying about his own beliefs in self-defense). It just doesn't even occur to him to use this offer to protect himself or that he needs to do so because this different, deluded other is there and has power over him. All of these possibilities completely elude him because of his fundamental lack of an ego, grounded in a relationship to a "you."

In court, he fails to say that he feels remorse that he killed a man and that he is sorry. Instead he tells the magistrate "more than sorry I felt kind of annoyed *(plutôt que du regret véritable, j'éprouvais un certain ennui*). (Camus, 70) He also fails explicitly to assure his defense lawyer that he loved his mother and that he is sad that she has died. Instead he says, "At one time or another all normal people have wished their loved ones were dead" and the day she was buried, he "was very tired and sleepy, so much so that I wasn't really aware of what was going on." (Camus, 65) These answers do not only point to characteristics of innocence, simplicity, and naiveté or honesty and truthfulness, as different critics have argued, but more fundamentally to an emotional, social, and symbolic impairment. He does not know how to use language as a tool for lying or conforming to social norms in order to save himself. Acts of symbolic self-preservation, such as lying or equivocating, are beyond his capacity.

The trial makes evident that his ego (*moi*) as distinct from his symbolic I (*je*) is almost nonexistent. The ego that would make all the language he hears impact *him* and make *him* the center of everything being said and done is missing. He has no imaginary ego (*moi*) to make apply to himself what the symbolic subject (*je*) hears. What he hears as a subject strikes him as distant, strange, and bizarre, as something in which he is not involved. This radical lack of an ego is what enables him at one point to follow the prosecutor's argument of his guilt unperturbed, and calmly term it "plausible." (Camus, 99) Egoless, he lacks the power of self-assertion as well as fear for his survival. The self-investment, narcissism, and self-love of the neurotic are absent in him. He has seemingly never identified with an other person as his mirror likeness nor has he made the turn away from the other back into himself, into self-centeredness and self-assurance. The first bond in his life seems to have been a very tenuous one, not strong enough to have structured him as an "I" in a relationship of desire to a "you." For him, others are simply not a primary source of interest, pleasure, or identificatory support or play. He is alone, a stranger to others.

In fact, at moments, other people do not even seem real to him. Thus, it is hard for him to believe that the people at the wake really exist. (Camus, 9) At the trial, the jurors seem to him like passengers on a streetcar looking to see if they could find something funny about him. He knows it a silly idea and that in fact they are looking for a crime rather than something to laugh at, but he adds, "there isn't much difference, though." (Camus, 83) All interactions cause him some anxiety. That he feels unease and distrust shows up, for example, in his sudden feeling that the mourners are there to judge him. (Camus, 10) This fundamental disrelationship to others, this perturbation or break in his link with them may be what underlies his sense that others expect more than he can deliver and that he will be found insufficient. Hence his attempted apologies ("It's not my fault") and explanations to others ("I thought he was criticizing me for something and I started to explain"). (Camus, 3,4)

It doesn't occur to him to make contact with any of his mother's friends at the wake or, in particular, with Pérez, his mother's so-called fiancé and most intimate friend, who is devastated by her loss and collapses from heat exhaustion and grief at the end of the burial. Meursault has no interest in other people, apart from his mother, and very little understanding of anyone else's psychology or motivation. He does not seem to register their affects, only some of his own in reaction to others. Awaiting execution, he tells the chaplain that he has been told he is guilty and that he is guilty, but "I was paying for it, and nothing more could be asked of me." (Camus, 118) He considers that enough. It's a matter *of quid pro quo*, a matter of payment. He understands it like numerical equation, but not at all emotionally. He is debarred from access to others by way of feeling or emotional identification. Compassion (from the Latin *com*, with + *passio*, suffering), in Kundera's sense of the word, and empathy (from the Greek *empatheia: em,* in + *pathos* feeling) are foreign to him. (Kundera, 19-21) He neither co-suffers nor co-feels with anyone, not even with or for himself. He does not know how to be with others, enjoy or love others, or use them instrumentally (as Machiavelli advised the Prince to do). He has no know-how with the imaginary other. (Jaanus, 323-6)

His imaginary incompetence and impairment is evident in his relationship with Marie. When she questions whether he loves her or not, he answers, "It didn't mean anything." (Camus, 35) Only in the presence of the momentary, mirroring example of Masson and his wife's domesticity, does it occur to him "for the first time maybe, I really thought I was going to get married." (Camus, 50) When she visits him in prison to tell him to have hope, he tells us: "I wanted to squeeze her shoulders through her dress. I wanted to feel the thin material and I didn't really know what else I had to hope for other than that." (Camus, 75) Touching the thinness of a material, visual perceptions, colors, sounds, changes of light or of temperature, such are the limits of his field of desire and hope. He seeks a sexual and sensual bodily relationship with Marie, but no other form of intimacy. His phallic jouissance (which always has been in tact, as we learn from his reflections in prison) is not joined to time, memory, emotion, belief, and the existence of others. (Camus, 77) He believes that "apart from our two bodies, now separated, there wasn't anything to keep us together or even to remind us of each other." After the cessation of her visits and his thought that she could even be dead, "remembering Marie meant nothing to me." (Camus, 115) Because of his symbolic and imaginary poverty, memories are of no interest to him. His memory theater is barren. Only in prison does he discover the advantage of learning "how to remember things," even if it is just all the objects in his former room. (Camus, 78-9)

That Meursault's is a bodily ego, centered in his body (rather than an imaginary ego focused on and inclusive of others) is also evident from the fact that he is not in a situation of rivalry with anyone. He does not measure himself by others or compare himself to others. He does not seek their recognition or to draw to himself their friendship, respect, or libidinal desires. His relationship to Raymond for one lacks such a rivalrous and mirroring dynamic. Raymond seeks his friendship and aid, and makes an appeal to him in the name of the image of macho manhood and bondedness. He tries to flatter Meursault by telling him that he is a man who understands things like a man. He pressures him to act with manly certitude, but all of this means little to Meursault. His response is minimal although he does almost everything Raymond asks him to do, but like an automaton: to write a letter for him; testify at the police station in his behalf; be his buddy; take on the other guy, if they are attacked; use Raymond's gun, if the Arabs pull a knife for the second time. Going to a whorehouse is the only thing he refuses to do because that directly concerns his own body, a terrain where he is at home and where he knows about his likes and dislikes. (Camus, 38) To all the rest, he agrees because it makes no difference to him and because he does not reflect on the consequences of doing so. It is particularly bad luck for him to get entangled with the likes of a Raymond, who is disrespectful of the law and also outside the social norm. Still, Raymond's insistence on their bond, which is seemingly new to Meursault, gives him some satisfaction. After spending an afternoon with Raymond, he says "I found him very friendly with me and I thought it was a nice moment." (Camus, 38)

Meursault's isolation and estrangement from others does not arise from misanthropy, hatred, or a will to dominate and crush others, but from an impediment, an emotional blockage. His own affective experiences are as distant, fragmentary, and hard for him to grasp as are those of others. For example, hearing Salamanco crying for his lost dog makes him think of Maman, but he doesn't know why. (Camus 39) There is a barrier, an obstruction, a blatant disconnection between his recognition of an other's carnal, wordless grieving such as crying expresses and his own capacity to do so. When a momentary identificatory connection comes suddenly into being as happens in court with Céleste's tearfully sincere attempt to defend him, Meursault says he wanted, for the first time in his life, to kiss a man. (Camus, 93) For him it is a novel experience of momentary emotional identification and solidarity. In court, surprised by the relentlessness of the prosecutor's attacks, he thinks, again as if for the first time, of his loss of "the right to show any feelings or good will." (Camus, 100) In court, he experiences "for the first time in years" a "stupid urge to cry because I could feel how much all these people hated me." (Camus, 89-90) The realization provokes a bodily reaction. It is a shock. Before when he encountered hate, such as that between Salamano and his dog and as evidenced by Salamano's abusive treatment of the animal, Meursault remained unperturbed. It meant nothing to him. (Camus, 28)

The court becomes for him, therefore, as if a very elementary schooling in feelings of hatred and compassion, more so than of the law and its function. In the forced testimony of those whom he had accidentally encountered and those in whose proximity he had been living without ever being attentive to them or knowing them – such as the caretaker, Pérez, Céleste, Marie, Masson, Salamano, and Raymond -- he confronts and sees mirrored something of himself. Their perceptions of his identity and failed attempts to define him, together with the perspectives of the lawyers, other court officials, and people in court, make small, initially almost imperceptible breaks and rifts in his being. They elicit emotional and mental effect and responses in him such he has not had in a long time or has never had before.

He has not wanted anything much from others. He has craved little that another has. He craves what is previous to the recognition of any other in the mirror. His concern is maintaining his relationship to the sky and to light. Basically, only he and the sky and the objects in nature really exist or, as he says, he could get used to living only in their company:

> At the time [in prison], I often thought that if I had to live in the trunk of a dead tree, with nothing to do but look up at the sky flowering overhead, little by little I would have gotten used to it. I would have waited for birds to fly by or clouds to mingle, just as here I waited to see my lawyer's ties and just as, in another world, I used to wait patiently until Saturday to hold Marie's body in my arms. (Camus, 77)

What the sky, the sun, and another body feel like and look like matters. That means something to him. The sun is his most basic compass, the very line of his desire. In his prison cell, we see him gripping the bars of his small window, straining his face to towards the light. (Camus, 73) Marie is a desired object for him because her face is as bright as "the color of the sun and flame of desire" *(la couleur du soleil et la flame du désir)*." (Camus, 119) That is the face he would look for on the stones of his cell, he shouts at the chaplain, not the face of Christ. The sun is for him a body, something he desires as he does the body of a woman, but it is also a force that can hit him "like a slap in the face" (Camus, 47) or become an antagonist, so that he has to strain "every nerve in order to overcome the sun and the thick drunkenness it was spilling over me." (Camus, 57) Sensuous objects give him his sense of being or nonbeing, not words.

Meursault lives in sensuous certitude. He lives the sensuous existence that Kierkegaard called the aesthetic, pagan stage of life, the stage previous to the ethical and the religious. The mind's insertion in corporeality, to speak with Merleau-Ponty, is something he experiences, something he has not yet lost contact with. (Merleau-Ponty, 4) He affirms what he has: his body with its perceptions. These are the differences that attract him, not lexical or linguistic differences. The roots of his mind *are* in his body and in his world. (Merleau-Ponty, 3) When the chaplain asks him how he "pictured this other life … . I shouted at him, 'One where I could remember this life!'" (Camus, 120) Meursault cannot feel much for others, but he can feel his own body in its environment. He is more attuned to the changes and fine differences in the phenomenological world than he is to changes in people. He cannot think much. But he is certain about his body and its different states. When the last speech, that of the defense, is over and he cannot register anything mental or emotional anymore, he does still clearly register that "it wasn't hot anymore" because the sun was getting low outside and "the sweetness of the evening [was] coming on." (Camus, 105) It is in such nuances, as he realizes later, that he had found, "the simplest and most lasting joys." (Camus, 104)

For Meursault it is true as Camus once wrote in *The Myth of Sisyphus*: "Even humiliated, the flesh is my only certainty. I can live only in it." (Camus, 1955: 64) But this will not remain so. It is a thesis Camus will question and disturb in this work. However, when we first encounter Meursault, his body is indeed his "central perspective." (Merleau-Ponty, 5) His anchorage is here, not in his ego. In so far as he has an ego, it is a bodily ego. The world that solicits him, that he grasps, and that gives him his soul, is not an imaginary or a symbolic one, but the one that his body and perceptions access. That is his world of *Da-sein*, the here and now in which he lives.

When this order of things fails him, when the sure, homeostatic world he relies on, breaks apart and seemingly turns against him, becoming a hostile, painful, and overwhelming excess of heat and light, blocking his perceptions and his access to what is his phenomenological reality, he has nothing with which to hold it together and mend it. He is unequal to the violence of the jouissance that the loss of this last boundary and defense against the real releases, and that is what triggers his move to a *passage à l'acte*. As the fragile barrier between his organism and the phenomenal world shatters, the elements seem to him to threaten his survival in a massive attack that becomes unbearable: the sun is burning him; the light, like a flashing blade, is cutting his forehead; the scorching blade of a spear is gouging out his eyes; he is blinded by tears and salty sweat; the sky rains down fire. "The trigger gave." He shoots four more times. (59) Why? And what is he shooting at?

"It was because of the sun"

"It was because of the sun" (*c'était à cause du soleil*) is the kind of irrational statement that the court and the world laugh at, term nonsense, and ignore. As Meursault says, "People laughed." (Camus, 103) But it is also exactly the kind of utterance that inaugurated psychoanalysis because Freud took such utterances seriously and attempted to interpret them. He was certain that they described the sense of another reality, finally, an other, a psychotic scene.

In the psychotic scene, the sun -- the form in the sky that is his compass and the partner of his bodily ego, supporting his reality -- splinters and crashes. As the sun shatters, his mind does. The bodily ego that organized and presented the forms of the world to him implodes into objectless, formless jouissance in the depth of the real of his organism. In the real, there are no forms. There are no objects. Forms come into being together with the bodily ego, shaped in the imaginary. His crisis entails the loss of the phenomenological reality that gave him his orientation and pleasures. The experience of the loss of all forms means a living encounter with the impossible, core jouissance that Lacan wrote with a capital J. (Lacan, 1998: 90) In schizophrenia, it appears as a painfully scattered jouissance such as the neurotic subject encounters only as a nightmare so horrible that it shakes him or her awake. Psychosis means that you cannot awaken, that you cannot return to reality. This is Meursault's state: he is in a nightmare from which he needs to awaken. This prompts his act.

His crisis is not a crisis on a voluntary level of thought or of the moral will (good or evil, lawful or unlawful), or on a voluntary level of the imaginary other (it's me or him, trust or distrust), or of imaginary affects (love or hate). These conscious levels barely exist for him and to the extent that they do, they are not operative at this moment. As Merleau-Ponty says, on the level of the perceiving and incarnated mind, "there is no question yet of a real self-awareness or of intentional activity…. "Perceptual behavior emerges from these relations to a situation and to an environment which are not the workings of a pure, knowing subject." (Merleau-Ponty, 1978: 4) Meursault is, indeed, not "a pure knowing subject," but questions have arisen as to whether he is a subject, either consciously or unconsciously, acting out a wish to kill someone, the Arab or some ethnically or racially other, as post-colonial critics imply, or his father in order to commit incest with his mother, as Stoltzfus and others oriented in psychoanalytic criticism argue? Such interpretations are hypothesis about his consciousness or what Lacan early on called the speaking unconscious: "this thing speaks (*ça parle*)" (Lacan, 1978: 24), but in *Seminar XXIV*, Lacan breaks definitively with this unconscious that constantly deciphers, interprets, and proposes reasons and causes. Miller distinguishes it from what he calls "the real unconscious" that is the elaboration of the last Lacan. (Miller, 2007: 3) Psychosis is the entry into the Hell and terror of the real unconscious and its amorphous, seemingly uncaused, and inexplicable jouissance.

Meursault shoots to stop his advance into this real unconscious and his imminent engulfment by it. He shoots to stop what is happening to him: to stop his loss of visual and aural contact with the world, which is so important a support for his bodily ego; to stop his temporary blindness due to the drowning of his vision in sweat, and his loss thereby of all contact with his world, which is only there for him when he can see, hear, touch, taste, or smell it. He needs to stop the glaring and flashing that shatters his world of images and objects on which he depends for his orientation, order, stability, and pleasure. To feel safe and stable, his perceptions need to be focused and localized on single phenomena, as the perceptions of an infant are. These images and objects yield the satisfaction of the drive and stabilize the infant before language does. Among these are above all the visual and aural object a to which the infant clings as much as to what it is given to touch and hold. Meursault's panic comes from the fact he has no psychic or perceptual images or forms to hold onto anymore. His mental forms are fractured and splintered, as is the jouissance they yielded. There are only shards and fragments as in a surrealist painting or melted pieces as in a Dali canvas. He needs his phenomenological world with its images and objects restored. He needs these perceptual forms that he can relate to to be there. He needs to stop this fall into a violent and amorphous jouissance where odd image pieces fuse and melt, strike, flash, and maim, and where there is only chaos and disintegration. This is what he has to bring to a halt.

The first shot does it. "I shook off the sweat and the sun." The sound breaks up his delusional chaos. How? From time immemorial, sound has closed off and ended the chaos of dreams and nightmares. Sound imposes itself on the image. It operates as a first, tyrannical, meaningless signifier that tears us away from images. We have eminent myths in which the advent of oracular sound overrides visionary and mental chaos. The oracles interpreted and turned dreams into meanings and directives, even if enigmatic ones. In the Bible, it is the voice of god that turns chaos into forms. In Vico, it is the thunderbolt of Jupiter that brings the first savage men to a halt. In Meursault's case, it is with what he has on hand, the object in his pocket, the only object he has, a gun. With the sound of the gun, he opposes a sea and a sun gone mad.

This question of a stop or what stops a mind approaching formlessness or moving towards an unbounded and traumatic sublime concerned Kant in the *Critique of Judgment.* Kant asked how is the sublime tolerable, especially the traumatic sublime, such as war or an omnipotent god are? Why do we not quake and breakdown before such an overwhelming force and power? (Kant, 219-20) Kant's answer was reason, a supersensible faculty, provided the halt; it gave the subject the superegonic category of totality by means of which to master and counteract fear and panic before a potential destruction by infinite size or might. Our own built-in rationality, a noumenal faculty and its categories, provided the stabilization. Kant's reason was a pre-Freudian fantasy, based in enlightenment idealism. It was a master signifier of extraordinary signification and immune to destruction by psychosis. For Lacan, such a master or primordial signifier is neither rational nor meaningful; it can become unmoored and may not even exist.

For a romantic realist, like Dostoevsky, it was active love and faith that could knot up Karamazov disorder, disintegration, and despair. Rationality, as exemplified in the brilliant Ivan Karamazov, was no guarantee against meaninglessness or a psychotic breakdown. Ivan's break happens in court when he is forced to confront the impotence of his reason. For the early Lacan, a master signifier, hooked to a signified that is believed, that has meaning and authority (or what he called the Name-of-the-Father) can introduce a stop. As Laurent aptly puts it, the father's word, like god's, says: "It's like that because that's how it is." (Laurent, 286). The Lacan of the middle period believed that the critical stop was on the object's side and that "interpretation must bear only on the object and the mode of jouissance." (Laurent, 282) Now it is no longer the signifier's bond to the signified that matters but its link to jouissance. As Laurent points out, a mere element of jouissance, such as an object a is, may be a barrier to a full-blown psychosis or may limit or arrest it. (Laurent, 286) Thus, the sight of even something like a small marble (as it is in the case of Marguerite Duras's mad heroine in the cellar in *Hiroshima Mon Amour*) may act as a stop, if it produces a condensation and localization of excessive jouissance. (Duras, 66, 91). Object a is a chance to isolate and collect jouissance so as to manage some extracted and limited part of it.

In his desperate effort to arrest and emerge from a bewildering and painful jouissance, Meursault cuts into it with the sound of his shot. The sound becomes an aural object a that stabilizes him and removes him from chaos. We know that he succeeds because, immediately after the first firing, he returns to consciousness and to knowing. He knows: *"I knew* that I had shattered the harmony of the day, the exceptional silence of a beach where I'd been happy." (My italics) (Camus, 59)

"Then I fired four more times." (Camus, 59) The four additional, seemingly identical shots that so disturb the court assert and impose a primitive, repetitious order onto chaos. If there is the repetition of the same, there is as if only one shot. But at the same time, the four shots also introduce a series of cuts or punctuations and a repeated alternations of sound and silence. Sound and silence are a foundational difference. According to Miller and Laurent such cuts and punctuations are necessary in the handling of psychotic jouissance. (Laurent, 283-293) Meursault has to punctuate or as if to cut up his madness so as to make it manageable and to stop it. The four gunshots do that. They establish difference and identity at the same time.

The sameness or the identical dimension of the four repeated shots might have a positive ordering or numbing or sedating effect such as four rhythmic, automatic, and mindlessly repeated drumbeats might have or that the rhythmic pulsation of the mother's blood that the fetus first hears might have. Or such a repetition of a fundamental sameness could also be the basis of a sense of " isness" or a return as if of one's sense of being. The repetition of the absolutely identical (if that were possible) would be as if the simplest, the most fundamental way to assert or even guarantee that a basic state or being as such existed or had returned. What now is, truly is. My "isness" is. And what now is cannot be changed. Absolute sameness would make only being be. It would abolish becoming. These are possible hypotheses (among others) about an act that extends into the openness of the real and our ignorance.

Meursault shoots indeed because of the sun, because of the disintegration of its body to which he is the delusional witness. Vico's savages cried out in fear at the thunder and uttered their first word, but Meursault uses an object, one that he can use, that he controls, as he realized shortly before at the first encounter: "Everything came to a stop there between the sea, the sand, and the sun…. It was then that I realized that you could either shoot or not shoot." (Camus, 56) This realization puts him in a new, dangerous terrain of physical action. To boot many objects are seemingly more effective or easier to act with and use than words are. The confrontation of all these men with each other is, in any case, silent and speechless. Even if Meursault could speak Arabic [Camus did not (Kaplan, 12)], these men do not reach out to each other with words on principle.. Their interaction is as speechless as is that of Meursault with his delusional opponents. It is an encounter of gazes as in the animal world. Meursault can only answer the phantasmagoric assault on his physical and psychic existence with those mindless, deadening sounds that are prior to any language.

Meursault shoots five times to exit madness and delirium, but the exit is at the same time an entrance into a new reality of unhappiness. "It was like knocking four quick times on the door of unhappiness." (Camus, 59) One knocks on a door in order that it be opened. He does so in order to escape what seems like imminent extinction, but this door also leads to death. He has knocked on the door of the unhappiness of knowing death. By shooting he chooses, unknowingly, to be a subject. Or to put it another way, he rejects what Lacan called "the place of *Plus-Personne*" or "the place of No One Anymore," (Lacan, 2006: 558-9) which, as Jacques-Alain Miller has elaborated, is the place in the real for the subject that doesn't yet exist or the place of an absent being. (Miller, June 2008) The shot is a *passage à l'acte,* with which he enacts his break with the natural world that he has loved and with the jouissance it has given him. It is his own castration and entry into the world of knowing by an unconscious act. "In the beginning was the act," as Goethe said. (Goethe, 19-20) The five shoots are his deadly punctuation marks or letters that signal both a founding of language and his loss of those cherished objects that the sun and the sea were for him.

Fundamentally, the shooting is at every moment about himself and for himself. It is not about his victim. The shots are not about killing an Arab or another man. They are not about hatred or indifference towards a racial or ethnic group or a class or anyone else, or about making sure a man is dead. It is an autistic shooting, radically disconnected from the murdered Arab victim. This is perhaps the most terrible thing about it. It is outside any imaginary *human* relationship altogether. His antagonist, his enemy is the delusionally disorganized and crazy visual plane of sea and sun, which mirrors his singular interiority in a psychotic state.

Ordinary Psychosis

Ordinary psychosis is "a word …an expression… a signifier… a very sketchy definition… not a concept," says Jacques-Alain Miller that he invented "just to attract … the various shades of meaning around the signifier. I didn't give any know-how as to how to use this signifier… I wanted it to grow and see how far this evasive expression would go." (Miller, 2009: 146) To me it seemed the very signifier I had been looking for to describe the strangeness of Camus's Meursault, in whom, as I have been trying to indicate, all kinds of insufficiencies and incapacities in the various Lacanian orders are clearly evident.

For Miller, the clinic of ordinary psychosis is "a clinic of the small clues of foreclosure." (Miller, 2009: 162) It could be that this or that might be cut out of a life due to a series of small bad encounters so that the openness to life is reduced. That seems to be the case of Meursault in whom various small breaks in different registers seem to have lead him to a diminished and carefully limited life, finally, literally and spatially limited to one room, (Camus, 21) but it is by these very acts of the exclusion of anything disturbing or excessive that he manages to maintain his existence.

Thus, ordinary psychosis and extraordinary psychosis differ as to the degree and form that foreclosure takes in each. Ordinary psychosis is not sudden and massive, as is a stroke that kills, but more like a series of minor ruptures that impairs and that may or may not also massively erupt at a later time. Ordinary psychosis, as Miller defines it, is precisely not extraordinary or spectacular. It is difficult to recognize as such and, therefore in fact, often not recognized, not even by professional clinicians. Meursault has none of the classical symptoms of psychosis: he does not hear voices or have delusional ideas or live in a delirious reality of his own invention. Before the triggering, his whole world has not yet imploded. (Anne-Lysy Stevens) His reality is a contracted one but not that different from a normal neurotic reality.

A diagnosis of ordinary psychosis indicates potentiality, not necessity. As Miller says, psychosis "is a vast continent…. An immense continent." "Not all psychoses take the form of a triggered, exploded psychosis. You have psychotics who will live all their lives of psychosis as a calm and ordinary psychosis. You have dormant psychoses … which will never awaken. You have a difference between psychoses that can be triggered and psychoses that cannot be triggered." (Miller, 2009: 161) Ordinary psychosis is for Miller a way to widen the field of psychosis that has been too narrowly defined. The category is a way to explain and explore why human being do not seem to be born psychotic and why psychotic breaks can come quite late in life, as did Schreber's at the age of fifty-one. His position is like that of the majority of geneticists today who say that even if a gene or genetic dispositions for something like alcoholism exists or is present, it still takes a triggering event to activate such a gene. The presence of a gene alone is not a sufficient condition, neither are minor breaks or signs of impairment in the various registers for a triggering of psychosis.

Because one is searching for small ruptures and nearly inaudible and invisible fractures, Miller calls the clinic of ordinary psychosis "a very delicate clinic." It is inferred "from various, very small clues…. It is more of an epistemic than an objective category. It concerns our way of knowing it." (Miller, 2009: 149) "Very often it's a question of intensity. It's a question of more or less." (Miller, 2009: 154) This seems to move this clinic closer to the study of the arts – to literature, music, painting, and dance -- studies of intensities that require a very slow and careful form of reading and sensing, of gathering meanings from other levels of hearing or seeing, from modulations in intonations or color and line, from the quality of a tone, the pitch pattern of the voice, its timbre, intensity, rhythm, volume, its rise and fall, and its pauses or silence. It is an attentiveness to the same qualities or similar ones in movement or vision and to how these modify or supersede meaning or point to a gap or to something else, something more essential that pertains to jouissance. These are "ways of knowing," ways of elaborating the processes of knowing rather than of positing an objective definition or objective known. These are demonstration of how a process of knowing is lived or how it accompanies living, experiencing, and doing. These are the determinants of a commentary on art or, in an analyst's case, of an intervention in a patient's life.

Miller invented ordinary psychosis to move away from the limits imposed by a binary diagnosis of neurosis and psychosis, while maintaining the accent on psychosis. (Miller, 2009: 148) It's "a third structure," says Miller. "But as a matter of fact, it's the same structure" as psychosis. (Miller, 2009: 161) In contrast to psychosis, Miller proposes, "a supposedly normal person is a neurotic who doesn't suffer from his neurosis, or who doesn't suffer too much from his neurosis, or who doesn't cures his neurosis through an analysis, who cures his neurosis through living." (Miller, 2009: 149)

In the case of ordinary psychosis, a self-prevention of the break (such as Lacan demonstrated was the case of Joyce) or a seeming self-cure after a break seems to require a compulsive limiting of life or an all-consuming working on or production of a suppleance or substitute. Joyce remained untriggered because his artwork was an obsessive object that focused and supported his ego and rewarded him with fame and a name that mattered in his world. (Stevens) Meursault's case is different. He manages to remain untriggered for a longtime by a reduction and contraction of his life to a minimum and to routine. He seems to believe, as did his mother, that getting used to anything is a matter of habituation. This belief in habituation is one of his few guidelines for living inherited from his mother: "It was one of Maman's ideas, and she often repeated it, that after a while you get used to anything." (Camus, 5, 77) It is a mantra that serves to calm him in the face of change, up to a point, until the changes become overwhelming.

Still, even when there is a psychotic break, "a kind of ordered world re-organizes itself," says Miller, and often it is somehow livable. Schreber, for one, "progressively manages to arrange for himself a livable world." He manages to create what Miller calls "a delusional symbolic order." (Miller, 2009: 152) Schreber's is a massive reorganization of the whole world and of the world beyond, supported by his megalomaniac ego, which assigns him the position of God's wife. As Brousse says, Schreber devotes himself to "to incarnating the exception function that is lacking." (Brousse, 12) This makes Schreber's "delusional symbolic order," a rather bizarre, singular and private order, where the traces of the mended breaks in his various relationships to God, others, and to his own body show up starkly, and which is without the general appeal and fascination that various other delusional systems -- religious, mythical, philosophical, psychological, and political – have had and continue to have. Schreber's world cannot readily be shared or identified with although today, given the rise of various forms of ordinary and extraordinary psychosis, psychotic art with its asocial singularity is ever more prevalent, sought after, and enjoyed.

Meursault's is an ordinary psychosis in crisis that he manages to interfere with. With a radical act, he arrests the continuation of his own break. Then, throughout the trial, he manages to exclude from his thoughts the fact that he has murdered a man and that he is on trial for this act. He proceeds as though no change has taken place and as if what is happening does not pertain to him. His interpreters have found various ways to account for or discount or avoid discussion of his reactions to the court proceedings so as to continue to assert his position and appeal as a literary icon of significant and even universal meanings of various kinds. Some have found his final state of mind and emotions life affirming and meaningful for their own psychic lives. Conor Cruise O'Brien for one expresses gratitude to Camus for offering to him in his youth "hope without reason" and "the joy of being alive, in the presence of death." (Conor Cruise O'Brien, 34)

A Stranger to Death

To live the most ordinary of ordinary lives, Meursault's has to be a life without any upheavals. He manages only to live by, in a sense, almost not living. For him any disruption in what is a precarious equilibrium is dangerous. His life has to be without major changes, emotionless and routinized, just as he tells himself it is after having buried his mother: "nothing had changed." (Camus, 24)

As is well known, change, whether positive or negative, disturbs everyone to a degree. Change inevitable goes together with a break, an ending, or a loss and, thus, a space in which something new or different can, possibly, come into being. However, for Meursault, the death of his mother is not a loss, but a hole that he does not confront. He does not experience it, not because it is too painfully traumatic for him to bear, but precisely because he is incapable of doing so. He is not open to the real of death because the structural difference between life and death is not present and active in him. Thus, his mother's death initiates no thoughts about his own, as it might in a neurotic subject. It does not, for example, make him think: "And I will die." It does not cause that inner splitting and ambivalence, that dialectical breaking apart, which, as Freud explicated, the death of a beloved or another human being close to us normally does. (Freud, 1915: 293-5) Though it may momentarily divide us, the death of others strikes our core only when there is an identification of love, when the loss is echoed as hole in our own bodies. But Meursault is as oblivious to the difference between living and dying as he is to killing or being killed or to loving and being loved. In the first scene on the beach with Raymond, he takes the gun and, unthinkingly, asserts that he will use it, "if the other one moves in, or if he draws the knife, I'll let him have it." (Camus, 56) Meursault seems never to have suffered thinking and feeling the absolute gap between life and death that neurotics need to invent ever-new ways of negating and filling. He is as if, above all, a stranger to his own death, which is for human beings the one thought approaching the real. We comprehend this when we see Meursault, in his final days in prison, begin like a child, terrified and exhilarated, to play the *fort-da* game of being dead or alive, with his own body as the object a. (Camus, 112-5)

The potential marriage with Marie and the new friendship with Raymond are, in comparison to the death of his mother and his act of murder, minor changes; nonetheless, they also suggest a lack or at least a space for something more. By putting pressure on him to respond, move, change -- emotionally and mentally -- in ways that are difficult for him, these events also contribute, though to a far lesser degree, to the triggering on the beach, a triggering which is essentially his failure to be able to respond realistically to the imperative of his own potential death. The delirious flood of hellish metaphors from his unconscious is the sign of this failure. There are twenty-five metaphors in this scene alone compared to fifteen in the remainder of the text, as my professor, William H. Frohock, was, it seems, the first to note. (Frohock) The metaphorical excess points to something beyond a neurotic sense of emptiness or nothingness and a need for massive substitutions. It points to the sudden opening up of a never before experienced psychotic hole that Meursault is both desperate to fill up and to express. This he does with the act of the multiple shots that both announces and makes five holes.

Ultimately, in a very general and conscious way, we are all strangers to death in that we do not know when or how we will die. In prison, Meursault tries to make this the basis of a rationale for accepting the refusal of his appeal and his execution: "Since we're all going to die, it's obvious that when and how don't matter. Therefore… I had to accept the rejection of my appeal." (Camus, 114) But, in fact, he cannot, and when the chaplain makes the same argument later, Meursault knows enough by then to say that it is not "the same thing." (Camus, 117) He has learned the difference by experiencing it in his flesh. An execution is real. It opens the real unconscious. Meursault's psychotic break just before the shooting propelled him suddenly and forcefully into this real. It was a first opening that his act closed. The court judgment that he be executed is a second real opening addressed to him.

From this time on, he thinks only about his execution – about what it actually is, how to escape it or somehow to confront it. To avoid another psychotic break, he has now, with the severely limited symbolic and imaginary means that he has, to knot his consciousness to the real of his imminent beheading by the guillotine. The gap between the two is abysmal. No bridge leads from the terrain of symbolic rationality to the real. There is no terrain of the real. His entire being becomes preoccupied with warding off the terror of death, and finally, with inventing an interpretation with which to face his impending execution. He is working against death, dread, and time to maintain and reinforce the shield of his being so as to confront the appalling hole of inexistence.

He stops being able to sleep at night, as he listens for footsteps and the slightest shuffle that might announce the approach of guards coming to get him: "With my ear pressed to the wood, I would wait frantically until I heard the sound of my own breathing, terrified to find it hoarse, like a dog's panting, my heart would not burst after all, and I would have gained another twenty-four hours." (Camus, 113) He knows what his organism tells him: that the terror of death makes his teeth chatter without stop and that a pardon with twenty more years of life makes for a "terrifying leap," with "hot blood" surging through his organism and stinging his eyes with "delirious joy." (Camus, 110, 114) He knows that even a reprieve of only twenty-four hours of more life is something he can be happy about. It is another of the few consolatory sayings that he retains from his mother: "Maman used to say that you can always find something to be happy about." (Camus, 113)

His repetitious *fort-da* game of dread and desire is about living or dying: he lives because his appeal is granted; he's executed because it is denied. Only now does he grasp that nothing is "more important" or "interesting" than an execution. That his father went to watch a murderer be executed, that the very idea of doing so made him sick to his stomach and that he "spent half the morning throwing up" when he returned, is no longer something that gives him the feeling he had as a child of being "a little disgusted by him." Now he tells us that if he got out of prison, he too would go to watch every execution. (Camus, 110) On the one hand, because this is the story of his father, not his own, Meursault is still holding the idea of execution at a distance from himself and his own organism. On the other, his appallingly belabored efforts to comprehend his father signifies a new connectedness, though it is only by means of an identificatory scarp that he has from a story told by his mother. The father and child meet as if for the first time in this carnal real of disgust, which is an intolerable incorporation followed by a reaction of extreme expulsion, and like anxiety, an unmistakable sign of the real. (Lacan, 1978: 172) Meursault recognizes his father for having tolerated this encounter with the real, even if at the price of disgust. The memory of the father is somewhat mended. He acquires new stature as a mediator of the horror of execution. Meursault's revaluation and acceptance of his father's disgust seems to signal his own advance towards the real that is the core of an execution.

It is shortly after these reflections on his father that he begins his *fort-da* game. The obsessively repeated game is as if a testimony to the birth of his unconscious as a binary temporal structure of opening and closing as Lacan, and subsequently, Miller has described it. (Miller, 1995). The game keeps his real unconscious open to excesses of terror and bliss that he has then to work hard to quiet and subdue. The mental strain on him is enormous. He cannot bring about a lasting or any kind of an anodyne closing. He cannot exit the game. His slow mental processes, his desperate attempts to remain lucid, and his fragmentary identifications with his mother and father yield only momentary reprieves. He cannot silence his unconscious. (Miller, Sept 2008)

He manages to close off the desire that he had for Marie by imagining that she may be dead. She becomes, as it were, "an object annulled by the signifier" (Miller, 1995) or a meaningless and empty signifier: "I was not interested in her dead. That seemed perfectly normal to me, since I understood very well that people would forget me when I was dead." (Camus, 115) But he cannot do this with himself as a living body. In the repetitious game of *fort-da*, the *tuché* is always his own body, which is for him an object of jouissance. He comes back to this body-object repeatedly in a state of great agitation, positive and negative, but he lacks signifiers that would annul him as an object or elevate him beyond this alternation of bliss and terror, where his teeth are chattering and he cannot make them stop. (Camus, 110) He cannot control the jouissance, either painful or blissful, coursing through his body. He cannot control the racing of his pulse or heart rate, and in part, he does not want to. His breath and his heartbeat are the *tuché* for which he aims. The body-object is his transferential goal as it is the fetus's to touch itself or the baby's to suck its thumb. As a real remainder, which is, as Miller says, "inassimilable to the signifier," it assures him of existing. (Miller, 1995)

The organism is a source of jouissance. The body as object is the first channel through which all jouissance passes. The jouissance shows itself as a variety of passions and moods. This body-object is what was at play in the Freudian *fort-da* game. As Lacan says, "The [child's] reel is not the mother…it is a small part of the subject that detaches itself from him, while still remaining his, still retained. This is the place to say … man thinks with his objects." (Lacan, 1978: 62) Later, Lacan will add, man "enjoys" with his objects. The partners in this play of transferential desire are the child's body-parts and its jouissance. In this circuit of bodily jouissance, the child's desire is, hopefully, to possess and to keep all parts of itself together but the circuit can also be an aggressive one. The child is enacting a circular, narcissistic, and auto-sexual transference between its bodily pieces. "Transference is the enactment of the reality of the unconscious," (Lacan, 1978: 146) but this "reality" as Miller points out, was for the later Lacan not only or primarily a "sexual reality," but the real of jouissance. (Miller, 1995) Thus, at a deeper level, transference is a reaching for a jouissance beyond sexual jouissance and for the real unconscious.

In Meursault's case, the Name-of-the-Father that imposes its order on the desire of the mother is foreclosed. The desire of the mother that imposes itself on the chaos of primal perceptual experience is also lacking. Only at the end of her life with Pérez, as Meursault notes, does the immobile and near dead-mother he remembers seem to have recovered her will to desire and to live. Thus, a larger, protective structure of desire and its objects, to which every healthy infant begins to cling as soon as it can and as comprehensively as it can, seems also not have been part of his experience. Instead he is dependent to an unusual degree on the instinctual, homeostatic order of his organism in its relations to light, water, air, and other such perceived phenomena in his immediate surroundings. Regularity and order in his instinctual and perceptual life is essential for him and almost his sole defense against chaos. It is the partner of what would otherwise be his wholly desireless, dead existence. The rupture of this shield means an opening to psychosis and to a neuronal-chemical failure we know as yet too little about. At this level, as best we know, there is crisis of connectivity. There are only unlinked or very weakly linked pieces or shards of what needs to be a more cohesive symbolic and imaginary reality.

Meursault cannot give up the jouissance of a repeated return to this primordial body-object that cannot and must not be lost, the narcissistic object par excellence that also assures him that he is still alive. His heartbeat, the racing and leaping of his heart, the chattering of his teeth, these are things he cannot stop or imagine being stopped: "I couldn't imagine that this sound which has been with me for so long could ever stop. I've never really had much of an imagination. But still I would try to picture the exact moment when the beating of my heart would no longer be going on inside my head. But it was no use." (Camus, 112) Without signifiers, there's no way out of the game of repetition. The hole remains open. The turbulent jouissance keeps rushing through.

For Lacan, from the perspective of the Borromean knot, the hole in the subject is an unavoidable real because no matter how tightly the strings are drawn together and no matter how many identifications the subject has or how many interpretations the subject constructs, the emptiness at the core can never be completely eliminated. (Lacan, 1998: 127) Lacking a chain of symbolic signifiers, in which he could believe, and an imaginary, genealogical chain of living bodies (strong images of a mother and father or other people) to arouse and bind his passions of love and hate and to identify him, such as the neurotic has, he has only his archaic, fragmentary perceptual experiences and forms with which to construct a defense and a minimal sense of self. He only has "identifications constructed with bits and pieces, with bric-a-brac, with flotsam and jetsam," which Miller says is very typical of ordinary psychosis. (Miller, 2009: 158) His construct of his mother is a composition of such pieced-together identificatory scraps and his father is no more than one such scrap. When the frail layer of his phenomenological reality and forms gives way, he is defenseless against the threat of his inexistence and his inner hole. He becomes subjected to passions in a way he never has been before in his life. He lives an alternation of excess terror and joy over which he has almost no control.

Meursault is learning that flesh is not "certitude." It is a site of terror. It is a terrifying thought that cannot be thought, because it is blocked from being thought by a panic so immense and solid as to be impenetrable. The gap between the general truth, "we all die," and the singular, "I will die," seems to be unbridgeable. It is an abyss. Hence the ancient pre-tragic wisdom of the Greeks that luck is never to have been born or to die as as soon as possible. However, all those, who do not die suddenly or accidentally, have to learn to die just as they had to learn to live. How does each subject do that? How will Meursault?

It is in the midst of his *fort-da* game, at a moment when he has denied his appeal and given up Marie, that the chaplain walks in, despite the fact that Meursault has just refused to see him for the fourth time. His unannounced and unwelcome entry sends a shudder through Meursault who knows a chaplain is sent at the time of execution. The presence of the chaplain's obdurate body in his cell, in which there is barely room for it, annoys him and what the chaplain says, eventually, enrages him. The negative transference that is there from the start becomes a torrential outpouring of hate for the chaplain's false certitudes, illusory beliefs, deluded desires, deadness to life, and perverse valuation of an "other life" over this life. Meursault yells at him at the top his lungs, and insults him (and his notions of sin, divine justice, and accountability to god), until the guards tear him away and threaten him. (Camus 120, 122)

Meursault has already told him that his god is an object he doesn't want and isn't interested in. He has already rejected all that the chaplain offers – otherworldly desires, friendship, an embrace, and a relationship between them of father and son. That the chaplain, deaf to all he has said, relentlessly persists with: "I shall pray for you," is what pushes Meursault from speaking to yelling, to verbal and physical assault. All these human and divine placebos offend him. They are useless to him as aids in his effort to confront the fearful certainty of the guillotine. What is their worth compared to the only certainty he has: that of his life and death. "But I was sure about me… surer than he could ever be, sure of my life and sure of the death I had waiting for me. Yes, that was all I had. But at least I had as much hold on it as it had on me." (Camus 120-1) What the chaplain offers are empty words that cannot be experienced or held.

His life is all he has and he refuses to be told, on the one hand that it is valueless and that he should stop loving it -- as the chaplain murmurs: "Do you really love this earth as much as all that?" (Camus, 119) -- and yet, on the other, that there is a god who values his life and that the chaplain's prayers may save him from losing it. His violent "no" to the chaplain is a break *(il y a quelque chose qui a crevé en moi)* that separated him as much from the chaplain as from who he had himself been. He discovers hatred and his right to it. By hatred, the strongest form of negation, he severs himself from the other, who is trying to make of him a mirror image of himself, (a believer in god and the afterlife), and establishes himself as a separated-off ego. A torrent of jouissance pours out of this new break in the form of rage, hatred, "cries of anger," and "cries of joy." (Camus, 120) Those strong, never before felt, negative and positive passions, finally become signifiers, pressing for speech and for his existence as a subject, who can speak for himself. "It was as if I had waited all this time for this moment and for the first light of this dawn to be vindicated." (Camus, 121)

This "dawn" is his awakening as a *parlêtre*, a speaking being, a subject, who seeks first of all to name his own meaning and to take possession of certain signifiers as his own, as signifiers of his beliefs. Fundamentally, Meursault is shouting, like a God, "I am that I am." It is the shout of primary narcissism and of a primitive sense of self-righteousness: "I had been right, I was still right, I was always right." (Camus, 121) Given what he has done and his circumstances, it is a delusional assertion, but it is what Meursault has never been able to feel or think or say. The world keeps making him wrong, but his existence is what it is. It is life of which his existence is a part, and his affirmation of life necessarily entails the affirmation, acceptance, and vindication of his own existence, justifying it and clearing it of blame.

Hating is jouissance; speaking is jouissance. The jouissance of rage, despair, and fierce enjoyment that he lets loose on the chaplain energizes him and pushes him to seek a new outlet for his passions in symbolic jouissance. The chaplain's unyielding resistance to and rejection of his reality makes him hate. The chaplain becomes an object to oppose and one against which he can form and declare himself. The chaplain is definitely not on his side. "I told him he wasn't my father; he wasn't even on my side." (Camus, 120) On his side are those who try to confront the fact of death as his father did. In the final moments of the encounter with the chaplain, he forgets his body. His excessive passions are dispersed in a field of new signifiers to which he suddenly gains access.

He finds release in a hatred that Lacan called one of the three great passions of being (Lacan, 2006: 524) and in the rudimentary symbolic subjectivity now shaping itself in him. He enters the house of language that Heidegger called the house of being, but that is, for Lacan, a mere semblance of being. The rage, and the explosive and vehement vociferation that the chaplain's relentless insistence and pressure unleash, end in a classic catharsis. The explosion enables him to empty and to close his unconscious, and to exit the repetition he was caught in. But no one who enters the house of language is exempt from a possible encounter with the real unconscious, with something truly inscrutable, undecipherable, and without causation -- such as an empty sound, an enigmatic image, a physical symptom. The subject can succumb to this mind-defying, uncaused, meaningless inscrutable sinthome and feel defeated by it or own it, accept it, or allow it to change his being and mode of living, as Meursault will.

His whole life, Meursault has avoided speaking or he has had little or "nothing" to say, as he tells the presiding judge after his condemnation. (Camus, 107) The Other in him has been nearly silent, desireless of saying, or unable to say. But now he has something to say. It seems he been as if "a waiting-to-say" for a long time. He has "what he is" to say, his existence to say, his jouissance to say, even though it cannot be said or integrated into language. (Miller, 2007: 6) Finally, now, what he manages to articulate for himself in opposition to the chaplain is first of all an understanding of what really is that indifference or sense of sameness that has always been his, and what it is that is excluded for him from that indifference. He understands at one and same time what sameness is and what difference is and he creates a metaphor by means of which to understand both:

> Nothing, nothing mattered, and I knew why. So did he. Throughout the whole absurd life I'd lived, *a dark wind* (*un souffle obscur*) had been rising towards me from somewhere deep in my future (*du fond de mon avenir*).... What did other people's deaths or a mother's love matter to me.... When we were all elected by the same fate.... Couldn't he see, couldn't he see that?... There were only privileged people. The others would all be condemned one day. And he [the chaplain] would be condemned too. What would it matter if he were accused of murder and then executed because he didn't cry at his mother's funeral? .... What did it matter that Raymond was as much my friend as Céleste, who was worth a lot more than him? What did it matter that Marie now offered her lips to a new Meursault? Couldn't he, couldn't this condemned man see...And that from somewhere deep in my future (*du fond de mon avenir*)...All the shouting had me gasping for air. (Camus, 121-2) (My italics)

There is only the privilege of life and the universal condemnation to death. The fundamental difference between life and death is what now opens itself up to Meursault at the same time as he sees this radical difference as a crossed indifference, as one in a chiasmus. Meursault ignores the difference between dying of old age, being murdered, or guillotined, etc. He stresses the universal: all are ultimately condemned whether guilty or innocent. Death is radically indifferent to differences. The real of death is not part of the symbolic and its binaries. However, Meursault's insistence on this idea ("Couldn't he [the chaplain] see, couldn't he see that?... Couldn't he, couldn't this condemned man see…") means also that he would like confirmation from someone else, because his own certainty, despite everything, is an uncertain certainty. He would like another subject to back him up by agreeing.

But as he is shouting all this, a strange image comes into being that interrupts his thinking. A metaphor of "a dark wind" *(un souffle obscur)* that has been rising towards him, since his beginning, from the depth of his future (*du fond de mon avenir*) interposes itself between his thoughts and words. The trope fuses beginnings and endings, birth and death, knotting them firmly. (115-22.) They are entwined and inseparable -- an undistinguishable chiasmus of existence and inexistence. This knot of life and death is like the wind, something baffling, defying lucidity and reason -- unseen, unidentified, formless, obscure, and strange. The wind comes and goes; it passes, as does a life, tied from its beginnings to death. His existence and inexistence conceived in this metaphor of the wind, as an unseen that has been with him throughout his time of life (*du fond de mon avenir)*, is different from a conception of life and death as separate and opposed. It translates and simplifies existence and inexistence into something more in line with classical fatality.

Because the phrase with its vague and indefinite space and time coordinates fascinates him, he repeats it, as if sensing that he has caught something in words that matters, that he wants to hang on to, that potentially means something to him. (Camus, 121, 122) It is a new symbolic formulation that pleases him. The fragment is poetic; it is on the rhetorical level of language, where tropes reign and where language acknowledges its fictionality and, thereby, at the same time, asserts its freedom. He is on that level of belief in language where there is, as Coleridge put it, a form of faith that he called poetic faith, which is "a willing suspension of disbelief" or a willingness to believe or be deluded (from the Latin *de*=completely and *ludere*= to play), or to be played on, exploited, even mocked, in order to gain pleasure. It liberates him from his incessant lucubration and his *fort-da* game because this imaginary and in part delusional idea that translates his existence and nonexistence into a phenomenon in nature, into a nonsensical metaphor of the wind as temporal entity, forged of his own compacted beginning and end, makes a kind of senseless sense to him. It arrests his thinking because it manages to formulate the fundamental paradox of our living as a form of dying or of our dying as living. The paradox catches an impenetrable chiasmus that stops further thought. It satisfies him because it strikes him as seemingly true and because it is his own work of art as it were, his poem. It gives him the satisfaction of a symbolic creation such as he seems never to have had before.

The human subject requires forms of defense that the animal seems not to need or have. We require more than food and shelter. We need a shelter against death. God and the afterlife are the best shelters ever invented, but Meursault rejects these. He has to construct his defense in other ways, by finding some meaning or community or love with which to oppose death's meaninglessness, solitude, and lovelessness. He has to find something felt and certain that can knot up the vague and uncertain or something solid that can defend him against the ungraspable. He has to oppose all the negativities that are connected to death or find a way to submit to dying. If he does not submit, he has to invent something -- some lie or delusion by which to fill the abyss of ignorance that death is. He has to do something to find a shelter and defense against the impossible.

In this image of death as born with his life, there is darkness and obscurity, but no terror. What Meursault seems to accomplish here is the making or turning of the ending or final cut into his first knot so that this paradoxical trope that conjoins ends and beginnings can metamorphoses their coexistence into something natural. The wind is something that Meursault is capable of accepting and believing. It is something familiar to Meursault, something he has always been aware of, something that has soothed and calmed him in the past. ("The summer air flowing over our brown bodies felt good.") (Camus, 35) The image announces that he is washed free of all others as well as of his own hopes for the success of his appeal. The encounter with the chaplain's beliefs has as if readied him to consider a life without appeal. In *The Myth of Sisyphus*, Camus wrote, "Knowing whether or not one can live a life *without appeal* is all that interests me." (Camus, 1955: 45)

The metaphor of the wind is about something only tactilely felt, barely audible, and amorphous. It is not linked to anything and without meaning, but caught in the drive of a circling repetition that cannot grasp it, and that he, therefore, feels the need to pursue and to repeat, until he runs out of breath and cannot go on speaking. *Du fond de mon avenir* is the repeated phrase that encircles the "obscure wind," searching for a significance and satisfaction, that though enigmatic and unreachable, is as if attained in the action of repeated reaching. The repetition establishes it as a sinthome, as a potential, as yet meaningless signifier, "a signifier all alone, in sufferance – waiting for the other signifier that would give it meaning." (Miller, 2007: 7)

In Lacan's Seminar XXIV, the sinthome definitively replaces the object a. The sinthome no longer has a relation to the symbolic as the object a does. The sinthome is the word for what there is -- for what "ex-sists" – when there is no interpreting unconscious. It is a signifier of unknown meaning, a new, radical signifier of "the fact that one speaks … all alone. One speaks all alone because one only ever says *the same thing*." (Lacan, January 11, 1977) (My italics) The sinthome is an autistic signifier. The logic of this autistic signifier is that of the same (A=A), whereas the logic of the signifier proper is that of difference (A ≠ A). But this is a ruptured same, and therefore one that can be repeated. The autistic sinthome relates to the bodily not only as an *en plus* of surplus jouissance but as a surplus of enigmatic and meaningless meaning. It replaces the signifier that is the exception, that is the lack in the big Other [S (Ø)]. It arises instead from the hole in the symbolic (Ø) and occupies it. Unlike Schreber, Meursault does not only "incarnate the exception." He comes to occupy the hole itself, which will, like a black hole in space, swallow him.

"The tender indifference of the world" (*la tendre indifférence du monde*)

The rage and arduous mental activity and shouting exhaust Meursault and enable him to fall asleep. In this rest, he gathers to himself something of that sweetness of the world that had previously comforted him and made him happy. Momentarily, he regains something of his former balance and calm. His earlier intimacy and close intercourse with the phenomenological world around him is restored. He wakes up with the stars in his face. (Camus, 122)

"Blind rage has washed me clean and rid me of hope for the first time," says Meursault. Hope as a desire is something disturbing. Purged of the hope for an appeal that drove his torturous and agitated *fort-da* game and calmed by the delusional and romantic trope he has given birth to, he is able to return to mindless, perceptual living and the phenomenological reality that is his home. He lets go once again of the symbolic and of its differences, with their taxing demand to reason, order, and choose or to live in ambivalence, doubt, and incertitude. Indifference is easier, softer, and gentler. It belongs to ignorance, contingency, and freedom. Freedom means release from "the prison house of language" (Jameson) and a return once again to the world of nature, with its familiar "sounds of the countryside," "smells of the night," and "salt air" that cools his temples. Meursault grasps again and feels grasped by these ever-changing phenomena in a marvelous chiasmus: "The wondrous peace of that sleeping summer flowed through me like a tide." (Camus, 122) But a very different sound -- of sirens – disrupts his feeling of accord. He associates the sound with departure from a world "that now and forever meant nothing to me." (Camus, 122) He wants to renounce sounds, especially those of language that impose reality and meaning on him. He wants a return to his *Dasei*n subjectivity where thoughts and meanings are suspended.

He thinks once again of his mother. Now he understands why his mother had at her end played at beginning again and why she had taken a fiancé. He identifies with her revived desire for life and love. He grasps that renunciation and loss arouse a desire for that which is renounced and lost. As the hole of loss by imminent death grows, the desire to fill it once again also gathers strength. He affirms his mother's will and right to live, together with his own: "I felt ready to live it all again too." (Camus, 122) He has made sporadic efforts before to understand his mother; in fact, she is the only person whose being and motivations have been in his thoughts at various moments, but these previous efforts were indirect. For example, at her funeral, it is the countryside of her evening walks with Pérez that mediates for him some sense of identification. It is the "cypress trees leading up to the hills next to the sky, and the houses standing out here and there against that red and green earth" that enables him "to understand Maman better." (Camus, 15) However, now he understands her experience directly and chiastically by means of his own. The understanding is for him an achievement and it gives him the satisfaction of an emotional identification with another human being in the imaginary.

Still, he turns back to the "night alive with signs and stars," where for him true living resides, but he does it in a way he never has before: "I opened myself *for the first time* to the tender indifference of the world" *(Je m'ouvrais pour la première fois à la tendre indifférence du monde*). (My italics) For him this "firstness" lies in the brotherhood he feels with the night. The universe seems to him "like a brother," and their kinship link is the "tender indifference of the world." It's not a Romantic universe of sympathetic identity. He finds comfort in its not being that. Rather it is the feeling of solidarity in "tender indifference" that makes him happy: "I felt that I had been happy and that I was happy again." (Camus, 123) The experience of the tenderness of this night is the closest Meursault comes to feeling what love is and to loving.

Indifference (ever paired with difference), but now traversed by tenderness, has as if become something gentler and softer, more like detachment (ever coupled with attachment). Indifference makes for closures as differences do; detachment is more open. His openness to the otherness of the night also signals oblivion to his own ego. He as if throws it away or breaks his ego boundaries to allow this tenderness in. Feeling the tenderness of this night is emotionally very different from simply feeling that the night air flowing over his body "felt good" or that the sun was doing him "a lot of good." (Camus, 50) The newness of this experience of tenderness, transferred and received, holds him spellbound for a moment and gives him the stillness of that kind of happiness that stops time and anxiety.

But this happiness, this beautiful and calm moment of detached attachment, this serene and tender ataraxia or state of near sleep, bordering on a submissiveness similar to a *Liebestod* or love-death cannot last because he has still the horror of the guillotine to confront.

The Jouissance of Hatred

There is love, hate, and indifference. Indifference or detachment is the freedom from love-hate or from what Lacan called hainamoration. (Lacan, 1998: 90) Love leads to egolessness, self-forgetting, and transference. By contrast, hate fixates the subject on its own imaginary ego, on its image, and on its rightness. Hate also fixates the subject on its hated object with dark and destructive intent and desire. It destroys its object, which need not be an other as object, but can be the self as well. The jouissance of hate goes beyond all limits or ends. It is limitless. It is the personification of unsatisfied desire. Death itself does not satisfy hate. Hate is implacable.

Hatred is Meursault's last word, the last word in the text, and the form of consummation that Meursault wishes for: "For everything to be consummated, for me to feel less alone, I had only to wish that there be a large crowd of spectators the day of my execution and that they greet me with cries of hate." (Camus, 123) Meursault's final wish, the first he has ever clearly articulated, is fierce, dark, and sad. He wishes to be greeted by a large crowd of spectators as the object of their murderous hatred, as which he now offers himself. He wishes to be recognized as an object, as a burning center and target of hatred. In this fantasy, he becomes the cause of the crowd's hatred. Their cries of hatred will as if provide the reason for his execution or an answer to its unreason. Their inordinate hatred beyond all measure is what will carry him together with them through to the final act of being beheaded. Their mad, passionate hatred will act as the psychical force that will accomplish the final deed that needs to be done. In this fantasy, he would not be enduring the execution alone with his executioner, but he and the violent crowd would as if be enacting it together. He is what the crowd needs to feel identified with the executioners so as to gain a partial, brutal satisfaction. And they are who give him his central place and role in being the executed. He is with them because they hold him with their hate. The relationship is the reverse of the psychoanalytic love transference. The violence of capital punishment pushes the law and everyone subsumed under it into a real of hatred. In the act of execution, the law throws off its veils of justice, objectivity, and rationality to reveal, momentarily, an incommensurable and limitless jouissance of pure destruction. It is an unfathomable hell that he is trying to demand and to accede to. But this delusional accretion and accession of perverse hatred provides the missing knowledge, the cause, or answer to why he is being executed.

In this, his final delusional scenario, he does not defiantly hate back. This is not a mirroring or warring situation of mutual hatred nor does it seem that he hates himself as the object that he now in fantasy is. He does not hate; he only wishes (souhaiter) to be hated so as not to be alone. His aloneness grounds and seemingly drives his delusional desire even more than his need for a deeper cause does. (The surface social-legal cause: his death is his payment for the crime of murder, is something he grasps.) On the one hand, his wish is shockingly negative and perverse, and on the other, it clearly expresses his fundamental symptom: his radical estrangement, a strangeness that he now, for the first time, recognizes as his inalienable and inexorable aloneness. He knows his aloneness, in a way he never has before, also because he has had some experiences of identification with others – with his mother, Céleste, the indifferent night and the stars, etc. The treatment of his symptom would be imaginary solidarity, but the immense sadness of his wish lies in that he can only imagine a solidarity of hatred. So as somehow to forge a human bond, so as to have some significance for others, he can only imagine being the necessary object of hate that their hatred craves. All he can affectively hope for is a transference of hate. He belongs because he is hated.

In court, he was moved by Céleste's compassion and friendship, but he felt an urge to cry when he felt hated. (Camus, 90) Now he feels strong enough to accept hate from a world he has renounced as meaningless. In his fantasy, he positions himself in a somewhat megalomaniac way as central and significant. This makes of his wish a defense, possibly against crying or breaking down and becoming an object of disgust as his father was for him as a child. He could in fantasy have chosen to be an object of disgust in a scenario that would make others vomit rather than hate, but he does not think of himself as the oral object of disgust that the society has to spit or vomit out. Earlier he had felt that his lawyer found him "slightly disgusting" without being disturbed. (Camus, 97) Being hated has made him cry but being an object of disgust has not. His challenge lies not in avoiding disgust but crying because he feels so alone. This symptom is at the core of his wish for a large crowd of spectators as well.

In his wish, his fantasy of a crowd, which is part of his symptom, his solitude, he makes himself something of an exception. He becomes the necessary exception on the basis of which the crowd attains its semblance of unity in hatred. But this is not the kind of psychotic, egomaniacal exception that Marie-Hélène Brousse analyzes in Schreber, where the subject devotes itself "to being the exception that is missing, the 'father who names' exception that is missing'" or "'The Woman that God Lacks.'" (Brousse, 11-12) Meursault does offers himself as the object of hatred that his society lacks in order to fantasize itself as a set of the good, beautiful, and justified. He is what contradicts the imaginary affects of love, justice, and goodness in which the symbolic veils itself in order to hide its ferocity and cruelty. He is as if a man on the cross of the guillotine, an object of exceptional hatred, not of exceptional love as was Christ. But contrary to what is the case in extraordinary psychosis, his fantasy is only a wish; it is not based in a psychotic certitude. He does not hear a voice, telling him that he is such an extraordinary or chosen object nor does he hear a command that orders him to be that. His sense of being does not depend on this fantasy. Yet, though it is only a wish, with it Meursault recovers something of that certitude of his flesh that he had lost after his condemnation by the court. With the aid of this fantasy, he stops his flesh from trembling.

In this fantasy scenario, he is an object, no longer a subject in the strict sense of the word or a subject of the signifier. But he is an important object, lost in a wish, a desire, a delusion that concerns his body, the substrate of his jouissance. He is what Lacan called "the subject of jouissance," sub-jected to jouissance. (Lacan, 1970) The touch of megalomania in this painful fantasy is his sense of the strength of this body-object and his control of it. He imagines being able to hold it up like a monstrance or an apotropaic figure, such as the Medusa head is, against the crowd's hate-bearing jouissance. But the dignity that he gives himself as an object comes at a price of self-loss and suffering of the body and mind that cannot be known. His final jouissance excludes the little subjectivity that he had and what he gained in addition from his trial and ordeal. Jouissance is the body laboring, alone. As Nasio says, "Something in us undergoes jouissance, without us." (Nasio, 40)

On the imaginary and symbolic side, solitude is related to solidarity and relationships, but on the symptomatic side of the real, it is related to nonrelationship, to a sense of being something that cannot be related, something alone and strange, something one's own being cannot grasp. It is the strangeness of the inscrutable core of the self as autistic jouissance. This is a jouissance that hooks to no one and nothing. It is not transferable or linkable to others, to language, or action. It is the singularity that is at the same time the subject's fundamental symptomatic identity and its alienation that cannot be eradicated (from the Latin eradicare, e=out + radix=root) because it is the root that each is. Even in analysis, this singularity is rarely reached. For Lacan, those who did were potential analysts. He invented the Pass as a way to test whether a contact with singularity -- a new, unheard of psychic singularity – has been made or not.

Art seems to attain this singularity. Goethe defined the novella form as a self-caused (or accidental), unheard-of event ("eine sich ereignete, unerhörte Begebenheit"). It is an apt definition for the Pass as well. As regards Meursault, significant is that he recognizes himself as the one whom Camus calls the stranger and that he wishes to go beyond his strangeness, which he renames his aloneness, at any price. He has lived in indifference and detachment. He has murdered a fellow man, but not out of hatred or indifference or detachment. His first experience of hating with the chaplain peters out into soft and obscure images of detached tenderness. He has painfully learnt that not to be alone, others must not be indifferent to him. They must hate him. Thus he delivers himself over to the hatred of others and their will to destroy a core that might make him want to cry because it is something unwanted by others as well as by himself, but this is the only form of connection, of coexistence, of transference that his social and legal experience has revealed as available to him. For Meursault, the other option, of love, is not available. It seems never to have been available. He is someone who seems never to have experienced being humanly loved or loving. He is a stranger to love.

A Psychoanalytic Interpretation

Quite a number of literary critics want to discount psychoanalytic interpretations altogether. For example, Mergerrison does so on the grounds that psychoanalytic interpretations "evacuate the significance of race from their considerations of the novel, and reduce all female figures (the Arab mistress included) to substitutes for the mother." (Margerrison, 63) Longstaffe discounts any psychoanalytic interpretations of abnormality because: "If he [Meursault] is to be considered psychologically abnormal, he can be neither example or lesson." (Longstaffe, 4) The first example indicates that many psychoanalytic interpretations are based in reductive readings of Freud. The second rejection of psychoanalysis is based on a high-minded, moral, and pre-modern conception of the function of art that has now been radically modified.

Ben Stoltzfus's "Lacanian Reading" summarizes many of the psychoanalytic interpretations that precede his own of 1989. He does a close and very interesting reading of the metaphoric flood of signifier fragments that pour out of Meursault at the triggering, but his reading is limited to the Oedipus complex or the libidinal triangle of mother, father, and child, and to phallic jouissance. Thus, Stoltzfus concludes: "Incest is the latent and repressed content of Camus's novel and it continues to fascinate reader who, as in a mirror ['this is you'], recognize in Meursault's actions the image of oedipal desire." (Stoltzfus, 136) Stoltzfus's focus is on the unconscious that interprets and gives meanings. His conception of the unconscious is not split between the deciphering unconscious and the real unconscious. He does not go beyond sexual fantasies. He does not recognize the other forms of jouissances that the body produces that are beyond sexuality. He does not search the text for the particular symptom or the sinthome that may uniquely be Meursault's.

For Stoltzfus, the sun is the father (more or less because *le soleil* is masculine); the sea is the mother (because the sea (*la mer*) is feminine and also the homonym for *la mère,* etc.), and Meursault is the child. "The drama is generated by… the perceived *alliance* between the mother and the father …. [Meursault's] anger, directed at the father and the law, illuminates the unconscious impulses that goad him to shoot at the sun, which is the 'mythical father,' if not 'our Father in Heaven." (Stoltzfus, 125-6; 135) For Stoltzfus the signifiers, "mother" and "father," are the absent and repressed referents in his unconscious to which many other signifiers and actions point. (Stoltzfus, 129-30) He reads the murder scene as an Oedipal battle between Meursault and his father over possession of the mother. He translates Meursault's experience with nature, with the sun and the sea, into mother and father figures. He has counted that the phoneme "*ma*" occurs 101 times in the first part of the text and assumes that this is each time an unconscious reference to *Maman*. (Stoltzfus, 114) He uses homophony, assonance, alliteration, and free association to connect as much of the verbal network in the text as possible to the Freudian bedrock of incest, castration anxiety, and the primal scene. In his analysis, the unconscious and its jouissance appear as rather limited and monomaniacal in their activity and aim. Stoltzfus's approach does not allow for the formation of any other forms of jouissance.

In this interpretation, the unconscious is in fact known, and it is universal. We all desire incest; we all want to murder one parent to possess the other. Meursault becomes representative of the universal desire and guilt that "implicate all of us" (Stoltzfus, 133). The "surfacing of the unconscious" is the surfacing of death and desire. Death is Meursault's only way, Stoltzfus argues, to attain unity with the mother. Only in death can he satisfy "his longing for the Edenic bond with the primal mother," and, at last, find "the love and the peace of his mother's embrace." (Stoltzfus, 131-2). This is why the question of why Meursault returns to the scene of confrontation on the beach is central for Stoltzfus. He argues that Meursault turns back to drink from the spring (*la source*), which also connotes the beginning (the source) or his mother. His unconscious wish for the mother drives him back. The mother operates like a divine force that determines and explains everything and that has designed every life in the unconscious to desire sex and death.

Cultural consciousness seemingly strives for simplicity and unity of structure. That is its pleasure and danger. It does not want to recognize a potentially infinite number of singular psychic structures. Thus, it forces Meursault into various, more general categories of meaning such as it has. To satisfy this want a generalization that a Lacanian orientation might possibly offer is to see Meursault as a harbinger of a fundamental shift in our psychic structure from the neurosis that dominated Freud's time to various forms of ordinary and extraordinary psychosis that dominate ours. It is a shift from a culture of discontents as described by Freud to a culture of the real and jouissance, such as Lacan investigations of the psyche opened up. Perhaps, if one wanted to generalize, one could say that Camus's work is also an extraordinary revelation of how a civilization operating and structured basically on the binary differences of the symbolic will fight to oppose the elimination of the necessary third fantasy term of god (or of some substitute for him) because it refuses to accept the real as its third term.

Identity Politics and Non-identity or "the Place of the No One Anymore": Said's Contrapuntal Criticism

La misère m'empâcha de croire que tout est bien sous le soleil et dans l'histoire; le soleil m'apprit que l'histoire n'est pas tout.
—Camus

Postcolonial criticism focuses on the clash of civilizations, East and West, colonizer and colonized, and on issues of race, sex, gender, ethnicity, and nationhood. For postcolonial criticism, what matters and what is central are the murdered Arab and the other Arab figures mentioned in the text. What Edward Said adds to this mix of politics and consciousness of identity is a demand for knowledge of Arab history and identity with Arab land. *Cultural and Imperialism* argues for "a wider optics" that must include geographical space and its history. (Said, 175) "I believe," says Said, that "it is a radical falsification of culture to strip it of its affiliations with its setting, or to pry it away from the terrain it contested or …. to deny its real influence." (Said 259) This is unarguably true, except that there are two terrains, the contested terrain of reality (in this instance Algeria) and the unconscious psychic terrain that, at a critical moment, as we see in Meursault's case, forecloses the actual terrain completely. Unconscious cartography, however, plays no role in Said's analysis of Camus's work. A tendency to stay away from the depths of solitude to which the unsayable dimensions of desire and jouissance lead is fairly common in post-colonial criticism (and given its foci, understandable), but the tendency to ignore psychoanalytic discourse, unfortunately implies that it is completely irrelevant or that its greatest challenge – the fact of psychosis -- does not exist.

For Said, the geographical terrain has more weight and solidity than consciousness. Compared to land, says Said, "Western consciousness" is a "relatively weightless" thing," a "receptacle emptied of all but its capacity for sentience and reflection." (Said, 173, 174) Said's dismissal of consciousness issues from the same conviction that drove Kierkegaard, Marx, Darwin, Freud, and Lacan before him to argue that something more material, substantial, and concrete than consciousness drives and accounts for historical change, evolution, and revolution. Every one of these critics, each in his own way, opposed the excesses of the rationalist tradition from Aristotle to Hegel that prioritized thought (or language) and mistakenly identified it with being. The rational tradition climaxed in Hegel's outrageously idealistic positing of consciousness as king, as history's true goal, leading to total enlightenment, because any thought produced by consciousness is superior to and of infinitely greater value than anything material or natural: "even a silly fancy such as may pass through a man's head is *higher* than any product of nature." (Hegel, 23)

For Said, what anchors this "empty receptacle" is land whereas ungrounded consciousness produces only "a detachable ethos … suggesting universality and humanism, deeply at odds with the descriptions of geographical locale plainly given in the fiction." (Said, 172) Said urges that the abstract semblances of language and thought be grounded in and balanced by the realities of geography and history. This avoids, as did the theories before him (excepting Lacan's), the possibility that there is no grounding. It forecloses the notion of a void, a real, unfulfillable hole that would be far more "deeply at odds" with "universality and humanism" than is the idea of geographic locale. For Said, land fills the void. It is as it were, his substitute god, and a capacity for bonding with land, even more so than with ethnicity or a language, is the test for belonging (or being native) rather than a colonizer or *colon* (settler). Identification with land crystallizes identity.

Said notes that only in two stories ("The Growing Stone" and "The Adulterous Woman") in *The Exile and the Kingdom* "is there any suggestion that Camus allowed himself to believe that Europeans might achieve sustained and satisfactory identification with the oversees territory." (Said, 178) As a demonstration, he offers an analysis of the climactic ending of "The Adulterous Woman," where Janine experiences an "almost pantheistic communion… with the sky and the desert," and a sense of timelessness, where "past and present drop away from her, as does the actuality of other beings." In her "communion with *this* piece of sky and desert…. Her *specific history* as a Frenchwoman in Algeria does not matter, for she has achieved a superveningly immediate and direct access to *that* particular earth and sky." (My italics) Oddly enough, Said reads this encounter as a purely sexual one: "Clearly, I think, Camus's intention is to present the relationship between woman and geography in sexual terms, as an alternative to her now nearly dead relationship with her husband." The narrative of her life is "sordid," he tells us, and he speculates about her identity: "What her real identity is or may be is judged later in the passage when she achieves what is an unmistakably sexual climax." (Said, 176-7) Ergo, if she has an identity at all, it is a sexual one or she has none. Thus, Said's analysis of Janine's story turns it into what is, in fact, not an example of a "sustained and satisfactory identification with the overseas territory," but the story of the loss of an identity in a sexual encounter with land because conscious identity is what matters to Said and sex is a loss of identity. "Loss of identity," such as occurs also in the story, "The Renegade," is "unacceptable," says Said.

(Said, 178) Said discounts the dialectical tie or logical link of connection and disconnection (<>) or of identity and nonidentity that is necessarily part of the structure of any subject.

For Said all that Janine achieves is "a sexual climax," but Camus writes that she achieves inner "silence," "stillness," freedom from "anguish" and "fear," and repossession of her independent being, her resources, her emotions, and happiness. Said's analysis devalues all that he himself in part grants her because, for him, an experience that is profoundly corporeal and erotic, must be necessarily be sexual. However, Janine is reaching for something beyond sex *(hors-sexe)* because sex does not give her all that she wants and needs to feel alive again. (Lacan, 1998: 85) Said's theory of the subject leaves no space for corporeal fantasies or encounters beyond the phallic. Corporeal resonances other than the sexual are as foreign to him as they were to Freud. (Freud, 1930: 64-5) The "oceanic" feeling, mysticism, self-forgetting, self-loss, or self-generated and autistic enjoyments and fantasms are dismissed as of little interest, significance, and consequence.

According to Said, Algeria is for Janine "an exotic locale" in which her "own spiritual problems can be addressed and therapeutically treated." (Said, 183) It is difficult to think how a locale, not matter how exotic, can become a kind of substitute therapist who might address Janine's neuroses (not to mention taking on psychosis). The locale seems rather to be as if only the flint that ignites Janine's own desire and initiates the work of rebuilding her own psychic terrain. Momentarily, this refound and recreated inner landscape -- singular, fantasmatic, and strange -- also re-ignites her passions. This inner land is nameless, timeless, placeless, ahistorical, lawless, solitary but impassioned; it fills her immense emptiness.

Camus's text does not say what Said's interpretation makes of it. Camus does not say that she has achieved "direct access" to "that particular earth and sky" or "with this piece of sky and desert" but that she has accessed within herself "*the obscure center of her being*" (*le centre obscur de son être*). Camus sees that in "*the obscure center of her being*," Janine can stop worrying about past and future and live in the now of her body, and her own, free, and mobile landscape of rising waters and falling stars. She does not crave "*that* particular earth and sky," but the experience of new psychic territory and state that would free and fulfill her, that would end the solitude of her desire and her sense of emptiness -- a territory that would be a satisfying one, attuned to her whole body, to its forms of jouissance and fantasy, and to her need for freedom and release from anxiety. Camus understands her experience as a catharsis. She is washed clean, momentarily, of her regrets and nostalgia, her memories, unfulfilled longings, and fear of old age and death.

Said immediately rejects all of this. To Said "*the obscure center of her being*" "suggests both her own sense of obscurity and ignorance and Camus's as well." (Said, 177) Said can seemingly not allow for a part of Janine to remain obscure, unknowable, and strange, yet alive and strong enough to restore her sense of aliveness. In Said's thinking there is no space for the Lacanian real. He seems to have no patience with the dialectical other side of identity or with a need for nonidentity, for disidentification as Camus does. Camus's notion of the "*obscure center*" is not of an ignorance that can or could be cured by knowledge and strong identifications, but rather as of something real and that needs nonetheless be encountered and acknowledged. Said cannot do that because for him recognizing such obscurity means the loss of "her specific history as a Frenchwoman in Algeria" and this conscious identity is what he believes matters most. But what really is "specific" about it? "French" is a national and rather general category that Janine shares with everyone who is French; "woman" is an anthropological category to which half the world belongs; and "Algeria," an area roughly 3.5 times the size of Texas, was a terrain, divided in Camus time, among a population of about 300,000 inhabitants. Her conscious identification "as a Frenchwoman in Algeria" does not, in fact, yield much historical specificity.

A conscious identity built on land and identification with a land certainly exists and has historically so for a long time, but an unconscious terrain is something else. It is a creation of libidinal investments, of primal markings and sources of jouissance, and fantasies. Janine is not libidinally invested in the same things or marked in the same way that Said is: not in her political history, or in her Frenchness, or in her womanhood as primarily sexual satisfaction. Hers is not a symbolically divided landscape between Arabs and French, It is neither a politicized or sexualized landscape. She is searching for more elementary symbolic coordinates such as a cut between the finite and the infinite in time and space. She knows her identity as an economically safe, secure, and cared for wife and needed sexual partner. She is not seeking more of what she has or more sex. She wants escape from these worldly coordinates; she wants the freedom of nonidentity, and something more, self-loss in the real of jouissance. In the unconscious terrain, what finally matter is how well, if at all, one can handle a nameless, silent, tumultuous obscurity within. For Said, this space of contradictory and dangerous living forces is not of much interest; it is, fundamentally, just an unacceptable dead end of "obscurity and ignorance." Said gives us an example of what the foreclosure of psychoanalysis entails. His criticism defines the limit where the work of psychoanalysis begins.

For Said "to resituate *L'Etranger* in the geographical nexus from which its narrative trajectory emerges is to interpret it as a heightened form of historical experience." (185) Granted, but what happens to the textual, literary, and subjective experience that the reader also wants and that artists, presumably also Camus, create? For Said Camus's novels and stories mainly and instead "very precisely distill the traditions, idioms, and discursive strategies of France's appropriation of Algeria." (Said, 184) They provide "an arresting account of the political and interpretative contest to represent, inhabit, and possess the territory itself." (Said, 176) It seems difficult to see Janine's suffering and her thoughtful efforts to find a self-cure as an attempt "to possess the territory itself," And the case of Meursault is similar. Nonetheless, Said believes that "It is accurate to say, therefore, that Camus's narratives lay severe and ontologically prior claims to Algeria's geography. …He inherits and uncritically accepts them [these claims to Algeria's geography] as conventions shaped in the long tradition of colonial writing on Algeria." (Said, 180) It goes without saying that I have difficulty, obviously, seeing Camus's intention in *The Stranger* (or that of his characters in this or any other artistic works of his) as being predominantly a laying of "severe and ontologically prior claims to Algeria's geography."

Camus did not need history to write his story, but Said seems to need it to do his interpretations. Why smoother this story in such a massive historical frame? Why bother to diminish and devalue it because of this absence of a history that matters very much to Said, but not to Camus here because he was focused on something else, something as important or perhaps ultimately more important, on the deep history of the psyche, on the unconscious history beyond words, which is read only in traces? Would a historical infusion of the kind Said demands, though highly significant in itself, illuminate the (arguably) deeper insights that Camus has into the singularity and madness of Meursault? Is not the imposition of a demand for such broad historical inclusion a questionable interference in and abridgement of the freedom of any writer? Said states: "Camus's writing is informed by an extraordinarily belated, in some way incapacitated colonial sensibility, which enacts an imperial gesture within and by means of a form, the realistic novel, well past its greatest achievements in Europe." (Said, 176) Everything about this august sentence is debatable. Even if Said were right to assert that Camus had an "extraordinarily belated, incapacitated colonial sensibility," can we assume that his artistic sensibility is incapacitated and belated as well? Is

Camus's artistic sensibility colonial? Is it incapacitated? Is Camus's *The Stranger* "enact[ing] an imperial gesture" or is it Said himself who is trying to do that with Camus? If the realistic novel is past its greatest achievements (an assertion that Sebald's works among others contests), and seemingly identified, for Said, with a master discourse capable of making "imperial gestures," why devalue Camus's minimalist, lyrical novella (not novel) that expressly refuses to make such gestures?

The main goal of what Said calls his "contrapuntal criticism" as regards Camus is a complete reevaluation of his politics and works. Camus's works are to be judged by a wider historical perspective that must include all of Algerian colonial history from 1830 to the liberation in 1962 and beyond that as it is and was written by both the Algerian and the French side. (Said, 66-7) To situate Camus properly in his actual history, contrapuntal criticism has "to be alert" to Camus's "true French antecedents, as well as the work of post-independence Algerian novelists, historians, sociologists, political scientists." (178) It has to demonstrate that Camus's most famous fiction "incorporates, intransigently recapitulates, and in many ways depends on a massive French discourse on Algeria, one that belongs to the language of French imperial attitudes and geographical reference." (Said, 181) It is "the post-colonial events," says Said, which "impose upon us both a longer narrative and more inclusive and demystifying interpretation." (Said, 183) Thus, contrapuntal criticism is an extended reading that aims "to include what was once forcibly excluded -- in *L'Etranger*, for example, the whole previous history of France's colonialism and its destruction of the Algerian State, and the later emergence of an independent Algeria (which Camus opposed)." (Said, 67)

The question is would we really want all that included in this novella or any other work of Camus's? Is the artist obliged to be a historian? Do we want to read our history as fiction? What would art be worth, if it were nothing but consciousness, nothing but history? If we do not grant that artists are driven to seek access by symbolic means to the as yet unsaid or the obscure unsayable, why bother with art? It would be just another, perhaps, more stylistically pleasing or pleasurable form of journalism or history. If we hold every artist responsible for knowing and representing a locale and its history, and for taking the right political side with political issues, how many artists would have to be demoted along with Camus?

Said wants to establish continuities and conjunctions between Camus's work and the horrors of French colonialism in Algeria and to ignore major discontinuities and disjunctions. He believes that "It would be correct to regard Camus's work as affiliated historically both with the French colonial adventure itself (since he assumes it to be immutable) and with outright opposition to Algerian independence." (Said, 175). He believes that Camus's work is representative of "Western *dominance* in the non-European world" (Said, 73) and that he survives only because he is in most critics' mistaken opinions a universalist writer.

Oddly, Said also believes, and this is in fact a central argument, that the inclusion of "this Algerian perspective" may "unblock and release aspects hidden, taken for granted or denied by Camus." (Said 175-6) (I won't ask how Camus hid or blocked off things that had not yet happened when he died in 1960?) Further, "interpretatively blocking off" is, according to Said, a "Eurocentric tradition" that one sees in Camus (and others) and in his fictional characters. (Said, 178) It's seemingly a purely cultural matter, limited to Europe, and disconnected from psychic structure.

Said allows for no gap or distance between Camus, the artist, and the consciously articulated political positions of Camus the citizen and public person. Thus, the public citizen, who, according to Said, lacked historical knowledge and political insight, and foresight, becomes identical to the artist, who must, therefore, have all the same flaws and weaknesses. It is one thing to say that Camus, the conscious, public man, blocked off, certain things, as we all do, but it is quite another thing to say that Camus, the artist, was blocked in his art in identical ways, as are his fictional. (It becomes somewhat absurd in the case of Meursault, whose problem is not neurotic negation or repression but psychotic foreclosure.) Yet, this is the all-important notion that underlies Said's reevaluation of Camus. His critical aim is to make this blocked off, imperial history in Camus's works patent and overt. By acting as if as Camus's Freud, he will demonstrate the presence of the "blocked off" material and enable its restoration. For Said, *The Stranger* as well as *The Plague* is "about the deaths of Arabs, deaths that highlight and silently inform the French character's difficulties of conscience and reflections." (Said, 181) Staying with *The Stranger* that seems simply to not be true. *The Stranger* is patently about Meursault and his death. Meursault does not reflect and is not able to on his murder of the Arab. This is a horrible fact of the real of psychosis. But for Said, the fact that "Meursault kills an Arab … that this Arab is not named and seems to be without a history, let alone a mother and father" are sufficient conditions to justify a claim that all of Algerian-French history is "projected into the composition of his [Camus] texts." Said demands that we see this as a fact: "But I want to insist that one finds in Camus's novels what they once were thought to have been cleared of -- detail about the very distinct French imperial conquest begun in 1830, continuing during Camus's life, and projecting into the composition of the texts." (Said, 176)

Since such details do not exist in the text, Said draws on Camus's politics and political statements to argue that Camus fiction (and its negative vitality, deadness, waste and sadness) (Said, 185) come from his refusal to accept Algerian independence (though for me, even in *The Plague*, it is hard to find this deadness). The refusal paralyzed and limited him, says Said, because he had the choice to oppose France's path.

Said does not want to allow for the simple fact that this is not a "contrapuntal" narrative of what Meursault is thinking and what the nameless Arab is thinking – that would be a different story -- but that the focus here is on a man who has to confront his death by the guillotine. Instead Said presses us to look at publications available to him, such as Marshall Bugeaud's incriminating letters, published about the same time as *The Stranger*, and a recent 1982 edition of the Sufi poetry of the relentless guerilla fighter Kadar, "to perceive the dynamic that makes Camus's diminishment of the Arab presence inevitable." (Said, 181) Relying for proof of his argument on documents that Camus may never have seen or had any interest in seeing, and some that he could not possibly have seen because they appeared after his death is not only logically unacceptable but damaging to the cause of art and the humanistic practices in that it distorts what they are have contributed, namely in the case of Camus, something deeper than history, something about the subjects that believe they are making history and structural flaws in their psyche's that we should not ignore. The "inevitability" of Camus's diminishment of the Arab is also hard to fit into a novella that gives so much space to chance and contingency, and that centers on an ordinary psychotic only dimly aware of anything at all in his environment.

Said's notion of blockage sounds like an attempted paraphrase of Freud's essay "On Negation." (Freud, 1925: 235-9) Said wants to make a case that the radical absence of Arabs and of Algeria's history in Camus's text is equivalent to a strong negation that can be read as an affirmation. But absence or something not present or missing or excluded is not the same as an act of negation, and negation is for Freud an act. This act has actually to be performed, to be made, in order to make possible the interpretation that it is an affirmation. But such an act of negation readily readable as an affirmation is not present in Camus's text. What we are dealing with here is not negation, but foreclosure, which produces a void from which affirmations do not easily emerge.

However, Said believes that Meursault's defiant declaration of his righteousness (that he terms a "suicidal self-acknowledgement") is such an enactment, which Said argues "could only have emerged out of *that* specific history and in *that* community and which makes him at this moment the representative of the *colon*, who "embodies both the real human effort his community contributed and the obstacle of refusing to give up a systematically unjust political system." (Said, 185)." (Said, 185) To hang all that on Meursault's one moment of liberated, though delusional self-assertion with the chaplain seems rather far-fetched. To suggest that Meursault, who can barely speak or think or participate in society and who knows nothing about history or politics, is in any sense speaking as *colon* or that he is aware of any superiority or power or justification derived from his position as *colon* is suggesting much too much. What Meursault manages to say to the chaplain is certainly not a declaration of his right to Algeria because he lives there or was perhaps born there (as Camus was though we cannot be sure about Meursault) etc. When he manages blunderingly to assert himself, it has nothing to do with politics. Meursault is not capable of being concerned with Algerian history or politics and he is not part of any community. He is almost totally incapable of understanding any kind of symbolic or imaginary realities and distinctions. Identity politics mean nothing to him. Finally, however, Said himself undermines his somewhat cloudy argument about hidden imperialistic desires and intentions in Camus's works that can and need to be uncovered with his sudden, blunt assertion that "Camus's obduracy accounts for the blankness and absence of background in the Arab killed by Meursault." (Said, 179) For Said, this "obduracy" is Camus's inability to acknowledge "*two* societies," the Arab and French in Algeria as Bourdieu did in 1958 in his *Sociologie de l'Algérie*. He only recognizes one history or ignores history altogether, "like Janine," adds Said, so that the French presence in Algeria becomes "in essence subject to neither time nor interpretation." This "obduracy" and Camus's politically "jejune formulae" are Said's explanation for why his eminence in the history of literature needs to be reevaluated and corrected. The question is the ancient one of art's relationship to reality and to subjectivity, the artist's as well as the reader's. But subjectivity, in Said, is limited to consciousness and knowledge, knowledge particularly of history and of causes. Said's notion of "obduracy" is a critique of the limitations of Camus's consciousness. It has nothing to do with Camus's notion of "obscurity" and its overlap with Lacan's order of the real. Said keeps away from acknowledging something unknowable. There is no real in his theory. He cannot allow for a hole, for a failure within his own or any structure as such.

Said says, "This restorative interpretation [of Camus] is not meant vindictively." (Said, 176) I believe that this is true, on one level, but on another level, Said is as if intentionally forging a method that could, if it held up, wrong Camus and his work. A certain forcing becomes evident from the logical lapses in the argument and the foreclosure of much that is valuable and significant at the core of Camus's artistic thought, including such matters as our "obscurity" and passion for "timelessness" and identitylessness. It begins to seem as if Said himself has problems with a *two*, with the dialectical two-sideness of the subject: his sociability and his radical solitude. Said refuses to address (to the point that strikes me as a foreclosing) what he calls "Meursault's astonishingly existential isolation." (Said, 172) That seems to be the point where Said cannot go and where Camus did go. It is the point of radical disjunction, the end of all connections, where everything does drop away – time, space, other people – a point of autistic isolation, to which some people are closer all their lives long than others, as Camus so brilliantly describes is the case with Meursault.

If I am at all correct in my analysis of Meursault, what on earth does the neoclassical Jane Austen, whose plots, thematics, and ironies depend on miniscule departures from reason, order, decorum, moderation, and other social and moral rules of conduct and whose characters never even approach madness, have to do with Camus? To be sure her world is filled with neurotics (and their anxieties that at rare and isolated moments approach the real), and I would include her model gentlemen and ladies among them, but they function collectively as mirrors and correctives for each other in a way that despite everything points to Austen's firm neoclassical ethical faith. Why then would one want to compare an artist like Camus who could produce such an exemplary description of the kind of person who might have a psychotic break to an artist like Austen, who, despite her ironic and astute attention to the many breaches, cracks, and discrepancies in her model ethical world, always returns to the safety of the symbolic and the authority of neoclassical rationality and its civilized values that had, as she believed, the power to correct immoderation, disorder, and fantasy? What has she to do with murder, death, and psychosis? Where are there twenty-five metaphors on one page in Austen?

Said makes the comparison because in both Austen and Camus "the facts of imperial actuality have dropped away… a detachable ethos has remained, an ethos suggesting universality and humanism…" (Said, 172) But what has Camus's fiction do with universality and humanism? Camus did not believe in universality, only in the particular. "The work of art," said Camus, "is born of the intelligence's refusal to reason the concrete. It marks the triumph of the carnal." (Camus, 72) For Camus, "Thinking is not unifying or making the appearance familiar under the guise of a great principle. Thinking is learning all over again how to see.… It is bad to stop, hard to be satisfied with a single way of seeing, to go without contradiction, perhaps the most subtle of all spiritual forces." (Camus, 1955: 32, 48)

Barthes once said of himself as a reader: "The pleasure of the text is that moment when my body pursues its own ideas – for my body does not have the same idea I do." (Barthes, 17) I think the same is true of not so much perhaps a writer's pleasure as more likely his jouissance. Jouissance seeks outlets in passions and experiences that consciousness blocks, that language cannot reach, and that certainly various social and cultural practices, requirements, and laws attempt to prohibit. Short of psychosis, art is where we come closest, sometimes, to seeing the lawlessness and indifference of the real.

The great artist always accesses something in himself of the real, disconnected from consciousness (the radical debility that we suffer from), and something of the jouissance that Lacan called "the place of Nonidentity," where, for Miller, "a ternary of three nouns can be placed: jouissance, truth, and madness." (Miller, June 2008)

A discussion of a literary text that does not begin, as does psychoanalysis for Lacan, with ignorance and the expectation of an encounter with singularity, but with preset binary differences and notions of our identities and their relative value makes an adequate critical and theoretical reading of a text improbable from the start. Such a reading fails to reach our madness.

Bibliography

Roland Barthes, *The Pleasure of the Text*, translated by Richard Miller, New York: Hill and Wang, 1975.

Brousse, Marie-Hélène. "Ordinary Psychosis in the Light of Lacan's Theory of Discourse," *Psychoanalytic Notebooks*. No. 19, 2009.

Camus, Albert. *The Stranger*, translated by Matthew Ward, New York: Vintage Books, 1989.

—. *The Myth of Sisyphus and other Essays*, translated by Justin O'Brien, New York: Vintage Books, 1955.

Coleridge, *Biographia Literaria or Biographical Sketches of My Literary Life and Opinions. www.online-literature.com/coleridge/biographia-literaria/14/*

Duras, Marguerite. *Hiroshima Mon Amour*, New York, New York: Grove Press, 1961.

Freud, Sigmund. 1915, *Thoughts for the Times on War and Death* in *The Standard Edition of the Complete Psychological Works of Sigmund*

Freud, Volume XIV (1914-1916): On the History of the Psycho-Analytic Movement, Papers on Metapsychology and Other Works, 289-302.

—. 1925, *Negation* in *The Standard Edition of the Complete Psychological Works of Sigmund Freud, Volume XIX (1923-1925): The Ego and the Id and Other Works*, 235-9.

—. 1930, *Civilization and Its Discontents* in *The Standard Edition of the Complete Psychological Works of Sigmund Freud, Volume XXI (1927-1931): The Future of an Illusion, Civilization and its Discontents, and Other Works*, 57-64.

Frohock, W.M. "Camus: Image, Influence and Sensibility," *Yale French Studies* 4 (1949): 93-94.

Wolfgang von Goethe, Johann. *Goethe's Faust*, translated by Barker Fairley, Toronto, Canada: University of Toronto Press, 1970.

Hegel, G.W.F. *On Art, Religion, Philosophy*, translated by Bernard Bosanquet, New York: Harper Torchbooks, 1970.

Heidegger, Martin. *Über den Humanismus*, Frankfurt am Main: Vittorio Klostermann, 1947.

Jameson, Fredric. *The Prison house of Language: A Critical Account of Structuralism and Russian Formalism,* Princeton, New Jersey: Princeton University Press, 1972.

Jaanus, Maire. " 'A Civilization of Hatred': The Other in the Imaginary," *Reading Seminars I and II: Lacan's Return to Freud*, edited by Richard Feldstein, Bruce Fink, & Maire Jaanus, Albany, New York: State University of New York Press, 1996.

Kaplan, Alice Yaeger. "The American Stranger," Marianna Torgovnick, ed. *Eloquent Obsessions: Writing Cultural Criticism*, Durham, North Carolina: Duke University Press, 1994.

Kundera, Milan. *The Unbearable Lightness of Being*, translated by Michael Henry Heim, New York: Harper & Row, 1985.

Kant, Immanuel. *Critique of Judgement* in *Philosophical Writings*, Vol. 13, New York: The Continuum Publishing Company, 1986.

Lacan, Jacques, "Structure as the Inmixing of an Otherness Prerequisite to Any Subject Whatever." 1970. http://www.lacan.com/hotel.htm

—. Le séminaire de Jacques Lacan livre XXIV: L'insu que sait de l'une-bévue s'aile à mourre (1976-1977), (unpublished), The lesson of 11 January 1977.

—. The Seminar of Jacques Lacan, Book XI. The Four Fundamental Concepts of Psychoanalysis, translated by Dennis Porter, New York: W.W. Norton & Company, 1978.

—. *The Seminar of Jacques Lacan, Book XX. Encore. On Feminine Sexuality: The Limits of Love and Knowledge*, translated by Bruce Fink, New York: W.W. Norton & Company, 1998.

—. *Écrits*, translated by Bruce Fink, New York: W.W. Norton & Company, 2006.

Laurent, Éric. "Ordinary Interpretation," *Psychoanalytic Notebooks*. No. 19, 2009.

Longstaffe, Moya. "A Happy Life and a Happy Death: The Quest of Camus's *Étranger*," *The French Review*, Vol. 64. No 1 (October 1990).

Margerrison, Christine. "The Dark Continent of Camus's *L'Étranger,*" *French Studies*, Vol. LV. No. 1 (January 2001). Available at http://fs.oxfordjournals.org/content/LV/1.toc

Merleu-Ponty, Maurice. *The Primacy of Perception and Other Essays on Phenomenological Psychology, the Philosophy of Art, History and Politics*, translated by James M. Edie, Evanston, Illinois: Northwestern University Press, 1964.

Miller, Jacques-Alain. "Interpretation in Reverse," *The Later Lacan: An Introduction*, edited by Véronique Voruz and Bogdan Wolf, Princton, New York: State University of New York Press, 2007.

—. *Tout le monde est fou*. Dix-septième séance du cours, 4 juin 2008.

—. "Rally of the Impossible Professions," Part 2, 20 Sept 2008 at the London Society of the New Lacanian School. London. Available at www.youtube.com/watch?v=2emnIlOhfzc

—. "Ordinary Psychosis Revisited," *Psychoanalytic Notebooks*. No. 19, 2009.

Nasio, Juan-David. *Five Lessons on the Psychoanalytic Theory of Jacques Lacan*, translated by David Pettigrew and François Raffoul, Albany, New York: New York State University Press, 1992.

O'Brien, Conor Cruise. *Albert Camus of Europe and Africa*, New York: The Viking Press, 1970.

Recalcati, Massimo. "The Empty Subject," translated by Jorge Jauregui, *lacanian ink,* 25 (2005).

Said, Edward W. *Culture and Imperialism*, New York: Vintage Books, 1994.

Stevens, Anne-Lysy. "What One Calls "Untriggered" Psychoses," http://ch-freudien-be.org/Papers/Txt/lysy-fc12.pdf

Stoltzfus, Ben. *Lacan & Literature: Purloined Pretexts*, New York: State University of New York Press, 1996.

Vico, Giambattista. *The New Science of Giambattista Vico*, translated by Thomas G. Bergin & Max H. Fish, Ithaca, New York: Cornell University Press, 1976.

INDEX